DB2 9 Fundamentals
Certification Study Guide

DB2 9
Fundamentals
Certification Study Guide

Roger E. Sanders

MC PRESS
MC Press Online, LP
Lewisville, TX 75077

DB2 9 Fundamentals Certification Study Guide
Roger E. Sanders

First Edition

First Printing—May 2007
Second Printing—April 2008

MC Press offers excellent discounts on this book when ordered in quantity for bulk purchases or special sales, which may include custom covers and content particular to your business, training goals, marketing focus, and branding interest.

For information regarding permissions or special orders, please contact:
    MC Press
    Corporate Offices
    125 N. Woodland Trail
    Lewisville, TX 75077 USA

For information regarding sales and/or customer service, please contact:
    MC Press
    P.O. Box 4300
    Big Sandy, TX 75755-4300 USA

ISBN: 1-58347-072-7

Dedication

To a good friend who has always been there when I needed him, Rev. Ross Marion

Acknowledgments

A project of this magnitude requires both a great deal of time and the support of many different individuals. I would like to express my gratitude to the following people for their contributions:

Susan Dykman—Information Management Certification Program Manager, IBM Information Management
Susan invited me to participate in the DB2 9 exam development process, and provided me with screen shots of the IBM Certification Exam Testing software. Susan also reviewed the first chapter of the book and provided valuable feedback.

Susan Visser—IBM Press, Data Management Program Manager IBM Toronto Lab
Once again, Susan's help was invaluable—without her help, this book would not have been written. Susan paved the way for me to acquire the rights to the Version 8.1 manuscript and move to MC Press when Pearson Education decided not to publish an updated version of my Version 8.1 book.

Dr. Arvind Krishna—Vice President, IBM Data Servers and Worldwide Information Management Development
Dr. Krishna provided me with the Foreword for this book.

Brant Davison—Program Director, IBM Information Management Software
Brant worked with Dr. Ambuj Goyal, Dr. Arvind Krishna, and me to ensure that IBM received the materials they needed to write the Foreword, and to make sure I received the Foreword for this book in a timely manner.

Rick Swagerman—Senior Technical Manager, DB2 SQL and Catalog Development IBM Toronto Lab
Rick provided me with detailed examples illustrating how the UPDATE/DELETE NO ACTION and UPDATE/DELETE RESTRICT rules of referential constraints work. His examples were converted into some of the illustrations you see in Chapter 6, and Rick reviewed the final draft of many of these drawings for accuracy and completeness.

I would also like to thank my wife, Beth, for her help and encouragement, and for once again overlooking all of the things that did not get done while I worked on yet another book.

About the Author

Roger E. Sanders is the President of Roger Sanders Enterprises, Inc. He has been designing and developing database applications for more than 20 years and has been working with DB2 and its predecessors since it was first introduced on the IBM PC (as part of OS/2 Extended Edition). He has written articles for publications such as *Certification Magazine* and *IDUG Solutions Journal*, authored tutorials for IBM's developerWorks Web site, presented at numerous International DB2 User's Group (IDUG) and Regional DB2 User's Group (RUG) conferences, taught classes on DB2 fundamentals and database administration (DB2 for Linux, UNIX, and Windows), writes a regular column (*Distributed DBA*) in *DB2 Magazine*, and is the author of the following books:

- *Using the IBM System Storage N Series with Databases* (IBM RedBook; co-author)

- *Integrating IBM DB2 with the IBM System Storage N Series* (IBM RedBook; co-author)

- *Using IBM DB2UDB with IBM System Storage N Series* (IBM RedBook; co-author)

- *DB2 Universal Database V8.1 Certification Exam 703 Study Guide*

- *DB2 Universal Database V8.1 Certification Exam 701 and 706 Study Guide*

- *DB2 Universal Database V8.1 Certification Exam 700 Study Guide*

- *DB2 UDB Exploitation of NAS Technology* (IBM RedBook; co-author)

- *All-In-One DB2 Administration Exam Guide*

- *DB2 Universal Database SQL Developer's Guide*

- *DB2 Universal Database API Developer's Guide*

- *DB2 Universal Database Call Level Interface Developer's Guide*

- *ODBC 3.5 Developer's Guide*

- *The Developer's Handbook to DB2 for Common Servers*

In addition, Roger holds the following professional certifications:

- IBM Certified Database Administrator—DB2 9 DBA for Linux, UNIX, and Windows
- IBM Certified Database Associate—DB2 9 Fundamentals
- IBM Certified Advanced Database Administrator—DB2 Universal Database V8.1 for Linux, UNIX, and Windows
- IBM Certified Database Administrator—DB2 Universal Database V8.1 for Linux, UNIX, and Windows
- IBM Certified Developer—DB2 Universal Database V8.1 Family
- IBM Certified Database Associate—DB2 Universal Database V8.1 Family
- IBM Certified Advanced Technical Expert—DB2 for Clusters
- IBM Certified Solutions Expert—DB2 UDB V7.1 Database Administration for UNIX, Windows, and OS/2
- IBM Certified Solutions Expert—DB2 UDB V6.1 Application Development for UNIX, Windows, and OS/2
- IBM Certified Specialist—DB2 UDB V6/V7 User

About This Book

This book is divided into two parts:

- Part 1: DB2 9 Certification (Chapter 1)

This section consists of one chapter (Chapter 1), which is designed to introduce you to the DB2 Professional Certification Program that is available from IBM. In this chapter, you will learn about the different certification roles available, along with the basic prerequisites and requirements for each role. This chapter also explains what's involved in the certification process, and it includes a tutorial on the IBM Certification Exam testing software, which you will encounter when you go to take any IBM certification exam.

- Part 2: DB2 9 Fundamentals (Chapters 2–7)

This section consists of six chapters (Chapters 2 through 7), which are designed to provide you with the concepts you will need to master before you can pass the DB2 9 Fundamentals exam (Exam 730).

Chapter 2 is designed to introduce you to the various products that make up the DB2 Family and to the comprehensive toolset provided with DB2. In this chapter, you will learn about the various editions of DB2 that are available, the functionality each edition provides, the functionality each DB2 client component provides, and the purpose of each of the more common add-on products that make up the remainder of the DB2 Family. You will also see what graphical user interface (GUI) tools are available and what each tool looks like on the Windows XP operating system, as well as learn what each tool is designed do.

Chapter 3 is designed to introduce you to the concept of database security and to the various authorization levels and privileges that are recognized by DB2. In this chapter, you will learn how and where users are authenticated, how authorities and privileges determine what a user can and cannot do while working with a database, and how authorities and privileges are given to and taken away from individual users and/or groups of individual users.

Chapter 4 is designed to introduce you to the concept of servers, instances, databases, and database objects. In this chapter, you will learn how to create a DB2 9 database, and you will see what a DB2 9 database's underlying structure looks like as well as how that structure is physically stored. You will also learn about the DB2 directory files, and you will see how to how to catalog and uncatalog DB2 databases and remote servers. Finally, you will see how to create the various data objects that can exist in a DB2 database, and you will discover what each object is used for.

Chapter 5 is designed to introduce you to the Structured Query Language (SQL) and XQuery statements that can be used to query and manipulate data. In this chapter, you will learn what SQL is, as well as which SQL statements are classified as Data Manipulation Language (DML) statements. You will also learn and how DML statements are used to store, manipulate, and retrieve relational data stored in tables and views. Finally, you will learn what XQuery is, and you will learn and how XQuery statements can be used to store, manipulate, and retrieve XML documents stored in tables and views.

Chapter 6 is designed to provide you with everything you need to know about DB2 data types and table constraints. In this chapter, you will learn about the various built-in data types available with DB2 9, as well as what constraints are and what types of constraints are available. You will also learn how data types and constraints can be incorporated into a table's definition, and you will see how constraints and triggers can be used to enforce business rules.

Chapter 7 is designed to introduce you to the concept of data consistency and to the various mechanisms that DB2 uses to maintain data consistency in both single- and multi-user environments. In this chapter, you will learn what isolation levels are, what isolation levels are available, and how isolation levels are used to keep transactions from interfering with each other in a multi-user environment. You will also learn how DB2 provides concurrency control through the use of locking, what types of locks are available, how locks are acquired, and what factors can influence locking performance.

The book is written primarily for IT professionals who have some experience working with DB2 9 and want to take (and pass) the DB2 9 Fundamentals exam (Exam 730). However, any individual who would like to learn the basic fundamentals of DB2 9 will benefit from the information found in this book.

Conventions Used

Many examples of DB2 9 administrative commands and SQL statements can be found throughout this book. The following conventions are used whenever a DB2 command or SQL statement is presented:

[ ]   Parameters or items shown inside of brackets are required and must be provided.

< >   Parameters or items shown inside of angle brackets are optional and do not have to be provided.

| Vertical bars are used to indicate that one (and only one) item in the list of items presented can be specified

, . . .A comma followed by three periods (ellipsis) indicate that multiple instances of the preceding parameter or item can be included in the DB2 command or SQL statement

The following examples illustrate each of these conventions:

Example 1

```
REFRESH TABLE [TableName,...]
<INCREMENTAL | NON INCREMENTAL>
```

In this example, at least one *TableName* value must be provided, as indicated by the brackets ([ ]), and more than one *TableName* value can be provided, as indicated by the comma and ellipsis (, ...) characters that follow the *TableName* parameter. INCREMENTAL and NON INCREMENTAL are optional, as indicated by the angle brackets (< >), and either one or the other can be specified, but not both, as indicated by the vertical bar (|).

Example 2

```
CREATE SEQUENCE [SequenceName]
<AS [SMALLINT | INTEGER | BIGINT | DECIMAL]>
<START WITH [StartingNumber]>
<INCREMENT BY [1 | Increment]>
<NO MINVALUE | MINVALUE [MinValue]>
<NO MAXVALUE | MAXVALUE [MaxValue]>
<NO CYCLE | CYCLE>
<NO CACHE | CACHE 20 | CACHE [CacheValue]>
<NO ORDER | ORDER>
```

In this example, a *SequenceName* value must be provided, as indicated by the brackets ([ ]). However, everything else is optional, as indicated by the angle brackets (< >), and in many cases, a list of available option values is provided (for example, NO CYCLE and CYCLE); however, only one can be specified, as indicated by the vertical bar (|). In addition, when some options are provided (for example, START WITH, INCREMENT BY, MINVALUE, MAXVALUE, and CACHE), a corresponding value must be provided for each option that is actually used, as indicated by the brackets ([ ]) that follow the option.

SQL is not a case-sensitive language, but for clarity, the examples provided are shown in mixed case – command syntax is presented in upper case while user-supplied elements such as table names and column names are presented in lower case. However, the examples shown can be entered in any case.

Contents

Foreword

There is justifiable excitement in today's technology world with topics such as Services Oriented Architectures, Open Source Development, Business Process Management, Radio Frequency Identification, Content Management, Regulatory Compliance or Data Warehousing. A technology that underpins all of those discussions is a topic near and dear to many of our hearts: database technology. In fact, databases play a bigger, more active role than ever.

Database technology was first introduced over 30 years ago with some simple objectives. Companies needed to abstract storage and retrieval of data to increase the productivity of their programmers and administrators and optimize the use of computing resources. Further, companies needed high levels of data integrity and reliability so they could entrust their transactional environments to computer automation. And, perhaps most importantly, companies needed to share information more effectively.

A continuum of advancements has allowed database technology make significant strides towards these objectives. But, while the basic objectives remain the same, the demands of business have raised the bar. Business demands have become global and the demands on data to be available 24 x 7 x 365. Business models must be flexible, allowing companies to quickly seize new opportunities. Costs relating to both computing resources and people must still be optimized.

So the challenge moves from having a database management system simply storing and retrieving data, to serving data in a networked, "always on, always available" world. Today's world demands a "data server." This is the driving concept behind DB2 9.

This means making data flow easily and dynamically to the applications, processes and people that need it, when they need it. It means supporting flexible architectures, like Services Oriented Architecture, optimizing support for new data types, like XML, and embracing new developer communities and development paradigms, like Ruby or PHP. It means integration with purchased application packages, like SAP. It means dynamically serving analytic insight from a warehouse in real time to the people who need it. It means all this and at the same time means optimizing the total cost of operations – from deep compression algorithms saving storage and processing costs, to increasing levels of automation to reduce skill levels and allow administrators to focus on high value tasks.

Like the last 30 years, the next 30 years will bring with it enormous change. Those years will also bring an incredible opportunity for information technology professionals and those who support data servers. Global businesses are based on information, and data server professionals will be the stewards of this critical corporate asset. I encourage you to take advantage of the opportunity that Roger Sanders is providing to learn more about DB2. You'll be learning skills you can both leverage across many technology settings and use to deliver more value to your business. Your time will be well spent. Enjoy the experience.

Dr. Arvind Krishna
Vice President,
IBM Data Servers and Worldwide Information Management Development

Preface

One of the biggest challenges computer professionals face today is keeping their skill sets current with the latest changes in technology. When the computing industry was in its infancy, it was possible to become an expert in several different areas, because the scope of the field was relatively small. Today, our industry is both widespread and fast paced, and the skills needed to master a single software package can be quite complex. Because of this complexity, many application and hardware vendors have initiated certification programs to evaluate and validate an individual's knowledge of their technology. Businesses benefit from these programs, because professional certification gives them confidence that an individual has the expertise needed to perform a specific job. Computer professionals benefit, because professional certification allows them to deliver high levels of service and technical expertise, and, more importantly, because professional certification can lead to advancement or new job opportunities within the computer industry.

If you've bought this book (or if you are thinking about buying this book), chances are you have already decided you want to acquire one or more of the IBM DB2 Professional Certifications available. As an individual who holds ten IBM DB2 professional certifications, let me assure you that the exams you must pass in order to become a certified DB2 professional are not easy. IBM prides itself on designing comprehensive certification exams that are relevant to the work environment an individual holding a particular certification will have had some exposure to. As a result, all of IBM's certification exams are designed with the following questions in mind:

- What are the critical tasks that must be performed by an individual who holds a particular professional certification?

- What skills must an individual possess in order to perform each critical task identified?

- How frequently will an individual perform each critical task identified?

You will find that to pass a DB2 certification exam, you must possess a solid understanding of DB2—and for some of the more advanced certifications, you must understand many of its nuances as well.

Now for the good news. You are holding in your hands what I consider to be the best tool you can use to prepare for the DB2 9 Fundamentals exam (Exam 730). When IBM began work on the DB2 9 certification exams, I was invited once again to participate in the exam development process. In addition to helping define the exam objectives, I authored several exam questions, and I provided feedback on many more before the final exams went into production. Consequently, I have seen every exam question you are likely to encounter, and I know every concept you will be tested on when you take the DB2 9 Fundamentals exam (Exam 730). Using this knowledge, along with copies of the actual exam questions, I developed this study guide, which not only covers every concept you must know in order to pass the DB2 9 Fundamentals exam (Exam 730) but also covers the exam process itself and the requirements for each DB2 9 certification role available. In addition, you will find, at the end of each chapter, sample questions that are worded just like the actual exam questions. In short, if you see it in this book, count on seeing it on the exam; if you don't see it in this book, it won't be on the exam. If you become familiar with the material presented in this book, you should do well on the exam.

CHAPTER 1

IBM DB2 9 Certification

Recognized throughout the world, the Professional Certification Program from IBM offers a range of certification options for IT professionals. This chapter is designed to introduce you to the various paths you can take to obtain DB2 9 Certification from IBM and to describe the testing software you will use when you sit down to take your first DB2 9 certification exam.

DB2 9 Certification Roles

One of the biggest trends in the IT industry today is certification. Many application and software vendors now have certification programs in place that are designed to evaluate and validate an individual's proficiency with the vendor's latest product release. In fact, one of the reasons the Professional Certification Program from IBM was developed was to provide a way for skilled technical professionals to demonstrate their knowledge and expertise with a particular version of an IBM product.

The Professional Certification Program from IBM is comprised of several distinct certification roles that are designed to guide you in your professional development. You simply select the role that's right for you, and then you begin the certification process by choosing the role you wish to pursue and familiarizing yourself with the requirements for that role. The following subsections are designed to help get you started by providing you with the prerequisites and requirements associated with each DB2 9 certification available.

IBM Certified Database Associate—DB2 9 Fundamentals

The *IBM Certified Database Associate—DB2 9 Fundamentals* certification is intended for entry-level DB2 9 users who are knowledgeable about the fundamental concepts of DB2 9 for Linux, UNIX, and Windows, DB2 9 for zSeries (OS/390), or DB2 9 for iSeries (AS/400). In addition to having some hands-on experience, some formal training, or both on DB2 9, individuals seeking this certification should:

- Know what DB2 9 products are available and be familiar with the various ways DB2 9 is packaged

- Know what DB2 9 products must be installed in order to create a desired environment

- Know what features and functions are provided by the various tools that are shipped with DB2 9

- Possess a strong knowledge about the mechanisms DB2 9 uses to protect data and database objects against unauthorized access and/or modification

- Know how to create, access, and manipulate basic DB2 objects, such as tables, views, and indexes

- Be familiar with the different types of constraints that are available and know how each is used

- Be familiar with how XML data can be stored and manipulated

- Possess an in-depth knowledge of Structured Query Language (SQL), Data Definition Language (DDL), Data Manipulation Language (DML), and Data Control Language (DCL) statements that are available with DB2 9

- Have a basic understanding of the methods used to isolate transactions from each other in a multi-user environment

- Be familiar with the methods used to control how locking is performed

In order to acquire the IBM Certified Database Associate—DB2 9 Fundamentals certification, candidates must take and pass one exam: the **DB2 9 Family Fundamentals** exam (Exam 730). The roadmap for acquiring the IBM Certified Database Associate—DB2 9 Fundamentals certification is illustrated in Figure 1–1.

Figure 1–1: IBM Certified Database Associate—DB2 9 Fundamentals certification roadmap.

IBM Certified Database Administrator—DB2 9 for Linux, UNIX, and Windows

The *IBM Certified Database Administrator—DB2 9 for Linux, UNIX, and Windows* certification is intended for experienced DB2 9 users who possess the knowledge and skills necessary to perform the day-to-day administration of DB2 9 instances and databases residing on Linux, UNIX, or Windows platforms. In addition to being knowledgeable about the fundamental concepts of DB2 9 and having significant hands-on experience as a DB2 9 Database Administrator (DBA), individuals seeking this certification should:

- Know how to configure and manage DB2 9 instances

- Know how to configure client/server connectivity

- Be able to obtain and modify the values of environment/Registry variables

- Be able to obtain and modify DB2 Database Manager (instance) and database configuration file parameter values

- Know how to use Automatic Maintenance and self-tuning memory

- Know how to create DB2 9 databases

- Possess a strong knowledge about SMS, DMS, and Automatic Storage table spaces, as well as be familiar with the management requirements of each

- Know how to create, access, modify, and manage the different DB2 objects available

- Know how to manage XML data

- Be able to create constraints on and between table objects

- Know how to capture and interpret snapshot monitor data

- Know how to create and activate event monitors, as well as capture and interpret event monitor data

- Know how to capture and analyze Explain information

- Know how to use the DB2 Control Center and other GUI tools available to manage instances and databases, create and access objects, create tasks, schedule jobs, and view Explain information

- Possess an in-depth knowledge of the EXPORT, IMPORT, and LOAD utilities

- Know how to use the REORGCHK, REORG, REBIND, RUNSTATS, db2look, db2move, and db2pd utilities

- Know how to perform database-level and table space-level backup, restore, and roll-forward recovery operations

- Have a basic understanding of transaction logging

- Be able to interpret information stored in the administration notification log

- Possess a strong knowledge about the mechanisms DB2 9 uses to protect data and database objects against unauthorized access and/or modification

Candidates who have either taken and passed the **DB2 V8.1 Family Fundamentals** exam (Exam 700) or acquired the IBM Certified Database Administrator—DB2 V8.1 for Linux, UNIX, and Windows certification (by taking and passing Exams 700 and 701) must take and pass the **DB2 9 for Linux, UNIX, and Windows Database Administration** exam (Exam 731) to acquire the IBM Certified Database Administrator—DB2 9 for Linux, UNIX, and Windows certification. All other candidates must take and pass both the **DB2 9 Family Fundamentals** exam (Exam 730) and the **DB2 9 for Linux, UNIX, and Windows Database Administration** exam (Exam 731). The roadmap for acquiring the IBM Certified Database Administrator—DB2 9 for Linux, UNIX, and Windows certification can be seen in Figure 1–2.

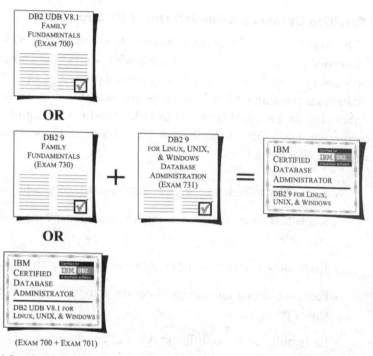

Figure 1–2: IBM Certified Database Administrator—DB2 9 for Linux, UNIX, and Windows certification roadmap.

Candidates who already hold the IBM Certified Database Administrator—DB2 V8.1 for Linux, UNIX, and Windows certification may opt to take the **DB2 9 for Linux, UNIX, and Windows Database Administration Upgrade** exam (Exam 736) to acquire the IBM Certified Database Administrator—DB2 9 for Linux, UNIX, and Windows certification. This exam, which is half the length and half the cost of the **DB2 9 for Linux, UNIX, and Windows Database Administration** exam (Exam 731), is designed to test a candidate's knowledge of the new features and functions that are provided in DB2 9. Essentially, the upgrade exam provides certified DB2 Version 8.1 DBAs an accelerated approach for acquiring an equivalent Version 9 certification. This accelerated approach is outlined in Figure 1–3.

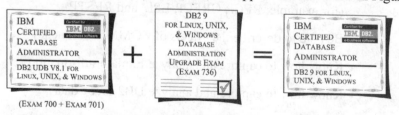

Figure 1–3: The accelerated approach for acquiring IBM Certified Database Administrator—DB2 9 for Linux, UNIX, and Windows certification.

IBM Certified Database Administrator—DB2 9 for z/OS

The *IBM Certified Database Administrator—DB2 9 for z/OS* certification is intended for experienced DB2 9 users who possess the knowledge and skills necessary to perform the day-to-day administration of DB2 9 instances and databases residing on OS/390 platforms. In addition to being knowledgeable about the fundamental concepts of DB2 9 and having significant hands-on experience as a DB2 9 Database Administrator, individuals seeking this certification should:

- Know how to convert a logical database design to a physical database design
- Know how to create, access, modify, and manage the various DB2 9 objects available
- Know how to interpret the contents of system catalogs and directories
- Possess a strong knowledge about the activities associated with enabling stored procedures
- Be familiar with the different types of constraints available and know how each is used
- Possess an in-depth knowledge of the Structured Query Language (SQL), Data Definition Language (DDL), Data Manipulation Language (DML), and Data Control Language (DCL) statements that are available with DB2 9
- Know the difference between static and dynamic SQL
- Know how to manage storage allocation with tools such as VSAM DELETE, VSAM DEFINE, and STOGROUP
- Be familiar with DB2 Disaster Recovery
- Possess a basic understanding of the different object statuses available (for example: RECP, GRECP, LPL, and RESTP)
- Be able to describe the effects of COMMIT frequency
- Know how to capture and analyze Explain information
- Know how to capture and analyze DB2 Trace data
- Be able to determine the best characteristics for an index

- Be able to describe the benefits of data sharing

- Be able to describe the features that enable around-the-clock availability

- Know how to use the REORG, BIND, REPAIR, UNLOAD, RUNSTATS, LOAD, and MODIFY utilities, including being able to restart a failed utility

- Know how to use the DISPLAY, START, STOP, ALTER, RECOVER, and TERM UTILITY commands

- Possess a basic understanding of the CHECK DATA/INDEX/LOB utility

- Be able to demonstrate how DB2I is used

- Be able to identify the functions of the Control Center

- Possess a strong knowledge about the mechanisms DB2 9 uses to protect data and database objects against unauthorized access and modification

Candidates who have either taken and passed the **DB2 V8.1 Family Fundamentals** exam (Exam 700) or acquired the IBM Certified Database Administrator—DB2 V8.1 for z/OS and OS/390 certification (by taking and passing Exams 700 and 702) must take and pass the **DB2 9 for z/OS Database Administration** exam (Exam 732) to acquire the IBM Certified Database Administrator—DB2 9 for z/OS certification. All other candidates must take and pass both the **DB2 9 Family Fundamentals** exam (Exam 730) and the **DB2 9 for z/OS Database Administration** exam (Exam 732). The roadmap for acquiring the IBM Certified Database Administrator—DB2 9 for z/OS certification can be seen in Figure 1–4.

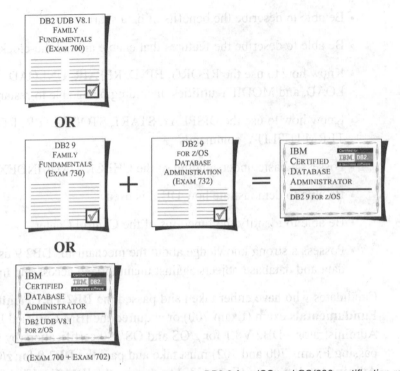

Figure 1–4: IBM Certified Database Administrator—DB2 9 for z/OS and OS/390 certification roadmap.

IBM Certified Application Developer—DB2 9 Family

The *IBM Certified Application Developer—DB2 9 Family* certification is intended for intermediate- to advanced-level application developers who possess the knowledge and skills necessary to create applications that interact with DB2 9 databases residing on supported platforms, including Linux, AIX, HP-UX, Sun Solaris, Windows, zSeries (z/OS, OS/390), and iSeries (AS/400). In addition to being knowledgeable about the fundamental concepts of DB2 9 and having strong skills in embedded SQL programming, ODBC/CLI programming, JDBC programming, or SQLJ programming, individuals seeking this certification should:

- Be familiar with the naming conventions used to identify DB2 9 objects

- Know what authorities and privileges are needed in order to access data with an application

- Possess an in-depth knowledge of the complex database objects available with DB2 9

- Possess an in-depth knowledge of the Structured Query Language (SQL), Data Definition Language (DDL), Data Manipulation Language (DML), and Data Control Language (DCL) statements that are available with DB2 9

- Know the difference between static and dynamic SQL

- Possess an in-depth knowledge of the SQL functions available

- Know when to use Embedded SQL, CLI/ODBC, JDBC, SQLJ, PHP, PERL, PYTHON, .NET, and XML

- Be able to query tables across multiple tables and views

- Be able to identify the types of cursors available, as well as know when to use cursors in an application and what their scope will be

- Be able to work with materialized query tables (MQTs)

- Be able to identify the results of XML parsing and XML serialization

- Possess an in-depth knowledge of XML document encoding management

- Know how XML schemas are validated

- Be able to execute and identify the results of an XQuery expression

- Be familiar with the SQL/XML functions that are available with DB2 9

- Be able to establish a connection to a database within an Embedded SQL, CLI/ODBC, JDBC, SQLJ, or .NET application

- Possess the ability to analyze the contents of an SQL Communications Area (SQLCA) data structure

- Possess the ability to obtain and analyze ODBC/CLI diagnostic information

- Possess the ability to obtain and analyze JDBC trace, SQL exception, and JDBC error log information

- Possess the ability to obtain and analyze .NET diagnostic information

- Be able to query tables across multiple databases, including federated databases

- Possess the ability to create triggers and identify their results

- Know how to cast data types

- Know when to use Compound SQL, parameter markers, and distributed units of work

- Know when to use user-defined functions (UDFs) and stored procedures

- Know how to create UDFs and stored procedures

- Be familiar with the DB2 Developer Workbench

Candidates who have either taken and passed the **DB2 V8.1 Family Fundamentals** exam (Exam 700) or acquired the IBM Certified Application Developer—DB2 V8.1 Family certification (by taking and passing Exams 700 and 703) must take and pass the **DB2 9 Family Application Development** exam (Exam 733) to acquire the IBM Certified Application Developer—DB2 9 Family certification. All other candidates must take and pass both the **DB2 9 Family Fundamentals** exam (Exam 730) and the **DB2 9 Family Application Development** exam (Exam 733). The roadmap for acquiring the IBM Certified Application Developer—DB2 9 Family certification can be seen in Figure 1–5.

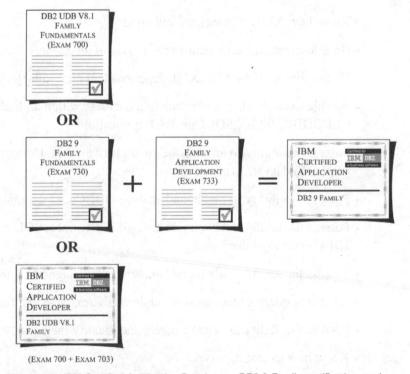

Figure 1–5: IBM Certified Application Developer—DB2 9 Family certification roadmap.

IBM Certified Advanced Database Administrator—DB2 9 for Linux, UNIX, and Windows

The *IBM Certified Advanced Database Administrator—DB2 9 for Linux, UNIX, and Windows* certification is intended for lead Database Administrators who possess extensive knowledge about DB2 9 and who have extensive experience using DB2 9 on one or more of the following supported platforms: Linux, AIX, HP-UX, Sun Solaris, and Windows. In addition to being knowledgeable about the more complex concepts of DB2 9 and having significant experience as a DB2 9 Database Administrator, individuals seeking this certification should:

- Know how to design, create, and manage both SMS and DMS tablespaces

- Know how to design, create, and manage buffer pools

- Be able to take full advantage of intrapartition parallelism and interpartition parallelism

- Be able to design and configure federated database access

- Know how to manage distributed units of work

- Be able to develop a logging strategy

- Be able to create constraints on and between table objects

- Know how to perform database-level and table-space-level backup, restore, and roll-forward recovery operations

- Be able to use the advanced backup and recovery features available

- Know how to implement a standby database using log shipping, replication, failover, and fault monitoring

- Be able to identify and modify the DB2 Database Manager and database configuration file parameter values that have the most impact on performance

- Possess a strong knowledge of query optimizer concepts

- Be able to correctly analyze, isolate, and correct database performance problems

- Know how to manage a large number of users and connections, including connections to host systems

- Know how to create, configure, and manage a partitioned database spanning multiple servers

- Be able to create and manage multidimensional clustered tables

- Know when the creation of an index will improve database performance

- Be able to identify and resolve database connection problems

- Possess a strong knowledge about the external authentication mechanisms DB2 9 uses to protect data and database objects against unauthorized access and/or modification

- Know how to implement data encryption using Label-Based Access Control (LBAC)

To acquire the IBM Certified Advanced Database Administrator—DB2 9 for Linux, UNIX, and Windows certification, candidates must hold the IBM Certified Database Administrator—DB2 9 for Linux, UNIX, and Windows certification, and they must take and pass the **DB2 9 for Linux, UNIX, and Windows Advanced Database Administration** exam (Exam 734). The roadmap for acquiring the IBM Certified Advanced Database Administrator—DB2 9 for Linux, UNIX, and Windows certification can be seen in Figure 1–6.

Figure 1–6: IBM Certified Advanced Database Administrator—DB2 9 for Linux, UNIX, and Windows certification roadmap.

IBM Certified Solution Designer—DB2 Data Warehouse Edition V9.1

The *IBM Certified Solution Designer—DB2 Data Warehouse Edition V9.1* certification is intended for individuals who are knowledgeable about the fundamental concepts of IBM's DB2 Data Warehouse Edition (DWE), Version 9.1. In addition to having the knowledge and skills necessary to design, develop, and support DB2 data warehouse environments using DB2 DWE, anyone seeking this certification should:

- Be able to explain how data warehouse and front-end analytics impact Business Intelligence Analytics architecture

- Know the difference between a multidimensional database and a relational database warehouse

- Know how metadata affects analytical queries

- Be able to select appropriate front-end features based on criteria such as presentation needed, level of interactivity required, Web versus FAT client, static versus dynamic, end user skill level

- Know how to translate data warehouse-based analytics into schémas, aggregations, and SQL

- Know when to use the DB2 Design Advisor versus the CV Advisor

- Be able to explain how the DB2 Query Patroller fits into warehouse-based analytics

- Be able to distinguish between logical and physical data models

- Be able to describe the architecture of DB2 DWE in terms of its components

- Be able to describe the architecture of DB2 DWE in terms of the three physical nodes used and where they are installed

- Be able to identify the hardware needed to install DB2 Data Warehouse Edition

- Know how to create a Data Design Project in the Project Engineer as a container for physical data modeling

- Know how to reverse-engineer an existing DB2 schema (or schema subset)

- Know how to design or modify a physical data model that describes a data warehouse (including constraints), as well as perform an impact analysis to identify all model/database dependencies

- Be able to view the contents of database objects

- Be able to identify candidate fact and dimension tables in a data warehouse

- Be able to create cube models and Cubes

- Know how to define levels and hierarchies

- Know how to define and create a dimension object

- Know how to create materialized query tables (MQTs), as well as troubleshoot ineffective MQTs

- Know how to perform Import and Export operations

- Be able to create a data mining project in the Project Explorer

- Know how to formulate a data mining task from a business problem, define a preprocessing function to prepare data for data mining, edit properties of mining operators, apply a visualizer operator to a data mining flow, run a data mining flow against a data warehouse, and view the results of any data mining flow run

- Be able to describe use cases for the SQL Warehousing Tool

- Know how to create, setup, and navigate a Data Warehouse Project using the DB2 DWE Design Studio

- Be able to describe the concepts of dataflows, subflows, and control flows, as well as build dataflows and subflows by adding, connecting, and defining properties of SQL Warehousing Dataflow Operators

- Know why, when, and how to use a data station in a dataflow

- Be able to prepare and deploy a Data Warehouse Project application to a test and/or production environment, using the DB2 DWE Administration Console

- Be able to set up and perform Query Workload Management

- Know how to setup and perform Historical Analysis

- Know how to administer, maintain, and tune the Query Patroller

In order to acquire the IBM Certified Solution Designer—DB2 Data Warehouse Edition V9.1 certification, candidates must take and pass one exam: the **DB2 Data Warehouse Edition V9.1** exam (Exam 716). The roadmap for acquiring the IBM Certified Solution Designer—DB2 Data Warehouse Edition V9.1 certification is illustrated in Figure 1–7.

Figure 1–7: IBM Certified Solution Designer—DB2 Data Warehouse Edition V9.1 certification roadmap.

The Certification Process

A close examination of the IBM certification roles available quickly reveals that, in order to obtain a particular DB2 9 certification, you must take and pass one or more exams that have been designed specifically for that certification role. (Each exam is a software-based exam that is neither platform- nor product-specific.) Thus, once you have chosen the certification role you wish to pursue and familiarized yourself with the requirements for that particular role, the next step is to prepare for and take the appropriate certification exams.

Preparing for the Certification Exams

If you have experience using DB2 9 in the context of the certification role you have chosen, you may already possess the skills and knowledge needed to pass the exam(s) required for that role. However, if your experience with DB2 9 is limited (and even if it is not), you can prepare for any of the certification exams available by taking advantage of the following resources:

- Formal Education

  IBM Learning Services offers courses that are designed to help you prepare for DB2 9 certification. A listing of the courses that are recommended for each certification exam can be found using the Certification Navigator tool provided on IBM's "Professional Certification Program from IBM" Web site (*www.ibm.com/certify*). Recommended courses can also be found at IBM's "DB2 Data Management" Web site (*www.ibm.com/software/data/education/ learningcontent.html*). For more information on course schedules, locations, and pricing, contact IBM Learning Services or visit their Web site.

- Online Tutorials

  IBM offers a series of seven interactive online tutorials designed to prepare you for the DB2 9 Fundamentals exam (Exam 730). These tutorials can be found at *www-128.ibm.com/developerworks/offers/lp/db2cert/db2-cert730.html.*

  IBM also offers a series of interactive online tutorials designed to prepare you for the DB2 9 for Linux, UNIX, and Windows Database Administration exam (Exam 731) and the DB2 9 Family Application Development exam (Exam 733). These tutorials can be found at *www-128.ibm.com/developerworks/offers/lp/db2cert/db2-cert731.html* and *www-128.ibm.com/developerworks/offers/lp/db2cert/db2-cert733.html.*

- Publications

  All the information you need to pass any of the available certification exams can be found in the documentation that is provided with DB2 9. A complete set of manuals comes with the product and are accessible through the Information Center once you have installed the DB2 9 software. DB2 9 documentation can also be downloaded from IBM's Web site in both HTML and PDF formats. (The IBM Web site that contains the DB2 9 documentation can be found at *www.ibm.com/software/data/db2/library.*)

  Self-study books (such as this one) that focus on one or more DB2 9 certification exams/roles are also available. Most of these books can be found at your local bookstore or ordered from many online book retailers. (A listing of possible reference materials for each certification exam can be found using the Certification Navigator tool provided on IBM's "Professional Certification Program from IBM" Web site (*http://www.ibm.com/certify*).

  In addition to the DB2 9 product documentation, IBM often produces manuals, known as "RedBooks," that cover advanced DB2 9 topics (as well as other topics). These manuals are available as downloadable PDF files on IBM's RedBook Web site (*www.redbooks.ibm.com*). Or, if you prefer to have a bound hard copy, you can obtain one for a modest fee by following the appropriate links on the RedBook Web site. (There is no charge for the downloadable PDF files.)

  A listing of possible reference materials for each certification exam can be found using the Certification Navigator tool provided on IBM's "Professional Certification Program from IBM" Web site (*www.ibm.com/certify*). Ordering information is often included with the listing.

- Exam Objectives
  Objectives that provide an overview of the basic topics that are covered on a particular certification exam can be found using the Certification Navigator tool provided on IBM's "Professional Certification Program from IBM" Web site (*www.ibm.com/certify*). Exam objectives for the DB2 9 Family Fundamentals exam (Exam 730) can also be found in Appendix A of this book.

- Sample Questions/Exams
  Sample questions and sample exams allow you to become familiar with the format and wording used on the actual certification exams. They can help you decide whether you possess the knowledge needed to pass a particular exam. Sample questions, along with descriptive answers, are provided at the end of every chapter in this book and in Appendix B. Sample exams for each DB2 9 certification role available can be found using the Certification Exam tool provided on IBM's "Professional Certification Program from IBM" Web site (*www.ibm.com/software/data/education/cert/assessment.html*). There is a $10 charge for each exam taken.

It is important to note that the certification exams are designed to be rigorous. Very specific answers are expected for most exam questions. Because of this, and because the range of material covered on a certification exam is usually broader than the knowledge base of many DB2 9 professionals, you should take advantage of the exam preparation resources available if you want to guarantee your success in obtaining the certification(s) you desire.

Arranging to Take a Certification Exam

When you are confident that you are ready to take a specific DB2 9 certification exam, your next step is to contact an IBM-authorized testing vendor. The DB2 9 certification exams are administered by Pearson VUE, by Thompson Prometric, and, in rare, cases by IBM (for example, IBM administers the DB2 9 certifications free of charge at some of the larger database conferences, such as the International DB2 User's Group North American conference). However, before you contact either testing vendor, you should visit their Web site (*www.vue.com/ibm* and *www.2test.com*, respectively) and use the navigation tools provided there to locate a testing center that is convenient for you to get to. Once you have located a testing center, you can then contact the vendor and make arrangements to take the certification exam. (Contact information for the testing vendors can also be found on their respective Web sites; in some cases, you can schedule an exam online.)

You must make arrangements to take a certification exam at least 24 hours in advance, and when you contact the testing vendor, you should be ready to provide the following information:

- Your name (as you want it to appear on your certification certificate)

- An identification number (if you have taken an IBM certification exam before, this is the number assigned to you at that time; if not, the testing vendor will supply one)

- A telephone number where you can be reached

- A fax number

- The mailing address to which you want all certification correspondence, including your certification welcome package, to be sent

- Your billing address, if it is different from your mailing address

- Your email address

- The number that identifies the exam you wish to take (for example, Exam 730)

- The method of payment (credit card or check) you wish to use, along with any relevant payment information (such as credit card number and expiration date)

- Your company's name (if applicable)

- The testing center where you would like to take the certification exam

- The date when you would like to take the certification exam

Before you make arrangements to take a certification exam, you should have pencil/pen and paper handy so you can write down the test applicant identification number the testing center will assign you. You will need this information when you arrive at the testing center to take the certification exam. (If time permits, you will be sent a letter of confirmation containing the number of the certification exam you have been scheduled to take, along with corresponding date, time, and location information; if you register within 48 hours of the scheduled testing date, you will not receive a letter).

If you have already taken one or more of the certification exams offered, you should make the testing vendor aware of this and ask the vendor to assign you the same applicant identification number that was used before. This will allow the certification team at IBM to quickly recognize when you have met all the exam requirements for a particular certification role. (If you were assigned a unique applicant identification number each time you took an exam, you should go to the IBM Professional Certification Member Web site (www.ibm.com/certify/members) and select Member Services to combine all of your exam results under one ID.)

With the exception of the DB2 9 for Linux, UNIX, and Windows Database Administration Upgrade Exam (Exam 736), each certification exam costs $150 (in the United States). Scheduling procedures vary according to how you choose to pay for the exam. If you decide to pay by credit card, you can make arrangements to take the exam immediately after providing the testing vendor with the appropriate information. However, if you elect to pay by check, you will be required to wait until the check has been received and payment has been confirmed before you will be allowed to make arrangements to take the exam. (Thompson Prometric recommends that if you pay by check, you write your registration ID on the front and contact them seven business days after the check is mailed. At that time, they should have received and confirmed your payment, and you should be able to make arrangements to take the exam you have paid for.)

If, for some reason, you need to reschedule or cancel your testing appointment after it is made, you must do so at least 24 hours before your scheduled test time. Otherwise, you will still be charged the price of the exam.

Taking an IBM Certification Exam

On the day you are scheduled to take a certification exam, you should arrive at the testing center at least 15 minutes before the scheduled start time to sign in. As part of the sign-in process, you will be asked to provide the applicant identification number you were assigned when you made arrangements to take the exam and two forms of identification. One form of identification must contain a recent photograph, and the other must contain your signature. Examples of valid forms of identification include a driver's license (photograph) and a credit card (signature).

Once you are signed in, the exam administrator will instruct you to enter the
testing area and select an available workstation. The exam administrator will then
enter your name and identification number into the workstation you have chosen,
provide you with a pencil and some paper, and instruct you to begin the exam
when you are ready. At that point, the title screen of the IBM Certification Exam
testing software should be displayed on the computer monitor in front of you.
Figure 1–8 illustrates what this screen looks like.

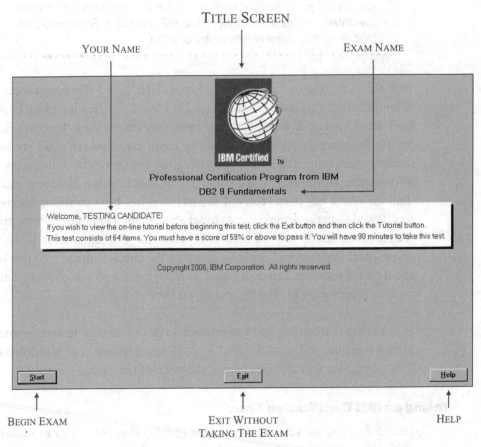

Figure 1–8: Title screen of the IBM Certification Exam testing software.

As you can see in Figure 1–8, the title screen of the IBM Certification Exam
testing software consists of the IBM Certification Logo along with the title
"Professional Certification Program from IBM," the name of the exam that is

about to be administered, (for example, the title screen shown in Figure 1–8 indicates that the DB2 9 Family Fundamentals exam is about to be administered), and a welcome message containing your name and some basic information on how to get started. Before proceeding, you should:

- Verify that the exam syou are about to take is indeed the exam you expected to take. If the name of the exam shown on the title screen is different from the name of the exam you had planned to take, bring this to the attention of the exam administrator immediately

- Verify that your name is spelled correctly. The way your name appears in the welcome message shown on the title screen reflects how it has been stored in the IBM Certification database. This is how all correspondence to you will be addressed, and more importantly, this is how your name will appear on the certification credentials you will receive if you pass the exam you are about to take

In addition to telling you which exam is about to be administered, the title screen of the IBM Certification Exam testing software lets you know how many questions you can expect to see on the exam you are about to take, what kind of score you must receive in order to pass, and the time frame in which the exam must be completed. With one exception, each exam contains between 50 and 70 questions and is allotted 90 minutes for completion. The DB2 9 for Linux, UNIX, and Windows Database Administration Upgrade exam (Exam 736) contains 38 questions and is allotted 60 minutes for completion. Although each certification exam must be completed within a predefined time limit, you should never rush through an exam just because the "clock is running"; the time limits imposed are more than adequate for you to work through the exam at a relaxed, but steady pace.

When you are ready, begin by selecting the "Start" push button located in the lower left corner of the screen (refer to Figure 1–9). If instead you would like a quick refresher course on how to use the IBM Certification Exam testing software, select the "Help" push button located in the lower right corner of the screen. (If you panic and decide you're not ready to take the exam, you can select the "Exit" push button located between the "Start" and "Help" push buttons at the bottom of the screen to get out of the testing software altogether, but I recommend you talk with the exam administrator about your concerns before selecting this push button).

If you plan to take a quick refresher course on how to use the IBM Certification Exam testing software, make sure you do so before you select the "Start" push button to begin the exam. Although help is available at any time, the clock does not start running until the "Start" push button is selected. By viewing help information before the clock is started, you avoid using what could prove to be valuable testing time reading documentation instead of test questions.

Once the "Start" button on the title screen of the IBM Certification Exam testing software is selected, the clock will start running, and the first exam question will be presented in a question panel that looks something like the screen shown in Figure 1–9.

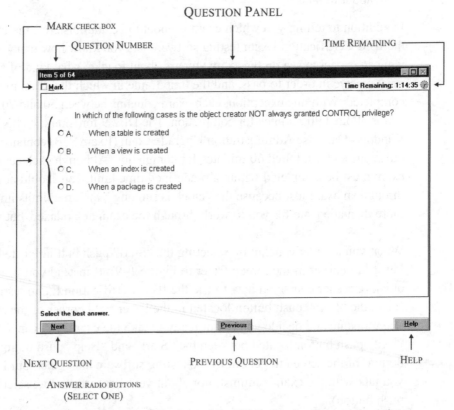

Figure 1–9: Typical question panel of the IBM Certification Exam testing software.

Aside from the question itself, one of the first things you may notice when you examine the question panel of the IBM Certification Exam testing software is the question number displayed in the top left corner of the screen. If you answer each question in the order they are presented, this portion of the screen can act as a progress indicator, because the current question number is displayed along with the total number of questions contained in the exam.

Immediately below the question number, you will find a special check box that is referred to as the "Mark" check box. If you would like to skip the current question for now and come back to it later, or if you're uncertain about the answer(s) you have chosen and would like to look at this question again after you have completed the rest of the exam, you should mark this check box (by placing the mouse pointer over it and pressing the left mouse button). When every question has been viewed once, you will be given the opportunity to review just the marked questions again. At that time, you can answer any unanswered questions remaining as well as re-evaluate any answers you provided about which you have some concerns.

Another important feature that can be found on the question panel is the "Time Remaining" information that is displayed in the top right corner of the screen. As the title implies, this area of the question panel provides continuous feedback on the amount of time you have available to finish and review the exam. If you would like to see more detailed information, such as the actual wall-clock time at which you began the exam and the time frame within which you are expected to complete the exam, you can view that information by selecting the clock icon located just to the right of the "Time Remaining" information. When this icon is selected (by placing the mouse pointer over it and pressing the left mouse button), a dialog similar to the one shown in Figure 1–10 is displayed.

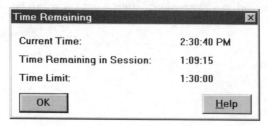

Figure 1–10: Time Remaining dialog.

Obviously, the most important part of the question panel is the exam question itself, along with the corresponding list of possible answers provided. Take the time to read each question carefully. When you have located the correct answer in the list provided, you should mark it by selecting the answer radio-button positioned just to the left of the answer text (by placing the mouse pointer over the desired answer radio-button and pressing the left mouse button). Once you have selected an answer for the question being displayed (or marked it with the "Mark" check box), you can move to the next question by selecting the "Next" push button, which is located in the lower left corner of the screen (refer to Figure 1–10).

If, at any time, you would like to return to the previous question, you can do so by pressing the "Previous" push button, located at the bottom of the screen, just to the right of the "Next" push button. Also, if you would like to access help on how to use the IBM Certification Exam testing software, you can do so by selecting the "Help" push button located in the lower right corner of the screen. It is important to note that, although the "Next" and "Previous" push buttons can be used to navigate through the questions provided with the exam, the navigation process itself is not cyclic in nature—that is, when you are on the first question, you cannot go to the last question by selecting the "Previous" push button (in fact the "Previous" push button will not be displayed if you are on the first question). Likewise, when you are on the last question, you cannot go to the first question simply by selecting the "Next" push button. However, there is a way to navigate quickly to a specific question from the item review panel, which we will look at shortly.

Although in most cases only one answer in the list provided is the correct answer to the question shown, there are times when multiple answers are valid. On those occasions, the answer radio-buttons will be replaced with answer check boxes, and the question will be worded in such a way that you will know how many answers are expected. An example of such a question can be seen in Figure 1–11.

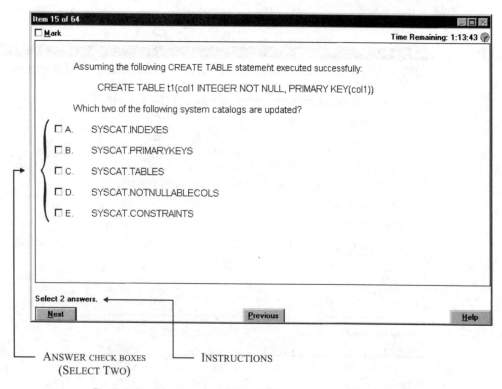

☐ **M**ark   Time Remaining: 1:13:43

Assuming the following CREATE TABLE statement executed successfully:

CREATE TABLE t1(col1 INTEGER NOT NULL, PRIMARY KEY(col1))

Which two of the following system catalogs are updated?

☐ A.   SYSCAT.INDEXES

☐ B.   SYSCAT.PRIMARYKEYS

☐ C.   SYSCAT.TABLES

☐ D.   SYSCAT.NOTNULLABLECOLS

☐ E.   SYSCAT.CONSTRAINTS

Select 2 answers.

Next   **P**revious   **H**elp

ANSWER CHECK BOXES   INSTRUCTIONS
(SELECT TWO)

Figure 1–11: Question panel for questions expecting multiple answers.

These types of questions are answered by selecting the answer check box positioned just to the left of the text *for every correct answer found.* (Again, this is done by placing the mouse pointer over each desired answer check box and pressing the left mouse button.)

Once in a while, an illustration or the output from some diagnostic tool will accompany a question. You will be required to view that illustration or output (referred to as an exhibit) before you can successfully answer the question presented. On those occasions, a message instructing you to display the exhibit for the question will precede the actual test question, and a special push button called the "Exhibit" push button will be positioned at the bottom of the screen, between the "Previous" push button and the "Help" push button. An example of such a question can be seen in Figure 1–12.

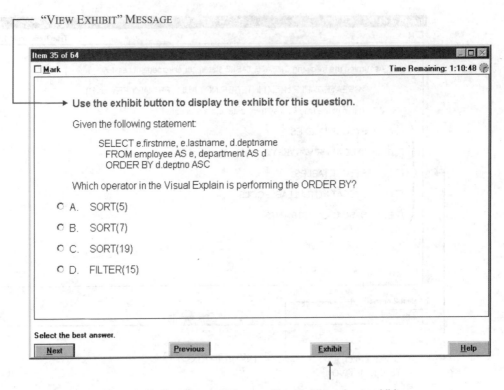

Figure 1–12: Question panel for questions that contain an exhibit.

To view the exhibit associated with such a question, you simply select the
"Exhibit" push button located at the bottom of the screen. This action will cause
the corresponding exhibit panel to be displayed. (A sample exhibit panel can be
seen in Figure 1–13.)

Exhibit panels are relatively simple. In fact, once an exhibit panel is displayed,
there are only two things you can do with it: You can close it by selecting the
"Close" push button located at the bottom of the screen, or you can tile it (i.e.,
make it share screen real estate) with its corresponding question panel by selecting
the "Tile" push button, which is located beside the "Close" push button. Aside from
having to view the exhibit provided, the process used to answer questions that have
exhibits is no different from the process used to answer questions that do not.

EXHIBIT PANEL

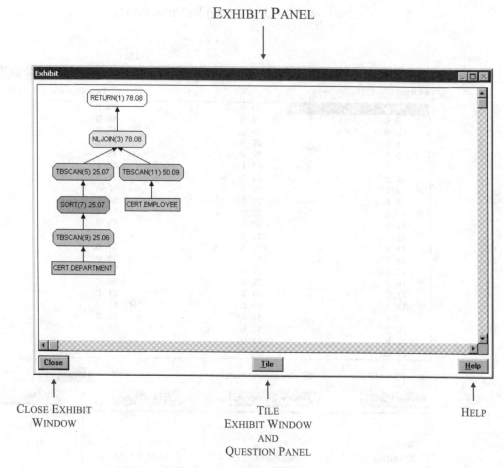

Figure 1–13: Sample exhibit panel.

When you have viewed every exam question available (by selecting the "Next" push button on every question panel shown), an item review panel that looks something like the panel shown in Figure 1–14 will be displayed.

ITEM (QUESTION) REVIEW PANEL

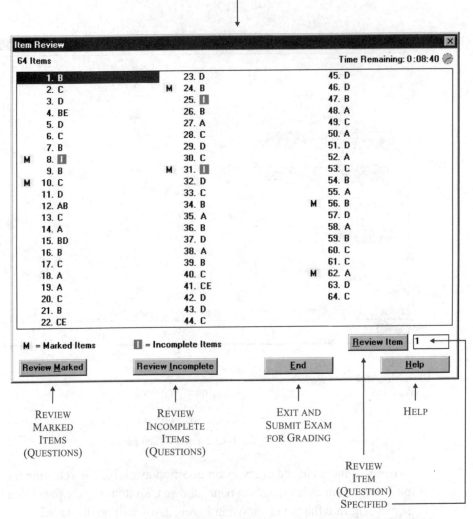

Figure 1–14: Item (question) review panel of the IBM Certification Exam testing software.

As you can see in Figure 1–14, the item review panel contains a numerical listing of the questions that make up the certification exam you are taking, along with the answers you have provided for each. Questions that you marked (by selecting the "Mark" check box) are preceded by the letter "M," and questions that you skipped or did not provide the correct number of answers for are assigned the answer "I" to indicate they are incomplete. By selecting the "Review Marked" push button located in the lower left corner of the screen (refer to Figure 1–15), you can quickly go back through just the questions that have been marked. When reviewing marked items in this manner, each time the "Next" push button is selected on a question panel, you are taken to the next marked question in the list until eventually you are returned to the item review panel. Likewise, by selecting the "Review Incomplete" push button located just to the right of the "Review Marked" push button, you can go back through just the questions that have been identified as being incomplete. (Navigation works the same as when the "Review Marked" push button is selected.) If, instead, you would like to review a specific question, you can do so by highlighting that question's number or typing that question's number in the entry field provided just to the right of the "Review Item" push button (which is located just above the "Help" push button in the lower right corner of the screen) and selecting the "Review Item" push button.

If you elect to use the "Review Item" push button to review a particular question, the only way you can return to the item review screen is by selecting the "Next" push button found on that question panel *and every subsequent question panel presented* until no more question panels exist.

One of the first things you should do when the item review panel is displayed is resolve any incomplete items found. (When the exam is graded, each incomplete item found is marked incorrect, and points are deducted from your final score.) Then, if time permits, you should go back and review the questions that you marked. It is important to note that when you finish reviewing a marked question, you should unmark it (by placing the mouse pointer over the "Mark" check box and pressing the left mouse button) before going on to the next marked question or returning to the item review panel. This will make it easier for you to keep track of which questions have been reviewed and which have not.

As soon as every incomplete item found has been resolved, the "Review Incomplete" push button is automatically removed from the item review panel. Likewise, when there are no more marked questions, the "Review Marked" push button is removed from the item review panel. Thus, when every incomplete and marked item found has been resolved, the item review panel will look similar to the one shown in Figure 1–15.

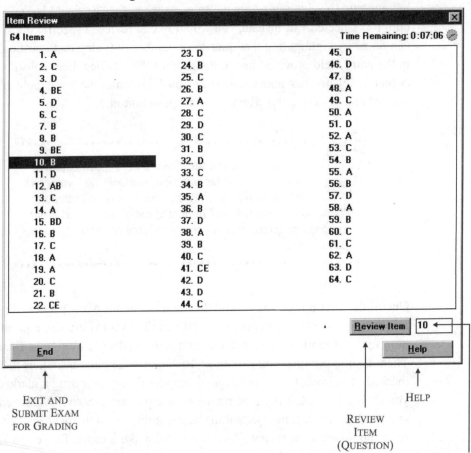

Figure 1–15: Item (question) review panel with all incomplete and marked items (questions) resolved.

Keep in mind that, even when the "Review Incomplete" and "Review Marked" push buttons are no longer available, you can still go back and review a specific question by highlighting that question's number or typing that question's number in the entry field provided and selecting the "Review Item" push button (refer to Figure 1–16).

As soon as you feel comfortable with the answers you have provided, you can end the exam and submit it for grading by selecting the "End" push button, which should now be located in the lower left corner of the item review panel. When this push button is selected (by placing the mouse pointer over it and pressing the left mouse button), a dialog similar to the one shown in Figure 1–16 should be displayed.

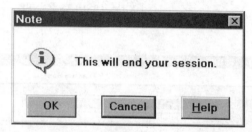

Figure 1–16: Confirmation dialog for end of exam session.

If you select the "End" push button on the item review panel before every incomplete item found has been resolved, a dialog similar to the one shown in Figure 1–17 will be displayed instead.

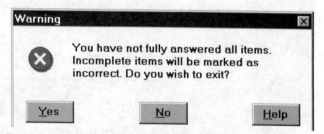

Figure 1–17: Warning dialog for ending exam with incomplete items.

Both of these dialogs give you the opportunity to confirm your decision to end the exam and submit it for grading or to reconsider and continue resolving and/or reviewing exam questions. If you wish to do the former, you should select the "OK" or the "Yes" push button when one of these dialogs is presented; if you wish to do the latter, you should select the "Cancel" or "No" push button, in which case you will be returned to the item review panel. Keep in mind that if you select the "Yes" push button when the dialog shown in Figure 1–18 is displayed, all incomplete items found will be marked as being wrong, and this will have a negative impact on your final score.

As soon as you confirm that you do indeed wish to end the exam, the IBM
Certification Exam testing software will evaluate your answers and produce a
score report that indicates whether or not you passed the exam. This report will
then be displayed on an exam results panel that looks something like the panel
shown in Figure 1–18, and a corresponding hard copy (printout) will be generated.

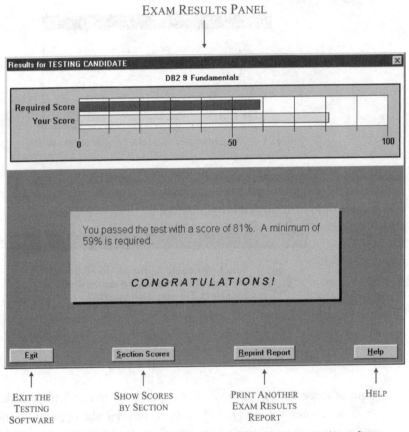

Figure 1–18: Exam results panel of the IBM Certification Exam testing software.

As you can see in Figure 1–19, the exam results panel shows the required score
along with your actual score in a horizontal percent bar graph. Directly below this
graph is a message that contains the percentage score you received, along with the
percentage score needed to pass the exam. If you received a passing score, this
message will end with the word "Congratulations!" However, if you received a
score that is below the score needed to pass, the message you see will begin with
the words "You did not pass the test," and your score will follow.

Each certification exam is broken into sections, and regardless of whether you pass or fail, you should take a few moments to review the score you received for each section. This information can help you evaluate your strengths and weaknesses; if you failed to pass the exam, it can help you identify the areas you should spend some time reviewing before you attempt to take the exam again. To view the section scores for the exam you have just completed, you simply select the "Section Scores" push button located at the bottom of the screen. This action will cause a section scores panel similar to the one shown in Figure 1–19 to be displayed.

SECTION SCORES PANEL

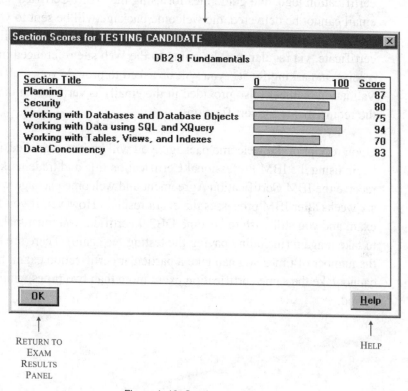

RETURN TO
EXAM
RESULTS
PANEL

HELP

Figure 1–19: Section scores panel.

When you have finished reviewing your section scores, you may return to the exam results panel by selecting the "OK" push button located at the bottom left corner of the screen. From there, you can exit the IBM Certification Exam testing software by selecting the "Exit" push button, which is also located at the bottom left corner of the screen.

Shortly after you take a certification exam (usually within five working days), the testing vendor sends your results, along with your demographic data (e.g., name, address, phone number) to the IBM Certification Group for processing. If you passed the exam, you will receive credit toward the certification role the exam was designed for, and if the exam you took completes the requirements that have been outlined for a particular certification role, you will receive an email (at the email address you provided during registration) that contains a copy of the IBM Certification Agreement and a welcome package that includes a certificate that is suitable for framing (as a .PDF file), camera-ready artwork of the IBM certification logo, and guidelines for using the "IBM Certified" mark. (If this email cannot be delivered, the welcome package will be sent to you via regular mail.) You can also receive a printed certificate, along with a wallet-sized certificate, via regular mail by going to the Web site referenced in the email you receive and asking for it—you will be asked to provide your Fulfillment ID and Validation Number (also provided in the email) as verification that you have met the requirements for certification.

Upon receipt of the welcome package, you will become certified, and you can begin using the IBM Professional Certification title and trademark. (You should receive the IBM Certification Agreement and welcome package within four to six weeks after IBM processes the exam results.) However, if you failed to pass the exam and you still wish to become DB2 9 certified, you must make arrangements to take it again (including paying the testing fee again). There are no restrictions on the number of times you can take a particular certification exam; however, you cannot take the same certification exam more than two times within a 30-day period.

2

Planning

Fourteen percent (14%) of the DB2 9 Fundamentals certification exam (Exam 730) is designeds to test your knowledge of the products that make up the DB2 Family as well as your ability to identify which products must be installed to create a desired environment or configuration. This portion of the exam is also designed to test your knowledge of the various tools that are provided with DB2. The questions that make up this portion of the exam are intended to evaluate the following:

- Your ability to identify the products that make up the DB2 Family

- Your knowledge of the different DB2 clients available

- Your knowledge of how nonrelational data is managed by the DB2 extenders

- Your knowledge of the implications of storing and managing Extensible Markup Language (XML) data

- Your knowledge of the features and functions available with the tools that are provided with DB2

- Your knowledge of data warehousing and On-Line Transaction Processing (OLTP) concepts

This chapter is designed to introduce you to the various products that make up the DB2 Family and to the comprehensive set of tools that are provided to assist in administering and managing DB2 servers, instances, databases, and database objects.

The DB2 Family

DB2, formally called DATABASE 2, was born on MVS in 1983. In 1987, DB2 arrived on the Personal Computer as the Database Manager in OS/2 1.3 Extended Edition; a year later, it emerged as SQL/400 for IBM's new AS/400 server. By 1992, DB2 had become a stand-alone product on OS/2 (it now had the name DB2/2), and in 1993, DB2 appeared on AIX; this port prompted another name change, and DB2/2 became DB2 for Common Servers. New editions of DB2 were introduced on HP-UX and Solaris in 1994, on Windows in 1995, and on Linux in 1999. Along the way the name changed again, and DB2 for Common Servers became DB2 Universal Database.

DB2 9 is the latest release of IBM's popular data management software for distributed systems, and with this release comes yet another name change. Like previous versions, DB2 runs on a wide variety of platforms (AIX, HP-UX, Linux, Solaris, Windows, i5/OS, and z/OS), and several editions are available—each of which has been designed to meet a specific business need. These editions, along with an extensive suite of add-on products that provide additional storage capability and advanced connectivity, are collectively known as the *DB2 Family*. The editions that make up the heart of the DB2 Family are:

- DB2 Everyplace
- DB2 Express
- DB2 Express-C
- DB2 Personal Edition
- DB2 Workgroup Server Edition
- DB2 Enterprise Server Edition
- DB2 Data Warehouse Edition
- DB2 Personal Developer's Edition
- DB2 Universal Developer's Edition
- DB2 Enterprise Developer's Edition
- DB2 for i5/OS
- DB2 for z/OS

All of the DB2 Family editions available, along with the type of computing environment each edition is primarily designed for, can be seen in Figure 2–1.

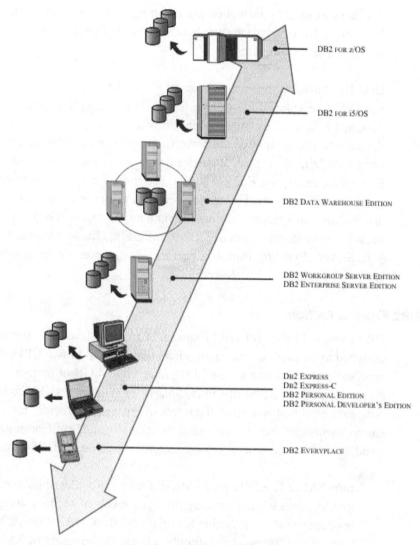

Figure 2–1: DB2 Family Editions.

DB2 Everyplace—Database Edition and Enterprise Edition

DB2 Everyplace is a small-footprint (approximately 350 KB) relational database and a high-performance data synchronization solution that allows enterprise applications and data to be extended to mobile devices such as personal digital assistants (PDAs), handheld personal computers (HPCs), and smart phones. DB2 Everyplace can be used as a local, stand-alone database that resides on a mobile device or to access information stored on remote servers whenever a connection is available. DB2 Everyplace can also be embedded directly into mobile devices to increase their functionality.

DB2 Everyplace is available in two editions: DB2 Everyplace Database Edition and DB2 Everyplace Enterprise Edition. DB2 Everyplace Database Edition is designed to be used by Independent Software Vendors (ISVs) and application developers who wish to create powerful mobile and embedded applications that work with DB2 Everyplace database data stored directly on a mobile device. DB2 Everyplace Enterprise Edition is designed to be a complete datacentric mobile synchronization server. This secure server is responsible for managing the distribution and synchronization of data between mobile device users and back-end data sources such as DB2 9, Informix, Oracle, Sybase, and Microsoft SQL Server. (Synchronization is performed whenever a connection to the back-end data source is detected.)

DB2 Express Edition

DB2 Express Edition (or DB2 Express) is an entry-level data server that is designed to be used on microcomputers that have up to two CPUs (a dual-core processor is treated as a single CPU), have up to 4 GB of memory, and are running a supported version of Linux, Solaris, or Windows. DB2 Express contains a rich feature set that will meet the needs of most deployments; for workloads or environments that require additional functionality, add-on features are available for an additional licensing fee. Add-on features available for DB2 Express include:

pureXML: The DB2 pureXML™ Feature provides simple, efficient access to XML data while providing the same levels of security, integrity, and resiliency that are available for relational data. DB2 9 stores XML data in a hierarchical format that naturally reflects the structure of XML. This storage approach, along with innovative XML indexing techniques, allows DB2 to manage XML data efficiently while eliminating the complex and time-consuming parsing that is typically required to store XML data in a relational database.

High Availability: The DB2 High Availability Feature provides 24 x 7 availability to a DB2 data server. Three packages that constitute this feature are High Availability Disaster Recovery (HADR), Online Reorganization, and IBM Tivoli System Automation for Multiplatforms (TSA MP). HADR allows failover to a standby system in the event that a software or hardware failure occurs on the primary system. Online Reorganization reconstructs the rows in a table to eliminate fragmentation and compacts information for better performance while permitting uninterrupted access to table data. TSA MP provides high availability by automating the control of IT resources such as processes, file systems, and IP addresses.

Workload Management: The DB2 Workload Management Feature leverages the Connection Concentrator in conjunction with either Query Patroller (QP) or the DB2 Governor to provide a more proactive, fail-safe workload environment. Connection Concentrator enables fail-safe operation and load balancing of a workload. Query Patroller is a powerful query workload management tool that proactively and dynamically controls submission and execution of queries to manage DB2 data server workloads better. The DB2 Governor monitors and changes the behavior of applications that run against the DB2 data server, depending on rules that you specify in the governor configuration file. For example, if an application is using too much of a particular resource, a rule might specify that the priority of the application is to be changed or that the application is to be forced to disconnect from the database.

Performance Optimization: DB2 Performance Optimization combines the functionality of three modules to provide performance optimizations for complex queries, data clustering for On-Line Analytical Processing (OLAP) applications, and high performance for machines with multiple processors. This feature consists of materialized query tables (MQTs), multidimensional clustering (MDC), and Query Parallelism. MQTs are tables whose definition is based on the result of a query; queries against an MQT can return results faster than would be possible if a normal table were used. MDC provides an elegant method for clustering data in tables along multiple dimensions. Query Parallelism allows for the simultaneous processing of parts of a single query by multiple processors, dramatically improving overall performance on multi-processor machines.

DB2 Homogenous Federation Feature: The DB2 Homogeneous Federation Feature provides the ability to manage and access remote DB2 and Informix data servers as if they were local tables; it also allows applications to access diverse types of data (mainframe and distributed, public and private) as if it were in a base table, regardless of where it physically resides. Homogeneous federation meets the needs of customers who require unified access to data managed by multiple data servers.

DB2 Express-C

DB2 Express-C is a no-charge entry-level data server that is designed to be used on microcomputers that have up to two CPUs, have up to 4 GB of memory, and are running a supported version of Linux or Windows. DB2 Express-C is intended to be used for evaluation purposes and for the development/deployment of C, C++, Java, .NET, PHP, and XQuery applications. Essentially, DB2 Express-C is a subset of DB2 Express Edition with one exception: Where pureXML is available as an add-on feature for DB2 Express, it is included with DB2 Express-C. Features found in DB2 Express that are not available with DB2 Express-C include:

- Spatial Extender Client and samples

- Microsoft Cluster Server support

- Informix Data Source support

- Replication Data Capture (both SQL Replication and Replication with MQ Server)

- DB2 Web Tools

- Global Secure Toolkit

- APPC and NetBios support

Additionally, the add-on features that are available for DB2 Express cannot be added to DB2 Express-C. If you wish to use any of those features, you must first purchase a license for DB2 Express Edition and then purchase the desired add-on features. Fortunately, DB2 Express-C can be seamlessly upgraded to DB2 Express without requiring modifications to existing databases or database applications.

DB2 Personal Edition

DB2 Personal Edition (PE) is a single-user, full-function relational database management system that is ideal for desktop or laptop-based deployments. Databases under its control can be managed remotely, making it the perfect edition for occasionally connected or remote office implementations that do not require multi-user capability.

With DB2 Personal Edition a user can create, manipulate, and administer any number of local databases; however, each database created must reside on a storage medium that is managed by the PC on which the DB2 software has been installed. Remote clients cannot access databases that are under DB2 Personal Edition's control, but PCs running DB2 Personal Edition can act as remote clients and access data stored on other DB2 servers.

DB2 Personal Edition can be deployed on any Personal Computer (PC) that is running Linux or Windows; however, you must acquire a separate license for each user who will have access to a database under its control.

DB2 Workgroup Server Edition

DB2 Workgroup Server Edition (WSE) is a multi-user, full-function client/server database management system designed to be used on microcomputers that have up to four CPUs, have up to 16 GB of memory, and are running any of the following operating systems:

- AIX 5.2 (64-bit)
- AIX 5.3 (64-bit)
- HP-UX 11iv2
- Solaris 10 (64-bit)
- Red Hat Enterprise Linux (RHEL) 4 (32-bit and 64-bit)
- SUSE Enterprise Linux Server (SLES) 9 (32-bit and 64-bit)
- SUSE Enterprise Linux Server (SLES) 10 (32-bit and 64-bit)
- Novell Enterprise Server 9 (32-bit)
- Windows 2000
- Windows NT
- Windows XP Professional Edition
- Windows XP Professional x64 Edition
- Windows 2003 Standard Edition (32-bit and 64-bit)

- Windows 2003 Enterprise Edition (32-bit and 64-bit)
- Windows 2003 Datacenter Edition (32-bit and 64-bit)

DB2 Workgroup Server Edition includes all of the features of DB2 Express, while providing scalability to larger servers. As with DB2 Express, the following add-on features are available for an additional licensing fee:

- pureXML
- High Availability
- Workload Management
- Performance Optimization
- DB2 Homogeneous Federation Feature

With or without these features, DB2 Workgroup Server Edition is the ideal data server for small- to medium-sized business environments and departments that comprise a small number of internal users.

DB2 Enterprise Server Edition

DB2 Enterprise Server Edition (ESE) is a multi-user, full-function, Web-enabled client/server database management system that easily scales to handle high-volume transaction processing, multi-terabyte data warehouses, and mission-critical applications from such vendors as SAP. It is designed to be used on any size of server (from one to hundreds of CPUs) that is running any of the following operating systems:

- AIX 5.2 (64-bit)
- AIX 5.3 (64-bit)
- HP-UX 11iv2
- Solaris 10 (64-bit)
- Red Hat Enterprise Linux (RHEL) 4 (32-bit and 64-bit)
- SUSE Enterprise Linux Server (SLES) 9 (32-bit and 64-bit)
- SUSE Enterprise Linux Server (SLES) 10 (32-bit and 64-bit)
- Novell Enterprise Server 9 (32-bit)
- Windows XP Professional Edition
- Windows XP Professional x64 Edition
- Windows 2003 Standard Edition (32-bit and 64-bit)
- Windows 2003 Enterprise Edition (32-bit and 64-bit)
- Windows 2003 Datacenter Edition (32-bit and 64-bit)

DB2 Enterprise Server Edition includes all of the functionality found in DB2 Workgroup Edition, plus features that are needed to handle high user loads and provide 24x7x365 availability, including:

- High Availability Disaster Recovery (HADR)
- Table (range) partitioning
- Online reorganization
- Materialized Query Tables
- Multi-dimensional data clustering
- Full intra-query parallelism
- Connection Concentrator
- The DB2 Governor
- Tivoli System Automation for Multiplatforms (TSA MP)

DB2 Enterprise Server Edition also comes packaged with a tightly integrated connectivity product (DB2 Connect) that allows it to participate in heterogeneous networks using the Distributed Relational Database Architecture (DRDA) protocol. This allows up to five users to interact with iSeries and zSeries-based DB2 databases, Informix Dynamic Server (IDS) databases, and non-database host resources such as CICS, VSAM, and IMS. (If more user connectivity is needed, you can purchase additional DB2 Connect user entitlements.)

Distributed Relational Database Architecture (DRDA) is comprised of two distinct components: an Application Requestor (AR) and an Application Server (AS). Any client that implements an Application Requestor can connect to any server that has implemented an Application Server, and any server that implements an Application Server can be accessed by any client that has implemented an Application Requestor. Thus, if only one DRDA component has been implemented on a client or a server, communication can flow only one way. With DB2 Enterprise Server Edition, both an Application Requestor and an Application Server are implemented, so communications can flow in both directions—provided the iSeries or zSeries server that DB2 Enterprise Server Edition is attempting to communicate with also has implemented both an Application Requestor and an Application Server.

In addition to many of the add-on features available for DB2 Express and DB2 Workgroup Edition, the following add-on features are available for DB2 Enterprise Server Edition (again, for an additional licensing fee):

Storage Optimization: The DB2 Storage Optimization Feature gives you the ability to compress data on disk in order to decrease disk space and storage infrastructure requirements. Since disk storage systems can often be the most expensive components of a database solution, even a small reduction in the storage subsystem can result in substantial cost savings for the entire database solution.

Advanced Access Control: The Advanced Access Control Feature lets you decide exactly who has write access and who has read access to individual rows and/or columns in one or more tables. Label-Based Access Control (LBAC), the package that provides this feature, controls access to table objects by attaching security labels to them. Users attempting to access an object must have been granted an appropriate security label. When an object protected by a security policy is accessed, DB2 applies the appropriate access rules to determine whether access should be granted or not. When there's a match, access is permitted; without a match, access is denied.

Database Partitioning: The DB2 Database Partitioning Feature (DPF) provides the ability to manage very large databases better by dividing them into multiple partitions and storing those partitions across a cluster of multiple inexpensive servers. DPF processes complex queries more efficiently, giving better performance with smaller systems, while providing an option to easily expand to a cluster of servers as the organization's data needs grow. DPF can also improve data availability by reducing the time required for, as well as the impact of, standard maintenance activities.

Geodetic Data Management: The Geodetic Data Management feature provides the ability to store, access, manage, and analyze geographic location–based, round earth information for weather, defense, intelligence, or natural resource applications. By treating the Earth as a continuous spherical coordinate system rather than a flat map, the Geodetic Data Management feature enables you to manage and analyze spatial information with accuracies in distance and area as well as to develop applications that require geographical location analysis.

Real-Time Insight: The DB2 Real-Time Insight feature is used to manage incoming data with message rates of tens to hundreds of thousands of messages per second. Such messages can come from multiple data streams and may be aggregated, filtered, and enriched in real time before being stored or forwarded to other servers. The DB2 Real-Time Insight feature is powered by the DB2 Data Stream Engine, which can be used to load large volumes of data with high throughput and low latency, store and publish data from multiple feeds (up to 100), and make data (both real-time and historical) available to queries through standard SQL, C-API, and Java API interfaces.

Designed for mid-size to large businesses, DB2 Enterprise Server Edition is the ideal foundation for building multi-terabyte data warehouses, high-availability, high-volume OLTP systems, or Web-based Business Intelligence (BI) solutions.

DB2 Data Warehouse Server Edition

DB2 Data Warehouse Edition (DWE) is the top-of-the-line DB2 Edition for dynamic data warehousing. It is designed for today's data center environments, where OLTP and decision support are merged into integrated information management systems. This integrated platform for developing warehouse-based analytics includes core components for warehouse construction and administration as well as Web-based applications with embedded data mining and multi-dimensional Online Analytical Processing (OLAP).

The core engine for DB2 Data Warehouse Edition is DB2 Enterprise Server Edition and the DB2 Data Partitioning Feature. (DB2 Enterprise Server Edition includes data warehouse enhancing features such as materialized query tables, the starburst optimizer, and multi-dimensional clusters; the DB2 Data Partitioning Feature provides increased parallelism to aid in performing administration tasks, as well as scalability to support very large databases and complex workloads.) Along with the core engine, DB2 Data Warehouse Edition is comprised of the following components:

DB2 DWE Design Studio: DB2 DWE Design Studio is a unified graphical development environment that can be used to build BI solutions. (DB2 DWE Design Studio is essentially an extension of Eclipse-based Rational Data Architect (RDA) modeling functions.) With DB2 DWE Design Studio, designers can connect to source and target databases, reverse-engineer physical data models, build DB2 SQL-based data flows and mining flows, set up OLAP cubes, and prepare applications for deployment to runtime systems.

DB2 DWE SQL Warehousing Tool: The DB2 DWE SQL Warehousing Tool provides a way to solve integration problems in a DB2 data warehouse environment. The tool provides a metadata system and an integrated development environment (IDE) to create, edit, and manage logical flows of higher-level operations, and a code generation system that understands the flows and translates them into optimized SQL code for execution. Once the development of the flows is complete, the second part of the SQL Warehousing Tool comes into play: the packaging of the code generated and any associated artifacts into a data warehouse application that can be deployed into various target runtime systems.

DB2 DWE Administration Console: The DB2 DWE Administration Console is a Web-based application that can be used to manage and monitor BI applications. Built upon the WebSphere Application Server, the DB2 DWE Administration Console uses Web clients to access and deploy data warehouse applications modeled and designed for DWE.

DB2 DWE OLAP Acceleration: DB2 DWE OLAP Acceleration provides a simple, efficient method for creating specialized relational structures that add OLAP functionality to a DB2 data warehouse. (Administrators simply drag objects onto predefined layouts to add OLAP functionality; no extensive knowledge of OLAP is needed.) DB2 DWE OLAP Acceleration also accelerates OLAP queries by analyzing dimensional models and recommending aggregates that will improve OLAP performance. Administrators can use the DB2 DWE OLAP Acceleration feature to show summarized, graphical views of business activity. End users, in turn, can experience faster cube loads and receive the ability to drill down into the data to get more detail than that provided in a summary.

DB2 DWE Data Mining and Visualization Features: DB2 DWE Data Mining and Visualization Features help you discover hidden relationships in your data, without requiring you to export the data to a special data mining computer or work with small samples of the data. The data mining process starts with historical data being gathered and put through a series of mathematical functions to derive business rules, which are then collected together to form a Model. Next, the Visualization feature provides data mining model analysis via a Java-based results browser. This is done to verify that the business rules derived are accurate. Finally, the verified business rules are applied to new data to determine the appropriate predicted outcome. This process of applying the business rules is called Scoring; Scoring in real time allows businesses to catch fraudulent records and defects faster.

DB2 DWE Alphablox Analytics: DB2 Alphablox provides the ability to rapidly create custom Web-based applications that fit into the corporate infrastructure and reach a wide range of users, inside and outside the corporate firewall. Applications built with the Alphablox platform run in standard Web browsers, allowing real-time, highly customizable multidimensional analysis from a client computer. DB2 Alphablox is tightly integrated with DB2 DWE OLAP Acceleration, which provides common metadata and database optimization for Alphablox multi-dimensional analysis.

DB2 Query Patroller: DB2 Query Patroller is a powerful query management system that can be used to control the flow of queries against a DB2 database dynamically. With the DB2 Query Patroller, an administrator can define separate query classes for queries of different sizes to share system resources better among queries; give queries submitted by certain users high priority so that they will run sooner, automatically put large queries on hold so that they can be canceled or scheduled to run during off-peak hours; and collect information about completed queries to determine trends and identify frequently used tables and indexes.

DB2 Personal Developer's Edition

DB2 Personal Developer's Edition contains both Linux and Windows versions of DB2 Personal Edition as well as the DB2 Extenders, DB2 Connect Personal Edition, and a software development toolkit (SDK) that can be used to develop applications that interact with databases that fall under DB2 Personal Edition's control. Using the tools provided with DB2 Personal Developer's Edition, an individual application developer can design, build, or prototype single-user desktop/laptop applications that interact with DB2 9 databases, using a wide variety of methods, including:

- Embedded Structured Query Language (SQL)
- IBM's Call Level Interface (CLI), which is comparable to Microsoft's Open Database Connectivity (ODBC) interface

- DB2 9's rich set of application programming interfaces (APIs)
- Java Database Connectivity (JDBC)
- SQLJ
- .NET
- PHP
- PYTHON

The toolkit provided with DB2 Personal Developer's Edition contains a set of libraries and header files for each programming language supported, a set of sample programs to help with your development efforts, and an SQL precompiler/binder, which is used to pre-process source code files containing embedded SQL so that they can be compiled and linked by a conventional compiler.

It is important to note that applications developed with the toolkit provided with DB2 Personal Developer's Edition can be run on any PC on which DB2 Personal Developer's Edition or DB2 Personal Edition has been installed. However, the DB2 software provided with this edition cannot be used for production systems.

DB2 Universal Developer's Edition

DB2 Universal Developer's Edition is designed to be used by application developers who wish to design, build, and prototype applications for deployment on any of the DB2 client or server platforms available. This comprehensive package contains versions of DB2 Everyplace, DB2 Express, DB2 Personal Edition, DB2 Workgroup Server Edition, and DB2 Enterprise Server Edition (along with all of the add-on features available) for each operating system supported. It also contains DB2 Extenders, DB2 Connect Personal Edition, DB2 Connect Enterprise Edition, and a software development toolkit (the same software development toolkit that comes with DB2 Personal Developer's Edition). This toolkit can be used to develop applications that utilize the latest DB2 9 technologies available.

As with DB2 Personal Developer's Edition, the DB2 software provided with DB2 Universal Developer's Edition cannot be used to create a production database system.

DB2 Enterprise Developer's Edition

DB2 Enterprise Developer's Edition is designed to be used by application developers who wish to design, build, and prototype applications for deployment on any of the IBM Information Management client or server platforms available. This comprehensive package contains everything found in the DB2 Universal Developer's Edition, along with versions of Informix Dynamic Server (IDS) Enterprise Edition, Cloudscape, and DB2 Connect Unlimited Edition for zSeries for each operating system supported.

As with DB2 Universal Developer's Edition, the DB2 software provided with DB2 Enterprise Developer's Edition cannot be used to create a production database system.

DB2 for i5/OS

DB2 for i5/OS is an advanced, 64-bit relational database management system that leverages the On-Demand capabilities of System i, such as Dynamic Logical Partitioning to respond quickly to changing workloads in order to ensure business continuity in a dynamic environment. Unlike other DB2 editions, DB2 for i5/OS is built directly into the operating system. As a result, Version/Release naming will differ because DB2 for i5/OS follows the i5/OS version/release numbering scheme, and not the DB2 for Linux, UNIX, and Windows version/release scheme. The current level of DB2 for i5/OS is Version 5 Release 4 (V5R4).

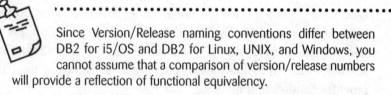

Since Version/Release naming conventions differ between DB2 for i5/OS and DB2 for Linux, UNIX, and Windows, you cannot assume that a comparison of version/release numbers will provide a reflection of functional equivalency.

Because of the unique architecture of IBM's System i5 and the way the DB2 database engine has been tightly integrated with the operating system, many of the traditional database-specific administration requirements associated with other database management systems either aren't necessary with DB2 for i5/OS or are provided through various operating system facilities. For example, graphical tools used to administer a DB2 for i5/OS database are provided as part of the iSeries Navigator component of the OS, whereas DB2's Control Center is used to administer DB2 editions that run on Linux, UNIX, and Windows. With iSeries Navigator, you can perform the following tasks:

- Create and/or work with DB2 database objects (tables, views, indexes, user-defined functions, etc.)

- Define referential integrity constraints

- Reverse-engineer a database to produce SQL DDL from existing data objects

- Create and debug SQL stored procedures

- Manage database logging (Journaling)

- Analyze SQL/Query performance using Visual Explain

- Use the Database Navigator to view and work with database objects and any related objects

DB2 for i5/OS's cost-based query optimizer, unique single-level-store architecture, and database parallelism feature allow it to scale nearly linearly within an iSeries SMP configuration. And if additional functionality is needed, there are several utilities available (including utilities for data replication, parallel processing, and query management) that either can be added to the core database functionality or included in the System i Enterprise Edition bundle.

DB2 for z/OS

DB2 for z/OS is a multi-user, full-function database management system that has been designed specifically for z/OS, IBM's flagship mainframe operating system. For over four decades the IBM mainframe has been a leader in data and transaction serving; DB2 9 for z/OS builds on the value delivered by the IBM mainframe and provides features that include:

- Rich hybrid data server support for both relational and XML data, along with the necessary services to support both (pureXML)

- New data types (DECFLOAT, BIGINT, and VARBINARY)

- Native SQL procedural language

- Improved security with roles, trusted context, and new encryption functions

- Extensions of DB2 for z/OS V8 capabilities

- Enhancements to large-object support and performance

- Volume-based copy and recover

- Refinements to optimization

- QMF interface design changes that provide on demand access to data, reports, and interactive visual solutions via a Web browser

- Enablement for IBM System z Integrated Information Processors (zIIP)

DB2 9 for z/OS is designed to cut IT infrastructure costs significantly, streamline efforts to meet compliance obligations, and simplify data serving on the System z9 operating system.

Other DB2 Products

Along with the DB2 editions that make up the core of the DB2 Family, several other products designed to expand and enhance the functionality and capabilities of DB2 are available. These products, which make up the remainder of the DB2 Family, are:

- DB2 Clients
- DB2 Connect
- DB2 Extenders

The following sections provide detailed descriptions of each of these products.

DB2 Clients

In order to create a DB2 client/server environment, you must have some type of client software installed on the workstation that will serve as the client before communications with a server can be established. Consequently, several of the DB2 editions available contain the software needed to set up and configure the following types of DB2 clients:

- DB2 Runtime Client
- DB2 Client

Each of these clients can be created (by installing the appropriate client software) on any number of workstations; however, the type of client you elect to create for a given workstation is often determined by the requirements of that workstation. For example, if a particular workstation will only be used to execute an application that interacts with a remote DB2 database stored on a server, it would need to be configured as a DB2 Runtime Client. This would be done by installing the DB2 Runtime Client software that is appropriate for the operating system being used on that workstation. Figure 2–2 shows how such a DB2 client/server environment might look.

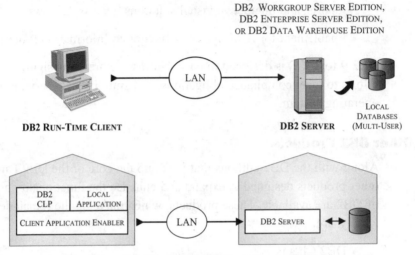

Figure 2–2: Simple DB2 client/server environment.

DB2 Runtime Client

The DB2 Runtime Client provides workstations running a variety of operating systems with the ability to access remote DB2 databases. This client is a light-weight client (having a smaller deployment footprint compared to the full DB2 Client in terms of install image size and disk space required) that provides the following features/capabilities:

- Support to handle database connections and process SQL statements, XQuery expressions, and DB2 commands.

- Support for common database access interfaces, including JDBC, ADO.NET, OLE DB, ODBC, and the DB2 Call Level Interface (CLI). This includes drivers and the capability to define data sources. For example, installing a DB2 client on a Windows workstation may cause the DB2 ODBC driver to be installed and registered. Application developers and other users can then use the Windows ODBC Data Source Administrator tool to define DB2 data sources.

- Support for common network communication protocols, including TCP/IP and Named Pipe.

- Support for installing multiple copies of a client on the same computer. These copies can be the same or different versions of DB2.

- Support for Lightweight Directory Access Protocol (LDAP).

- Versions that run on both 32-bit and 64-bit operating systems.

- License terms that allow free redistribution of the DB2 Runtime Client with any applications you develop.

In addition, the DB2 Runtime Client provided for Windows can be packaged with an application to provide database connectivity for that application; the Windows DB2 Runtime Client is available in the form of Windows Installer merge modules that enable you to include the DB2 Runtime Client DLL files in any application install package you create.

DB2 Client

Like the DB2 Runtime Client, the DB2 Client provides workstations running a variety of operating systems with the ability to access remote DB2 databases. However, where the DB2 Runtime Client provides basic connectivity capabilities, the DB2 Client delivers the same functionality as the DB2 Runtime Client, plus the tools needed to perform client/server configuration, database administration, and application development. Features/capabilities provided by the DB2 Client include:

- The Configuration Assistant to assist with cataloging remote databases and configuring database servers.

- The Control Center and other graphical tools for database administration. It is important to note that these tools are only available for 32-bit and 64-bit versions of Linux and Windows.

- First Steps for new users.

- Application development tools.

The application development tools provided with the DB2 Client are the same as those provided with the various DB2 Developer's editions: a set of libraries and header files for each programming language supported, a set of sample programs and tutorials to assist with your development efforts, and an SQL precompiler/binder, which is used to process source code files containing embedded SQL so that they can be compiled and linked by a conventional high-level programming language compiler.

DB2 Connect

For information technology professionals who have made DB2 on iSeries and zSeries servers the cornerstone of their business, DB2 Connect provides a robust, highly scalable communications infrastructure for connecting Linux, UNIX, Windows, and mobile applications to data stored in z/OS (mainframe) and i5/OS (minicomputer) databases. DB2 Connect can be used seamlessly with some of the more common standard interfaces for database access, including ODBC, OLE DB, JDBC, SQLJ, ADO, ADO.NET, RDO, DB2 CLI, and Embedded SQL. DB2 Connect (and DB2) also delivers full support for the Microsoft .NET programming model, along with its respective IDE, Visual Studio.NET. DB2 Connect can also be used to access nondatabase resources such as CICS, WebSphere MQ, IMS, or VSAM.

DB2 Connect is an add-on product that must be purchased separately unless DB2 Enterprise Server Edition, which provides a limited-use version, is installed. DB2 Connect is available in several editions, and each is designed to address specific data access and usage needs. The DB2 Connect editions that are available are:

DB2 Connect Personal Edition: DB2 Connect Personal Edition is intended to be used by a single user on a single workstation who needs connection to any number of mainframe and/or minicomputer database servers.

DB2 Connect Enterprise Edition: DB2 Connect Enterprise Edition is intended to be used by multiple users on multiple workstations who need connection to any number of mainframe and/or minicomputer database servers. DB2 Connect Enterprise Edition is priced using the Standard server/user model that is used to price DB2 Enterprise Edition. Therefore, this edition is not suitable in environments where multi-tier client/server applications or Web-based applications are used, because determining the number of concurrent users in such environments is not practical and licensing every registered user may be cost-prohibitive.

DB2 Connect Application Server Edition: DB2 Connect Application Server Edition provides the same functionality as DB2 Connect Enterprise

Edition, however, license charges are based on the number of processors being used by Web or application servers that are connecting to mainframe and/or minicomputer database servers. This edition is designed to provide a cheaper alternative to DB2 Connect Unlimited Edition for environments in which one or more multi-tier applications will access enterprise data with regular frequency, and the growth of the number of users of these applications is expected to be slow or minimal over time.

DB2 Connect Unlimited Edition: DB2 Connect Unlimited Edition provides the same functionality as DB2 Connect Enterprise Edition, however, license charges are based on Millions of Service Units (MSUs) per hour. This edition is designed to provide an attractive pricing alternative for environments where a large amount of access to enterprise data is needed today or will be needed sometime in the future.

DB2 Extenders

In most relational database systems, including DB2, data is stored according to its data type. Therefore, in order to store a wide variety of data, DB2 contains a rich set of built-in data types, along with a set of functions that are designed to work with each data type provided. DB2 also allows users to create their own data types (known as user-defined types) and supporting functions (known as user-defined functions) to handle data that does not map directly to one of the built-in data types available. Building on this capability, the developers of DB2 created several sets of user-defined data types and user-defined functions for the sole purpose of managing specific kinds of data. Collectively, these sets of user-defined data types and functions are referred to as *extenders*, because they extend the basic functionality and capabilities of a DB2 database. Currently, six different extender products are available. They are:

- DB2 Audio, Video, and Image (AVI) Extender
- DB2 Text Extender
- DB2 Net Search Extender
- DB2 XML Extender
- DB2 Spatial Extender
- DB2 Geodetic Extender

DB2 Audio, Video, and Image Extender: As the name implies, the DB2 Audio, Video, and Image Extender contains a set of user-defined data types and functions that allow a DB2 database to store and manipulate nontraditional data such as audio clips, movies, and pictures. The data types and functions that are provided by the DB2 Audio, Video, and Image Extender can be used in SQL statements just like any of the built-in data types and functions available. And because SQL can be used to construct multi-data-type queries, this extender provides a lot of flexibility when searching for information. For example, a query could be written to locate a particular movie by searching for its description, the date it was recorded, or its total playing time. Additionally, the Query By Image Content (QBIC) capability provided with this extender can be used to locate images that have a particular color combination or that have colors and/or textures that are similar to those of another image.

DB2 Text Extender: The DB2 Text Extender contains a set of user-defined data types that can store complex text documents in a DB2 database and a set of user-defined functions that can extract key information from such documents, regardless of where they are stored (text documents can be stored directly in a DB2 database or in a file system that is accessible to the DB2 Database Manager). This extender's strength comes from IBM's powerful linguistic search and text-mining technology; this technology allows users to construct queries that will search through any kind of text document, including most word processing documents, for:

- A specific word
- A specific phrase
- A particular word sequence
- Word variations (such as plural forms of a word or the word in a different tense)
- Synonyms of a particular word
- Similar-sounding words
- Words that have a similar spelling
- Words that have a particular pattern (for example, all words that begin with the characters "data")

DB2 Net Search Extender: The DB2 Net Search Extender provides application developers with a way to integrate the search functionality provided by the DB2 Text Extender into their applications. Unlike the DB2 Text Extender, the DB2 Net Search Extender does not provide linguistic processing support. However, it does provide better query performance and scalability by means of its caching and optimization techniques. For this reason, the DB2 Net Search Extender is well suited for high-end e-business applications where search performance on large indexes can be critical and the ability to scale the processing of concurrent queries is needed. Key features the DB2 Net Search Extender provides include:

- The ability to create multiple indexes on a single column (indexing proceeds without acquiring row-level locks)
- The ability to create indexes across multiple processors
- The ability to search for a particular word or phrase
- The ability to search for words that have a similar spelling
- The ability to perform wildcard searches (for example, search for all words that begin with the characters "net")
- The ability to control how search results are sorted
- The ability to limit the number of search results returned
- The ability to search for tags or sections (with or without using Boolean operations)

DB2 XML Extender: The DB2 XML Extender contains a set of user-defined data types and functions that can be used to store XML documents in a DB2 database (as character data or in external files) and to manipulate such documents, regardless of where they are stored. The DB2 XML Extender can be used to decompose ("shred") XML elements from a document and store them in columns and tables; it can also compose (create) new XML documents from existing character and numerical data or previously shredded XML documents. And because the DB2 XML Extender is compatible with the DB2 Net Search Extender, the powerful search capabilities provided by the DB2 Net Search Extender can be used to quickly locate information stored in one or more sections within a set of XML documents. (Retrieval functions let you retrieve complete documents or individual elements within a document.)

DB2 Spatial Extender: Traditionally, geospatial data has been managed by specialized Geographic Information Systems (GISs) that, because of their design, have been unable to integrate their spatial data with business data stored in other relational database management systems or data sources. Shortly after DB2 Universal Database, Version 5.0 was released, IBM, together with Environmental Systems Research Institute (ESRI), a leading manufacturer of spatial database systems, created a set of user-defined data types for describing spatial data (for example points, lines, and polygons) and a set of user-defined functions to query spatial objects (for example to find area, endpoints, and intersects). This set of user-defined data types and functions make up the DB2 Spatial Extender.

At the basic level, the DB2 Spatial Extender allows you to store spatial data in a DB2 database. With this capability, you can generate, analyze, and exploit spatial information about geographic features, such as the locations of office buildings or the size of a flood zone, and present it in a three-dimensional format. The DB2 Spatial Extender also enables you to add another element of intelligence to your database by integrating spatial information with business data (text and numbers).

DB2 Geodetic Extender: Although many organizations rely on traditional two-dimensional map-based technology (which the DB2 Spatial Extender is designed to support), some need to treat the world as round rather than flat; a round Earth is paramount for calculations and visualizations in such disciplines as military command/control and asset management, meteorology and oceanography (scientific, government, or commercial), and satellite imagery. The DB2 Geodetic Extender contains a set of user-defined data types and functions that treat the Earth like a globe rather than a flat map (it can construct a virtual globe at any scale), thus making it easier to develop applications for business intelligence and e-government that require geographical location analysis.

The DB2 Geodetic Extender is best used for global data sets and applications. It has the capability to manage geospatial information referenced by latitude and longitude coordinates and support global spatial queries without the limitations inherent in two-dimensional map projections. To handle objects defined on the Earth's surface with precision, the DB2 Geodetic Extender uses a latitude/longitude coordinate system on an ellipsoidal earth model—or geodetic datum—rather than a planar, x- and y-coordinate system. This avoids the distortions, inaccuracies, and imprecision inevitably introduced by planar projections.

The Geodetic Extender provides a cost-effective solution for global, spherical coordinate (latitude/longitude)–based problems, because it models a spherical problem with a spherical solution.

A Word About XML Data

XML is a simple, very flexible text format derived from Standard Generalized Markup Language (SGML, ISO 8879). Originally designed to meet the challenges of large-scale electronic publishing, XML is playing an increasingly important role in the exchange of a wide variety of data on the Web and elsewhere. Why? Because XML provides a neutral, flexible way to exchange data between different devices, systems, and applications; data is maintained in a self-describing format that accommodates a wide variety of ever-evolving business needs.

One approach to storing XML data in a relational database has been to "shred" or decompose XML documents and store their contents across multiple columns in one or more tables. (This is the functionality provided by the DB2 XML Extender.) The shredding of XML documents enables users to leverage their existing SQL programming skills, as well as popular query and reporting tools, to work directly with selected portions of the "converted" XML data. This approach is ideal if the XML data being stored is tabular in nature. However, the cost associated with decomposing XML data often depends on the structure of the underlying XML document. XML documents are composed of a hierarchical set of entities, and many XML documents contain heavily nested parent/child relationships and/or irregular structures. Shredding such documents may require a large number of tables, some of which may need to have values generated for foreign keys in order to capture the relationships and ordering that is inherent in the original documents. Moreover, querying a "shredded" document can require complex SQL statements that contain many joins.

Another popular method is to use character and binary large object (CLOB and BLOB) data types to store the entire contents of an XML file in a single column of a row within a table. With this approach, the overhead required to break a document into pieces and store the pieces in various columns of one or more tables is eliminated. Additionally, complex joins aren't needed to reconstruct the original XML document, because it was never decomposed for storage. However, the use of large objects—character or binary—to store XML documents has its drawbacks as well. Searching and retrieving a subset of an XML document can be resource intensive. And when performing updates, the entire document must be replaced, even if only a small portion of the original document has been changed. This can result in unacceptably high processing costs, particularly if the XML document is large.

DB2 9 is the first IBM implementation of a "hybrid" or multi-structured database management system. In addition to supporting the traditional tabular, relational data model, DB2 9 supports the native hierarchical data model found in XML documents and messages. With DB2 9, XML documents are stored in tables that contain one or more columns that are based on a new XML data type. (Tables created with XML data types may also contain columns with traditional SQL data types, including numeric data, character strings, and date/time/timestamp data.) This "pure" support for XML includes new storage techniques for efficient management of hierarchical structures inherent in XML documents, new indexing technology to speed up retrieval of subsets of XML documents, new capabilities for validating XML data and managing changing XML schemas, new query language support (including native support for XQuery as well as new SQL/XML enhancements), new query optimization techniques, integration with popular application programming interfaces (APIs), and extensions to popular database utilities. The result is a single DBMS platform that offers the benefits of a relational database environment and a pure XML data store.

DB2 9's Comprehensive Tool Set

With the exception of DB2 Everyplace, DB2 for i5/OS, and DB2 for z/OS, each edition of DB2 and the DB2 Client comes with a comprehensive set of tools designed to assist in administering and managing DB2 instances, databases, and database objects. The majority of these tools have a graphical user interface (GUI); however, most of the tasks that can be performed with the GUI tools provided can also be performed by issuing equivalent DB2 commands from the operating system prompt or the DB2 Command Line Processor (another tool that we'll look at later in this section). The following subsections describe the most commonly used GUI tools available.

The Control Center

Of all the DB2 GUI tools available, the Control Center is the most important and versatile one provided. The Control Center presents a clear, concise view of an entire system and serves as the central point for managing DB2 systems and performing common administration tasks. With the Control Center, users can:

- Create and delete instances

- Create and delete (drop) DB2 databases

- Catalog and uncatalog databases

- Configure instances and databases

- Create, alter, and drop buffer pools, table spaces, tables, views, indexes, aliases, triggers, schemas, and user-defined data types (UDTs)

- Grant and revoke authorities and privileges

- Export, import, or load data

- Reorganize tables and collect table statistics

- Back up and restore databases and table spaces

- Replicate data between systems

- Manage database connections

- Monitor resources and track events as they take place

- Analyze queries

- Schedule jobs to run unattended

The Control Center interface presents itself using one of three different views:

Basic: The basic view displays essential objects such as databases, tables, views, and stored procedures, and limits the actions you can perform on those objects. This is the view you should use if you only want to perform core DB2 database operations.

Advanced: The advanced view displays all objects available in the Control Center and allows you to perform all actions available. This is the view you should use if you are working in an enterprise environment or if you want to connect to DB2 for i5/OS or DB2 for z/OS.

Custom: The custom view gives you the ability to tailor the object tree and actions allowed to meet your specific needs.

Figure 2–3 shows how the Control Center looks on a Windows XP server when the advanced view is used.

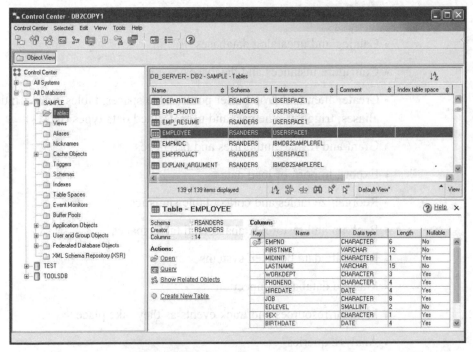

Figure 2–3: The Control Center (advanced view).

If you look closely at Figure 2–3, you will notice that the Control Center is comprised of the following elements:

- A *menu bar*, which allows users to perform any of the Control Center functions available.

- A *toolbar*, which can be used to launch the other DB2 GUI tools available. Figure 2–4 identifies the tools that can be invoked directly from the Control Center toolbar. It is important to note that every tool that can be invoked from the Control Center toolbar can also be invoked from the Control Center's menu bar.

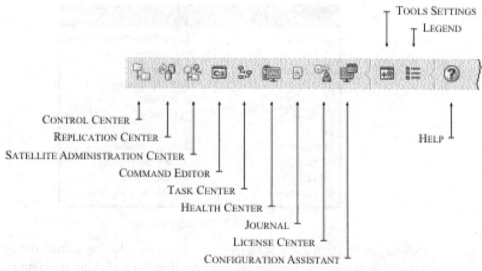

Figure 2–4: The Control Center Toolbar.

- An *objects pane* (located on the left-hand side of the Control Center), which contains a hierarchical representation of every object type that can be managed from the Control Center.

- A *contents pane* (located on the upper right-hand side of the Control Center), which contains a listing of existing objects that correspond to the object type selected in the objects pane. (For example, if the Tables object type were selected in the objects pane, a list of all tables available would be listed in the contents pane.)

- An *object details pane* (located on the lower right-hand side of the Control Center), which contains detailed information about the object selected in the object tree or contents pane.

As you can see in Figure 2–3, every object listed in the contents pane is preceded by an icon intended to identify the type of object being described in the list. A wide variety of icons are used, and a list of all icons available, along with their corresponding object type, can be seen by viewing the Legend dialog, which can be accessed from the Control Center's menu and toolbar. Figure 2–5 shows what the Legend dialog looks like on a Windows XP server.

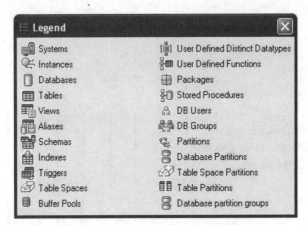

Figure 2–5: The Legend dialog.

Users can perform specific tasks on an object by selecting it from the list provided (either in the objects pane or the contents pane) and clicking the right mouse button; when the right mouse button is clicked, a pop-up menu that lists every action available for that particular object will be displayed, and the user simply selects the desired action from the menu.

The Replication Center

The Replication Center is an interactive GUI application that allows users to administer data replication between a DB2 database and any other relational database—whether that database is a DB2 database or not. From the Replication Center, users can:

- Define replication environments
- Create replication control tables
- Register replication sources
- Create subscription sets
- Add members to a subscription set
- Apply designated changes from one location to another
- Synchronize data in two locations
- Monitor the replication process
- Perform basic troubleshooting for replication operations

Figure 2–6 shows how the Replication Center looks when it is first invoked on a Windows XP server.

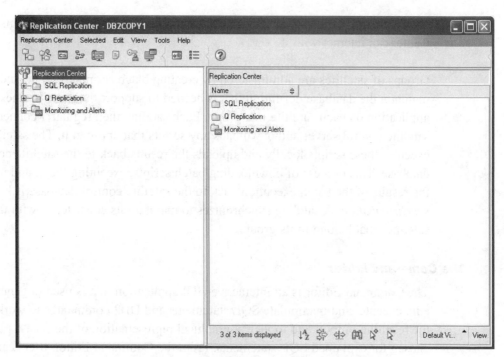

Figure 2–6: The Replication Center.

The Satellite Administration Center

The Satellite Administration Center is a GUI application that allows users to set up and administer a group of DB2 servers that perform the same business function. These servers, known as *satellites*, all run the same application and have the same DB2 database definition needed to support a particular application. With the Satellite Administration Center, users create a group and then define satellites as members of this group. This group of satellites can then be administered as a single entity, as opposed to each satellite having to be administered separately. If additional DB2 servers that perform the same business function are acquired later, they are simply added to the group as additional satellites.

Information about a satellite environment is stored in a central database referred to as the *satellite control database*. This database records, among other things, which satellites are in the environment, the group each satellite belongs to, and which version of an end-user business application a satellite is currently running. This database resides on a DB2 server known as the *DB2 control server*, and it must be cataloged and accessible to the Control Center before the Satellite Administration Center can interact with it.

Groups of satellites are administered by creating batch scripts to set up and maintain the database definition that is needed to support the same business application on each satellite in a group. Each satellite then regularly connects to its satellite control server and downloads any scripts that apply to it. The satellite executes these scripts locally and uploads the results back to the satellite control database. This process of downloading batch scripts, executing them, and reporting the results of the batch execution back to the satellite control database is known as *synchronization*. A satellite synchronizes to maintain its consistency with the other satellites that belong to its group.

The Command Editor

The Command Editor is an interactive GUI application that is used to generate, edit, execute, and manipulate SQL statements and DB2 commands; to work with the resulting output; and to view a graphical representation of the access plan chosen for explained SQL statements. From the Command Editor, users can:

- Execute SQL statements, DB2 commands, and operating system commands—operating system commands must be preceded by an exclamation point (!).

- View the results of the execution of SQL statements and DB2 commands and see the result data set produced in response to a query.

- Save the results of the execution of SQL statements and DB2 commands to an external file.

- Create and save a sequence of SQL statements and DB2 commands to a script file that can be invoked by the Task Center. (Such a script file can then be scheduled to run at a specific time or frequency.)

- Use the SQL Assist tool to build complex queries.

- Examine the execution plan and statistics associated with a SQL statement before (or after) it is executed.

Figure 2–7 shows how the Command Editor looks on a Windows XP server after a database connection has been established.

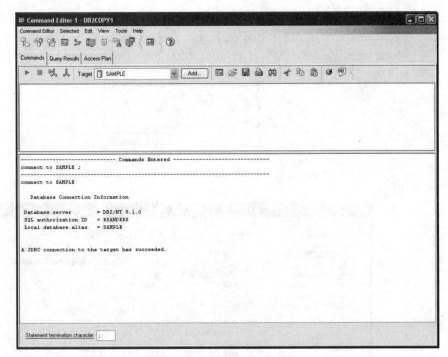

Figure 2–7: The Command Editor.

As you can see in Figure 2–7, the Command Editor is comprised of three different individual pages (which are accessed by tabs): the *Commands* page, the *Query Results* page, and the *Access Plan* page. Users can enter and execute an SQL statement or a DB2 command, create and save a script, run an existing script, or schedule a task from the Commands page. Once a query has been executed, users can see the results, if any, on the Query Results page. And on the Access Plan page, users can see the access plan for any explainable statement that was specified on the Commands page. (If more than one SQL statement is specified on the Commands page, an access plan will only be created for the first statement encountered.)

SQL Assist

SQL Assist is an interactive GUI application that allows users to visually construct complex SELECT, INSERT, UPDATE, and DELETE SQL statements and examine the results of their execution. SQL Assist is invoked directly from the Command Editor, either by selecting the appropriate menu option or by selecting the appropriate toolbar icon (this icon will not be available until a database connection is established). Figure 2–8 identifies the Command Editor toolbar icon that is used to activate the SQL Assist dialog; Figure 2–9 shows how the SQL Assist dialog might look on a Windows XP server after it has been used to build a complex query.

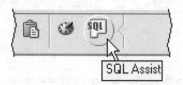

Figure 2–8: The SQL Assist icon on the Command Editor toolbar.

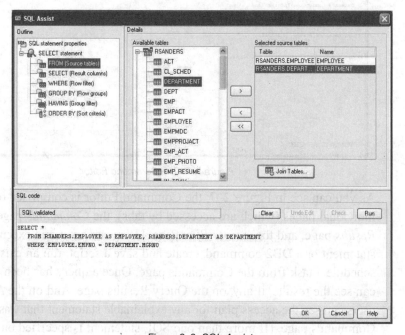

Figure 2–9: SQL Assist.

Once the desired SQL statement been constructed inside SQL Assist, it can be written back to the Command Editor, where it can then be executed immediately or saved to a script file where it can be executed later using the Task Center.

Visual Explain

Visual Explain is a GUI tool that provides database administrators and application developers with the ability to view a graphical representation of the access plan that has been chosen by the DB2 Optimizer for a particular SQL statement. In addition, Visual Explain allows you to:

- See the database statistics that were used to optimize the SQL statement.

- Determine whether or not an index was used to access table data. (If an index was not used, Visual Explain can help you determine which columns might benefit from being indexed.)

- View the effects of performance tuning by allowing you to make "before" and "after" comparisons.

- Obtain detailed information about each operation that is performed by the access plan, including the estimated cost of each.

Figure 2–10 shows how the Visual Explain tool might look like on a Windows XP server when it is displayed by selecting the Access Plan page from the Command Editor.

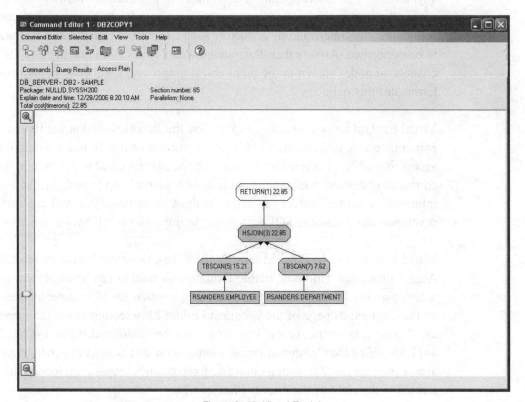

Figure 2–10: Visual Explain.

The output provided by Visual Explain consists of a hierarchical graph that represents the various components that are needed to process the access plan that has been chosen for a particular SQL statement. Each component is represented as a graphical object known as a *node*, and two types of nodes can exist:

Operator: An operator node is used to identify either an action that must be performed on data, or output produced from a table or index.

Operand: An operand node is used to identify an entity on which an operation is performed (for example, a table would be the operand of a table scan operator).

Typically, operand nodes are used to identify tables (symbolized in the hierarchical graph by rectangles), indexes (symbolized by diamonds), and table queues (symbolized by parallelograms—table queues are used when intrapartition parallelism is used). Operator nodes, on the other hand, are used to identify anything from an insert operation to an index or table scan. Operator nodes, which are symbolized in the hierarchical graph by ovals, indicate how data is accessed, how tables are joined, and other factors such as whether or not a sort operation is to be performed. Arrows that illustrate how data flows from one node to the next connect all nodes shown in the hierarchical graph, and a RETURN operator normally terminates this path.

Visual Explain allows users to quickly view the statistics used at the time a particular query was optimized, determine whether or not an index would improve access to a table, obtain information about the cost required to perform a particular operation, and understand how tables have been joined. Armed with this information, administrators can make database design changes, and application developers can fine-tune SQL statements to improve overall performance.

Visual Explain can be invoked directly from the Command Editor by selecting the Access Plan page. However, before Explain information can be displayed, an access plan must exist; access plans can be generated for SQL statements entered on the Commands page of the Command Editor by selecting either the Execute and Access plan or the Access Plan icon from the Command Editor toolbar. Figure 2–11 identifies the Command Editor toolbar icon that is used to generate an access plan for an SQL statement. (The Execute and Access plan icon is the icon located to the right of the Access Plan icon.)

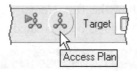

Figure 2–11: The Access Plan icon on the Command Editor toolbar

Before Visual Explain can be used, Explain tables must be added to the appropriate database. Often, the DB2 Database Manager will attempt to create Explain tables automatically the first time Visual Explain is used. However, Explain tables can also be created by executing the script EXPLAIN.DDL, which can be found in the *misc* subdirectory of the *sqllib* directory where the DB2 product was installed. Refer to the header portion of this file for information for specific information on how to execute it.

The Task Center

The Task Center is an interactive GUI application that allows users to schedule tasks, run tasks, and send notifications about completed tasks to other users. A *task* is a script together with any associated success conditions, schedules, and notifications. Users can create a task within the Task Center, generate a task by saving the results from a DB2 dialog or wizard, create a script within another tool and save it to the Task Center, or import an existing script. Such scripts can contain DB2 commands, SQL statements, operating system commands, or any combination of the three.

The Task Center uses success code sets (the return codes or range of return codes that, if received, indicate the task was executed successfully) to evaluate the success or failure of any task it executes. Return codes that fall outside the range specified are considered failures. In addition, the Task Center evaluates the SQLCA return code of every SQL statement executed in a DB2 script, and if any statement fails, the entire task fails. As well as evaluating the success or failure of a particular task, the Task Center can perform one or more actions if a particular task succeeds and perform other actions if the same task fails. The Task Center can also be configured to perform one or more actions each time a scheduled task completes, regardless of the outcome of that task (success or failure).

Figure 2–12 shows how the Task Center might look on a Windows XP server after a Database Backup task has been created.

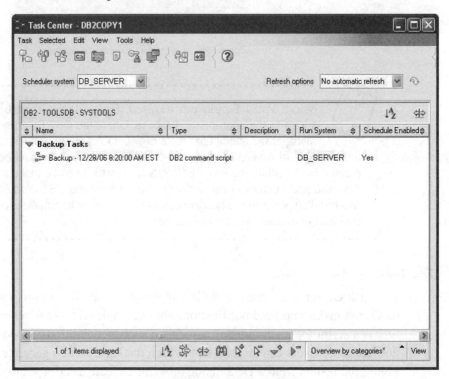

Figure 2–12: The Task Center.

If you run a script from the Task Center instead of from the Command Editor or a command prompt, the results will be logged in the Journal. By viewing the Journal, you can see a list of jobs that use a particular script, along with the status of all jobs that either already have been executed or are scheduled to be executed.

The Health Center

Database monitoring is such an integral part of database administration that DB2 comes equipped with a monitoring utility, which is known as the Database System Monitor. Although the name suggests that only one monitoring tool is provided, in reality the Database System Monitor is composed of two distinct types of tools—a *snapshot monitor* and one or more *event monitors*—that can be used to capture and return system monitor information. The snapshot monitor allows you to capture a picture of the state of a database (along with all database activity) at a specific point in time, while event monitors capture and log data as specific database events occur. Along with the Database System Monitor, DB2 provides two additional tools that are designed to help database administrators monitor DB2 systems under their control. These tools are known as the *Health Monitor* and the *Health Center*. Together, these tools provide a *management by exception* capability that enables administrators to address system health issues before they become real problems.

The Health Monitor is a server-side tool that constantly monitors the health of a DB2 Database Manager instance without a need for user interaction; the Health Monitor uses several *health indicators* to evaluate specific aspects of instance and database performance. A health indicator is a system characteristic that the Health Monitor monitors continuously to determine whether or not an object is operating normally; each health indicator has a corresponding set of predefined threshold values, and the Health Monitor compares the state of the system against these health-indicator thresholds to see whether they have been exceeded. If the Health Monitor finds that a predefined threshold has been surpassed (for example, if the amount of log space available is insufficient), or if it detects an abnormal state for an object (for example, if the instance is down), it will automatically raise an alert.

The Health Center is a GUI tool that is designed to interact with the Health Monitor. Using the Health Center, you can select the instance and database objects that you want to monitor, customize the threshold settings of any health indicator, and specify where notifications are to be sent and what actions are to be taken if an alert is issued. The Health Center also allows you to start and stop the Health Monitor as well as access details about current alerts and obtain a list of recommended actions that describe how to resolve the situation that caused an alert to be generated. Figure 2–13 shows how the Health Center looks on a Windows XP server (in this case, after two warning-type alerts have been generated).

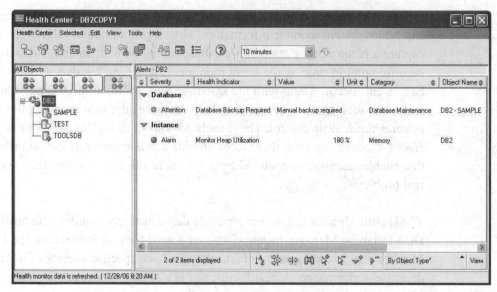

Figure 2–13: The Health Center.

A Word about the SQL Performance Monitor

If you are running DB2 for i5/OS, the SQL Performance Monitor is a valuable tool that can be used to keep track of the resources SQL statements use. Information on resource usage can help you determine whether your system and/or your SQL statements are performing at optimum level or whether they need to be tuned. There are two types of monitors you can elect to use:

Summary SQL Performance Monitor: The Summary SQL Performance Monitor is the iSeries Navigator version of the Memory Resident Database Monitor, found on the system interface. As the name implies, this monitor resides in memory and only retains a summary of the data collected. When the monitor is paused or ended, this data is written to disk; once written to disk, the data collected can be analyzed. Because the Summary SQL Performance Monitor stores its information in memory, the performance impact to the system is minimized. However, some of the details are lost.

Detailed SQL Performance Monitor: The detailed SQL performance monitor is the iSeries Navigator version of the Database Monitor, found on the system interface. This monitor saves detailed data to disk, as it is collected, and does not need to be paused or ended in order to analyze the results. Data collected by this monitor can also be used as input to Visual Explain, whereas data collected by the Summary SQL Performance Monitor cannot. However, since this monitor does save data in real time, it may have a negative impact on system performance.

The Journal

The Journal is an interactive GUI application that tracks historical information about tasks, database actions and operations, Control Center actions, messages, and alerts. To present this information in an organized manner, the Journal uses several different views. They are:

- Task History
- Database History
- Messages
- Notification Log

The *Task History* view shows the results of tasks that have already been executed. This view contains one entry for each individual task (regardless of how many times the task was executed) and allows users to:

- View details of any task that has been executed
- View the results any task that has been executed
- Edit any task that has been executed
- View execution statistics associated with any task that has been executed
- Remove any task execution record from the Journal

The *Database History* view shows information stored in a database's recovery history file. The recovery history file is automatically updated whenever any of the following operations are performed:

- Database or table space backup
- Database or table space restore
- Roll-forward recovery
- Load
- Table reorganization

The *Messages* view shows a running history of messages that were issued from the Control Center and any other GUI tool, and the *Notification Log* view shows information from the administration notification log.

Figure 2–14 shows how the Messages view of the Journal might look on a Windows XP server.

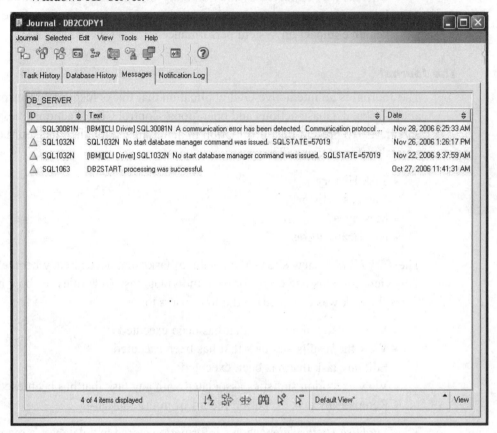

Figure 2–14: The Messages view of the Journal.

The License Center

The License Center is an interactive GUI application that allows users to view information about the license associated with each DB2 product installed on a particular system. Such information includes processor status information, concurrent users policy information, license information, and user statistics or details. This tool can also be used to add or remove licenses or registered users, change license type policies, change the number of concurrent users, change the number of licensed processors, change the number of Internet processor licenses, and configure a particular system for proper license monitoring. Figure 2–15 shows how the License Center might look on a Windows XP server.

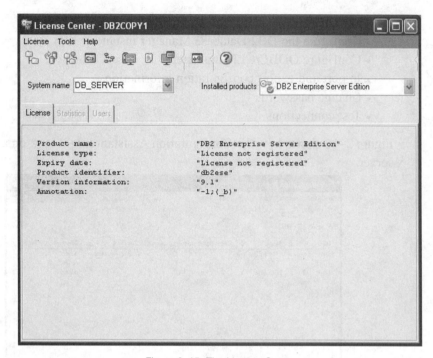

Figure 2–15: The License Center.

The Configuration Assistant

The Configuration Assistant is an interactive GUI application that allows users to configure clients so that they can access databases stored on remote DB2 servers. In order to access an instance or database on another server or system, that system must first be cataloged in the node directory of the client workstation, and information about the remote database must be cataloged in the database directory (and on the client workstation). The Configuration Assistant provides a way to catalog nodes and databases quickly without having to know the inherent complexities involved with performing these tasks. And because the Configuration Assistant maintains a list of databases to which users and applications can connect, it can act as a lightweight alternative to the Control Center in situations where the complete set of GUI tools available has not been installed.

From the Configuration Assistant, users can:

- Catalog new databases
- Work with or uncatalog existing databases
- Bind applications

- Set DB2 environment/registry variables
- Configure the DB2 Database Manager instance
- Configure ODBC/CLI parameters
- Import and export configuration information
- Change passwords
- Test connections

Figure 2–16 shows how the Configuration Assistant might look on a Windows XP server.

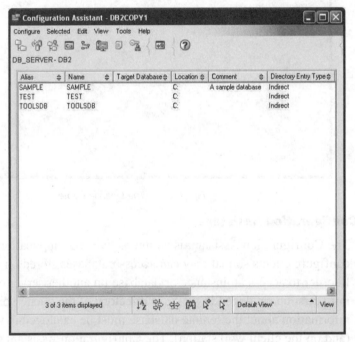

Figure 2–16: The Configuration Assistant.

The Design Advisor

As with other relational database systems, the primary purpose of an index in a DB2 database is to help the database engine quickly locate records stored in a table; if a table is referenced in a query and no corresponding index exists, the entire table must be scanned sequentially to locate the desired data. And if the table contains a large amount of data, such a scan can take a significant amount of time. In most cases, if an index is created for frequently used columns in a table, performance can often be greatly improved for data access operations. That's because index files are generally smaller and require less time to read than their corresponding table files, particularly as tables grow in size. Furthermore, the entire index may not need to be scanned; predicates can be applied to an index to reduce the number of rows that must actually be read.

Therefore, indexes are important because they:

- Provide a fast, efficient method for locating specific rows of data in very large tables.

- Provide a logical ordering of the rows of a table. Data is stored in a table in no particular order; when indexes are used, the values of one or more columns can be sorted in ascending or descending order. This is very beneficial when processing queries that contain ORDER BY and GROUP BY clauses.

- Improve overall query performance. If no index exists on a table, a table scan must be performed for each table referenced in a query. The larger the table, the longer a table scan takes because a table scan requires each table row to be accessed sequentially.

- Can be used to enforce the uniqueness of records stored in a table.

- Can require a table to use *clustering* storage, which causes the rows of a table to be physically arranged according to the ordering of their index column values. Although all indexes provide a logical ordering of data, only a clustering index provides a physical ordering of data.

- Can provide greater concurrency in multi-user environments. Because records can be located faster, acquired locks do not have to be held as long.

However, there is a price to pay for these benefits:

- Each index created requires additional storage or disk space. The exact amount of space needed is dependent upon the size of the associated table, along with the size and number of columns contained in the index.

- Every insert and update operation performed on a table requires additional updating of the indexes associated with that table. This is also true when data is bulk-loaded into a table using DB2's LOAD utility.

- Each index potentially adds an alternative access path that the DB2 optimizer must consider when generating the optimum access plan to use to resolve a query. This in turn increases compilation time when static queries are embedded in an application program.

So how do you decide when having an index would be beneficial and how do you determine what indexes should exist? And how do you decide whether to use materialized query tables (MQTs), partitioning, or both to help improve index performance? Even if you have a lot of experience with database and database application design, the task of selecting which indexes, MQTs, clustering dimensions, or database partitions to create for a complex workload can be quite daunting. That's where the Design Advisor comes in.

The Design Advisor is a special tool that is designed to capture specific information about typical workloads (queries or sets of SQL operations) performed against your database and recommend changes based upon the information provided. When given a set of SQL statements in a workload, the Design Advisor will make recommendations for:

- New indexes

- New materialized query tables (MQTs).

- Conversions of base tables to multidimensional clustering (MDC) tables

- Redistribution of table data

- Deletion of indexes and MQTs that are not being used by the specified workload

You can have the Design Advisor implement some or all of these recommendations immediately or arrange for them to be applied at a later time. Furthermore, the Design Advisor can be used to aid in the design of a new database or to improve performance of a database that is already in operation. For example, in designing a database, the Design Advisor can be used to:

- Generate design alternatives of a partitioned database environment and of indexes, MQTs, and MDC tables.

- Determine the best database partitioning strategy to use (in a partitioned environment).

- Assist in migrating from another database product to a multiple-partition DB2 database.

Once a database is in production, the Design Advisor can be used to:

- Improve performance of a particular SQL statement or workload

- Improve general database performance, using the performance of a sample workload as a gauge

- Improve performance of the most frequently executed queries, for example, as identified by the Activity Monitor

- Determine how to optimize the performance of a new key query

- Respond to Health Center recommendations regarding shared memory utility or sort heap problems encountered by a sort-intensive workload

- Find objects such as indexes and MQTs that are not used in a workload

- Assist in migrating from a single-partition DB2 database to a multiple-partition DB2 database

- Evaluate indexes, MQTs, MDC tables, or database partitioning strategies that have been generated manually

Figure 2–17 shows how the second page of the Design Advisor looks on a Windows XP server.

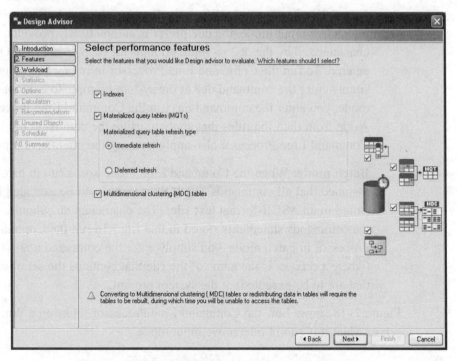

Figure 2–17: The second page of the Design Advisor wizard.

The Command Line Processor

The Command Line Processor (CLP) is a text-oriented application that allows users to issue DB2 commands, system commands, and SQL statements, as well as view the results of the statements/commands executed. The Command Line Processor can be run in three different modes:

Command mode: When the Command Line Processor is run in command mode, the user simply enters a DB2 command or SQL statement, preceded by the characters db2, followed by a space, at the system prompt. (For example, the command "CONNECT TO sample" would be entered as "db2 CONNECT TO sample"). If the command contains characters that have a special meaning to the operating system being used, it must be enclosed in quotation marks to ensure that it will be properly executed (for example, db2 "SELECT COUNT(*) FROM employee"). If the command to be executed is too long to fit on a single line, a space followed by the line continuation character (\) can be placed at the end of the line that is to be continued, and the rest of the command can follow on a new line.

Interactive Input mode: When the Command Line Processor is run in interactive input mode, the db2 prefix is automatically provided (as characterized by the db2 => input prompt) for each command/SQL statement entered. To run the Command Line Processor in interactive input mode, you simply enter the command db2 at the system prompt. To exit out of interactive mode, you enter the command quit at the Command Line Processor prompt. Aside from that, the rules that apply to using the command mode of the Command Line Processor also apply to using the interactive input mode.

Batch mode: When the Command Line Processor is run in batch mode, it is assumed that all commands and SQL statements to be executed have been stored in an ASCII-format text file. (The characters db2 should *not* precede the commands/statements stored in this file.) To run the Command Line Processor in batch mode, you simply enter the command db2 -f *xxxxxxxx* (where *xxxxxxxx* is the name of the file that contains the set of commands that are to be executed) at the system prompt.

Figure 2–18 shows how the Command Line Processor looks on a Windows XP server when it is run in interactive input mode.

Figure 2–18: The Command Line Processor (in interactive input mode).

There are various command-line options that can be specified when the Command Line Processor is invoked; a list of all options available can be obtained by executing the command LIST COMMAND OPTIONS, either from the system prompt or from the Command Line Processor prompt (when the Command Line Processor is run in interactive input mode).

The Developer Workbench

When you set up a remote DB2 database server and access it from one or more DB2 client workstations, you have, in essence, established a basic DB2 client/server environment. In such an environment, each time an SQL statement is executed against the database on the remote server, the statement itself is sent through a network from the client workstation to the database server. The database server then processes the statement, and the results are sent back, again through the network, to the client workstation. (This means that two messages must go through the network for every SQL statement executed.)

To take advantage of this architecture, client/server application development focuses on breaking an application into two parts, storing those parts on two platforms (the client and the server), and having them communicate with each other as the application executes. This allows the code that interacts directly with a database to reside on a database server or midrange computer, where computing power and centralized control can be used to provide quick, coordinated data access. At the same time, the application logic can reside on one or more smaller (client) workstations so that it can make effective use of all the resources the client workstation has to offer without causing a bottleneck at the server.

If you have an application that contains one or more transactions that perform a relatively large amount of database activity with little or no user interaction, each transaction can be stored on the database server as a *stored procedure*. With a stored procedure, all database processing done by the transaction can be performed directly at the database server. Because a stored procedure is invoked by a single SQL statement, fewer messages have to be transmitted across the network—only the data that is actually needed at the client workstation has to be sent across.

As you might imagine, the complexity of developing, debugging, and deploying stored procedures increases as the amount of work a stored procedure is expected to do increases. However, this complexity can be greatly reduced when stored procedures are developed using a special tool known as the Developer Workbench.

The Developer Workbench is an Eclipse-based, comprehensive development environment that can be used to create, edit, debug, deploy, and test DB2 stored procedures and user-defined functions. The Developer Workbench can also be used to develop SQLJ applications and to create, edit, and run SQL statements and XQuery expressions. Figure 2–19 shows how the Developer Workbench looks when it is first activated on a Windows XP server.

By using the Developer Workbench, application developers can focus on creating and testing stored procedures and user-defined functions without having to concern themselves with the details of registering, building, and installing the procedures and functions on a DB2 server. When the Developer Workbench is used to build a stored procedure or user-defined function, it compiles the source code on the client workstation (Java routines) or server (SQL routines), copies the source code and resulting library to the server, and registers the routine in the system catalog of the database being used.

Figure 2–19: The Developer Workbench.

A Word About Database Workloads

When you look closely at the type of processing that is done by most relational databases on a day-to-day basis, you will discover that they tend to support one of two types of workloads: On-Line Transaction Processing (OLTP) and data warehousing. Earlier, we saw that DB2 Data Warehouse Server Edition is the top-of-the-line DB2 Edition for dynamic data warehousing and that it is designed for today's data center environments, where OLTP and decision support are merged into single, integrated information management systems. But just what characteristics does a data warehouse have, and how are they different from the characteristics of an OLTP database?

Data warehousing involves storing and managing large volumes of data (often historical in nature) that is used primarily for analysis. Workloads in a data warehouse vary; they can consist of bulk load operations, short-running queries, long-running complex queries, random queries, occasional updates to data, and the execution of online utilities. To handle these types of workloads, most data warehouse environments have the following characteristics:

Performance: Population of a data warehouse and incremental updates should be performed as fast as possible. Any query should be satisfied at any time without degrading the performance of mission-critical or time-sensitive workloads. Complex queries should handle aggregations, full-table scans, and multiple table joins with little or no performance impact. Likewise, multidimensional queries should be satisfied without any impact. Database is optimized for query processing; multiple indexes are used.

Scalability: Both the hardware and the software components used in building a data warehouse should be scalable. Scalability enables you to grow your data warehouse without impacting performance and throughput rates.

Availability: A data warehouse should be available 24 hours a day, 7 days a week, 365 days a year.

Manageability: A data warehouse environment should be flexible and extensible, while minimizing the administrative costs of a high-volume database.

In contrast, OLTP systems are designed to support day-to-day, mission-critical business activities such as order entry, stock trading, inventory management, and banking. This typically involves hundreds to thousands of users issuing millions of transactions per day against databases that vary in size. Response time requirements tend to be subsecond, and workloads tend to be a mix of real-time Data Manipulation Language (DML) operations (inserts, updates, and deletes).

OLTP workloads tend to have the following characteristics:

High Performance: High throughput, measured in hundreds of transactions per second, with the requirement for subsecond end-user response time. Simple transactions, with each transaction issuing a limited number of straightforward SQL statements that access a small number of rows, and perform few, if any I/Os. Transactions perform a great deal of concurrent read and update activity. Database is optimized for transaction processing—performance of OLTP workloads is considerably enhanced by minimizing I/Os, optimizing CPU utilization, eliminating sorts, and improving concurrency between transactions.

High Volume: Volume of data may be very large (hundreds of gigabytes to a few terabytes) or just tens of gigabytes. (Data tends to be current.) Hundreds to thousands of concurrent users.

High Availability: An OLTP environment must be available 24 hours a day, 7 days a week, 365 days a year.

Practice Questions

Question 1

> Which of the following is the lowest cost DB2 product that can be legally installed on a Windows server that has 2 CPUs?
>
> ○ A. DB2 Everyplace
>
> ○ B. DB2 Express Edition
>
> ○ C. DB2 Workgroup Server Edition
>
> ○ D. DB2 Enterprise Server Edition

Question 2

> Which of the following is the lowest cost DB2 product that can be legally installed on an HP-UX server?
>
> ○ A. DB2 Express-C
>
> ○ B. DB2 Express
>
> ○ C. DB2 Personal Edition
>
> ○ D. DB2 Enterprise Server Edition

Question 3

> Which of the following DB2 products can only be installed on a System i server?
>
> ○ A. DB2 for z/OS
>
> ○ B. DB2 for i5/OS
>
> ○ C. DB2 Data Warehouse Edition
>
> ○ D. DB2 Enterprise Server Edition

Question 4

> What is the purpose of the Design Advisor?
>
> ○ A. To analyze workloads and make recommendations for indexes and MQTs
>
> ○ B. To present a graphical representation of a data access plan and recommend design changes that will improve performance
>
> ○ C. To replicate data between a DB2 database and another relational database
>
> ○ D. To configure clients so they can access databases stored on remote servers

Question 5

Which of the following DB2 tools allows a user to set DB2 registry parameters?

○ A. Task Center

○ B. Visual Explain

○ C. Configuration Assistant

○ D. Satellite Administration Center

Question 6

What is the SQL Performance Monitor used for?

○ A. To examine the health of a DB2 Database Manager instance

○ B. To visually construct complex DML statements and examine the results of their execution

○ C. To schedule tasks, run tasks, and send notifications about completed task s to other users

○ D. To analyze database operations performed against a DB2 for i5/OS database

Question 7

Which of the following tasks can NOT be performed using the Developer Workbench?

○ A. Develop and debug an SQL stored procedure

○ B. Develop and debug a user-defined data type

○ C. Develop and debug a user-defined function

○ D. Develop and run XML queries

Question 8

Which of the following tools can be used to automate table reorganization operations?

○ A. Control Center

○ B. Command Center

○ C. Command Line Processor

○ D. Task Center

Question 9

Which of the following can be viewed with the Journal?

○ A. Historical information about tasks, database changes, messages, and notifications

○ B. Information about licenses associated with each DB2 9 product installed on a particular system

○ C. Graphical representations of data access plans chosen for SQL statements

○ D. Warning and alarm thresholds for database indicators

Question 10

Which of the following is NOT a characteristic of an OLTP database?

○ A. Granular transactions

○ B. Current data

○ C. Optimized for queries

○ D. Frequent updates

Question 11

Which of the following is NOT a characteristic of a data warehouse?

○ A. Summarized queries that perform aggregations and joins

○ B. Heterogeneous data sources

○ C. Voluminous historical data

○ D. Sub-second response time

Question 12

Which of the following products is used to shred extensible markup language documents?

○ A. DB2 AVI Extender

○ B. DB2 Text Extender

○ C. DB2 XML Extender

○ D. DB2 Spatial Extender

Question 13

Which of the following best describes the difference between the DB2 Spatial Extender and the DB2 Geodetic Extender?

○ A. The DB2 Spatial Extender uses a latitude-longitude coordinate system; the DB2 Geodetic Extender uses a planar, x- and y-coordinate system

○ B. The DB2 Geodetic Extender is used to describe points, lines, and polygons; the DB2 Spatial Extender is used to find area, endpoints, and intersects

○ C. The DB2 Spatial Extender treats the world as a flat map; the DB2 Geodetic Extender treats the world as a round globe

○ D. The DB2 Geodetic Extender can be used to manage information like the locations of office buildings or the size of a flood zone; the DB2 Spatial Extender can be used for calculations and visualizations in disciplines like military command/control and asset management, meteorology and oceanography

Question 14

Which of the following is true about XML columns?

○ A. XML columns are used to store XML documents as a hierarchical set of entities

○ B. Only XQuery can be used to retrieve an XML document from an XML column

○ C. XML columns must be altered to accommodate additional parent/child relationships if they are used in referential constraints

○ D. In order to access any portion of an XML document stored in an XML column, the entire document must be retrieved

Question 15

Which of the following is the major difference between relational data and XML data?

○ A. Relational data is self-describing; XML data is not

○ B. Relational data has inherent ordering; XML data does not

○ C. Relational data must be tabular; XML data does not have to be tabular

○ D. Relational data is comprised of entities; XML data is comprised of numbers, characters, and dates

Answers

Question 1

The correct answer is **B**. DB2 Express Edition (or DB2 Express) is an entry-level data server that is designed to be used on microcomputers that have up to two CPUs (a dual-core processor is treated as a single CPU), up to 4 GB of memory, and are running a supported version of Linux, Solaris, or Windows. DB2 Everyplace is a small footprint (approximately 350 KB) relational database and a high performance data synchronization solution that allows enterprise applications and data to be extended to mobile devices like personal digital assistants (PDAs), handheld personal computers (HPCs), and smart phones; DB2 Workgroup Server Edition (WSE) is a multi-user, full-function, client/server database management system designed to be used on microcomputers that have up to four CPUs, up to 16 GB of memory, and are running any of the following operating systems: AIX, HP-UX, Solaris, Linux, and Windows; and DB2 Enterprise Server Edition (ESE) is a multi-user, full-function, Web-enabled client/server database management system that is designed to be used on any size server (from one to hundreds of CPUs) that is running any of the following operating systems: AIX, HP-UX, Solaris, Linux, and Windows.

Question 2

The correct answer is **D**. DB2 Enterprise Server Edition (ESE) is designed to be used on a server that is running any of the following operating systems: AIX, HP-UX, Solaris, Linux, and Windows. DB2 Express-C is designed to be used on microcomputers that are running a supported version of Linux or Windows; DB2 Express is designed to be used on microcomputers that are running a supported version of Linux, Solaris, or Windows; and DB2 Personal Edition can be deployed on any Personal Computer (PC) that is running Linux or Windows.

Question 3

The correct answer is **B**. DB2 for i5/OS is an advanced, 64-bit relational database management system that leverages the On-Demand capabilities of System i to quickly respond to changing workloads. DB2 for z/OS is a multi-user, full-function, database management system that has been designed specifically for z/OS, IBM's flagship mainframe operating system. DB2 Data Warehouse Edition (DWE) is comprised of, among other things, DB2 Enterprise Server Edition and the DB2 Data Partitioning Feature - DB2 Enterprise Server Edition (ESE) is designed to be used on a server that is running any of the following operating systems: AIX, HP-UX, Solaris, Linux, and Windows.

Question 4

The correct answer is **A**. The Design Advisor is a special tool that is designed to capture specific information about typical workloads (queries or sets of SQL operations) performed against your database and recommend changes based upon the information provided. When given a set of SQL statements in a workload, the Design Advisor will make recommendations for new indexes, new materialized query tables (MQTs), conversions of base tables to multi-dimensional clustering (MDC) tables, redistribution of table data, and deletion of indexes and MQTs that are not being used by the workload specified. Visual Explain is used to present a graphical representation of a data access plan but it does not recommend design changes; the Replication Center allows users to administer data replication between a DB2 database and any other relational database; and the Configuration Assistant allows users to configure clients so they can access databases stored on remote DB2 servers.

Question 5

The correct answer is **C**. The Configuration Assistant is an interactive GUI application that allows users to configure clients so they can access databases stored on remote DB2 servers. From the Configuration Assistant, users can: catalog new databases, work with or uncatalog existing databases, bind applications, *set DB2 environment/registry variables*, configure the DB2 Database Manager instance, configure ODBC/CLI parameters, import and export configuration information, change passwords, and test database connections. The Task Center allows users to schedule tasks, run tasks, and send notifications about completed tasks to other users; Visual Explain provides database administrators and application developers with the ability to view a graphical representation of the access plan that has been chosen by the DB2 Optimizer for a particular SQL statement; and the Satellite Administration Center is a GUI application that allows users to set up and administer a group of DB2 servers that perform the same business function.

Question 6

The correct answer is **D**. If you are running DB2 for i5/OS, the SQL Performance Monitor is a valuable tool that can be used to keep track of the resources SQL statements use. The Health Monitor is a server-side tool that constantly monitors the health of a DB2 Database Manager instance without a need for user interaction; SQL Assist is an interactive GUI application that allows users to visually construct complex SELECT, INSERT, UPDATE, and DELETE SQL statements and examine the results of their execution; and the Task Center is allows users to schedule tasks, run tasks, and send notifications about completed tasks to other users.

Question 7

The correct answer is **B**. The Developer Workbench is a comprehensive development environment that can be used to create, edit, debug, deploy, and test DB2 stored procedures and user-defined functions. The Developer Workbench can also be used to develop SQLJ applications, and to create, edit, and run SQL statements and XML queries (XQuery expressions).

Question 8

The correct answer is **D**. The Task Center allows users to schedule tasks, run tasks, and send notifications about completed tasks to other users. Users can create a task within the Task Center, generate a task by saving the results from a DB2 dialog or wizard, create a script within another tool and save it to the Task Center, or import an existing script. Thus, it is possible to create a script that calls the REORG command and have the Task Center to execute that script on a routine basis.

Question 9

The correct answer is **A**. The Journal is an interactive GUI application that tracks historical information about tasks, database actions and operations, Control Center actions, messages, and alerts. The License Center allows users to view information about the license associated with each DB2 9 product installed on a particular system; Visual Explain provides database administrators and application developers with the ability to view a graphical representation of the access plan that has been chosen by the DB2 Optimizer for a particular SQL statement; and the Health Center is used to select the instance and database objects that you want to monitor, customize the threshold settings of any health indicator, and specify where notifications are to be sent and what actions are to be taken if an alert is issued.

Question 10

The correct answer is **C**. OLTP systems are designed to support day-to-day, mission-critical business activities such as order entry, stock trading, inventory management, and banking. This typically involves hundreds to thousands of users issuing millions of transactions per day against databases that vary in size. Response time requirements tend to be sub-second and workloads tend to be a mix of real-time DML operations (inserts, updates, and deletes). Workloads in a data warehouse can consist of bulk load operations, short running queries, long running complex queries, random queries, occasional updates to data, and the execution of online utilities. Thus, data warehouses are optimized for queries.

Question 11

The correct answer is **D**. Data Warehousing involves storing and managing large volumes of data (often historical in nature) that is used primarily for analysis. Workloads in a data warehouse vary; they can consist of bulk load operations, short running queries, long running complex queries, random queries, occasional updates to data, and the execution of online utilities. OLTP workloads, on the other hand, tend to be a mix of real-time DML operations (inserts, updates, and deletes) and often require sub-second end-user response time.

Question 12

The correct answer is **C**. The DB2 XML Extender can be used to decompose (shred) XML elements from a document and store them in columns and tables; it can also compose (create) new XML documents from existing character and numerical data or previously shredded XML documents. (If the DB2 XML extender is not used, XML documents are stored hierarchically in columns with the XML data type.) The DB2 Audio, Video, and Image (AVI) Extender contains a set of data types and functions that can be used to store and manipulate nontraditional data such as audio clips, movies, and pictures in a DB2 UDB database; the DB2 Text Extender contains a set of data types and functions that can be used to store complex text documents in a DB2 UDB database and to extract key information from such documents; and the DB2 Spatial Extender contains a set of user-defined data types that can be used to describe spatial data (for example, points, lines, and polygons) and a set of user-defined functions that can be used to query spatial objects (for example, to find area, endpoints, and intersects).

Question 13

The correct answer is **C**. The DB2 Spatial Extender contains a set of user-defined data types that can be used to describe spatial data (for example, points, lines, and polygons) and a set of user-defined functions that can be used to query spatial objects (for example, to find area, endpoints, and intersects). With this capability, you can generate, analyze, and exploit spatial information about geographic features, such as the locations of office buildings or the size of a flood zone and present it in a three-dimensional format. The DB2 Geodetic Extender contains a set of user-defined data types and functions that treat the Earth like a globe rather than a flat map (it can construct a virtual globe at any scale); a round earth is paramount for calculations and visualizations for users in disciplines like military command/control and asset management, meteorology and oceanography (scientific, government, and commercial), and satellite imagery. The DB2 Geodetic Extender has the capability to manage geospatial information referenced by latitude-longitude coordinates and support global spatial queries without the limitations inherent in map projections. To handle objects defined on the earth's surface with precision, the DB2 Geodetic Extender uses a latitude-longitude coordinate system on an ellipsoidal earth model—or geodetic datum—rather than a planar, x- and y-coordinate system.

Question 14

The correct answer is **A**. With DB2 9, XML documents are stored in tables that contain one or more columns that are based on the new XML data type. Along with the XML data type, support for XML data includes new storage techniques for efficient management of the hierarchical entities that inherent in XML documents, new indexing technology to speed up retrieval of subsets of XML documents (entire documents do not have to be read in order to retrieve specific information), new capabilities for validating XML data and managing changing XML schemas, new query language support (including native support for XQuery as well as new SQL/XML enhancements), new query optimization techniques, integration with popular application programming interfaces (APIs), and extensions to popular database utilities.

Question 15

The correct answer is **C**. Extensible Markup Language (XML) is a simple, very flexible text format that provides a neutral, flexible way to exchange data between different devices, systems, and applications because data is maintained in a self-describing format. XML documents are comprised of a hierarchical set of entities and many XML documents contain heavily nested parent/child relationships and/or irregular structures. Relational data, on the other hand, is a collection of numeric values, character strings, and date/time/timestamp values that must be stored in a tabular format. (XML documents can be "shredded" or decomposed and their contents stored across multiple columns in one or more tables and this approach is ideal if the XML data being stored is tabular in nature. However, the cost associated with decomposing XML data often depends on the structure of the underlying XML document and may require a large number of tables, some of which may need to have values generated for foreign keys in order to capture the relationships and ordering that is inherent in the original documents.)

CHAPTER 3

Security

Eleven percent (11%) of the DB2 9 Fundamentals certification exam (Exam 730) is designed to test your knowledge about the mechanisms DB2 uses to protect data and database objects against unauthorized access and modification. The questions that make up this portion of the exam are intended to evaluate the following:

- Your ability to identify the methods that can be used to restrict access to data stored in a DB2 database

- Your ability to identify the authorization levels used by DB2

- Your ability to identify the privileges used by DB2

- Your ability to identify how specific authorizations and/or privileges are given to a user or group

- Your ability to identify how specific authorizations and/or privileges are taken away from a user or group

This chapter is designed to introduce you to the various authorizations and privileges that are available with DB2 9 and to the tools that are used to give (grant) one or more of these authorizations and/or privileges to various users and groups. This chapter will also show you how to revoke one or more authorizations or privileges a user or group currently holds.

Controlling Database Access

Identity theft—a crime in which someone wrongfully obtains another person's personal data (such as a Social Security number, bank account number, and credit card number) and uses it in some way that involves fraud or deception for economic gain—is the fastest-growing crime in our nation today. Criminals are stealing information by overhearing conversations made on cell phones, from faxes and emails, by hacking into computers, from telephone and email scams, by stealing wallets and purses, by stealing discarded documents from trash bins, by stealing mail, and by taking advantage of careless online shopping and banking habits. But more frightening is the fact that studies show up to 70 percent of all identity theft cases are inside jobs—perpetrated by a co-worker or an employee of a business you patronize. In these cases, all that is needed is access to your personal data, which can often be found in a company database.

Every database management system must be able to protect data against unauthorized access and modification. DB2 uses a combination of external security services and internal access control mechanisms to perform this vital task. In most cases, three different levels of security are employed: The first level controls access to the instance a database was created under, the second controls access to the database itself, and the third controls access to the data and data objects that reside within the database.

Authentication

The first security portal most users must pass through on their way to gaining access to a DB2 instance or database is a process known as *authentication*. The purpose of authentication is to verify that users really are who they say they are. Normally, authentication is performed by an external security facility that is not part of DB2. This security facility may be part of the operating system (as is the case with AIX, Solaris, Linux, HP-UX, Windows 2000/NT, and many others), may be a separate add-on product (for example, Distributed Computing Environment [DCE] Security Services), or may not exist at all (which is the case with Windows 95, Windows 98, and Windows Millennium Edition). If a security facility does exist, it must be presented with two specific items before a user can be authenticated: a unique *user ID* and a corresponding *password*. The user ID identifies the user to the security facility, while the password, which is information that is known only by both the user and the security facility, is used to verify that the user is indeed who he or she claims to be.

....

Because passwords are a very important tool for authenticating users, you should always require passwords at the operating system level if you want the operating system to perform the authentication for your database. Keep in mind that on most UNIX operating systems, undefined passwords are treated as NULL, and any user who has not been assigned a password will be treated as having a NULL password. From the operating system's perspective, if no password is provided when a user attempts to log on, this will evaluate to being a valid match.

....

Where Does Authentication Take Place?

Because DB2 can reside in environments comprised of multiple clients, gateways, and servers, each of which may be running on a different operating system, deciding where authentication is to take place can be a daunting task. To simplify things, DB2 uses a parameter in each DB2 Database Manager configuration file (such a file is associated with every instance) to determine how and where users are authenticated. The value assigned to this configuration parameter, often referred to as the *authentication type*, is set initially when an instance is created. (On the server side, the authentication type is specified during the instance creation process; on the client side, the authentication type is specified when a remote database is cataloged.) Only one authentication type exists for each instance, and it controls access to that instance, as well as to all databases that fall under that instance's control.

With DB2 9, the following authentication types are available:

SERVER: Authentication occurs at the server workstation, using the security facility provided by the server's operating system. (The user ID and password provided by the user wishing to attach to an instance or connect to a database are compared to the user ID and password combinations stored at the server to determine whether the user is permitted to access the instance or database.) By default, this is the authentication type used when an instance is first created.

SERVER_ENCRYPT: Authentication occurs at the server workstation, using the security facility that is provided by the server's operating system. However, the password provided by the user wishing to attach to an instance or connect to a database stored on the server may be encrypted at the client workstation before it is sent to the server workstation for validation.

CLIENT: Authentication occurs at the client workstation or database partition where a client application is invoked, using the security facility that is provided by the client's operating system, assuming one is available. If no security facility is available, authentication is handled in a slightly different manner. The user ID and password provided by the user wishing to attach to an instance or connect to a database are compared to the user ID and password combinations stored at the client or node to determine whether the user is permitted to access the instance or the database.

KERBEROS: Authentication occurs at the server workstation, using a security facility that supports the Kerberos security protocol. This protocol performs authentication as a third-party service by using conventional cryptography to create a shared secret key. The key becomes the credentials used to verify the identity of the user whenever local or network services are requested; this eliminates the need to pass a user ID and password across the network as ASCII text. (If both the client and the server support the Kerberos security protocol, the user ID and password provided by the user wishing to attach to an instance or connect to a database are encrypted at the client workstation and sent to the server for validation.) It should be noted that the KERBEROS authentication type is supported only on clients and servers that are using the Windows 2000, Windows XP, or Windows .NET operating system. In addition, both client and server workstations must either belong to the same Windows domain or belong to trusted domains.

KRB_SERVER_ENCRYPT: Authentication occurs at the server workstation, using either the KERBEROS or the SERVER_ENCRYPT authentication method. If the client's authentication type is set to KERBEROS, authentication is performed at the server using the Kerberos security system. On the other hand, if the client's authentication type is set to anything other than KERBEROS or if the Kerberos authentication service is unavailable, the server acts as if the SERVER_ENCRYPT authentication type was specified, and the rules of this authentication method apply.

DATA_ENCRYPT: Authentication occurs at the server workstation, using the SERVER_ENCRYPT authentication method. In addition, all user data is encrypted before it is passed from client to server and from server to client.

DATA_ENCRYPT_CMP: Authentication occurs at the server workstation, using the SERVER_ENCRYPT authentication method; all user data is encrypted before it is passed from client to server and from server to client. In addition, this authentication type provides compatibility for down-level products that do not support the DATA_ENCRYPT authentication type. Such products connect using the SERVER_ENCRYPT authentication type, and user data is not encrypted.

GSSPLUGIN: Authentication occurs at the server workstation, using a *Generic Security Service Application Program Interface* (GSS-API) plug-in. If the client's authentication type is not specified, the server returns a list of server-supported plug-ins (found in the srvcon_gssplugin_list database manager configuration parameter) to the client. The client then selects the first plug-in found in the client plug-in directory from the list. If the client does not support any plug-in in the list, the client is authenticated using the KERBEROS authentication method.

GSS_SERVER_ENCRYPT: Authentication occurs at the server workstation, using either the GSSPLUGIN or the SERVER_ENCRYPT authentication method. That is, if client authentication occurs through a GSS-API plug-in, the client is authenticated using the first client-supported plug-in found in the list of server-supported plug-ins. If the client does not support any of the plug-ins found in the server-supported plug-in list, the client is authenticated using the KERBEROS authentication method. If the client does not support the Kerberos security protocol, the client is authenticated using the SERVER_ENCRYPT authentication method.

It is important to note that if the authentication type used by the client workstation encrypts user ID and password information before sending it to a server for authentication (i.e., SERVER_ENCRYPT, KRB_SERVER_ENCRYPT, etc.), the server must be configured to use a compatible authentication method. Otherwise, it will not be able to process the encrypted data received and an error will occur.

It is also important to note that if the authentication type is not specified for a client workstation, the SERVER_ENCRYPT authentication method is used by default. If such a client tries to communicate with a server that does not support the

SERVER_ENCRYPT authentication method, the client will attempt to use the authentication type that is being used by the server—provided the server has been configured to use only one authentication type. If the server supports multiple authentication types, an error will be generated.

Trusted Clients versus Untrusted Clients

If both the server and the client are configured to use the CLIENT authentication type, authentication occurs at the client workstation (if the database is a nonpartitioned database) or at the database partition from which the client application is invoked (if the database is a partitioned database), using the security facility provided by the client workstation's operating system. But what happens if the client workstation is using an operating system that does not contain a tightly integrated security facility, and no separate add-on security facility has been made available? Does such a configuration compromise security? The answer is no. However, in such environments, the DB2 Database Manager for the instance at the server must be able to determine which clients will be responsible for validating users and which clients will be forced to let the server handle user authentication. To make this distinction, clients that use an operating system that contains a tightly integrated security facility (for example, Windows NT, Windows 2000, all supported versions of UNIX, MVS, OS/390, VM, VSE, and AS/400) are classified as *trusted clients*, whereas clients that use an operating system that does not provide an integrated security facility (for example, Windows 95, Windows 98, and Windows Millennium Edition) are treated as *untrusted clients*.

The trust_allclnts parameter of a DB2 Database Manager configuration file helps the DB2 Database Manager for an instance on a server anticipate whether its clients are to be treated as trusted or untrusted. If this configuration parameter is set to YES (which is the default), the DB2 Database Manager assumes that any client that accesses the instance is a trusted client and that some form of authentication will take place at the client. However, if this configuration parameter is set to NO, the DB2 Database Manager assumes that one or more untrusted clients will try to access the server; therefore, all users must be authenticated at the server. (If this configuration parameter is set to DRDAONLY, only MVS, OS/390, VM, VSE, and OS/400 clients will be treated as trusted clients.) It is important to note that, regardless of how the trust_allclnts parameter is set, whenever an untrusted client attempts to access an instance or a database, user authentication always takes place at the server.

In some situations, it may be desirable to authenticate users at the server, even when untrusted clients will not be used. In such situations, the `trust_clntauth` configuration parameter of a DB2 Database Manager configuration file can be used to control where trusted clients are to be validated. By accepting the default value for this parameter (which is `CLIENT`), authentication for trusted clients will take place at the client workstation. If however, the value for this parameter is changed to `SERVER`, authentication for all trusted clients will take place at the server.

Authorities and Privileges

Once a user has been authenticated and an attachment to an instance or a connection to a database has been established, the DB2 Database Manger evaluates any *authorities* and *privileges* that have been assigned to the user to determine what operations the user is allowed to perform. Privileges convey the rights to perform certain actions against specific database resources (such as tables and views). Authorities convey a set of privileges or the right to perform high-level administrative and maintenance/utility operations on an instance or a database. Authorities and privileges can be assigned directly to a user, or they can be obtained indirectly from the authorities and privileges that have been assigned to a group of which the user is a member. Together, authorities and privileges act to control access to the DB2 Database Manager for an instance, to one or more databases running under that instance's control, and to a particular database's objects. Users can only work with those objects for which they have been given the appropriate authorization—that is, the required authority or privilege. Figure 3–1 provides a hierarchical view of the authorities and privileges that are recognized by DB2 9.

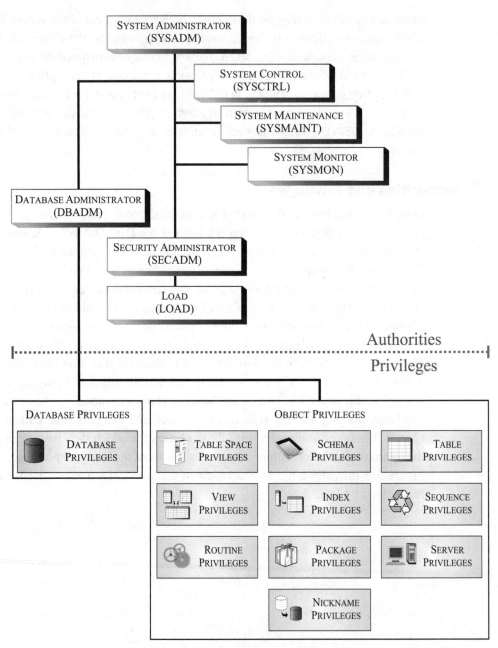

Figure 3–1: Hierarchy of the authorities and privileges available with DB2 9.

Authorities

DB2 9 uses seven different levels of authority to control how users perform administrative and/or maintenance operations against an instance or a database. These levels are:

- System Administrator (SYSADM) authority
- System Control (SYSCTRL) authority
- System Maintenance (SYSMAINT) authority
- System Monitor (SYSMON) authority
- Database Administrator (DBADM) authority
- Security Administrator (SECADM) authority
- Load (LOAD) authority

Four of these levels apply to the DB2 Database Manager instance (and to all databases that are under that instance's control), while three apply only to specific databases within a particular instance. The instance-level authorities can only be assigned to groups; the names of the groups that are assigned these authorities are stored in the DB2 Database Manager configuration file that is associated with the instance. Conversely, the database-level authorities can be assigned to individual users and, in some cases, groups; groups and users that have been assigned database-level authorities are recorded in the system catalog tables of the database to which the authority applies.

System Administrator authority

System Administrator (SYSADM) authority is the highest level of administrative authority available. Users who have been given this authority are allowed to run any DB2 utility, execute any DB2 command, and perform any SQL/XQuery operation that does not attempt to access data that is protected by Label-Based Access Control (LBAC). Users with this authority also have the ability to control all database objects within an instance, including databases, database partition groups, buffer pools, table spaces, schemas, tables, views, indexes, aliases, servers, data types, functions, procedures, triggers, packages, and event monitors. Additionally, users who have been given this authority are allowed to perform the following tasks:

- Migrate an existing database from a previous version of DB2 to DB2 Version 9.

- Modify the parameter values of the DB2 Database Manager configuration file associated with an instance—including specifying which groups have System Administrator, System Control, System Maintenance, and System Monitor authority. (The DB2 Database Manager configuration file is used to control the amount of system resources allocated to a single instance.)

- Give (grant) Database Administrator authority and Security Administrator authority to individual users and/or groups.

- Revoke Database Administrator authority and/or Security Administrator authority from individual users and/or groups.

System Administrator authority can only be assigned to a group; this assignment is made by storing the appropriate group name in the `sysadm_group` parameter of the DB2 Database Manager configuration file associated with an instance. Individual membership in the group itself is controlled through the security facility provided by the operating system used on the workstation where the instance has been defined. Users who possess System Administrator authority are responsible both for controlling the DB2 Database Manager associated with an instance and for ensuring the safety and integrity of the data contained in databases that fall under the instance's control.

Users who hold System Administrator authority are implicitly given the rights granted by System Control, System Maintenance, System Monitor, and Database Administrator authority. However, they are not implicitly given the rights granted by Security Administrator authority.

System Control authority

System Control (`SYSCTRL`) authority is the highest level of system or instance control authority available. Users who have been given this authority are allowed to perform maintenance and utility operations both on a DB2 Database Manager instance and on any databases that fall under that instance's control. However, because System Control authority is designed to allow special users to maintain an instance that contains sensitive data that they most likely do not have the right to view or modify, users who are granted this authority do not implicitly receive authority to access the data stored in the databases that are controlled by the instance. On the other hand, because a connection to a database is required in order to perform some of the utility operations available, users who are granted System Control authority for a particular instance also receive the privileges needed to connect to each database under that instance's control.

Users with System Control authority (or higher) are allowed to perform the following tasks:

- Update a database, node, or database connection services (DCS) directory (by cataloging/uncataloging databases, nodes, or DCS databases).

- Modify the parameter values in one or more database configuration files. (A database configuration file is used to control the amount of system resources that are allocated to a single database during normal operation.)

- Force users off the system.

- Create or destroy (drop) a database.

- Create, alter, or drop a table space.

- Make a backup image of a database or a table space.

- Restore an existing database using a backup image.

- Restore a table space using a backup image.

- Create a new database from a database backup image.

- Perform a roll-forward recovery operation on a database.

- Start or stop a DB2 Database Manager instance.

- Run a trace on a database operation.

- Take database system monitor snapshots of a DB2 Database Manager instance or any database under the instance's control.

- Query the state of a table space.

- Update recovery log history files.

- Quiesce (restrict access to) a table space.

- Reorganize a table.

- Collect catalog statistics using the RUNSTATS utility.

Like System Administrator authority, System Control authority can only be assigned to a group. This assignment is made by storing the appropriate group name in the sysctrl_group parameter of the DB2 Database Manager configuration file that is associated with a particular instance. Again, individual membership in the group itself is controlled through the security facility that is used on the workstation where the instance has been defined.

System Maintenance authority

System Maintenance (SYSMAINT) authority is the second highest level of system or instance control authority available. Users who have been given this authority are allowed to perform maintenance and utility operations both on a DB2 Database Manager instance on and any databases that fall under that instance's control. System Maintenance authority is designed to allow special users to maintain a database that contains sensitive data that they most likely do not have the right to view or modify. Therefore, users who are granted this authority do not implicitly receive authority to access the data stored in the databases they are allowed to perform maintenance on. However, because a connection to a database must exist before some utility operations can be performed, users who are granted System Maintenance authority for a particular instance automatically receive the privileges needed to connect to each database that falls under that instance's control.

Users with System Maintenance authority (or higher) are allowed to perform the following tasks:

- Modify the parameter values of one or more DB2 database configuration files.

- Make a backup image of a database or a table space.

- Restore an existing database using a backup image.

- Restore a table space using a backup image.

- Perform a roll-forward recovery operation on a database.

- Start or stop a DB2 Database Manager instance.

- Run a trace on a database operation.

- Take database system monitor snapshots of a DB2 Database Manager instance or any database under the instance's control.

- Query the state of a table space.

- Update recovery history log files.

- Quiesce (restrict access to) a table space.

- Reorganize a table.

- Collect catalog statistics using the RUNSTATS utility.

Like System Administrator and System Control authority, System Maintenance authority can only be assigned to a group. This assignment is made by storing the appropriate group name in the sysmaint_group parameter of the DB2 Database Manager configuration file that is associated with a particular instance. Again, individual membership in the group itself is controlled through the security facility that is used on the workstation where the instance has been defined.

System Monitor authority

System Monitor (SYSMON) authority is the third highest level of system or instance control authority available with DB2. Users who have been given this authority are allowed to take system monitor snapshots for a DB2 Database Manager instance and/or for one or more databases that fall under that instance's control. System Monitor authority is designed to allow special users to monitor the performance of a database that contains sensitive data that they most likely do not have the right to view or modify. Therefore, users who are granted this authority do not implicitly receive authority to access the data stored in the databases they are allowed to collect snapshot monitor information on. However, because a connection to a database must exist before the snapshot monitor SQL table functions can be used, users who are granted System Monitor authority for a particular instance automatically receive the privileges needed to connect to each database under that instance's control.

Users with System Monitor authority (or higher) are allowed to perform the following tasks:

- Obtain the current settings of the snapshot monitor switches.
- Modify the settings of one or more snapshot monitor switches.
- Reset all counters used by the snapshot monitor.

- Obtain a list of active databases.
- Obtain a list of active applications, including DCS applications.
- Collect snapshot monitor data.
- Use the snapshot monitor SQL table functions.

Like System Administrator, System Control, and System Maintenance authority, System Monitor authority can only be assigned to a group. This assignment is made by storing the appropriate group name in the sysmon_group parameter of the DB2 Database Manager configuration file that is associated with a particular instance. Again, individual membership in the group itself is controlled through the security facility that is used on the workstation where the instance has been defined.

Database Administrator authority

Database Administrator (DBADM) authority is the second highest level of administrative authority available (just below System Administrator authority). Users who have been given this authority are allowed to run most DB2 utilities, issue database-specific DB2 commands, perform most SQL/XQuery operations, and access data stored in any table in a database—provided that data is not protected by LBAC. (To access data protected by LBAC, a user must have the appropriate LBAC credentials.) However, they can perform these functions only on the database for which Database Administrator authority is held.

Additionally, users with Database Administrator authority (or higher) are allowed to perform the following tasks:

- Read database log files.
- Create, activate, and drop event monitors.
- Query the state of a table space.
- Update recovery log history files.
- Quiesce (restrict access to) a table space.
- Reorganize a table.
- Collect catalog statistics using the RUNSTATS utility.

Unlike System Administrator, System Control, System Maintenance, and System Monitor authority, Database Administrator authority can be assigned to both individual users and groups. This assignment is made by executing the appropriate form of the GRANT SQL statement (which we will look at shortly). When a user is given Database Administrator authority for a particular database, they automatically receive all database privileges available for that database as well.

• •

Any time a user with SYSADM or SYSCTRL authority creates a new database, that user automatically receives DBADM authority on that database. Furthermore, if a user with SYSADM or SYSCTRL authority creates a database and is later removed from the SYSADM or SYSCTRL group (i.e., the user's SYSADM or SYSCTRL authority is revoked), the user retains DBADM authority for that database until it is explicitly removed (revoked).removed (revoked).

• •

Security Administrator authority

Security Administrator (SECADM) authority is a special database level of authority that is designed to allow special users to configure various label-based access control (LBAC) elements to restrict access to one or more tables that contain data to which they most likely do not have access themselves. Users who are granted this authority do not implicitly receive authority to access the data stored in the databases for which they manage data access. In fact, users with Security Administrator authority are only allowed to perform the following tasks:

- Create and drop security policies.

- Create and drop security labels.

- Grant and revoke security labels to/from individual users.

- Grant and revoke LBAC rule exemptions.

- Grant and revoke SETSESSIONUSER privileges.

- Transfer ownership of any object not owned by the Security Administrator by executing the TRANSFER OWNERSHIP SQL statement.

No other authority provides a user with these abilities, including System Administrator authority.

Security Administrator authority can only be assigned to individual users; it cannot be assigned to groups (including the group PUBLIC). This assignment is made by executing the appropriate form of the GRANT SQL statement, and only users with System Administrator authority are allowed to grant this authority.

Load authority

Load (LOAD) authority is a special database level of administrative authority that has a much smaller scope than DBADM authority. Users that have been given this authority, along with INSERT and in some cases DELETE privileges, on a particular table are allowed to bulk-load data into that table, using either the AutoLoader utility (db2atld command) or the LOAD command/API. Load authority is designed to allow special users to perform bulk-load operations against a database that they most likely cannot do anything else with. This authority provides a way for Database Administrators to allow more users to perform special database operations, such as Extraction-Transform-Load (ETL) operations, without having to sacrifice control.

In addition to being able to load data into a database table, users with Load authority (or higher) are allowed to perform the following tasks:

- Query the state of a table space using the LIST TABLESPACES command.

- Quiesce (restrict access to) a table space.

- Perform bulk load operations using the LOAD utility. (If exception tables are used as part of a load operation, the user must have INSERT privilege on the exception tables used as well as INSERT privilege on the table being loaded.)

- Collect catalog statistics using the RUNSTATS utility.

Like Database Administrator authority, Load authority can be assigned to both individual users and groups. This assignment is made by executing the appropriate form of the GRANT SQL statement.

Privileges

As mentioned earlier, privileges are used to convey the rights to perform certain actions on specific database resources to both individual users and groups. With DB2 9, two distinct types of privileges exist: *database privileges* and *object privileges*.

Database privileges

Database privileges apply to a database as a whole, and in many cases, they act as a second security checkpoint that must be cleared before access to data is provided. Figure 3–2 shows the different types of database privileges available.

As you can see in Figure 3–2, eight different database privileges exist. They are:

CONNECT: Allows a user to establish a connection to the database.

QUIESCE_CONNECT: Allows a user to establish a connection to the database while it is in a quiesced state (i.e., while access to it is restricted).

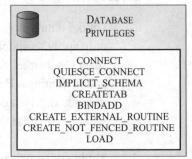

DATABASE PRIVILEGES

CONNECT
QUIESCE_CONNECT
IMPLICIT_SCHEMA
CREATETAB
BINDADD
CREATE_EXTERNAL_ROUTINE
CREATE_NOT_FENCED_ROUTINE
LOAD

Figure 3–2: Database privileges available with DB2 9.

IMPLICIT_SCHEMA: Allows a user to create a new schema in the database implicitly by creating an object and assigning that object a schema name that is different from any of the schema names that already exist in the database.

CREATETAB: Allows a user to create new tables in the database.

BINDADD: Allows a user to create packages in the database (by precompiling embedded SQL application source code files against the database or by binding application bind files to the database).

CREATE_EXTERNAL_ROUTINE: Allows a user to create user-defined functions (UDFs) and/or procedures and store them in the database so that they can be used by other users and applications.

CREATE_NOT_FENCED_ROUTINE: Allows a user to create unfenced UDFs and/or procedures and store them in the database. (Unfenced UDFs and stored procedures are UDFs/procedures that are considered "safe" enough to be run in the DB2 Database Manager operating environment's process or address space. Unless a UDF/procedure is registered as unfenced, the DB2 Database Manager insulates the UDF/procedure's internal resources in such a way that it cannot be run in the DB2 Database Manager's address space.)

LOAD: Allows a user to bulk-load data into one or more existing tables in the database.

At a minimum, a user must have CONNECT privilege on a database before he can work with any object contained in that database.

Object privileges

Unlike database privileges, which apply to a database as a whole, object privileges only apply to specific objects within a database. These objects include table spaces, schemas, tables, views, indexes, sequences, routines, packages, servers, and nicknames. Because the nature of each database object available varies, the individual privileges that exist for each object can vary as well. The following sections describe the different sets of object privileges that are available with DB2 9.

Table space privileges: Table space privileges control what users can and cannot do with a particular table space. (Table spaces are used to control where data in a database physically resides.) Figure 3–3 shows the only table space privilege available.

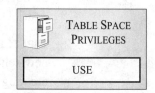

Figure 3–3: Table space privilege available with DB2 9.

As you can see in Figure 3–3, only one table space privilege exists. That privilege is the USE privilege, which, when granted, allows a user to create tables and indexes in the table space. The owner of a table space (usually the individual who created the table space) automatically receives USE privilege for that table space.

The USE privilege cannot be used to provide a user with the ability to create tables in the SYSCATSPACE table space or in any temporary table space that might exist.

Schema privileges: Schema privileges control what users can and cannot do with a particular schema. (A schema is an object that is used to logically classify and group other objects in the database; most objects are named using a naming convention that consists of a schema name, followed by a period, followed by the object name.) Figure 3–4 shows the different types of schema privileges available.

As you can see in Figure 3–4, three different schema privileges exist. They are:

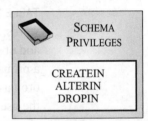

Figure 3–4: Schema privileges available with DB2 9.

CREATEIN: Allows a user to create objects within the schema.

ALTERIN: Allows a user to change the comment associated with any object in the schema or to alter any object that resides within the schema.

DROPIN: Allows a user to remove (drop) any object within the schema.

Objects that can be manipulated within a schema include tables, views, indexes, packages, user-defined data types, user-defined functions, triggers, stored procedures, and aliases. The owner of a schema (usually the individual who created the schema) automatically receives all privileges available for that schema, along with the right to grant any combination of those privileges to other users and groups.

Table privileges: Table privileges control what users can and cannot do with a particular table in a database. (A table is a logical structure that is used to present data as a collection of unordered rows with a fixed number of columns.) Figure 3–5 shows the different types of table privileges available.

As you can see in Figure 3–5, eight different table privileges exist. They are:

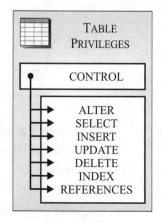

Figure 3–5: Table privileges available with DB2 9.

CONTROL: Provides a user with every table privilege available, allows the user to remove (drop) the table from the database, and gives the user the ability to grant and revoke one or more table privileges (except the CONTROL privilege) to/from other users and groups. (CONTROL privilege is not recognized by DB2 for iSeries and DB2 for zSeries.)

ALTER: Allows a user to execute the ALTER TABLE SQL statement against the table. In other words, allows a user to add columns to the table, add or change comments associated with the table or any of its columns, create a primary key for the table, create a unique constraint for the table, create or drop a check constraint for the table, and create triggers for the table (provided the user holds the appropriate privileges for every object referenced by the trigger).

SELECT: Allows a user to execute a SELECT SQL statement against the table. In other words, this privilege allows a user to retrieve data from a table, create a view that references the table, and run the EXPORT utility against the table.

INSERT: Allows a user to execute the INSERT SQL statement against the table. In other words, this privilege allows a user to add data to the table and run the IMPORT utility against the table.

UPDATE: Allows a user to execute the UPDATE SQL statement against the table. In other words, this privilege allows a user to modify data in the table. (This privilege can be granted for the entire table or limited to one or more columns within the table.)

DELETE: Allows a user to execute the DELETE SQL statement against the table. In other words, allows a user to remove rows of data from the table.

INDEX: Allows a user to create an index for the table.

REFERENCES: Allows a user to create and drop foreign key constraints that reference the table in a parent relationship. (This privilege can be granted for the entire table or limited to one or more columns within the table, in which case only those columns can participate as a parent key in a referential constraint.)

The owner of a table (usually the individual who created the table) automatically receives all privileges available for that table (including CONTROL privilege), along with the right to grant any combination of those privileges (except CONTROL privilege) to other users and groups. If the CONTROL privilege is later revoked from the table owner, all other privileges that were automatically granted to the owner for that particular table are not automatically revoked. Instead, they must be explicitly revoked in one or more separate operations.

View privileges: View privileges control what users can and cannot do with a particular view. (A view is a virtual table residing in memory that provides an alternative way of working with data that resides in one or more base tables. For this reason, views can be used to prevent access to select columns in a table.) Figure 3–6 shows the different types of view privileges available.

As you can see in Figure 3–6, five different view privileges exist. They are:

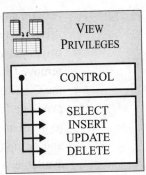

Figure 3–6: View privileges available with DB2 9.

CONTROL: Provides a user with every view privilege available, allows the user to remove (drop) the view from the database, and gives the user the ability to grant and revoke one or more view privileges (except the CONTROL privilege) to/from other users and groups. (CONTROL privilege is not recognized by DB2 for iSeries and DB2 for zSeries.)

SELECT: Allows a user to retrieve data from the view, create a second view that references the view, and run the EXPORT utility against the view.

INSERT: Allows a user to execute the INSERT SQL statement against the view. In other words, allows a user to add data to the view.

UPDATE: Allows a user to execute the UPDATE SQL statement against the view. In other words, this privilege allows a user to modify data in the view. (This privilege can be granted for the entire view or limited to one or more columns within the view.)

DELETE: Allows a user to execute the DELETE SQL statement against the views. In other words, this privilege allows a user to remove rows of data from the view.

In order to create a view, a user must hold appropriate privileges (at a minimum, SELECT privilege) on each base table the view references. The owner of a view (usually the individual who created the view) automatically receives all privileges available—with the exception of the CONTROL privilege—for that view, along with the right to grant any combination of those privileges (except CONTROL privilege) to other users and groups. A view owner will only receive CONTROL privilege for a view if they also hold CONTROL privilege for every base table the view references.

Index privileges: Index privileges control what users can and cannot do with a particular index. (An index is an ordered set of pointers that refer to one or more key columns in a base table; indexes are used to improve query performance.) Figure 3–7 shows the only index privilege available.

Figure 3–7: Index privilege available with DB2 9.

As you can see in Figure 3–7, only one index privilege exists. That privilege is the CONTROL privilege, which, when granted, allows a user to remove (drop) the index from the database. Unlike the CONTROL privilege for other objects, the CONTROL privilege for an index does not give a user the ability to grant and revoke index privileges to/from other users and groups. That's because the CONTROL privilege is the only index privilege available, and only users who hold System Administrator or Database Administrator authority are allowed to grant and revoke CONTROL privileges for an object.

The owner of an index (usually the individual who created the index) automatically receives CONTROL privilege for that index.

It is important to note that this index privilege is available only with DB2 for Linux, UNIX, and Windows; CONTROL privilege is not recognized by DB2 for iSeries and DB2 for zSeries.

Sequence privileges: Sequence privileges control what users can and cannot do with a particular sequence. (A sequence is an object that can be used to generate values automatically. Sequences are ideal for generating unique key values, and they can be used to avoid the possible concurrency and performance problems that can occur when unique counters residing outside the database are used for data generation.) Figure 3–8 shows the different types of sequence privileges available.

As you can see in Figure 3–8, two different sequence privileges exist. They are:

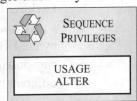

USAGE: Allows a user to use the PREVIOUS VALUE and NEXT VALUE expressions that are associated with the sequence. (The PREVIOUS VALUE expression returns the most recently generated value for the specified sequence; the NEXT VALUE expression returns the next value for the specified sequence.)

Figure 3–8: Sequence privileges available with DB2 9.

ALTER: Allows a user to perform administrative tasks such as restarting the sequence, changing the increment value for the sequence, and adding or changing the comment associated with the sequence.

The owner of a sequence (usually the individual who created the sequence) automatically receives all privileges available for that sequence, along with the right to grant any combination of those privileges to other users and groups.

Routine privileges: Routine privileges control what users can and cannot do with a particular routine. (A routine can be a user-defined function, a stored procedure, or a method that can be invoked by several different users.) Figure 3–9 shows the only routine privilege available.

As you can see in Figure 3–9, only one routine privilege exists. That privilege is the EXECUTE privilege, which, when granted, allows a user to invoke the routine, create a function that is sourced from the routine (provided the routine is a function), and reference the routine in any Data Definition Language SQL statement (for example, CREATE VIEW and CREATE TRIGGER).

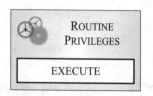

Figure 3–9: Routine privilege available with DB2 9.

The owner of a routine (usually the individual who created the routine) automatically receives EXECUTE privilege for that routine.

Package privileges: Package privileges control what users can and cannot do with a particular package. (A package is an object that contains the information needed by the DB2 Database Manager to process SQL statements in the most efficient way possible on behalf of an embedded SQL application.) Figure 3–10 shows the different types of package privileges available.

As you can see in Figure 3–10, three different package privileges exist. They are:

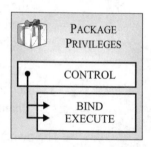

Figure 3–10: Package privileges available with DB2 9.

CONTROL: Provides a user with every package privilege available, allows the user to remove (drop) the package from the database, and gives the user the ability to grant and revoke one or more table privileges (except the CONTROL privilege) to/from other users and groups. (CONTROL privilege is not recognized by DB2 for iSeries and DB2 for zSeries.)

BIND: Allows a user to rebind or add new package versions to a package that has already been bound to a database. (In addition to the BIND package privilege, a user must hold the privileges needed to execute the SQL statements that make up the package before the package can be successfully rebound.)

EXECUTE: Allows a user to execute the package. (A user that has EXECUTE privilege for a particular package can execute that package, even if the user does not have the privileges that are needed to execute the SQL statements stored in the package. That is because any privileges needed to execute the SQL statements are implicitly granted to the package user. It is important to note that for privileges to be implicitly granted, the creator of the package must hold privileges as an individual user or as a member of the group PUBLIC—not as a member of another named group.)

The owner of a package (usually the individual who created the package) automatically receives all privileges available for that package (including CONTROL privilege), along with the right to grant any combination of those privileges (except CONTROL privilege) to other users and groups. If the CONTROL privilege is later revoked from the package owner, all other privileges that were automatically granted to the owner for that particular package are not automatically revoked. Instead, they must be explicitly revoked in one or more separate operations.

> Users who have EXECUTE privilege for a package that contains nicknames do not need additional authorities or privileges for the nicknames in the package; however, they must be able to pass any authentication checks performed at the data source(s) in which objects referenced by the nicknames are stored and they must hold the appropriate authorizations and privileges needed to access all objects referenced.

Server privileges: Server privileges control what users can and cannot do with a particular federated database server. (A DB2 federated system is a distributed computing system that consists of a DB2 server, known as a *federated server,* and one or more data sources to which the federated server sends queries. Each data source consists of an instance of some supported relational database management system—such as Oracle—plus the database or databases that the instance supports.) Figure 3–11 shows the only server privilege available.

As you can see in Figure 3–11, only one server privilege exists. That privilege is the PASSTHRU privilege, which, when granted, allows a user to issue Data Definition Language (DDL) and Data Manipulation Language (DML) SQL statements (as pass-through operations) directly to a data source via a federated server.

Figure 3–11: Server privilege available with DB2 9.

Nickname privileges: Nickname privileges control what users can and cannot do with a particular nickname. (When a client application submits a distributed request to a federated database server, the server forwards the request to the appropriate data source for processing. However, such a request does not identify the data source itself; instead, it references tables and views within the data source by using *nicknames* that map to specific table and view names in the data source. Nicknames are not alternate names for tables and views in the same way that aliases are; instead, they are pointers by which a federated server references external objects.) Figure 3–12 shows the different types of nickname privileges available.

As you can see in Figure 3–12, eight different nickname privileges exist. They are:

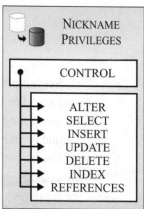

CONTROL: Provides a user with every nickname privilege available, allows the user to remove (drop) the nickname from the database, and gives the user the ability to grant and revoke one or more nickname privileges (except the CONTROL privilege) to/from other users and groups. (CONTROL privilege is not recognized by DB2 for iSeries and DB2 for zSeries.)

ALTER: Allows a user to execute the ALTER NICKNAME SQL statement against the nickname. In other words, this privilege allows a user to change column names in the nickname, add or change the DB2 data type that a particular nickname column's data type maps to, and specify column options for a specific nickname column.

Figure 3–12: Nickname privileges available with DB2 9.

SELECT: Allows a user to execute a SELECT SQL statement against the nickname. In other words, this privilege allows a user to retrieve data from the table or view within a federated data source that the nickname refers to.

INSERT: Allows a user to execute the INSERT SQL statement against the nickname. In other words, this privilege allows a user to add data to the table or view within a federated data source that the nickname refers to.

UPDATE: Allows a user to execute the UPDATE SQL statement against the nickname. In other words, this privilege allows a user to modify data in the table or view within a federated data source that the nickname refers to. (This privilege can be granted for the entire table or limited to one or more columns within the table.)

DELETE: Allows a user to execute the DELETE SQL statement against the nickname. In other words, allows a user to remove rows of data from the table or view within a federated data source that the nickname refers to.

INDEX: Allows a user to create an index specification for the nickname.

REFERENCES: Allows a user to create and drop foreign key constraints that reference the nickname in a parent relationship.

The owner of a nickname (usually the individual who created the table) automatically receives all privileges available for that nickname (including CON-TROL privilege), along with the right to grant any combination of those privileges (except CONTROL privilege) to other users and groups. If the CONTROL privilege is later revoked from the nickname owner, all other privileges that were automatically granted to the owner for that particular table are not automatically revoked. Instead, they must be explicitly revoked in one or more separate operations.

Granting Authorities and Privileges

There are three different ways that users (and in some cases, groups) can obtain database-level authorities and database/object privileges. They are:

Implicitly: When a user creates a database, that user implicitly receives Database Administrator authority for that database, along with most database privileges available. Likewise, when a user creates a database object, that user implicitly receives all privileges available for that object, along with the ability to grant any combination of those privileges (with the exception o the CONTROL privilege) to other users and groups. Privileges can also be implicitly given whenever a higher-level privilege is explicitly granted to a user (for example, if a user is explicitly given CONTROL privilege for a table space, the user will implicitly receive the USE privilege for that table space as well). It's important to remember that such implicitly assigned privileges are not automatically revoked when the higher-level privilege that caused them to be granted is revoked.

Indirectly: Indirectly assigned privileges are usually associated with packages; when a user executes a package that requires additional privileges that the user does not have (for example, a package that deletes a row of data from a table requires the DELETE privilege on that table), the user is indirectly given those privileges for the express purpose of executing the package. Indirectly granted privileges are temporary and do not exist outside the scope in which they are granted.

Explicitly: Database-level authorities, database privileges, and object privileges can be explicitly given to or taken from an individual user or a group of users by anyone who has the authority to do so. To grant privileges explicitly on most database objects, a user must have System Administrator authority, Database Administrator authority, or CONTROL privilege on that object. Alternately, a user can explicitly grant any privilege that user was assigned with the WITH GRANT OPTION specified. To grant CONTROL privilege for any object, a user must have System Administrator authority or Database Administrator authority; to grant Database Administrator authority or Security Administrator authority, a user must have System Administrator authority.

Granting and Revoking Authorities and Privileges from the Control Center

One way to explicitly grant and revoke database-level authorities, as well as many of the object privileges available, is by using the various authorities and privileges management dialogs that are provided with the Control Center. These dialogs are activated by highlighting the appropriate database or object name shown in the Control Center panes and selecting either Authorities or Privileges from the corresponding database or object menu. Figure 3–13 shows the menu items that must be selected in the Control Center in order to activate the Table Privileges dialog for a particular table. Figure 3–14 shows how the Table Privileges dialog might look immediately after a table is first created. (A single check mark under a privilege means that the individual or group shown has been granted that privilege; a double check mark means the individual or group has also been granted ability to grant that privilege to other users and groups.)

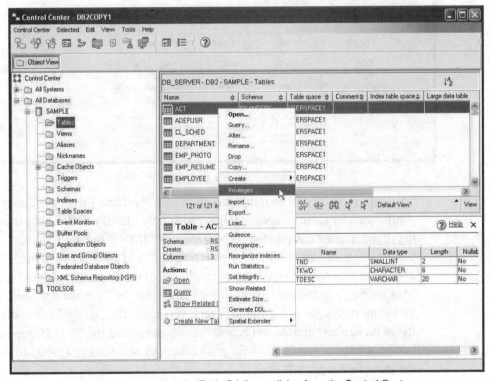

Figure 3–15: Invoking the Table Privileges dialog from the Control Center.

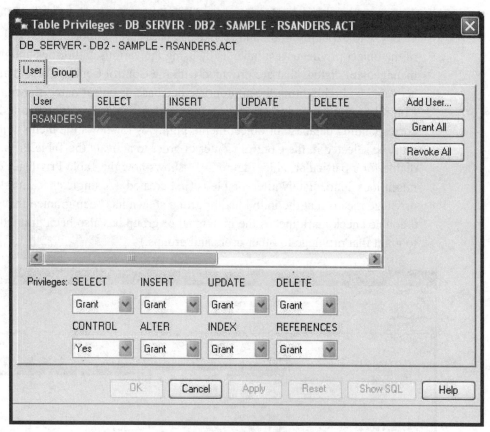

Figure 3–16: The Table Privileges dialog.

To assign privileges to an individual user from the Table Privileges dialog (or a
similar authorities/privileges dialog), you simply identify a particular user by
highlighting their entry in the recognized users list—if the desired user is not in
the list, the user can be added by selecting the "Add User" push button—and
assign the appropriate privileges (or authorities) using the "Privileges" (or
"Authorities") drop-down list(s) or the "Grant All" or "Revoke All" push buttons.
To assign privileges to a group of users, you select the "Group" tab to display a
list of recognized groups and repeat the process (using the "Add Group" push
button instead of the "Add User" push button to add a desired group to the list if
the group is not already there).

Granting Authorities and Privileges with the GRANT SQL Statement

Not all privileges can be explicitly given to users/groups with the privileges management dialogs available. In situations where no privileges dialog exists (and in situations where you elect not to use the privileges dialogs available), database-level authorities and database/object privileges can be explicitly given to users and/or groups by executing the appropriate form of the GRANT SQL statement. The syntax for the GRANT SQL statement varies according to the authority or privilege being granted. The following subsections show the syntax used to grant each database-level authority and database/object privilege available.

Database-level authorities and privileges

```
GRANT [Privilege, ...] ON DATABASE
TO [Recipient, ...]
```

where:

Privilege   Identifies one or more database privileges that are to be given to one or more users and/or groups. The following values are valid for this parameter: DBADM, SECADM, CONNECT, CONNECT_QUIESCE, IMPLICIT_SCHEMA, CREATETAB, BINDADD, CREATE_EXTERNAL_ROUTINE, CREATE_NOT_FENCED_ROUTINE, and LOAD.

Recipient   Identifies the name of the user(s) and/or group(s) that are to receive the database privileges specified. The value specified for the *Recipient* parameter can be any combination of the following:

    <USER> [*UserName*]   Identifies a specific user that the privileges specified are to be given to.

    <GROUP> [*GroupName*]   Identifies a specific group that the privileges specified are to be given to.

    PUBLIC   Indicates that the specified privilege(s) are to be given to the group PUBLIC. (All users are a member of the group PUBLIC.)

Table space privileges

```
GRANT USE OF TABLESPACE [TablespaceName]
TO [Recipient, ...]
<WITH GRANT OPTION>
```

where:

TablespaceName Identifies by name the table space that the USE privilege is to be associated with.

Recipient Identifies the name of the user(s) and/or group(s) that are to receive the USE privilege. Again, the value specified for the *Recipient* parameter can be any combination of the following: <USER> [*UserName*], <GROUP> [*GroupName*], and PUBLIC.

If the WITH GRANT OPTION clause is specified, each *Recipient* is given the ability to grant the privilege received to others.

Schema privileges

```
GRANT [Privilege, ...] ON SCHEMA [SchemaName]
TO [Recipient, ...]
<WITH GRANT OPTION>
```

where:

Privilege Identifies one or more schema privileges that are to be given to one or more users and/or groups. The following values are valid for this parameter: CREATIN, ALTERIN, and DROPIN.

SchemaName Identifies by name the schema that all schema privileges specified are to be associated with.

Recipient Identifies the name of the user(s) and/or group(s) that are to receive the schema privileges specified. The value specified for the *Recipient* parameter can be any combination of the following: <USER> [*UserName*], <GROUP> [*GroupName*], and PUBLIC.

Table privileges

```
GRANT [ALL <PRIVILEGES> |
        Privilege <( ColumnName, ... )> , ...]
ON TABLE [TableName]
TO [Recipient, ...]
<WITH GRANT OPTION>
```

where:

Privilege   Identifies one or more table privileges that are to be given to one or more users and/or groups. The following values are valid for this parameter: CONTROL, ALTER, SELECT, INSERT, UPDATE, DELETE, INDEX, and REFERENCES. (CONTROL privilege is not recognized by DB2 for iSeries and DB2 for zSeries.)

ColumnName Identifies by name one or more specific columns that UPDATE or REFERENCES privileges are to be associated with. This option is only used when *Privilege* contains the value UPDATE or REFERENCES.

TableName Identifies by name the table that all table privileges specified are to be associated with.

Recipient   Identifies the name of the user(s) and/or group(s) that are to receive the table privileges specified. The value specified for the *Recipient* parameter can be any combination of the following: <USER> [*UserName*], <GROUP> [*GroupName*], and PUBLIC.

It is important to note that only users who hold System Administrator or Database Administrator authority are allowed to grant CONTROL privilege for a table. For this reason, when the ALL PRIVILEGES clause is specified, all table privileges *except* CONTROL privilege are granted to each *Recipient*; CONTROL privilege must be granted separately.

View privileges

```
GRANT [ALL <PRIVILEGES> |
       Privilege <( ColumnName, ... )> , ...]
ON [ViewName]
TO [Recipient, ...]
<WITH GRANT OPTION>
```

where:

Privilege   Identifies one or more view privileges that are to be given to
                  one or more users and/or groups. The following values are valid
                  for this parameter: CONTROL, SELECT, INSERT, UPDATE, and
                  DELETE. (CONTROL privilege is not recognized by DB2 for iSeries
                  and DB2 for zSeries.)

ColumnName   Identifies by name one or more specific columns that UPDATE
                  privileges are to be associated with. This option is only used
                  when *Privilege* contains the value UPDATE.

ViewName   Identifies by name the view that all view privileges specified are
                  to be associated with.

Recipient   Identifies the name of the user(s) and/or group(s) that are to
                  receive the view privileges specified. The value specified for the
                  Recipient parameter can be any combination of the following:
                  <USER> [*UserName*], <GROUP> [*GroupName*], and PUBLIC.

Again, only users who hold System Administrator or Database Administrator
authority are allowed to grant CONTROL privilege for a view. Therefore, when the
ALL PRIVILEGES clause is specified, all view privileges *except* CONTROL privilege
are granted to each *Recipient*; CONTROL privilege must be granted separately.

Index privileges

```
GRANT CONTROL ON INDEX [IndexName]
TO [Recipient, ...]
```

where:

IndexName   Identifies by name the index that the CONTROL privilege is to be associated with. (CONTROL privilege is not recognized by DB2 for iSeries and DB2 for zSeries.)

Recipient   Identifies the name of the user(s) and/or group(s) that are to receive the CONTROL privilege. The value specified for the *Recipient* parameter can be any combination of the following: <USER> [*UserName*], <GROUP> [*GroupName*], and PUBLIC.

Sequence privileges

```
GRANT [Privilege, ...] ON SEQUENCE [SequenceName]
TO [Recipient, ...]
<WITH GRANT OPTION>
```

where:

Privilege   Identifies one or more sequence privileges that are to be given to one or more users and/or groups. The following values are valid for this parameter: USAGE and ALTER.

SequenceName   Identifies by name the sequence that all sequence privileges specified are to be associated with.

Recipient   Identifies the name of the user(s) and/or group(s) that are to receive the sequence privileges specified. Again, the value specified for the *Recipient* parameter can be any combination of the following: <USER> [*UserName*], <GROUP> [*GroupName*], and PUBLIC.

Routine privileges

```
GRANT EXECUTE ON [RoutineName |
    FUNCTION <SchemaName.> * |
    METHOD * FOR [TypeName] |
    METHOD * FOR <SchemaName.> * |
    PROCEDURE <SchemaName.> *]
TO [Recipient, ...]
<WITH GRANT OPTION>
```

where:

RoutineName   Identifies by name the routine (user-defined function, method, or stored procedure) that the EXECUTE privilege is to be associated with.

TypeName   Identifies by name the type in which the specified method is found.

SchemaName   Identifies by name the schema in which all functions, methods, or procedures—including those that may be created in the future—are to have the EXECUTE privilege granted on.

Recipient   Identifies the name of the user(s) and/or group(s) that are to receive the EXECUTE privilege. The value specified for the *Recipient* parameter can be any combination of the following: <USER> [*UserName*], <GROUP> [*GroupName*], and PUBLIC.

On DB2 for iSeries and DB2 for zSeries, the command for granting routine privileges is:

```
GRANT EXECUTE ON [FunctionName]([ParameterType],...)|
              SPECIFIC FUNCTION [SpecificName] |
              PROCEDURE [ProcedureName]
TO [Recipient, ...]
<WITH GRANT OPTION>
```

where:

FunctionName   Identifies by name the user-defined function that the EXECUTE privilege is to be associated with.

ParameterType   Identifies one or more parameter data types used by the function.

SpecificName   Identifies by specific name the user-defined function that the EXECUTE privilege is to be associated with.

> *Recipient*   Identifies the name of the user(s) and/or group(s) that are to receive the EXECUTE privilege. The value specified for the *Recipient* parameter can be any combination of the following: [*UserName*] and PUBLIC.

Package privileges

```
GRANT [Privilege, ...] ON PACKAGE <SchemaName.>[PackageID]
TO [Recipient, ...]
<WITH GRANT OPTION>
```

where:

> *Privilege*   Identifies one or more pckage privileges that are to be given to one or more users and/or groups. The following values are valid for this parameter: CONTROL, BIND, and EXECUTE. (CONTROL privilege is not recognized by DB2 for iSeries and DB2 for zSeries.)

> *SchemaName*   Identifies by name the schema in which the specified package is found.

> *PackageName*   Identifies by name the package that all package privileges specified are to be associated with.

> *Recipient*   Identifies the name of the user(s) and/or group(s) that are to receive the package privileges specified. The value specified for the *Recipient* parameter can be any combination of the following: <USER> [*UserName*], <GROUP> [*GroupName*], and PUBLIC. (DB2 for iSeries and DB2 for zSeries allow users to grant package privileges to themselves; DB2 for Linux, UNIX, and Windows does not.)

Server privileges

```
GRANT PASSTHRU ON SERVER [ServerName]
TO [Recipient, ...]
```

where:

ServerName	Identifies by name the server that the PASSTHRU privilege is to be associated with.
Recipient	Identifies the name of the user(s) and/or group(s) that are to receive the PASSTHRU privilege. The value specified for the *Recipient* parameter can be any combination of the following: <USER> [*UserName*], <GROUP> [*GroupName*], and PUBLIC.

Nickname privileges

```
GRANT [ALL <PRIVILEGES> |
       Privilege <( ColumnName, ... )>  , ...]
ON [Nickname]
TO [Recipient, ...]
<WITH GRANT OPTION>
```

where:

Privilege	Identifies one or more nickname privileges that are to be given to one or more users and/or groups. The following values are valid for this parameter: CONTROL, ALTER, SELECT, INSERT, UPDATE, DELETE, INDEX, and REFERENCES. (CONTROL privilege is not recognized by DB2 for iSeries and DB2 for zSeries.)
ColumnName	Identifies by name one or more specific columns that UPDATE or REFERENCES privileges are to be associated with. This option is only used when *Privilege* contains the value UPDATE or REFERENCES.
Nickname	Identifies by name the nickname that all privileges specified are to be associated with.
Recipient	Identifies the name of the user(s) and/or group(s) that are to receive the nickname privileges specified. The value specified for the *Recipient* parameter can be any combination of the following: <USER> [*UserName*], <GROUP> [*GroupName*], and PUBLIC.

Only users who hold System Administrator or Database Administrator authority are allowed to grant CONTROL privilege for a nickname. Therefore, when the ALL

PRIVILEGES clause is specified, all nickname privileges *except* CONTROL privilege are granted to each *Recipient*; CONTROL privilege must be granted separately.

Distinct type privileges (DB2 for iSeries and DB2 for zSeries only)

```
GRANT USAGE ON DISTINCT TYPE [TypeName]
TO [Recipient, ...]
<WITH GRANT OPTION>
```

where:

TypeName Identifies by name the distinct type that the USAGE privilege is to be associated with.

Recipient Identifies the name of the user(s) and/or group(s) that are to receive the distinct type privileges specified. The value specified for the *Recipient* parameter can be any combination of the following: [*UserName*] and PUBLIC.

It is important to note that this statement is not supported by DB2 for Linux, UNIX, and Windows. Instead, with DB2 for Linux, UNIX, and Windows the group PUBLIC is implicitly granted USAGE privilege on all distinct types.

GRANT SQL statement examples

Now that we've seen the basic syntax for the various forms of the GRANT SQL statement, let's take a look at some examples.

Example 1: A server has both a user and a group named TESTER. Give the group TESTER the ability to bind applications to the database SAMPLE:

```
CONNECT TO sample;
GRANT BINDADD ON DATABASE TO GROUP tester;
```

Example 2: Give all table privileges available for the table
PAYROLL.EMPLOYEE (except CONTROL privilege) to the group
PUBLIC:

```
GRANT ALL PRIVILEGES ON TABLE payroll.employee TO PUBLIC
```

Example 3: Give user USER1 and user USER2 the privileges needed to
perform DML operations on the table DEPARTMENT using the
view DEPTVIEW:

```
GRANT SELECT, INSERT, UPDATE, DELETE ON deptview
TO USER user1, USER user2
```

Example 4: Give user JOHN_DOE the privileges needed to query the table
INVENTORY, along with the ability to give these privileges to
other users whenever appropriate:

```
GRANT SELECT ON TABLE inventory
TO john_doe
WITH GRANT OPTION
```

Example 5: Give user USER1 the ability to run an embedded SQL application
that requires a package named GET_INVENTORY:

```
GRANT EXECUTE ON PACKAGE get_inventory TO USER user1
```

Example 6: Give user USER1 the ability to use a stored procedure named
PAYROLL.CALC_SALARY in a query:

```
GRANT EXECUTE ON PROCEDURE payroll.calc_salary TO user1
```

Example 7: Give user USER1 and group GROUP1 the ability to define a referential constraint between the tables EMPLOYEE and DEPARTMENT
using column EMPID in table EMPLOYEE as the parent key:

```
GRANT REFERENCES(empid) ON TABLE employee TO USER user1,
GROUP group1
```

Example 8: Give the group PUBLIC the ability to modify information stored in the ADDRESS and HOME_PHONE columns of the table EMP_INFO:

```
GRANT UPDATE(address, home_phone) ON TABLE emp_info TO
PUBLIC
```

Revoking Authorities and Privileges with the REVOKE SQL Statement

Just as there is an SQL statement that can be used to grant database-level authorities and database/object privileges, there is an SQL statement that can be used to revoke database-level authorities and database/object privileges. This statement is the REVOKE SQL statement, and, as with the GRANT statement, the syntax for the REVOKE statement varies according to the authority or privilege being revoked. The following sections show the syntax used to revoke each database-level authority and database/object privilege available.

Database-level authorities and privileges

```
REVOKE [Privilege, ...] ON DATABASE
FROM [Forfeiter, ...] <BY ALL>
```

where:

Privilege   Identifies one or more database privileges that are to be taken from one or more users and/or groups. The following values are valid for this parameter: DBADM, SECADM, CONNECT, CONNECT_QUIESCE, IMPLICIT_SCHEMA, CREATETAB, BINDADD, CREATE_EXTERNAL_ROUTINE, CREATE_NOT_FENCED_ROUTINE, and LOAD.

Forfeiter   Identifies the name of the user(s) and/or group(s) that are to lose the database privileges specified. The value specified for the *Forfeiter* parameter can be any combination of the following:

         <USER> [*UserName*]   Identifies a specific user that the privileges specified are to be taken from.

         <GROUP> [*GroupName*]   Identifies a specific group that the privileges specified are to be taken from.

PUBLIC   Indicates that the specified privilege(s) are to be taken from the group PUBLIC. (All users are members of the group PUBLIC.)

The BY ALL clause is optional and is provided as a courtesy for administrators who are familiar with the syntax of the DB2 for OS/390 REVOKE SQL statement. Whether it is included or not, all privileges specified will be revoked from all users and/or groups specified.

Table space privileges

```
REVOKE USE OF TABLESPACE [TablespaceName]
FROM [Forfeiter, ...] <BY ALL>
```

where:

TablespaceName   Identifies by name the table space that the USE privilege is to be associated with.

Forfeiter   Identifies the name of the user(s) and/or group(s) that are to lose the USE privilege. Again, the value specified for the *Forfeiter* parameter can be any combination of the following: <USER> [*UserName*], <GROUP> [*GroupName*], and PUBLIC.

Schema privileges

```
REVOKE [Privilege, ...] ON SCHEMA [SchemaName]
FROM [Forfeiter, ...] <BY ALL>
```

where:

Privilege   Identifies one or more schema privileges that are to be taken from one or more users and/or groups. The following values are valid for this parameter: CREATIN, ALTERIN, and DROPIN.

SchemaName   Identifies by name the schema that all schema privileges specified are to be associated with.

Forfeiter   Identifies the name of the user(s) and/or group(s) that are to lose the schema privileges specified. The value specified for the *Forfeiter* parameter can be any combination of the following: <USER> [*UserName*], <GROUP> [*GroupName*], and PUBLIC.

Table privileges

```
REVOKE [ALL <PRIVILEGES> |
        Privilege, ...]
ON TABLE [TableName]
FROM [Forfeiter, ...] <BY ALL>
```

where:

Privilege   Identifies one or more table privileges that are to be taken from one or more users and/or groups. The following values are valid for this parameter: CONTROL, ALTER, SELECT, INSERT, UPDATE, DELETE, INDEX, and REFERENCES. (CONTROL privilege is not recognized by DB2 for iSeries and DB2 for zSeries.)

TableName   Identifies by name the table that all table privileges specified are to be associated with.

Forfeiter   Identifies the name of the user(s) and/or group(s) that are to lose the table privileges specified. The value specified for the *Forfeiter* parameter can be any combination of the following: <USER> [*UserName*], <GROUP> [*GroupName*], and PUBLIC.

It is important to note that only users who hold System Administrator or Database Administrator authority are allowed to revoke CONTROL privilege for a table. For this reason, when the ALL PRIVILEGES clause is specified, all table privileges *except* CONTROL privilege are revoked from each *Forfeiter*; CONTROL privilege must be revoked separately.

View privileges

```
REVOKE [ALL <PRIVILEGES> |
           Privilege, ...]
ON [ViewName]
FROM [Forfeiter, ...] <BY ALL>
```

where:

Privilege   Identifies one or more view privileges that are to be taken from one or more users and/or groups. The following values are valid for this parameter: CONTROL, SELECT, INSERT, UPDATE, and DELETE. (CONTROL privilege is not recognized by DB2 for iSeries and DB2 for zSeries.)

ViewName   Identifies by name the view that all view privileges specified are to be associated with.

Forfeiter   Identifies the name of the user(s) and/or group(s) that are to lose the view privileges specified. The value specified for the *Forfeiter* parameter can be any combination of the following: <USER> [*UserName*], <GROUP> [*GroupName*], and PUBLIC.

Again, only users who hold System Administrator or Database Administrator authority are allowed to revoke CONTROL privilege for a table. For this reason, when the ALL PRIVILEGES clause is specified, all table privileges *except* CONTROL privilege are revoked from each *Forfeiter*; CONTROL privilege must be revoked separately.

Index privileges

```
REVOKE CONTROL ON INDEX [IndexName]
FROM [Forfeiter, ...] <BY ALL>
```

where:

IndexName   Identifies by name the index that the CONTROL privilege is to be associated with. (CONTROL privilege is not recognized by DB2 for iSeries and DB2 for zSeries.)

Forfeiter   Identifies the name of the user(s) and/or group(s) that are to lose the CONTROL privilege. The value specified for the *Forfeiter* parameter can be any combination of the following: <USER> [*UserName*], <GROUP> [*GroupName*], and PUBLIC.

Sequence privileges

```
REVOKE [Privilege, ...] ON SEQUENCE [SequenceName]
FROM [Forfeiter, ...] <BY ALL>
```

where:

Privilege   Identifies one or more sequence privileges that are to be taken from one or more users and/or groups. The following values are valid for this parameter: USAGE and ALTER.

SequenceName   Identifies by name the sequence that all sequence privileges specified are to be associated with.

Forfeiter   Identifies the name of the user(s) and/or group(s) that are to lose the sequence privileges specified. The value specified for the *Forfeiter* parameter can be any combination of the following: <USER> [*UserName*], <GROUP> [*GroupName*], and PUBLIC.

Routine privileges

```
REVOKE EXECUTE ON [RoutineName |
        FUNCTION <SchemaName.> * |
        METHOD * FOR [TypeName] |
        METHOD * FOR <SchemaName.> * |
        PROCEDURE <SchemaName.> *]
FROM [Forfeiter, ...] <BY ALL>
RESTRICT
```

where:

RoutineName   Identifies by name the routine (user-defined function, method, or stored procedure) that the EXECUTE privilege is to be associated with.

TypeName	Identifies by name the type in which the specified method is found.
SchemaName	Identifies by name the schema in which all functions, methods, or procedures—including those that may be created in the future—are to have the EXECUTE privilege revoked from the *Forfeiter*.
Forfeiter	Identifies the name of the user(s) and/or group(s) that are to lose the routine privileges specified. The value specified for the *Forfeiter* parameter can be any combination of the following: <USER> [*UserName*], <GROUP> [*GroupName*], and PUBLIC.

The RESTRICT clause guarantees EXECUTE privilege will not be revoked if the routine specified is used in a view, trigger, constraint, index, SQL function, SQL method, transform group, or is referenced as the source of a sourced function. Additionally, EXECUTE privilege will not be revoked if the loss of the privilege would prohibit the routine definer from executing the routine (i.e., if the user who created the routine is identified as a *Forfeiter*).

On DB2 for iSeries and DB2 for zSeries, the command for revoking routine privileges is:

```
REVOKE EXECUTE ON [FunctionName]([ParameterType], ...)|
                  SPECIFIC FUNCTION [SpecificName] |
                  PROCEDURE [ProcedureName]
TO )[Forfeiter, ...]
```

where:

FunctionName	Identifies by name the user-defined function that the EXECUTE privilege is to be associated with.
ParameterType	Identifies one or more parameter data types used by the function.
SpecificName	Identifies by specific name the user-defined function that the EXECUTE privilege is to be associated with.

Forfeiter	Identifies the name of the user(s) and/or group(s) that are to loose the EXECUTE privilege. The value specified for the *Forfeiter* parameter can be any combination of the following: [*UserName*] and PUBLIC.

Package privileges

```
REVOKE [Privilege, ...] ON PACKAGE <SchemaName.>[PackageID]
FROM [Forfeiter, ...] <BY ALL>
```

where:

Privilege	Identifies one or more package privileges that are to be taken from one or more users and/or groups. The following values are valid for this parameter: CONTROL, BIND, and EXECUTE. (CONTROL privilege is not recognized by DB2 for iSeries and DB2 for zSeries.)
SchemaName	Identifies by name the schema in which the specified package is found.
PackageName	Identifies by name the specific package that all package privileges specified are to be associated with.
Forfeiter	Identifies the name of the user(s) and/or group(s) that are to lose the package privileges specified. The value specified for the *Forfeiter* parameter can be any combination of the following: <USER> [*UserName*], <GROUP> [*GroupName*], and PUBLIC.

Server privileges

```
REVOKE PASSTHRU ON SERVER [ServerName]
FROM [Forfeiter, ...] <BY ALL>
```

where:

ServerName	Identifies by name the server that the PASSTHRU privilege is to be associated with.

Forfeiter   Identifies the name of the user(s) and/or group(s) that are to lose the PASSTHRU privilege. The value specified for the *Forfeiter* parameter can be any combination of the following: <USER> [*UserName*], <GROUP> [*GroupName*], and PUBLIC.

Nickname privileges

```
REVOKE [ALL <PRIVILEGES> |
        Privilege, ...]
ON [Nickname]
FROM [Forfeiter, ...] <BY ALL>
```

where:

Privilege   Identifies one or more nickname privileges that are to be taken from one or more users and/or groups. The following values are valid for this parameter: CONTROL, ALTER, SELECT, INSERT, UPDATE, DELETE, INDEX, and REFERENCES. (CONTROL privilege is not recognized by DB2 for iSeries and DB2 for zSeries.)

Nickname   Identifies by name the nickname that all privileges specified are to be associated with.

Forfeiter   Identifies the name of the user(s) and/or group(s) that are to lose the nickname privileges specified. The value specified for the *Forfeiter* parameter can be any combination of the following: <USER> [*UserName*], <GROUP> [*GroupName*], and PUBLIC.

Only users who hold System Administrator or Database Administrator authority are allowed to revoke CONTROL privilege for a nickname. For this reason, when the ALL PRIVILEGES clause is specified, all nickname privileges *except* CONTROL privilege are revoked from each *Forfeiter*; CONTROL privilege must be revoked separately.

Distinct type privileges (DB2 for iSeries and DB2 for zSeries only)

```
REVOKE USAGE ON DISTINCT TYPE [TypeName]
FROM [Forfeiter, ...]
```

where:

TypeName   Identifies by name the distinct type that the USAGE privilege is to be associated with.

Forfeiter   Identifies the name of the user(s) and/or group(s) that are to lose the distinct type privileges specified. The value specified for the *Forfeiter* parameter can be any combination of the following: [*UserName*] and PUBLIC.

It is important to note that this statement is not supported by DB2 for Linux, UNIX, and Windows. Instead, with DB2 for Linux, UNIX, and Windows the group PUBLIC is implicitly granted USAGE privilege on all distinct types, and that privilege cannot be revoked.

REVOKE SQL statement examples

Now that we've seen the basic syntax for the various forms of the REVOKE SQL statement, let's take a look at some examples.

Example 1: A server has both a user and a group named Q045. Remove the ability to connect to the database named SAMPLE from the group Q045:

```
CONNECT TO sample;
REVOKE CONNECT ON DATABASE FROM GROUP q045;
```

Example 2: Revoke all table privileges available for the table DEPARTMENT (except CONTROL privilege) from the user USER1 and the group PUBLIC:

```
REVOKE ALL PRIVILEGES ON TABLE department FROM user1, PUBLIC
```

· ·

If all table privileges are revoked from the group PUBLIC, all views that reference the table will become inaccessible to the group PUBLIC. That's because SELECT privilege must be held on a table in order to access a view that references the table.

· ·

Example 3: Take away user USER1's ability to use a user-defined function named CALC_BONUS:

```
REVOKE EXECUTE ON FUNCTION calc_bonus FROM user1
```

Example 4: Take away user USER1's ability to modify information stored in the ADDRESS and HOME_PHONE columns of the table EMP_INFO:

```
REVOKE UPDATE(address, home_phone) ON TABLE emp_info FROM user1
BY ALL
```

Example 5: Take away USER1's ability to read data stored in a table named INVENTORY:

```
REVOKE SELECT ON TABLE inventory FROM user1
```

Example 6: Prevent users in the group PUBLIC from adding or changing data stored in a table named EMPLOYEE:

```
REVOKE INSERT, UPDATE ON TABLE employee FROM PUBLIC
```

Requirements for Granting and Revoking Authorities and Privileges

Not only do authorization levels and privileges control what a user can and cannot do; they also control what authorities and privileges a user is allowed to grant and revoke. A list of the authorities and privileges a user who has been given a specific authority level or privilege is allowed to grant and revoke can be seen in Table 3–1.

Table 3-1: Requirements for Granting/Revoking Authorities and Privileges

If a User Holds ...	The User Can Grant ...	The User Can Revoke ...
System Administrator (SYSADM) authority	System Control (SYSCTRL) authority	System Control (SYSCTRL) authority
	System Maintenance (SYSMAINT) authority	System Maintenance (SYSMAINT) authority
	System Monitor (SYSMON) authority	System Monitor (SYSMON) authority
	Database Administrator (DBADM) authority	Database Administrator (DBADM) authority
	Security Administrator (SECADM) authority	Security Administrator (SECADM) authority
	Load (LOAD) authority	Load (LOAD) authority
	Any database privilege, including CONTROL privilege	Any database privilege, including CONTROL privilege
	Any object privilege, including CONTROL privilege	Any object privilege, including CONTROL privilege
System Control (SYSCTRL) authority	The USE table space privilege	The USE table space privilege
System Maintenance (SYSMAINT) authority	No authorities or privileges	No authorities or privileges
System Monitor (SYSMON) authority	No authorities or privileges	No authorities or privileges
Database Administrator (DBADM) authority	Any database privilege, including CONTROL privilege Any object privilege, including CONTROL privilege	Any database privilege, including CONTROL privilege Any object privilege, including CONTROL privilege
Security Administrator (SECADM) authority	No authorities or privileges; only security labels	No authorities or privileges; only security labels
Load (LOAD) authority	No authorities or privileges	No authorities or privileges
CONTROL privilege on an object (but no other authority)	All privileges available (with the exception of the CONTROL privilege) for the object the user holds CONTROL privilege on	All privileges available (with the exception of the CONTROL privilege) for the object the user holds CONTROL privilege on
A privilege on an object that was assigned with the WITH GRANT OPTION option specified	The same object privilege that was assigned with the WITH GRANT OPTION option specified.	No authorities or privileges

Authorities and Privileges Needed to Perform Common Tasks

So far, we have identified the authorities and privileges that are available, and we have examined how these authorities and privileges are granted and revoked. But to use authorities and privileges effectively, you must be able to determine which authorities and privileges are appropriate for an individual user and which are not. Often, a blanket set of authorities and privileges are assigned to an individual, based on his or her job title and/or job responsibilities. Then, as the individual begins to work with the database, the set of authorities and privileges he or she has is modified as appropriate. Some of the more common job titles used, along with the tasks that usually accompany them and the authorities/privileges needed to perform those tasks, can be seen in Table 3–2.

Table 3-2: Common Job Titles, Tasks, and Authorities/Privileges Needed

Job Title	Tasks	Authorities/Privileges Needed
Department Administrator	Oversees the departmental system; designs and creates databases	System Control (SYSCTRL) authority or System Administrator (SYSADM) authority (if the department has its own instance)
Security Administrator	Grants authorities and privileges to other users and revokes them, if necessary	System Administrator (SYSADM) authority or Database Administrator (DBADM) authority (Security Administrator [SECADM] authority if label-based access control is used)
Database Administrator	Designs, develops, operates, safeguards, and maintains one or more databases	Database Administrator (DBADM) authority over one or more databases and System Maintenance (SYSMAINT) authority, or in some cases System Control (SYSCTRL) authority, over the instance(s) that control the databases
System Operator	Monitors the database and performs routine backup operations. Also performs recovery operations if needed	System Maintenance (SYSMAINT) authority or System Monitor (SYSMON) authority

Job Title	Tasks	Authorities/Privileges Needed
Table 3-2: Common Job Titles, Tasks, and Authorities/Privileges Needed (continued)		
Application Developer/ Programmer	Develops and tests database/DB2 Database Manager application programs; may also create test tables and populate them with data	CONNECT and CREATE_TAB privilege for one or more databases, BINDADD and BIND privilege on one or more packages, one or more schema privileges for one or more schemas, and one or more table privileges for one or more tables; CREATE_EXTERNAL_ROUTINE privilege for one or more databases may also be required
User Analyst	Defines the data requirements for an application program by examining the database structure using the system catalog views	CONNECT privilege for one or more databases and SELECT privilege on the system catalog views
End User	Executes one or more application programs	CONNECT privilege for one or more databases and EXECUTE privilege on the package associated with each application used; if an application program contains dynamic SQL statements, SELECT, INSERT, UPDATE and DELETE privileges for one or more tables may be needed as well
Information Center Consultant	Defines the data requirements for a query user; provides the data needed by creating tables and views and by granting access to one or more database objects	Database Administrator (DBADM) authority for one or more databases
Query User	Issues SQL statements (usually from the Command Line Processor) to retrieve, add, update, or delete data (may also save results of queries in tables)	CONNECT privilege on one or more databases, SELECT, INSERT, UPDATE, and DELETE privilege on each table used, and CREATEIN privilege on the schema in which tables and views are to be created
Adapted from Table 78 on pages 608-609 of the *IBM DB2 Version 9 for Linux, UNIX, and Windows Administration Guide-Implementation Manual.*		

Practice Questions

Question 1

Which of the following is NOT a valid method of authentication that can be used by DB2 9?

○ A. SERVER

○ B. SERVER_ENCRYPT

○ C. CLIENT

○ D. DCS

Question 2

In a client-server environment, which two of the following can be used to verify passwords?

❑ A. System Catalog

❑ B. User ID/password file

❑ C. Client Operating System

❑ D. Communications layer

❑ E. Application Server

Question 3

A table named DEPARTMENT has the following columns:

```
DEPT_ID
DEPT_NAME
MANAGER
AVG_SALARY
```

Which of the following is the best way to prevent most users from viewing AVG_SALARY data?

○ A. Encrypt the table's data

○ B. Create a view that does not contain the AVG_SALARY column

○ C. Revoke SELECT access for the AVG_SALARY column from users who should not see AVG_SALARY data

○ D. Store AVG_SALARY data in a separate table and grant SELECT privilege for that table to the appropriate users

Question 4

Assuming USER1 has no authorities or privileges, which of the following will allow USER1 to create a view named VIEW1 that references two tables named TAB1 and TAB2?

○ A. CREATEIN privilege on the database

○ B. REFERENCES privilege on TAB1 and TAB2

○ C. CREATE_TAB privilege on the database

○ D. SELECT privilege on TAB1 and TAB2

Question 5

On which two of the following database objects may the SELECT privilege be controlled?

❑ A. Sequence

❑ B. Nickname

❑ C. Schema

❑ D. View

❑ E. Index

Question 6

After the following SQL statement is executed:

```
GRANT ALL PRIVILEGES ON TABLE employee TO USER user1
```

Assuming user USER1 has no other authorities or privileges, which of the following actions is USER1 allowed to perform?

○ A. Drop an index on the EMPLOYEE table

○ B. Grant all privileges on the EMPLOYEE table to other users

○ C. Alter the table definition

○ D. Drop the EMPLOYEE table

Question 7

A user wishing to invoke an SQL stored procedure that queries a table must have which of the following privileges?

○ A. CALL privilege on the procedure; SELECT privilege on the table

○ B. CALL privilege on the procedure; REFERENCES privilege on the table

○ C. EXECUTE privilege on the procedure; SELECT privilege on the table

○ D. EXECUTE privilege on the procedure; REFERENCES privilege on the table

Question 8

User USER1 wants to utilize an alias to remove rows from a table. Assuming USER1 has no authorities or privileges, which of the following privileges are needed?

○ A. DELETE privilege on the table

○ B. DELETE privilege on the alias

○ C. DELETE privilege on the alias; REFERENCES privilege on the table

○ D. REFERENCES privilege on the alias; DELETE privilege on the table

Question 9

Which of the following statements allows user USER1 to take the ability to create packages in a database named SAMPLE away from user USER2?

○ A. REVOKE CONNECT ON DATABASE FROM user2

○ B. REVOKE CREATETAB ON DATABASE FROM user2

○ C. REVOKE BIND ON DATABASE FROM user2

○ D. REVOKE BINDADD ON DATABASE FROM user2

Question 10

Which of the following will allow user USER1 to change the comment associated with a table named TABLE1?

○ A. GRANT UPDATE ON TABLE table1 TO user1

○ B. GRANT CONTROL ON TABLE table1 TO user1

○ C. GRANT ALTER ON TABLE table1 TO user1

○ D. GRANT REFERENCES ON TABLE table1 TO user1

Question 11

Which of the following will provide user USER1 and all members of the group GROUP1 with the ability to perform DML, but no other operations on table TABLE1?

○ A. GRANT INSERT, UPDATE, DELETE, SELECT ON TABLE table1 TO user1 AND group1

○ B. GRANT INSERT, UPDATE, DELETE, SELECT ON TABLE table1 TO USER user1, GROUP group1

○ C. GRANT ALL PRIVILEGES EXCEPT ALTER, INDEX, REFERENCES ON TABLE table1 TO USER user1, GROUP group1

○ D. GRANT CONTROL ON TABLE table1 TO user1 AND group1

Question 12

What does the following statement do?

```
GRANT ALTER ON SEQUENCE gen_empid TO user1 WITH GRANT OPTION
```

○ A. Gives USER1 the ability to change the comment associated with a sequence named GEN_EMPID, along with the ability to give this CONTROL authority for the sequence to other users and groups.

○ B. Gives USER1 the ability to change the values returned by the PREVIOUS_VALUE and NEXT_VALUE expressions associated with a sequence named GEN_EMPID, along with the ability to give CONTROL authority for the sequence to other users and groups.

○ C. Gives USER1 the ability to change the comment associated with a sequence named GEN_EMPID, along with the ability to give this authority to other users and groups.

○ D. Gives USER1 the ability to change the values returned by the PREVIOUS_VALUE and NEXT_VALUE expressions associated with a sequence named GEN_EMPID, along with the ability to give this authority to other users and groups.

Question 13

USER1 is the owner of TABLE1. Assuming USER1 only holds privileges for TABLE1, which of the following is the best way to remove all privileges USER1 holds?

○ A. REVOKE CONTROL ON table1 FROM user1

○ B. REVOKE ALL PRIVILEGES ON table1 FROM user1

○ C. REVOKE CONTROL ON table1 FROM user1;
REVOKE ALL PRIVILEGES ON table1 FROM user1;

○ D. REVOKE CONTROL, ALL PRIVILEGES ON table1 FROM user1

Question 14

User USER1 has the privileges needed to invoke a stored procedure named
GEN_RESUME. User USER2 needs to be able to call the procedure – user USER1
and all members of the group PUBLIC should no longer be allowed to call the
procedure. Which of the following statement(s) can be used to accomplish this?

○ A. GRANT EXECUTE ON ROUTINE gen_resume TO user2 EXCLUDE user1,
PUBLIC

○ B. GRANT EXECUTE ON PROCEDURE gen_resume TO user2;
REVOKE EXECUTE ON PROCEDURE gen_resume FROM user1,
PUBLIC;

○ C. GRANT CALL ON ROUTINE gen_resume TO user2 EXCLUDE user1,
PUBLIC

○ D. GRANT CALL ON PROCEDURE gen_resume TO user2;
REVOKE CALL ON PROCEDURE gen_resume FROM user1, PUBLIC;

Answers

Question 1

The correct answer is **D**. In DB2 9, the following authentication types are available:
SERVER, SERVER_ENCRYPT, CLIENT, KERBEROS, KRB_SERVER_ENCRYPT,
DATA_ENCRYPT, DATA_ENCRYPT_CMP, GSSPLUGIN, and GSS_SERVER_ENCRYPT.
(Although DCS was a valid method of authentication in DB2 UDB Version 7.x, it is no
longer supported.)

Question 2

The correct answers are **C** and **E**. Authentication is usually performed by an external security
facility that is not part of DB2. This security facility may be part of the operating system (as
is the case with AIX, Solaris, Linux, HP-UX, Windows 2000/NT, and many others), may be
a separate add-on product (for example, Distributed Computing Environment (DCE)
Security Services), or may not exist at all (which is the case with Windows 95, Windows 98,
and Windows Millennium Edition). The combination of authentication types specified at
both the client and the server determine which authentication method is actually used.

Question 3

The correct answer is **B**. A view is a virtual table residing in memory that provides an
alternative way of working with data that resides in one or more base tables. For this reason,
views can be used to prevent access to select columns in a table. While it is possible to
encrypt the data stored in the DEPARTMENT table or move the AVG_SALARY data to a separate table (you cannot revoke SELECT privilege for a column), the best solution is to create a
view for the DEPARTMENT table that does not contain the AVG_SALARY column, revoke
SELECT privilege on the DEPARTMENT table from users who are not allowed to see
AVG_SALARY data, and grant SELECT privilege on the new view to users who need to access
the rest of the data stored in the DEPARTMENT table.

Question 4

The correct answer is **D**. In order to create a view, a user must hold appropriate privileges (at a minimum, SELECT privilege) on each base table the view references. CREATEIN is a schema privilege – not a database privilege; REFERENCES privilege allows a user to create and drop foreign key constraints that reference the table in a parent relationship; and CREATETAB privilege allows a user to create new tables in the database (there is no CREATE_TAB privilege).

Question 5

The correct answers are **B** and **D**. SELECT privilege is available for tables, views, and nicknames. The SELECT table privilege allows a user to retrieve data from a table, create a view that references the table, and run the EXPORT utility against the table; the SELECT view privilege allows a user to retrieve data from a view, create a second view that references the view, and run the EXPORT utility against the view; and the SELECT privilege for a nickname allows a user to retrieve data from the table or view within a federated data source that the nickname refers to.

Question 6

The correct answer is **C**. The GRANT ALL PRIVILEGES statement gives USER1 the following privileges for the EMPLOYEE table: ALTER, SELECT, INSERT, UPDATE, DELETE, INDEX, and REFERENCES. To drop an index, USER1 would need CONTROL privilege on the index – not the table the index is based on; USER1 cannot grant privileges to other users because the WITH GRANT OPTION clause was not specified with the GRANT ALL PRIVILEGES statement used to give USER1 table privileges; and in order to drop the EMPLOYEE table, USER1 would have to have CONTROL privilege on the table – CONTROL privilege is not granted with the GRANT ALL PRIVILEGES statement.

Question 7

The correct answer is **C**. The EXECUTE privilege, when granted, allows a user to invoke a routine (a routine can be a user-defined function, a stored procedure, or a method that can be invoked by several different users), create a function that is sourced from the routine (provided the routine is a function), and reference the routine in a Data Definition Language SQL statement (for example, **CREATE VIEW** and **CREATE TRIGGER**) statement. When the EXECUTE privilege is granted for a routine, any privileges needed by the routine must also be granted – in this case, the SELECT privilege is needed for the table the procedure will query.

Question 8

The correct answer is **A**. The DELETE table privilege allows a user to remove rows of data from a table. Aliases are publicly-referenced names, so no special authority or privilege is required to use them. However, tables or views referred to by an alias have still have the authorization requirements that are associated with these types of objects.

Question 9

The correct answer is **D**. The BINDADD database privilege allows a user to create packages in a database by precompiling embedded SQL application source code files against the database and/or by binding application bind files to the database. The CONNECT database privilege allows a user to establish a connection to a database and the CREATETAB database privilege allows a user to create new tables in the database. The BIND privilege is a package privilege – not a database privilege – and it allows a user to rebind a package that has already been bound to a database.

Question 10

The correct answer is **C**. The ALTER table privilege allows a user to add columns to the table, *add or change comments associated with the table and/or any of its columns*, create a primary key for the table, create a unique constraint for the table, create or drop a check constraint for the table, and create triggers for the table (provided the user holds the appropriate privileges for every object referenced by the trigger). The UPDATE table privilege allows a user to modify data in a table; the CONTROL table privilege allows a user to remove (drop) a table from a database and gives the user the ability to grant and revoke one or more table privileges (except the CONTROL privilege) to/from other users and groups; the REFERENCES table privilege allows a user to create and drop foreign key constraints that reference the table in a parent relationship.

Question 11

The correct answer is **B**. The syntax used to grant table privileges is:

```
GRANT [ALL <PRIVILEGES> |
        Privilege <( ColumnName, ... )> , ...]
ON TABLE [TableName]
TO [Recipient, ...]
<WITH GRANT OPTION>
```

where:

Privilege   Identifies one or more table privileges that are to be given to one or more users and/or groups. The following values are valid for this parameter: CONTROL, ALTER, SELECT, INSERT, UPDATE, DELETE, INDEX, and REFERENCES. (CONTROL privilege is not recognized by DB2 for iSeries and DB2 for zSeries.)

ColumnName   Identifies by name one or more specific columns that UPDATE or REFERENCES privileges are to be associated with. This option is only used when *Privilege* contains the value UPDATE or REFERENCES.

TableName   Identifies by name the table that all table privileges specified are to be associated with.

Recipient   Identifies the name of the user(s) and/or group(s) that are to receive the table privileges specified. The value specified for the *Recipient* parameter can be any combination of the following: <USER> [*UserName*], <GROUP> [*GroupName*], and PUBLIC.

CONTROL PRIVILEGE allows a user to remove (drop) a table from a database and gives the user the ability to grant and revoke one or more table privileges (except the CONTROL privilege) to/from other users and groups; granting ALL PRIVILEGES gives a user the right to perform other operations besides DML operations.

Question 12

The correct answer is **C**. The ALTER sequence privilege allows a user to perform administrative tasks like restarting the sequence, changing the increment value for the sequence, and *adding or changing the comment associated with the sequence*. And when the GRANT statement is executed with the **WITH GRANT OPTION** clause is specified, the user/group receiving privileges is given the ability to grant the privileges received to others. There is no CONTROL privilege for a sequence and the USAGE privilege is the sequence privilege that allows a user to use the **PREVIOUS VALUE** and **NEXT VALUE** expressions that are associated with the sequence. (The **PREVIOUS VALUE** expression returns the most recently generated value for the specified sequence; the **NEXT VALUE** expression returns the next value for the specified sequence.)

Question 13

The correct answer is **C**. The owner of a table automatically receives CONTROL privilege, along with all other table privileges available for that table. If the CONTROL privilege is later revoked from the table owner, all other privileges that were automatically granted to the owner when the table was created are not automatically revoked. Instead, they must be explicitly revoked in one or more separate operations. Therefore, both REVOKE statements shown in answer C must be executed in order to completely remove all privileges user USER1 holds on table TABLE1. If an attempt is made to try to combine both operations in a single statement as shown in answer **D**, an error will be generated.

Question 14

The correct answer is **B**. The syntax used to grant the only procedure privilege available is:

```
GRANT EXECUTE ON [RoutineName] |
      [PROCEDURE <SchemaName.> *]
TO [Recipient, ...]
<WITH GRANT OPTION>
```

The syntax used to revoke the only stored procedure privilege available is:

```
REVOKE EXECUTE ON [RoutineName |
       [PROCEDURE <SchemaName.> *]
FROM [Forfeiter, ...] <BY ALL>
RESTRICT
```

where:

RoutineName   Identifies by name the routine (user-defined function, method, or stored procedure) that the EXECUTE privilege is to be associated with.

TypeName   Identifies by name the type in which the specified method is found.

SchemaName   Identifies by name the schema in which all functions, methods, or procedures—including those that may be created in the future—are to have the EXECUTE privilege granted on.

Recipient   Identifies the name of the user(s) and/or group(s) that are to receive the EXECUTE privilege. The value specified for the *Recipient* parameter can be any combination of the following: <USER> [*UserName*], <GROUP> [*GroupName*], and PUBLIC.

Forfeiter   Identifies the name of the user(s) and/or group(s) that are to lose the EXECUTE privilege. The value specified for the *Forfeiter* parameter can be any combination of the following: <USER> [*UserName*], <GROUP> [*GroupName*], and PUBLIC.

Thus, the proper way to grant and revoke stored procedure privileges is by executing the GRANT EXECUTE … and REVOKE EXECUTE … statements.

4

Working with Databases and Database Objects

Seventeen percent (17%) of the DB2 9 Fundamentals certification exam (Exam 730) is designed to test your knowledge of the different objects that are available with DB2 9 and to test your ability to create a DB2 9 database. The questions that make up this portion of the exam are intended to evaluate the following:

- Your ability to identify and connect to DB2 servers and databases

- Your ability to construct a DB2 9 database

- Your ability to identify DB2 objects

- Your knowledge of the basic characteristics and properties of DB2 objects

- Your ability to identify the Data Definition Language (DDL) statements available with DB2 9

- Your ability to identify the results produced when a DDL statement is executed

This chapter is designed to introduce you to instances and databases, to walk you through the database creation process, and to provide you with an overview of the various objects that can be developed once a database has been created.

Servers, Instances, and Databases

DB2 sees the world as a hierarchy of objects. Workstations (or servers) on which DB2 9 has been installed occupy the highest level of this hierarchy. During the installation process, program files for a background process known as the *DB2*

Database Manager are physically copied to a specific location on the server, and an *instance* of the DB2 Database Manager is created. Instances occupy the second level in the hierarchy and are responsible for managing system resources and databases that fall under their control. Although only one instance is created initially, several instances can exist. Each instance behaves like a separate installation of DB2 9, even though all instances within a system share the same DB2 Database Manager program files (unless each instance is running a different version of DB2). And although multiple instances share the same binary code, each runs independently of the others and has its own environment, which can be modified by altering the contents of its associated configuration file.

Every instance controls access to one or more databases. Databases make up the third level in the hierarchy and are responsible for managing the storage, modification, and retrieval of data. Like instances, databases work independently of each other. Each database has its own environment (also controlled by a set of configuration parameters), as well as its own set of grantable authorities and privileges to govern how users interact with the data and database objects it controls. From a user's perspective, a database is a collection of tables (preferably related in some way) that are used to store data. However, from a database administrator's viewpoint, a DB2 database is much more; a database is an entity that is composed of many physical and logical components. Some of these components help determine how data is organized, while others determine how and where data is physically stored. Figure 4–1 shows the hierarchical relationship between systems, instances, and databases.

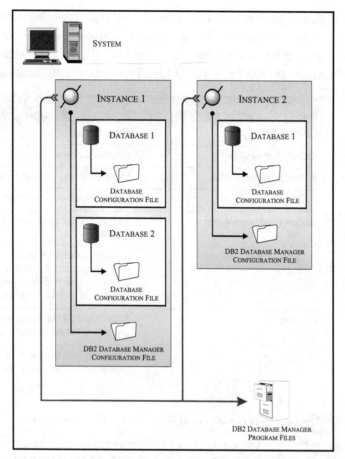

Figure 4–1: Hierarchical relationship between systems, instances, and databases.

Managing Instances

The default instance for a particular system is defined by the DB2INSTANCE
environment variable, and this is the instance used for most operations. However,
as mentioned earlier, there are times when it is advantageous to create multiple
instances on the same physical workstation (server). Reasons for creating multiple
instances include:

- To separate your production environment from your development environment

- To obtain optimum performance for special applications (for example, you
  may choose to create multiple instances for several applications and
  fine-tune each instance specifically for the application(s) it will service)

As you might imagine, DB2 provides several commands that are used to create and manage instances. These commands, which are referred to as *system commands* because they are executed from the system command prompt rather than from the DB2 Command Line Processor (CLP), are listed in Table 4–1.

Table 4-1: DB2 9 Instance Management Commands	
Command ...	**Purpose ...**
db2icrt [*InstanceName*]	Creates a new instance
db2idrop [*InstanceName*]	Deletes (drops) an existing instance
db2ilist	Lists all instances that have been defined
db2imigr [*InstanceName*]	Migrates an existing instance to a newer version of DB2 9
db2iupdt [*InstanceName*]	Updates an existing instance to take advantage of new functionality that is provided when product fix packs are installed (also used to convert a 32-bit instance to a 64-bit instance)
db2start	Starts the DB2 Database Manager background processes for the current instance
db2stop	Stops the DB2 Database Manager background processes for the current instance

Although basic syntax is presented for the instance management commands shown in Table 4–1, the actual syntax supported may be more complex. To view the complete syntax for or to obtain more information about a specific DB2 command, refer to the *IBM DB2 9 Command Reference.*

Creating a DB2 9 Database

Now that you have a basic understanding of servers, instances, and databases, let's look at how a DB2 9 database is created. There are two ways to create a DB2 9 database: by using the Create Database Wizard or by using the CREATE DATABASE command. Because the Create Database Wizard is essentially a graphical user interface (GUI) for the CREATE DATABASE command, we will look at the command method first.

In its simplest form, the syntax for the CREATE DATABASE command is:

```
CREATE [DATABASE | DB] [DatabaseName]
```

where:

DatabaseName   Identifies a unique name that is to be assigned to the database
                 once it is created.

The only value you must provide when executing this command is a name to
assign to the new database. This name:

- Can consist of only the characters **a** through **z**, **A** through **Z**, **0** through **9**, **@**,
  #, **$**, and _ (underscore)

- Cannot begin with a number

- Cannot begin with the letter sequences "SYS", "DBM", or "IBM"

- Cannot be the same as the name already assigned to another database within
  the same instance

Of course, a much more complex form of the CREATE DATABASE command that
provides you with much more control over database parameters is available, and
we will examine it shortly. But for now, let's look at what happens when this form
of the CREATE DATABASE command is executed.

What Happens When a DB2 9 Database Is Created

Regardless of how the process is initiated, whenever a new DB2 9 database is
created, the following tasks are performed, in the order shown:

1. All directories and subdirectories needed are created in the appropriate
   location.

Information about every DB2 9 database created is stored in a special hierarchical
directory tree. Where this directory tree is actually created is determined by
information provided with the CREATE DATABASE command. If no location information is provided, this directory tree is created in the location specified by the
dftdbpath DB2 Database Manager configuration parameter associated with the
instance the database is being created under. The root directory of this hierarchical
tree is assigned the name of the instance the database is associated with. This

directory will contain a subdirectory that has been assigned a name corresponding to the partition's node. If the database is a partitioned database, this directory will be named NODE*xxxx*, where *xxxx* is the unique node number that has been assigned to the partition; if the database is a nonpartitioned database, this directory will be named NODE0000. This node-name directory, in turn, will contain one subdirectory for each database that has been created, along with one subdirectory that contains the containers that are used to hold the database's data.

The name assigned to the subdirectory that holds the containers that are used to house the database's data is the same as that specified for the database; the name assigned to the subdirectory that contains the base files for the database corresponds to the database token that is assigned to the database during the creation process. Thus the subdirectory for the first database created will be named SQL00001, the subdirectory for the second database will be named SQL00002, and so on. Figure 4–2 illustrates how this directory hierarchy typically looks in a nonpartitioned database environment.

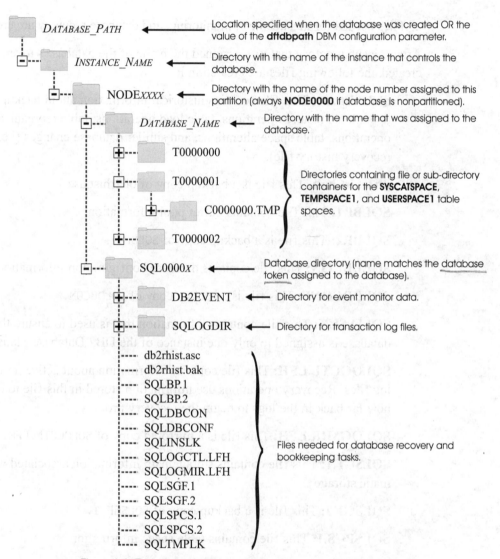

Figure 4–2: *Typical directory hierarchy tree for a nonpartitioned database.*

Never attempt to modify this directory structure or any of the files stored in it. Such actions could destroy one or more databases or make them unusable.

2. Files needed for management, monitoring, and database recovery are created.

After the subdirectory that was assigned the name of the database's token is created, the following files are created in it:

db2rhist.asc: This file contains historical information about backup operations, restore operations, table load operations, table reorganization operations, table space alterations, and similar database changes (i.e., the recovery history file).

db2rhist.bak: This file is a backup copy of db2rhist.asc.

SQLBP.1: This file contains buffer pool information.

SQLBP.2: This file is a backup copy of SQLBP.1.

SQLDBCON: This file contains database configuration information.

SQLDBCONF: This file is a backup copy of SQLDBCON.

SQLINSLK: This file contains information that is used to ensure that the database is assigned to only one instance of the DB2 Database Manager.

SQLOGCTL.LFH: This file contains information about active transaction log files. Recovery operations use information stored in this file to determine how far back in the logs to begin the recovery process.

SQLOGMIR.LFH: This file is a mirrored copy of SQLOGCTL.LFH.

SQLSGF.1: This file contains storage path information associated with automatic storage.

SQLSGF.2: This file is a backup copy of SQLSGF.1.

SQLSPCS.1: This file contains table space information.

SQLSPCS.2: This file is a backup copy of SQLSPCS.1.

SQLTMPLK: This file contains information about temporary table spaces.

Two subdirectories named DB2EVENT and SQLOGDIR are also created; a detailed deadlocks event monitor is created and stored in the DB2EVENT subdirectory, and three files named S0000000.LOG, S0000001.LOG, and S0000002.LOG are created and stored in the SQLLOGDIR subdirectory. These three files are used to store transaction log records as SQL operations are performed against the database.

3. A buffer pool is created for the database.   *Cache in memory*

During the database creation process, a buffer pool is created and assigned the name IBMDEFAULTBP. By default, on Linux and UNIX platforms, this buffer pool is 1,000 4K (kilobyte) pages in size; on Windows platforms, this buffer pool is 250 4K pages in size. The actual memory used by this buffer pool (and for that matter, by any other buffer pools that may exist) is allocated when the first connection to the database is established, and it is freed when all connections to the database have been terminated.

4. Two regular table spaces and one system temporary table space are created.

Immediately after the buffer pool IBMDEFAULTBP is created, three table spaces are created and associated with this buffer pool. These three table spaces are:

A tablespace is a layer between the logical table definitions & physical disk storage & memory (BP)

- A regular table space named SYSCATSPACE, which is used to store the system catalog tables and views associated with the database. *AKA: Dictionary, Metadata*
- A regular table space named USERSPACE1, which is used to store all user-defined objects (such as tables, indexes, and so on) along with user data, index data, and long value data. *Also used for sorts & joins*
- A system temporary table space named TEMPSPACE1, which is used as a temporary storage area for operations such as sorting data, reorganizing tables, and creating indexes.

Unless otherwise specified, SYSCATSPACE and USERSPACE1 will be database-managed (DMS) FILE table spaces, while TEMPSPACE1 will be a system-managed (SMS) table space; characteristics for each of these table spaces can be provided as input to the CREATE DATABASE command or the Create Database Wizard.

5. The system catalog tables and views are created.

After the table space SYSCATSPACE is created, a special set of tables, known as the *system catalog tables*, is constructed within that table space. The DB2 Database Manager uses the system catalog tables to keep track of such information as database object definitions, database object dependencies, database object privileges, column data types, table constraints, and object relationships. A set of system catalog views is created along with the system catalog tables, and these views are typically used when accessing data stored in the system catalog tables. The system catalog tables and views cannot be modified with SQL statements (however, their contents can be viewed). Instead, they are modified by the DB2 Database Manager whenever:

- A database object (such as a table, view, or index) is created, altered, or dropped.

- Authorizations and/or privileges are granted or revoked.

- Statistical information is collected for a table.

- Packages are bound to the database.

In most cases, the complete characteristics of a database object are stored in one or more system catalog tables when the object is created. However, in some cases, such as when triggers and constraints are defined, the actual SQL used to create the object is stored instead.

6. The database is cataloged in the system and local database directory (the system and local database directory are created first if they don't already exist).

DB2 uses a set of special files to keep track of where databases are stored and to provide access to those databases. Because the information stored in these files is used in the same way as the information stored in an office building directory is used, these files are referred to as *directory files*. Whenever a database is created, these directories are updated with the database's name and alias. If specified, a comment and code set values are also stored in these directories.

7. The database configuration file for the database is initialized.

Some of the parameters in the database configuration file (such as code set, territory, and collating sequence) will be set using values that were specified as input for the CREATE DATABASE command or the Create Database Wizard; others are assigned system default values.

8. Four schemas are created.

Once the system catalog tables and views are created, the following schemas are created: SYSIBM, SYSCAT, SYSSTAT, and SYSFUN. A special user named SYSIBM is made the owner of each.

9. A set of utility programs are bound to the database.

Before some of the DB2 9 utilities available can work with a database, the packages needed to run those utilities must be created. Such packages are created by binding a set of predefined DB2 Database Manager bind files to the database (the set of bind files used are stored in the utilities bind list file *db2ubind.lst*).

10. Authorities and privileges are granted to the appropriate users.

To connect to and work with a particular database, a user must have the authorities and privileges needed to use that database. Therefore, whenever a new database is created, unless otherwise specified, the following authorities and privileges are granted:

- DBADM authority, along with CONNECT, CREATETAB, BINDADD, CREATE_NOT_FENCED, IMPLICIT_SCHEMA, and LOAD privileges, are granted to the user who created the database.

- USE privilege on the table space USERSPACE1 is granted to the group PUBLIC.

- CONNECT, CREATETAB, BINDADD, and IMPLICIT_SCHEMA privileges are granted to the group PUBLIC.

- SELECT privilege on each system catalog table is granted to the group PUBLIC.

- EXECUTE privilege on all procedures found in the SYSIBM schema is granted to the group PUBLIC.

- EXECUTE WITH GRANT privilege on all functions found in the SYSFUN schema is granted to the group PUBLIC.

- BIND and EXECUTE privileges for each successfully bound utility are granted to the group PUBLIC.

11. The Configuration Advisor is launched.

The Configuration Advisor is a tool that is designed to help you to tune performance and balance memory requirements for a database by suggesting which configuration parameters to modify based on information you provide about the database. In DB2 9, the Configuration Advisor is automatically invoked whenever you create a database, unless the default behavior is changed by assigning the value NO to the DB2_ENABLE_AUTOCONFIG_DEFAULT registry variable.

The Complete CREATE DATABASE Command

When the simplest form of the CREATE DATABASE command is executed, the characteristics of the database created, such as the storage and transaction logging method used, are determined by several predefined defaults. If you wish to change any of the default characteristics, you must specify one or more options available when executing the CREATE DATABASE command. The complete syntax for this command is:

```
CREATE [DATABASE | DB] [DatabaseName] <AT DBPARTITIONNUM>
```

or

```
CREATE [DATABASE | DB] [DatabaseName]
<AUTOMATIC STORAGE [YES | NO]>
<ON [StoragePath, ...] <DBPATH [DBPath]>>
<ALIAS [Alias]>
<USING CODESET [CodeSet] TERRITORY [Territory]>
<COLLATE USING [CollateType]>
<PAGESIZE [4096 | Pagesize <K>]>
<NUMSEGS [NumSegments]>
<DFT_EXTENT_SZ [DefaultExtSize]>
<RESTRICTIVE>
<CATALOG TABLESPACE [TS_Definition]>
<USER TABLESPACE [TS_Definition]>
<TEMPORARY TABLESPACE [TS_Definition]>
<WITH "[Description]">
<AUTOCONFIGURE <USING [Keyword] [Value], ... >
<APPLY [DB ONLY | DB AND DBM | NONE>>
```

where:

DatabaseName	Identifies the unique name that is to be assigned to the database to be created.
StoragePath	If AUTOMATIC STORAGE NO is specified, identifies the location (drive and/or directory) where the directory hierarchy and files associated with the database to be created are to be physically stored; otherwise, identifies one or more storage paths that are to be used to hold table space containers used by automatic storage.
DBPath	If AUTOMATIC STORAGE YES (the default) is specified, identifies the location (drive or directory) where the directory hierarchy and files associated with the database to be created are to be physically stored.
Alias	Identifies the alias to be assigned to the database to be created.

CodeSet	Identifies the code set to be used for storing data in the database to be created. (In a DB2 9 database, each single-byte character is represented internally as a unique number between 0 and 255. This number is referred to as the *code point* of the character; assignments of code points to every character in a particular character set are called the *code page*; and the International Organization for Standardization term for a code page is *code set.*)
Territory	Identifies the territory to be used for storing data in the database to be created.
CollateType	Specifies the collating sequence (i.e., the sequence in which characters are ordered for the purpose of sorting, merging, and making comparisons) that is to be used by the database to be created. The following values are valid for this parameter: `COMPATIBILITY`, `IDENTITY`, `IDENTITY_16BIT`, `UCA400_NO`, `UCA400_LSK`, `UCA400_LTH`, `NLSCHAR`, and `SYSTEM`.
NumSegments	Specifies the number of directories that are to be created and used to store files for the default SMS table space used by the database to be created (`TEMPSPACE1`).
DefaultExtSize	Specifies the default extent size to be used whenever a table space is created and no extent size is specified during the creation process.
Description	A comment used to describe the database entry that will be made in the database directory for the database to be created. The description must be enclosed by double quotation marks.
Keyword	One or more keywords recognized by the `AUTOCONFIGURE` command. Valid values include `mem_percent`, `workload_type`, `num_stmts`, `tpm`, `admin_priority`, `is_populated`, `num_local_apps`, `num_remote_apps`, `isolation`, and `bp_resizable`. Refer to the *DB2 9 Command Reference* for more information on how the `AUTOCONFIGURE` command is used.

Value   Identifies the value that is to be associated with the *Keyword* specified.

TS_Definition   Specifies the definition that is to be used to create the table space that will be used to hold the system catalog tables (SYSCATSPACE), user-defined objects (USERSPACE1), and/or temporary objects (TEMPSPACE1).

The syntax used to define a system managed (SMS) table space is:

```
MANAGED BY SYSTEM
USING ( '[Container]', ... )
<EXTENTSIZE [ExtentSize]>
<PREFETCHSIZE [PrefetchSize]>
<OVERHEAD [Overhead]>
<TRANSFERRATE [TransferRate]>
```

The syntax used to define a database managed (DMS) table space is:

```
MANAGED BY DATABASE
USING ([FILE | DEVICE] '[Container]' NumberOfPages, ... )
<EXTENTSIZE [ExtentSize]>
<PREFETCHSIZE [PrefetchSize]>
<OVERHEAD [Overhead]>
<TRANSFERRATE [TransferRate]>
<AUTORESIZE [NO | YES]>
<INCREASESIZE [Increment] <PERCENT | K | M | G>>
<MAXSIZE [NONE | MaxSize <K | M | G> ]>
```

And the syntax used to define an automatic storage table space is:

```
MANAGED BY AUTOMATIC STORAGE
<EXTENTSIZE [ExtentSize]>
<PREFETCHSIZE [PrefetchSize]>
<OVERHEAD [Overhead]>
<TRANSFERRATE [TransferRate]>
<AUTORESIZE [NO | YES]>
<INITIALSIZE [InitialSize] <K | M | G>>
<INCREASESIZE [Increment] <PERCENT | K | M | G>>
<MAXSIZE [NONE | MaxSize <K | M | G> ]>
```

where:

Container   Identifies one or more containers to be used to store data that will be assigned to the table space specified. For SMS table spaces, each container specified must identify a valid directory; for DMS FILE containers, each container specified must identify a valid file; and for DMS DEVICE containers, each container specified must identify an existing device.

NumberOfPages   Specifies the number of pages to be used by the table space container.

ExtentSize   Specifies the number of pages of data that will be written in a round-robin fashion to each table space container used.

PrefetchSize   Specifies the number of pages of data that will be read from the specified table space when data prefetching is performed.

Overhead   Identifies the I/O controller overhead and disk-seek latency time (in number of milliseconds) associated with the containers that belong to the specified table space.

TransferRate   Identifies the time, in number of milliseconds, that it takes to read one page of data from a table space container and store it in memory.

InitialSize   Specifies the initial size an automatic storage table space should be.

Increment   Specifies the amount by which a table space that has been enabled for automatic resizing will be increased when the table space becomes full and a request for space is made.

MaxSize   Specifies the maximum size to which a table space that has been enabled for automatic resizing can be increased.

Thus, if you wanted to create a DB2 database that has the following characteristics:

- It will be physically located on drive E:.

- It will not use automatic storage.

- It will be assigned the name SAMPLEDB.

- It will recognize the United States/Canada code set. (The code set or code page, along with the territory, is used to convert alphanumeric data to binary data that is stored in the database.)

- It will use a collating sequence that is based on the territory used (which in this case is United States/Canada).

- It will store the system catalog in a DMS table space that uses the file SYSCATSPACE.DAT as its container. (This file is stored on drive E: and is capable of holding up to 5,000 pages that are 4K in size.)

You would execute a CREATE DATABASE command that looks something like this:

```
CREATE DATABASE sampledb
AUTOMATIC STORAGE NO
ON E:
USING CODESET 1252 TERRITORY US
COLLATE USING SYSTEM
PAGESIZE 4096
CATALOG TABLESPACE MANAGED BY DATABASE
  (FILE 'E:\syscatspace.dat', 5000)
```

Creating a DB2 9 Database with the Create Database Wizard

If you are the type of individual who prefers using graphical user interfaces to typing long commands, you can use the Create Database Wizard to construct a DB2 9 database. The Create Database Wizard is designed to collect information that defines the characteristics of a database and then create a database that has those characteristics. (These same characteristics can be specified through the various options that are available with the CREATE DATABASE command.)

In Chapter 2, we saw that the Control Center is the most important and versatile GUI tool DB2 9 has to offer. We also saw that the Control Center is comprised of several elements, including:

- An objects pane (located on the left-hand side of the Control Center), which contains a hierarchical representation of every object type that can be managed from the Control Center.

- A contents pane (located on the right-hand side of the Control Center), which contains a listing of existing objects that correspond to the object type selected in the objects pane. (For example, if the Tables object type were selected in the objects pane, a list of all tables available would be listed in the contents pane.)

By highlighting the All Databases object shown in the objects pane of the Control Center and right-clicking the mouse button, you will bring up a menu that contains a list of options available for database objects. The Create Database Wizard is invoked by selecting "Create Database", followed by "Standard..." from this menu. Figure 4–3 shows the Control Center menu items that must be selected in order to activate the Create Database Wizard; Figure 4–4 shows what the first page of the Create Database Wizard looks like when it is first initiated.

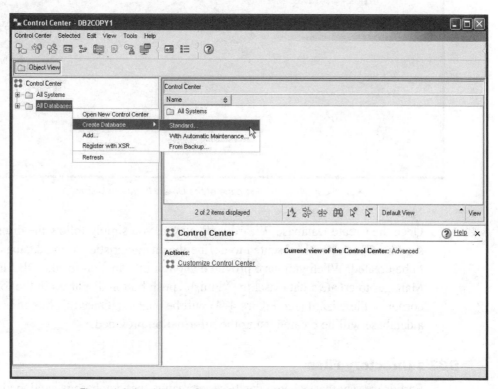

Figure 4–3: Invoking the Create Database Wizard from the Control Center.

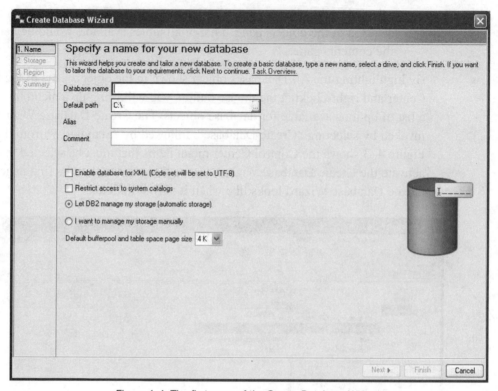

Figure 4–4: The first page of the Create Database Wizard.

Once the Create Database Wizard is displayed, you simply follow the directions shown on each panel presented to define the characteristics of the database that is to be created. When you have provided enough information for the DB2 Database Manager to create a database, the "Finish" push button displayed in the lower right corner of the wizard (see Figure 4–4) will be enabled. Once this button is selected, a database will be created using the information provided.

DB2's Directory Files

Earlier we saw that, when a database is created, that database is cataloged in the system and local database directories. So what are the system and local database directories, and why must a database be cataloged in them? If you recall, when we examined the CREATE DATABASE command, we saw that a database can physically reside anywhere on a system. Because of this, each DB2 Database Manager instance must know where databases that fall under its control physically reside, as well as how to establish connections to those databases on behalf of users and applications. To keep track of this information, DB2 uses a special set of files known as *directory files* (or *directories*). Four types of directories exist:

- System database directory
- Local database directory
- Node directory
- Database Connection Services (DCS) directory

[handwritten annotation: Table of Contents - Lists all databases that you can connect to, whether local or remote]

The System Database Directory

The system database directory resides in a file named *sqldbdir* that is created automatically when the first database for an instance is created. Information about the new database is then recorded in the system database directory, and as additional databases are cataloged, information about those databases is recorded as well. (Databases are implicitly cataloged when they are created; databases can be explicitly cataloged using the Control Center or the CATALOG DATABASE command.) Each entry recorded in the system database directory contains the following information:

- The name assigned to the database when the database was created (or explicitly cataloged)

- The alias assigned to the database (which is the same as the database name, if no alias was specified when the database was created/cataloged)

- Descriptive information about the database (if that information is available)

- The location of the local database directory file that contains additional information about the database

- The database entry type, which tells whether or not the database is an indirect database (which means that it resides on the same workstation as the system database directory file)

- Other system information, including the code page under which the database was created

The contents of the system database directory or a local database directory file can be viewed by executing the LIST DATABASE DIRECTORY command. The syntax for this command is:

```
LIST [DATABASE | DB] DIRECTORY <ON [Location]>
```

where:

Location   Identifies the drive or directory where one or more databases are
                    stored.

If no location is specified when this command is executed, the contents of the
system database directory file will be displayed. On the other hand, if a location is
specified, the contents of the local database directory file that exists at that
particular location will be displayed.

The Local Database Directory

Any time a DB2 database is created in a new location (i.e., a drive or a directory), a
local database directory file is also created at that location. Information about that
database is then recorded in the local database directory, and as other databases are
created in that location, information about those databases is recorded in the local
database directory as well. Thus, while only one system database directory exists
for a particular instance, several local database directories can exist, depending
upon how databases have been distributed across the storage available.

Each entry recorded in a local database directory contains the following
information:

- The name assigned to the database when the database was created (or
  explicitly cataloged)
- The alias assigned to the database (which is the same as the database name,
  if no alias was specified when the database was created/cataloged)
- Descriptive information about the database (if that information is available)
- The name of the root directory of the hierarchical tree used to store
  information about the database
- Other system information, including the code page under which the database
  was created

As mentioned earlier, the contents of a local database directory file can be viewed
by executing the LIST DATABASE DIRECTORY command.

The Node Directory

Unlike the system database directory and the local database directory, which are used to keep track of what databases exist and where they are stored, the node directory contains information that identifies how and where remote systems or instances can be found. A node directory file is created on each client workstation the first time a remote server or instance is cataloged. As other remote instances/servers are cataloged, information about those instances/servers is recorded in the node directory as well. Entries in the node directory are then used in conjunction with entries in the system database directory to make connections and instance attachments to DB2 databases stored on remote servers.

Each entry in the node directory contains, among other things, information about the type of communication protocol to be used to communicate between the client workstation and the remote database server. DB2 9 supports the following communications protocols:

- Named pipe

- Transmission Control Protocol/Internet Protocol (TCP/IP) (which is used today in an overwhelming majority of cases)

- Lightweight Directory Access Protocol (LDAP)

The contents of the node directory file can be viewed by executing the LIST NODE DIRECTORY command. The syntax for this command is

```
LIST <ADMIN> NODE DIRECTORY <SHOW DETAIL>
```

(If the ADMIN option is specified when this command is executed, information about administration servers will be displayed.)

The Database Connection Services (DCS) Directory

Using an add-on product called DB2 Connect, it is possible for DB2 for Linux, UNIX, and Windows clients to establish a connection to a DRDA Application Server, such as:

- DB2 for OS/390 or z/OS databases on System/370 and System/390 architecture host computers

- DB2 for VM and VSE databases on System/370 and System/390 architecture host computers

- iSeries databases on Application System/400 (AS/400) and iSeries computers

Because the information needed to connect to DRDA host databases is different from the information used to connect to LAN-based databases, information about remote host or iSeries databases is kept in a special directory known as the Database Connection Services (DCS) directory. If an entry in the DCS directory has a database name that corresponds to the name of a database stored in the system database directory, the specified Application Requester (which in most cases is DB2 Connect) can forward SQL requests to the database that resides on a remote DRDA server.

The contents of the DCS directory file can be viewed by executing the LIST DCS DIRECTORY command. The syntax for this command is:

```
LIST DCS DIRECTORY
```

It is important to note that the DCS directory exists only if the DB2 Connect product has been installed.

Cataloging and Uncataloging a DB2 Database

Because a database is implicitly cataloged as soon as it is created, most users never have to concern themselves with the cataloging process. However, if you need to catalog a previously uncataloged database, if you want to set up an alternate name for an existing database, or if you need to access a database stored on a remote server, you will need to become familiar with the tools that can be used to catalog DB2 databases. Fortunately, cataloging a database is a relatively straightforward process and can be done by using the Control Center, by using the Configuration Assistant, or by executing the CATALOG DATABASE command.

Earlier, we saw that by highlighting the *Databases* object shown in the objects pane of the Control Center and right-clicking the mouse button, it is possible to bring up a menu that contains a list of options available for database objects. The dialog used to catalog databases (the Add Database dialog) is invoked by selecting "Add..." from this menu. Figure 4–5 shows the Control Center menu items that must be selected in order to activate the Add Database dialog; Figure 4–6 shows what the Add Database dialog looks like when it is first activated.

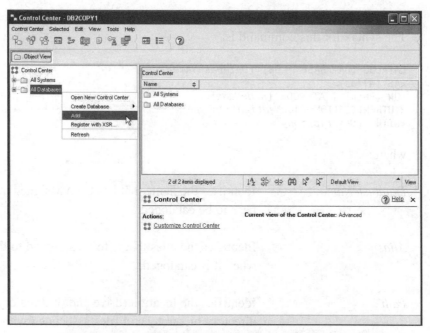

Figure 4–5: Invoking the Add Database dialog from the Control Center.

Figure 4–6: The Add Database dialog.

You can also catalog a database by executing the CATALOG DATABASE command. The syntax for this command is:

```
CATALOG [DATABASE | DB] [DatabaseName]
<AS [Alias]>
<ON [Path] | AT NODE [NodeName]>
<AUTHENTICATION [AuthenticationType]>
<WITH "[Description]">
```

where:

DatabaseName   Identifies the name that has been assigned to the database to be cataloged.

Alias   Identifies the alias that is to be assigned to the database when it is cataloged.

Path   Identifies the location (drive and/or directory) where the directory hierarchy and files associated with the database to be cataloged are physically stored.

NodeName   Identifies the node where the database to be cataloged resides. The node name specified should match an entry in the node directory file (i.e., should correspond to a node that has already been cataloged).

AuthenticationType   Identifies where and how authentication is to take place when a user attempts to access the database. The following values are valid for this parameter: SERVER, CLIENT, SERVER_ENCRYPT, KERBEROS TARGET PRINCIPAL [PrincipalName] (where *PrincipalName* is the fully qualified Kerberos principal name for the target server), DATA_ENCRYPT, and GSSPLUGIN.

Description   A comment used to describe the database entry that will be made in the database directory for the database to be cataloged. The description must be enclosed by double quotation marks.

Thus, if you wanted to catalog a database that physically resides in the directory */home/db2data* and has been given the name TEST_DB, you could do so by executing a CATALOG DATABASE command that looks something like this:

```
CATALOG DATABASE test_db AS test
ON /home/db2data
AUTHENTICATION SERVER
```

Since a database must be cataloged before a user or application can connect to it, you're probably wondering why you would ever want to uncatalog a database. Suppose you are running an older version of DB2, and when you upgrade, you decide to uninstall the old DB2 software completely before installing the latest release. To prevent this software upgrade from having an impact on existing databases, you could simply uncatalog them before you uninstall the old version of DB2, then catalog them again after the new DB2 software has been installed. (Migration may or may not be necessary.)

Just as there are multiple ways to catalog a DB2 database, there are multiple ways to uncatalog one: by using the Control Center, by using the Configuration Assistant, or by executing the UNCATALOG DATABASE command. By highlighting the object shown in the objects pane of the Control Center that corresponds to the database to be uncataloged and right-clicking the mouse button, you can display a menu that contains a list of options that are available for that particular database. If you then select the "Remove" item from this menu, you will be presented with a Confirmation dialog, where you will be asked to confirm your decision to uncatalog the database (the name of the database you are about to uncatalog will be displayed in this dialog in an effort to prevent you from accidentally uncataloging the wrong one). Once you confirm that the database specified is to be uncataloged, its entry is removed from both the system and the local database directory; however, the database itself is not destroyed, nor are its table space storage containers made available for other databases to use.

A database can also be uncataloged by executing the UNCATALOG DATABASE command. The syntax for this command is:

```
UNCATALOG [DATABASE | DB] [DatabaseAlias]
```

where:

DatabaseAlias   Identifies the alias assigned to the database to be uncataloged.

So, if you wanted to uncatalog a database that has the name and alias TEST_DB, you could do so by executing an UNCATALOG DATABASE command that looks like this:

```
UNCATALOG DATABASE test_db
```

Cataloging and Uncataloging a Node

The process used to catalog nodes (servers) is significantly different from the process used to catalog databases. Instead of being explicitly cataloged as needed, nodes are usually implicitly cataloged whenever a remote database is cataloged via the Configuration Assistant. However, if you desire to explicitly catalog a particular node (server), you can do so by executing the CATALOG...NODE command that corresponds to the communications protocol that will be used to access the server being cataloged. Several forms of the CATA-LOG...NODE command are available, including:

- CATALOG LOCAL NODE
- CATALOG LDAP NODE
- CATALOG NAMED PIPE NODE
- CATALOG TCPIP NODE

The syntax for all of these commands is very similar, the major difference being that many of the options available with each are specific to the communications protocol the command has been tailored for. Because TCP/IP is probably the most common communications protocol in use today, let's take a look at the syntax for that form of the CATALOG...NODE command.

The syntax for the CATALOG TCPIP NODE command is:

```
CATALOG <ADMIN> [TCPIP | TCPIP4 | TCPIP6] NODE [NodeName]
REMOTE [IPAddress | HostName]
SERVER [ServiceName | PortNumber]
<SECURITY SOCKS>
<REMOTE INSTANCE [InstanceName]>
<SYSTEM [SystemName]>
<OSTYPE [SystemType]>
<WITH "[Description]">
```

where:

NodeName	Identifies the alias to be assigned to the node to be cataloged. This is an arbitrary name created on the user's workstation and used to identify the node.
IPAddress	Identifies the IP address of the server where the remote database you are trying to communicate with resides.
HostName	Identifies the host name, as it is known to the TCP/IP network. (This is the name of the server where the remote database you are trying to communicate with resides.)
ServiceName	Identifies the service name that the DB2 Database Manager instance on the server uses to communicate with.
PortNumber	Identifies the port number that the DB2 Database Manager instance on the server uses to communicate with.
InstanceName	Identifies the name of the server instance to which an attachment is to be made.
SystemName	Identifies the DB2 system name that is used to identify the server workstation.
SystemType	Identifies the type of operating system being used on the server workstation. The following values are valid for this parameter: AIX, WIN, HPUX, SUN, OS390, OS400, VM, VSE, and LINUX.
Description	A comment used to describe the node entry that will be made in the node directory for the node being cataloged. The description must be enclosed by double quotation marks.

Thus, if you wanted to catalog a node for an AS/400 server workstation named DB2HOST that has a DB2 instance that listens on port 5000 and assign it the alias RMT_SERVER, you could do so by executing a CATALOG TCPIP NODE command that looks something like this:

```
CATALOG TCPIP NODE rmt_server
REMOTE db2host
SERVER 5000
OSTYPE OS400
WITH "A remote TCP/IP node"
```

Regardless of how a node was cataloged, it can be uncataloged at any time by executing the UNCATALOG NODE command. The syntax for this command is:

```
UNCATALOG NODE [NodeName]
```

where:

NodeName   Identifies the alias assigned to the node to be uncataloged.

So if you wanted to uncatalog the node that was cataloged in the previous example, you could do so by executing an UNCATALOG NODE command that looks like this:

```
UNCATALOG NODE rmt_server
```

Cataloging and Uncataloging a DCS Database

Aside from the fact that neither the Control Center nor the Configuration Assistant can be used, the process for cataloging a Database Connection Services (DCS) database is very similar to that used to catalog a regular DB2 database. A DCS database is cataloged by executing the CATALOG DCS DATABASE command. The syntax for this command is:

```
CATALOG DCS [DATABASE | DB] [Alias]
<AS [TargetName]>
<AR [LibraryName]>
<PARMS "[ParameterString]">
<WITH "[Description]">
```

where:

Alias   Identifies the alias of the target database that is to be cataloged. This name should match an entry in the system database directory associated with the remote node.

TargetName   Identifies the name of the target host or iSeries database to be cataloged.

LibraryName   Identifies the name of the Application Requester library that is to be loaded and used to access the remote database listed in the DCS directory.

ParameterString Identifies a parameter string to be passed to the Application Requestor when it is invoked. The parameter string must be enclosed by double quotation marks.

Description   A comment used to describe the database entry that will be made in the DCS directory for the database to be cataloged. The description must be enclosed by double quotation marks.

So, if you wanted to catalog a DCS database that has the alias TEST_DB and is a DB2 for z/OS database, you could do so by executing a CATALOG DCS DATABASE command that looks something like this:

```
CATALOG DCS DATABASE test_db
AS dsn_db
WITH "DB2 z/OS database"
```

Keep in mind that an entry for the database TEST_DB would also have to exist in the system database directory before the entry in the DCS database directory could be used to connect to the z/OS database.

Entries in the DCS database directory can be removed by executing the UNCATALOG DCS DATABASE command. The syntax for this command is:

```
UNCATALOG [DCS DATABASE | DB] [DatabaseAlias]
```

where:

DatabaseAlias   Identifies the alias assigned to the DCS database to be uncataloged.

Thus, if you wanted to uncatalog the DCS database cataloged in the previous example, you could do so by executing an UNCATALOG DCS DATABASE command that looks like this:

```
UNCATALOG DCS DATABASE test_db
```

Establishing a Database Connection

When a database is first created, it does not contain anything except the system catalog; before it can be used to store data, data objects such as tables, views, and indexes must be defined. And before new data objects can be defined (or anything else can be done with the database, for that matter), a connection to the database must be established. In most cases, a database connection will be established automatically if the Control Center is used to create data objects and work with data. If the Command Line Processor is used instead, a database connection can be established by executing the CONNECT SQL statement. The basic syntax for this statement is:

```
CONNECT
<TO [ServerName]>
<IN SHARE MODE | IN EXCLUSIVE MODE>
<USER [UserID] USING [Password]>
<NEW PASSWORD [NewPassword] CONFIRM [NewPassword]>
```

or

```
CONNECT
<USER [UserID] USING [Password]>
<NEW PASSWORD [NewPassword] CONFIRM [NewPassword]>
```

where:

ServerName Identifies the name assigned to the application server a connection is to be established with. (A database alias is often used to identify an application server.)

UserID Identifies the authentication ID (or user ID) assigned to the user attempting to establish the database connection.

Password Identifies the password assigned to the user trying to establish the database connection. (It is important to note that passwords are case sensitive.)

NewPassword Identifies the new password the user trying to establish the database connection wishes to have associated with his/her authentication ID.

Thus, in order for a user whose authentication ID is DB2USER and whose password is IBMDB2 to establish a connection to a database named SAMPLE, a CONNECT statement that looks something like this would need to be executed:

```
CONNECT TO sample USER db2user USING ibmdb2
```

And as soon as the CONNECT statement is successfully executed, you might see a message that looks something like this:

```
Database Connection Information

Database server       = DB2/NT 9.1.0
SQL authorization ID  = DB2USER
Local database alias  = SAMPLE
```

The CONNECT statement can be executed without specifying a user ID and password (since these are optional parameters). When the CONNECT statement is executed without this information, the DB2 Database Manager will either attempt to use the user ID and password you provided to gain access to the system or prompt you for this information. Such a connect operation is called an implicit connect, as it is implied that the credentials of the current user are to be used; on the other hand, when a user ID and password are specified, the connect operation is called an explicit connect, because the required user credentials have been explicitly provided.

Once a database connection has been established, it will remain in effect until it is explicitly terminated or until the application that established the connection ends. Database connections can be explicitly terminated at any time by executing a special form of the CONNECT statement. The syntax for this form of the CONNECT statement is:

```
CONNECT RESET
```

Creating Database (Data) Objects

Database objects, also known as data objects, are used to control how all user data (and some system data) is stored and organized within a DB2 database. Data objects include:

- Schemas
- Tables
- Views
- Indexes
- Aliases
- Sequences
- Triggers
- User-defined data types
- User-defined functions
- Stored procedures
- Packages

Schemas

Schemas are objects that are used to logically classify and group other objects in the database. Because schemas are objects themselves, they have privileges associated with them that allow the schema owner to control which users can create, alter, and drop objects within them.

Most objects in a database are named using a two-part naming convention. The first (leftmost) part of the name is called the *schema name* or *qualifier*, and the second (rightmost) part is called the *object name*. Syntactically, these two parts are concatenated and delimited with a period (for example, HR.EMPLOYEES). When any object that can be qualified by a schema name (such as a table, view, index, user-defined data type, user-defined function, nickname, package, or trigger) is first created, it is assigned to a particular schema based on the qualifier in its name. Figure 4–7 illustrates how a table named STAFF would be assigned to the PAYROLL schema during the table creation process.

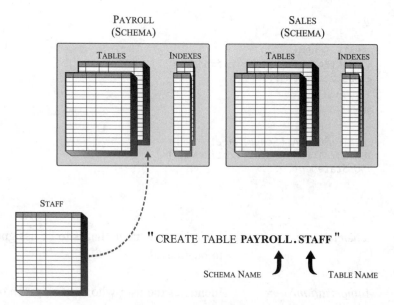

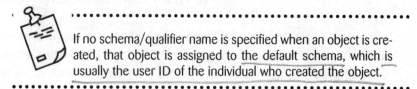

Figure 4–7: Assigning a table object to a schema.

Some schema names are reserved and cannot be used. An example includes the names assigned to the four schemas that are automatically created when a database is created—SYSIBM, SYSCAT, SYSSTAT, and SYSFUN.

> If no schema/qualifier name is specified when an object is created, that object is assigned to the default schema, which is usually the user ID of the individual who created the object.

Schemas are implicitly created whenever a data object that has been assigned a qualifier that is different from existing schema names is created—provided the user creating the object holds IMPLICIT_SCHEMA privilege. (Unless otherwise specified, when a new database is created, the group PUBLIC is given IMPLICIT_SCHEMA privilege. This allows any user to create objects in any schema not already in existence.) Schemas can be explicitly created by executing the CREATE SCHEMA SQL statement. The basic syntax for this statement is:

```
CREATE SCHEMA [SchemaName]
<SQLStatement, ...>
```

or

```
CREATE SCHEMA
AUTHORIZATION [AuthorizationName]
<SQLStatement, ...>
```

or

```
CREATE SCHEMA [SchemaName]
AUTHORIZATION [AuthorizationName]
<SQLStatement, ...>
```

where:

SchemaName   Identifies the name that is to be assigned to the schema
                         to be created.

AuthorizationName   Identifies the user who is to be given ownership of the
                         schema once it is created.

SQLStatement   Specifies one or more SQL statements that are to be exe-
                         cuted together with the CREATE SCHEMA statement. (Only
                         the following SQL statements are valid: CREATE TABLE,
                         CREATE VIEW, CREATE INDEX, COMMENT ON, and GRANT).

If a schema name is specified, but no authorization name is provided, the
authorization ID of the user who issued the CREATE SCHEMA statement is given
ownership of the newly created schema; if an authorization name is specified but
no schema name is provided, the new schema is assigned the same name as the
authorization name used.

So, if you wanted to explicitly create a schema named PAYROLL and give
ownership of the schema to the user DB2ADMIN, you could do so by executing a
CREATE SCHEMA SQL statement that looks something like this:

```
CREATE SCHEMA payroll
AUTHORIZATION db2admin
```

On the other hand, if you wanted to explicitly create a schema named INVENTORY,
along with a table named PARTS inside the schema named INVENTORY, you

could do so by executing a CREATE SCHEMA SQL statement that looks something like this:

```
CREATE SCHEMA inventory
CREATE TABLE parts (partno      INTEGER NOT NULL,
                    description  VARCHAR(50),
                    quantity     SMALLINT)
```

Schemas can also be created using the Create Schema dialog, which can be activated by selecting the appropriate action from the Schemas menu found in the Control Center. Figure 4–8 shows the Control Center menu items that must be selected to activate the Create Schema dialog; Figure 4–9 shows how the Create Schema dialog looks when it is first activated.

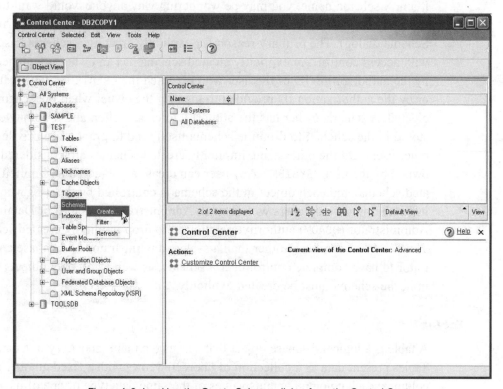

Figure 4–8: Invoking the Create Schema dialog from the Control Center.

Figure 4–9: The Create Schema dialog.

Given that schemas can be implicitly created by creating an object and assigning it a new schema name, you may be wondering why anyone would want to explicitly create a schema using the CREATE SCHEMA statement (or the Create Schema dialog). The primary reason for explicitly creating a schema has to do with access control. An explicitly created schema has an owner, identified either by the authorization ID of the user who executed the CREATE SCHEMA statement or by the authorization ID provided to identify the owner when the schema was created. A schema owner has the authority to create, alter, and drop any object stored in the schema; to drop the schema itself; and to grant these privileges to other users. On the other hand, implicitly created schemas are considered to be owned by the user "SYSIBM." Any user can create an object in an implicitly created schema, and each object in the schema is controlled by the user who created it. Furthermore, only users with System Administrator (SYSADM) or Database Administrator (DBADM) authority are allowed to drop implicitly created schemas. Thus, in order for a user other than a system administrator or database administrator to have complete control over a schema, as well as all data objects stored in it, the schema must be created explicitly.

Tables

A table is a logical database object that acts as the main repository in a database. Tables present data as a collection of unordered rows with a fixed number of columns; each column contains values of the same data type or one of its subtypes, and each row contains a set of values for each column available. Usually, the columns in a table are logically related, and additional relationships can be defined between two or more tables. The storage representation of a row is called a *record,* the storage representation of a column is called a *field*, and each intersection of a row and column is called a *value*. Figure 4–10 shows the structure of a simple database table.

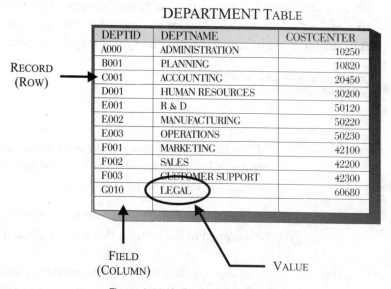

Figure 4–10: A simple database table.

With DB2 9, five types of tables are available:

Base tables: User-defined tables designed to hold persistent user data.

Result tables: DB2 Database Manager-defined tables populated with rows retrieved from one or more base tables in response to a query.

Materialized query tables: User-defined tables whose definition is based on the result of a query, and whose data is in the form of precomputed results that are taken from one or more tables upon which the materialized query table definition is based. Materialized query tables (MQTs) are used during query optimization to improve the performance of a subset of queries.

Declared temporary tables: User-defined tables used to hold nonpersistent data temporarily, on behalf of a single application. Declared temporary tables are explicitly created by an application when they are needed and implicitly destroyed when the application that created them terminates its last database connection.

Typed tables: User-defined tables whose column definitions are based on the attributes of a user-defined structured data type.

Because tables are the basic data objects used to store information, many are often created for a single database. Tables are created by executing the CREATE TABLE SQL statement. In its simplest form, the syntax for this statement is:

```
CREATE TABLE [TableName]
([ColumnName] [DataType], ...)
```

where:

TableName   Identifies the name that is to be assigned to the table to be created. (The table name specified must be unique within the schema the table is to be created in.)

ColumnName   Identifies the unique name (within the table definition) that is to be assigned to the column that is to be created.

DataType   Identifies the data type (built-in or user-defined) to be assigned to the column to be created; the data type specified determines the kind of data values that can be stored in the column. (Table 4–2 contains a list of valid built-in data type definitions.)

Table 4-2: Built-In Data Type Definitions That Can Be Used with the CREATE TABLE Statement (continued)	
Definition(s) ...	**Data Type ...**
SMALLINT	Numeric
INTEGER INT	Numeric
BIGINT	Numeric
DECIMAL(*Precision, Scale*) DEC(*Precision, Scale*) NUMERIC(*Precision, Scale*) NUM(Precision, Scale) where *Precision* is any number between 1 and 31; *Scale* is any number between 0 and *Precision*	Numeric
REAL FLOAT(*Precision*) where *Precision* is any number between 1 and 24	Numeric

Table 4-2: Built-In Data Type Definitions That Can Be Used with the CREATE TABLE Statement (continued)

Definition(s) ...	Data Type ...
DOUBLE DOUBLE PRECISION FLOAT(*Precision*) where *Precision* is any number between 25 and 53	Numeric
CHARACTER(*Length*) <FOR BIT DATA> CHAR(*Length*) <FOR BIT DATA> where *Length* is any number between 1 and 254. See note at bottom of table for the FOR BIT DATA clause.	Character/Character string
CHARACTER VARYING(*MaxLength*) <FOR BIT DATA> CHAR VARYING(*MaxLength*) <FOR BIT DATA> VARCHAR(*MaxLength*) <FOR BIT DATA> where *MaxLength* is any number between 1 and 32,672. See note at bottom of table for the FOR BIT DATA clause.	Character string
LONG VARCHAR <FOR BIT DATA>	Character string
GRAPHIC(*Length*) where *Length* is any number between 1 and 127	Double-byte character string
VARGRAPHIC(*MaxLength*) where *MaxLength* is any number between 1 and 16,336	Double-byte character string
LONG VARGRAPHIC	Double-byte character string
DATE	Date
TIME	Time
TIMESTAMP	Date and time
BINARY LARGE OBJECT(*Size* <K | M | G>) BLOB(*Size* <K | M | G>) where *Length* is any number between 1 and 2,147,483,647; if K (for kilobyte) is specified, Length is any number between 1 and 2,097,152; if M (for megabyte) is specified, *Length* is any number between 1 and 2,048; if G (for gigabyte) is specified, Length is any number between 1 and 2.	Binary

Table 4-2: Built-In Data Type Definitions That Can Be Used with the CREATE TABLE Statement (continued)

Definition(s) ...	Data Type ...
CHARACTER LARGE OBJECT(*Size* <K | M | G>) CHAR LARGE OBJECT(*Size* <K | M | G>) CLOB(*Size* <K | M | G>) where *Length* is any number between 1 and 2,147,483,647; if K (for kilobyte) is specified, Length is any number between 1 and 2,097,152; if M (for megabyte) is specified, *Length* is any number between 1 and 2,048; if G (for gigabyte) is specified, Length is any number between 1 and 2.	Character string
DBCLOB(*Size* <K | M | G>) where *Length* is any number between 1 and 1,073,741,823; if K (for kilobyte) is specified, *Length* is any number between 1 and 1,048,576; if M (for megabyte) is specified, *Length* is any number between 1 and 1,024; if G (for gigabyte) is specified, *Length* is must be 1.	Double-byte character string
CHARACTER VARYING(*MaxLength*) <FOR BIT DATA> CHAR VARYING(*MaxLength*) <FOR BIT DATA> VARCHAR(*MaxLength*) <FOR BIT DATA> where *MaxLength* is any number between 1 and 32,672. See note at bottom of table for the FOR BIT DATA clause.	Character string
XML	XML Document

Note: If the FOR BIT DATA option is used with any character string data type definition, the contents of the column the data type is assigned to are treated as binary data.

Thus, if you wanted to create a table named EMPLOYEES that had three columns in it, two of which are used to store numeric values and one that is used to store character string values, you could do so by executing a CREATE TABLE SQL statement that looks something like this:

```
CREATE TABLE employees
    (empid  INTEGER,
     name   CHAR(50),
     dept   INTEGER)
```

It is important to note that this is an example of a relatively simple table. Table definitions can be quite complex; therefore, the CREATE TABLE statement has several different permutations. Because the definition for a table object can be quite complex, and because the syntax for the CREATE TABLE SQL statement can be complex as well, the CREATE TABLE SQL statement is covered in much more detail in Chapter 6, "Working with DB2 Tables, Views, and Indexes." (A detailed description of the data types available is presented in Chapter 6 as well.)

Like schemas, tables can be created using a GUI tool that is accessible from the Control Center. In this case, the tool is the Create Table Wizard, and it can be activated by selecting the appropriate action from the Tables menu found in the Control Center. Figure 4–11 shows the Control Center menu items that must be selected to activate the Create Table Wizard; Figure 4–12 shows how the first page of the Create Table Wizard looks when it is first activated.

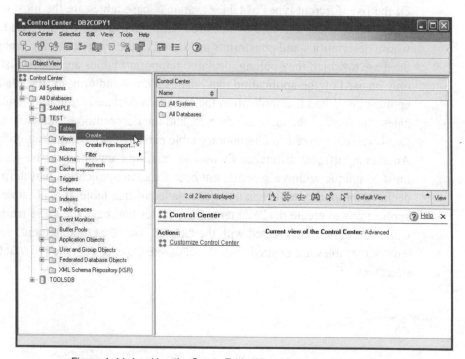

Figure 4–11: Invoking the Create Table Wizard from the Control Center.

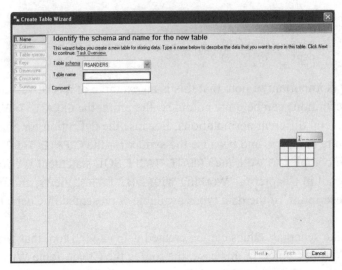

Figure 4–12: The first page of the Create Table Wizard.

A word about declared temporary tables

Of the five different types of tables available, base tables are the most common type of table used, followed by declared temporary tables. Unlike base tables, whose descriptions and constraints are stored in the system catalog tables of the database to which they belong, declared temporary tables are not persistent and can only be used by the application that creates them—and only for the life of the application. When the application that creates a declared temporary table terminates, the rows of the table are deleted, and the description of the table is dropped. (However, data stored in a temporary table can exist across transaction boundaries.) Another significant difference focuses on naming conventions: base table names must be unique within a schema, but because each application that defines a declared temporary table has its own instance of that table, it is possible for many applications to create declared temporary tables that have the same name. Finally, while base tables are created with the CREATE TABLE SQL statement, declared temporary tables are created with the DECLARE GLOBAL TEMPORARY TABLE statement.

Cursor

> Before an application can create and use a declared temporary
> table, a user temporary table space must be defined for the
> database the application will be working with.

Views

Views are used to provide a different way of looking at the data stored in one or more base tables. Essentially, a view is a named specification of a result table that is populated whenever the view is referenced in an SQL statement. (Each time a view is referenced, a query is executed and the results are returned in a table-like format.) Like base tables, views can be thought of as having columns and rows. And in most cases, data can be retrieved from a view the same way it can be retrieved from a table. However, whether or not a view can be used in insert, update, and delete operations depends upon how it was defined—views can be defined as being insertable, updatable, deletable, and read-only.

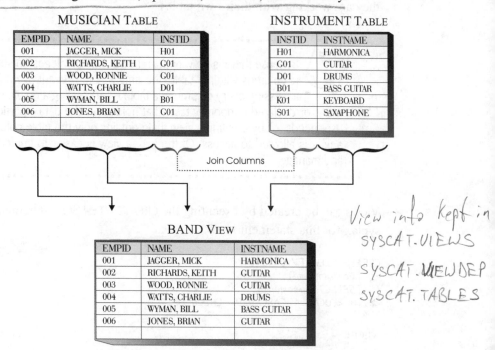

MUSICIAN TABLE

EMPID	NAME	INSTID
001	JAGGER, MICK	H01
002	RICHARDS, KEITH	G01
003	WOOD, RONNIE	G01
004	WATTS, CHARLIE	D01
005	WYMAN, BILL	B01
006	JONES, BRIAN	G01

INSTRUMENT TABLE

INSTID	INSTNAME
H01	HARMONICA
G01	GUITAR
D01	DRUMS
B01	BASS GUITAR
K01	KEYBOARD
S01	SAXAPHONE

Join Columns

BAND VIEW

EMPID	NAME	INSTNAME
001	JAGGER, MICK	HARMONICA
002	RICHARDS, KEITH	GUITAR
003	WOOD, RONNIE	GUITAR
004	WATTS, CHARLIE	DRUMS
005	WYMAN, BILL	BASS GUITAR
006	JONES, BRIAN	GUITAR

View info kept in
SYSCAT.VIEWS
SYSCAT.VIEWDEP
SYSCAT.TABLES

Figure 4–13: A simple view that references two base tables.

Although views look similar to base tables, they do not contain real data. Instead, views refer to data stored in other base tables. Only the view definition itself is actually stored in the database. (In fact, when changes are made to the data presented in a view, the changes are actually made to the data stored in the base table(s) the view references.) Figure 4–13 shows the structure of a simple view, along with its relationship to two base tables.

Because views allow different users to see different presentations of the same data, they are often used to control access to data. For example, suppose you had a table that contained information about all employees who worked for a particular company. Department managers could be given access to this table using a view that allows them to see only information about the employees who work in their department. Members of the payroll department, on the other hand, could be given access to the table using a view that allows them to see only the information needed to generate employee paychecks. Both sets of users are given access to the same table; however, because each user works with a different view, it appears that they are working with their own tables.

Because there is no way to grant SELECT privileges on specific columns within a table, the only way to prevent users from accessing every column in a table is by creating a result, summary, or declared temporary table that holds only the data a particular user needs, or by creating a view that contains only the table columns a user is allowed to access. Of the two, a view is easier to implement and manage.

Views can be created by executing the CREATE VIEW SQL statement. The basic syntax for this statement is:

```
CREATE VIEW [ViewName]
<( [ColumnName], ... )>
AS [SELECTStatement]
<WITH <LOCAL | CASCADED> CHECK OPTION>
```

where:

ViewName   Identifies the name that is to be assigned to the view to be created.

ColumnName   Identifies the names of one or more columns that are to
                            be included in the view to be created. If a list of column
                            names is specified, the number of column names
                            provided must match the number of columns that will
                            be returned by the SELECT statement used to create the
                            view. (If a list of column names is not provided, the
                            columns of the view will inherit the names that are
                            assigned to the columns returned by the SELECT
                            statement used to create the view.)

SELECTStatement   Identifies a SELECT SQL statement that, when executed,
                            will produce data that will populate the view.

Thus, if you wanted to create a view that references all data stored in a table
named DEPARTMENT and assign it the name DEPT_VIEW, you could do so by
executing a CREATE VIEW SQL statement that looks something like this:

```
CREATE VIEW dept_view
AS SELECT * FROM department
```

On the other hand, if you wanted to create a view that references specific data
values stored in the table named DEPARTMENT and assign it the name
ADV_DEPT_VIEW, you could do so by executing a CREATE VIEW SQL statement that
looks something like this:

```
CREATE VIEW adv_dept_view
AS SELECT (dept_no, dept_name, dept_size) FROM department
    WHERE dept_size > 25
```

The view created by this statement would contain only department number,
department name, and department size information for each department that has
more than 25 people in it.

Views can also be created using the Create View dialog, which can be activated by
selecting the appropriate action from the Views menu found in the Control Center.
Figure 4–14 shows the Control Center menu items that must be selected to activate
the Create View dialog; Figure 4–15 shows how the Create View dialog looks
when it is first activated.

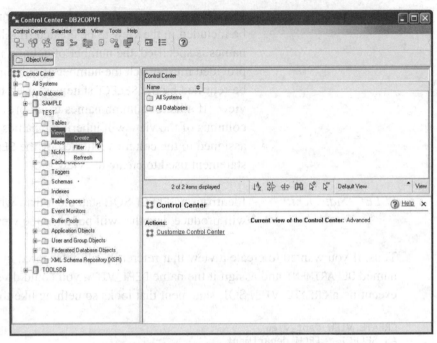

Figure 4–14: Invoking the Create View dialog from the Control Center.

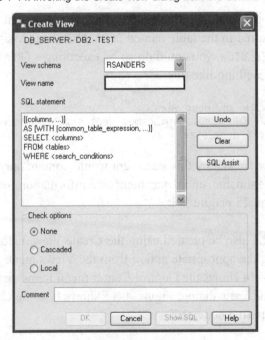

Figure 4–15: The Create View dialog.

If the WITH LOCAL CHECK OPTION clause of with the CREATE VIEW SQL statement is specified (or if the Local Check option is selected on the Create View dialog), insert and update operations performed against the view that is created are validated to ensure that all rows being inserted into or updated in the base table the view refers to conform to the view's definition (otherwise, the insert/update operation will fail). So what exactly does this mean? Suppose a view was created using the following CREATE VIEW statement:

```
CREATE VIEW priority_orders
AS SELECT * FROM orders WHERE response_time < 4
WITH LOCAL CHECK OPTION
```

Now, suppose a user tries to insert a record into this view that has a RESPONSE_TIME value of 6. The insert operation will fail because the record violates the view's definition. Had the view not been created with the WITH LOCAL CHECK OPTION clause, the insert operation would have been successful, even though the new record would not be visible to the view that was used to add it. Figure 4–16 illustrates how the WITH LOCAL CHECK OPTION clause works.

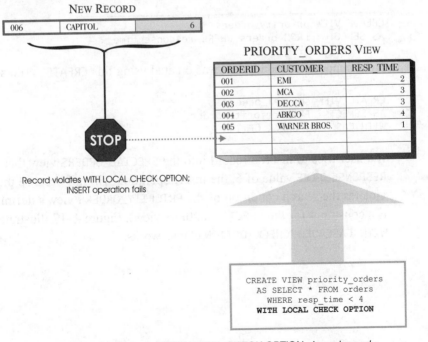

Figure 4–16: How the WITH LOCAL CHECK OPTION clause is used to ensure that insert and update operations conform to a view's definition.

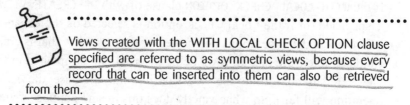

Views created with the WITH LOCAL CHECK OPTION clause specified are referred to as symmetric views, because every record that can be inserted into them can also be retrieved from them.

If the WITH CASCADED CHECK OPTION clause of with the CREATE VIEW SQL statement is specified (or if the Cascaded Check option is selected on the Create View dialog), the view created will inherit the search conditions of the *parent view* upon which the view is based and treat those conditions as one or more constraints that are used to validate insert and update operations that are performed against the view. Additionally, every view created that is a child of the view that was created with the WITH CASCADED CHECK OPTION clause specified will inherit those constraints; the search conditions of both parent and child views are ANDed together to form the constraints. To understand better what this means, let's look at an example. Suppose a view was created using the following CREATE VIEW statement:

```
CREATE VIEW priority_orders
AS SELECT * FROM orders WHERE response_time < 4
```

Now, suppose a second view was created using this CREATE VIEW statement:

```
CREATE VIEW special_orders
AS SELECT * FROM priority_orders
WITH CASCADED CHECK OPTION
```

If a user tries to insert a record into the SPECIAL_ORDERS view that has a RESPONSE_TIME value of 6, the insert operation will fail because the record violates the search condition of the PRIORITY_ORDERS view's definition (which is a constraint for the SPECIAL_ORDERS view). Figure 4–17 illustrates how the WITH CASCADED CHECK OPTION clause works.

```
CREATE VIEW priority_orders
   AS SELECT * FROM orders
      WHERE resp_time < 4
```

PRIORITY_ORDERS View

ORDERID	CUSTOMER	RESP_TIME
001	EMI	2
002	MCA	3
003	DECCA	3
004	ABKCO	4
005	WARNER BROS.	1

NEW RECORD

006	CAPITOL	6

SPECIAL_ORDERS View

ORDERID	CUSTOMER	RESP_TIME
001	EMI	2
002	MCA	3
003	DECCA	3
004	ABKCO	4
005	WARNER BROS.	1

STOP

Record violates WITH CASCADED CHECK OPTION;
INSERT operation fails

```
CREATE VIEW special_orders
   AS SELECT * FROM primary_orders
   WITH CASCADED CHECK OPTION
```

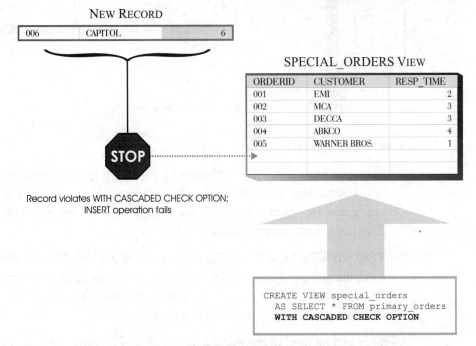

*Figure 4–17: How the WITH CASCADED CHECK OPTION clause is used
to ensure insert and update operations conform to a parent view's definition.*

Indexes

An index is an object that contains an ordered set of pointers that refer to rows in a base table. Each index is based upon one or more columns in the base table it refers to (known as *keys*), yet it is stored as separate entities. Figure 4–18 shows the structure of a simple index, along with its relationship to a base table.

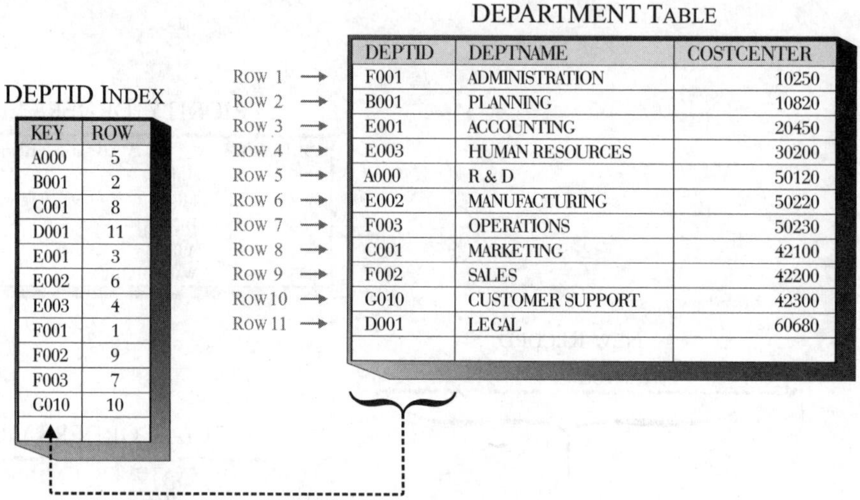

DEPARTMENT TABLE

DEPTID INDEX

KEY	ROW
A000	5
B001	2
C001	8
D001	11
E001	3
E002	6
E003	4
F001	1
F002	9
F003	7
G010	10

	DEPTID	DEPTNAME	COSTCENTER
Row 1 →	F001	ADMINISTRATION	10250
Row 2 →	B001	PLANNING	10820
Row 3 →	E001	ACCOUNTING	20450
Row 4 →	E003	HUMAN RESOURCES	30200
Row 5 →	A000	R & D	50120
Row 6 →	E002	MANUFACTURING	50220
Row 7 →	F003	OPERATIONS	50230
Row 8 →	C001	MARKETING	42100
Row 9 →	F002	SALES	42200
Row 10 →	G010	CUSTOMER SUPPORT	42300
Row 11 →	D001	LEGAL	60680

Figure 4–18: A simple index.

Indexes are important because:

- They provide a fast, efficient method for locating specific rows of data in very large tables. (In some cases, all the information needed to resolve a query may be found in the index itself, in which case the actual table data does not have to be accessed.)

- They provide a logical ordering of the rows of a table. (When indexes are used, the values of one or more columns can be sorted in ascending or descending order; this property is very beneficial when processing queries that contain ORDER BY and GROUP BY clauses.)

- They can be used to enforce the uniqueness of records stored in a table.

- They can force a table to use *clustering* storage, which causes the rows of a table to be physically arranged according to the ordering of their index column values. (Although all indexes provide a logical ordering of data, only a clustering index provides a physical ordering of data.)

A clustering index usually increases performance by decreasing the amount of I/O required to access data: When a logical set of rows are physically stored close together, a read operation on the set of rows will require less I/O, because adjacent rows are more likely to be found within the same extent (remember, data pages are written in batches called extents) instead of being widely distributed across multiple extents.

Whereas some indexes are created implicitly to provide support for a table's definition (for example, to provide support for a *primary key*), indexes are typically created explicitly, using tools available with DB2. One way to explicitly create an index is by executing the CREATE INDEX SQL statement. The basic syntax for this statement is:

```
CREATE <UNIQUE> INDEX IndexName]
ON [TableName] ( [PriColumnName] <ASC | DESC>, ... )
<INCLUDE ( [SecColumnName], ... )>
<CLUSTER>
<DISALLOW REVERSE SCANS | ALLOW REVERSE SCANS>
```

where:

IndexName   Identifies the name that is to be assigned to the index to be created.

TableName   Identifies the name assigned to the base table with which the index to be created is to be associated.

PriColumnName   Identifies one or more primary columns that are to be part of the index's key. (The combined values of each primary column specified will be used to enforce data uniqueness in the associated base table.)

SecColumnName   Identifies one or more secondary columns whose values are to be stored with the values of the primary columns specified, but are not to be used to enforce data uniqueness.

If the UNIQUE clause is specified when the CREATE INDEX statement is executed, rows in the table associated with the index to be created must not have two or more occurrences of the same values in the set of columns that make up the index key. If the base table the index is to be created for contains data, this uniqueness is checked when the DB2 Database Manager attempts to create the index specified; once the index has been created, this uniqueness is enforced each time an insert or update operation is performed against the table. In both cases, if the uniqueness of the index key is compromised, the index creation, insert, or update operation will fail and an error will be generated. It is important to keep in mind that when the UNIQUE clause is used, it is possible to have an index key that contains one (and only one) NULL value.

So, if you had a base table named EMPLOYEES that has the following characteristics:

Column Name ...	Data Type ...
EMPNO	INTEGER
FNAME	CHAR(20)
LNAME	CHAR(30)
TITLE	CHAR(10)
DEPARTMENT	CHAR(20)
SALARY	DECIMAL(6,2)

and you wanted to create a index such that the index key consists of the column named EMPNO and all employee numbers entered will be guaranteed to be unique, you could do so by executing a CREATE INDEX statement that looks something like this:

```
CREATE UNIQUE INDEX empno_indx
ON employees(empno)
```

Indexes can also be created using the Create Index wizard, which can be activated by selecting the appropriate action from the Indexes menu found in the Control Center. Figure 4–19 shows the Control Center menu items that must be selected to activate the Create Indexes dialog; Figure 4–20 shows how the Create Index wizard might look when it is first activated.

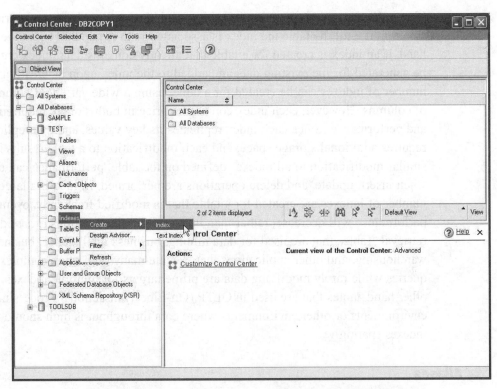

Figure 4–19: Invoking the Create Index dialog from the Control Center.

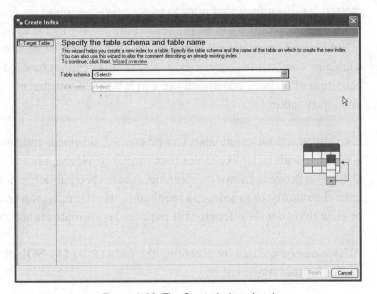

Figure 4–20: The Create Index wizard.

If an index is created for an empty table, that index will not have any entries stored in it until the table the index is associated with is populated. On the other hand, if an index is created for a table that already contains data, index entries will be generated for the existing data and added to the index upon its creation. Any number of indexes can be created for a table, using a wide variety of combinations of columns. However, each index comes at a price in both storage requirements and performance. Since each index replicates its key values, and this replication requires additional storage space, and each modification to a table results in a similar modification to all indexes defined on the table, performance can decrease when insert, update, and delete operations are performed. In fact, if a large number of indexes are created for a table that is modified frequently, overall performance will decrease, rather than increase, for all operations *except* data retrieval. Tables that are used for data mining, business intelligence, business warehousing, and other applications that execute many (and often complex) queries while rarely modifying data are prime targets for multiple indexes. On the other hand, tables that are used in OLTP (On-Line Transactional Processing) environments or other environments where data throughput is high should use indexes sparingly.

Aliases

An alias is simply an alternate name for a table or view. (Aliases can also be created for *nicknames* that refer to tables or views found on federated systems.) Once created, an alias can be referenced the same way the table or view the alias refers to can be referenced. However, an alias cannot be used in every context that a table or view name can. For example, an alias cannot be used in the check condition of a check constraint, nor can it be used to reference a user-defined temporary table.

Like tables and views, an alias can be created, dropped, and have comments associated with it. Unlike tables (but similar to views), aliases can refer to other aliases—a process known as *chaining*. Aliases are publicly referenced names, so no special authority or privilege is required to use them. However, access to the table or view that an alias refers to still requires appropriate authorization.

Aliases can be created by executing the CREATE ALIAS SQL statement. The basic syntax for this statement is:

```
CREATE [ALIAS | SYNONYM] [AliasName]
FOR [TableName | ViewName | Nickname | ExistingAlias]
```

where:

AliasName   Identifies the name that is to be assigned to the alias to be created.

TableName   Identifies the table, by name, that the alias to be created is to reference.

ViewName   Identifies the view, by name, that the alias to be created is to reference.

Nickname   Identifies the nickname that the alias to be created is to reference.

ExistingAlias   Identifies an existing alias, by name, that the alias to be created is to reference.

Thus, if you wanted to create an alias that references a table named EMPLOYEES and you wanted to assign it the name EMPINFO, you could do so by executing a CREATE ALIAS SQL statement that looks something like this:

```
CREATE ALIAS empinfo FOR employees
```

Aliases can also be created using the Create Alias dialog, which can be activated by selecting the appropriate action from the Alias menu found in the Control Center. Figure 4–21 shows the Control Center menu items that must be selected to activate the Create Alias dialog; Figure 4–22 shows how the Create Alias dialog might look when it is first activated.

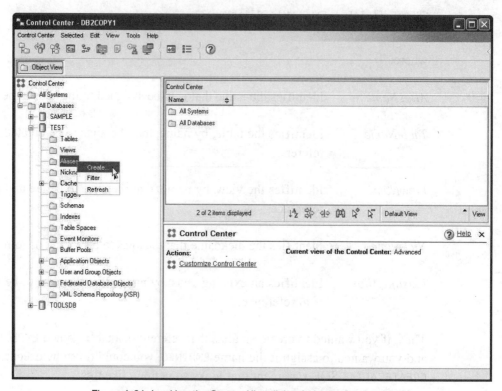

Figure 4–21: Invoking the Create Alias dialog from the Control Center.

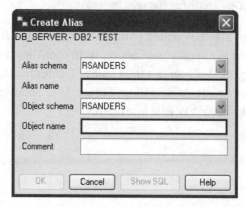

Figure 4–22: The Create Alias dialog.

So why would you want use an alias instead of the actual table/view name? By using aliases, SQL statements can be constructed such that they are independent of the qualified names that identify the base tables or views they reference.

Whenever an alias is used in an SQL statement, the behavior is the same as when the target (source table or view) of the alias is used instead. Therefore, any application that uses an alias to access data can easily be made to work with many different targets. That's because, when the target of an alias is changed, no changes to applications that use the alias are necessary.

Sequences

 A sequence is an object that is used to generate data values automatically. Unlike an identity column, which is used to generate data values for a specific column in a table, a sequence is not tied to any specific column or any specific table. Instead, a sequence behaves like a unique counter that resides outside the database, with the exception that it does not introduce the concurrency and performance problems that can exist when external counters are used.

Sequences have the following characteristics:

- Values generated can be any exact numeric data type that has a scale of zero (SMALLINT, BIGINT, INTEGER, or DECIMAL).

- Consecutive values can differ by any specified increment value. The default increment value is 1.

- Counter values are recoverable. Counter values are reconstructed from logs when recovery is required.

- Values generated can be cached to improve performance.

In addition, sequences can generate values in one of three ways:

- By incrementing or decrementing by a specified amount, without bounds

- By incrementing or decrementing by a specified amount to a user-defined limit and stopping

- By incrementing or decrementing by a specified amount to a user-defined limit, and then cycling back to the beginning and starting again

To facilitate the use of sequences in SQL operations, two expressions are available: PREVIOUS VALUE and NEXT VALUE. The PREVIOUS VALUE expression returns the most recently generated value for the specified sequence, while the NEXT VALUE expression returns the next sequence value.

One important difference between a sequence and an identity column is that an identity column cannot be referenced by an INSERT SQL statement; a sequence, on the other hand, can.

Sequences can be created by executing the CREATE SEQUENCE SQL statement. The basic syntax for this statement is:

```
CREATE SEQUENCE [SequenceName]
<AS INTEGER | AS [DataType]>
<START WITH [StartingNumber]>
<INCREMENT BY [1 | IncrementValue]>
<NO MINVALUE | MINVALUE [MinValue]>
<NO MAXVALUE | MAXVALUE [MaxValue]>
<NO CYCLE | CYCLE>
<CACHE 20 | CACHE [CacheValue] | NO CACHE>
<NO ORDER | ORDER>
```

where:

SequenceName   Identifies the name that is to be assigned to the sequence to be created.

DataType   Identifies the data type to be used for the sequence's value. The data type specified can be any built-in numeric type with a scale of zero (SMALLINT, INTEGER, BIGINT, or DECIMAL), or a user-defined data type whose source is a built-in numeric type with a scale of zero.

StartingValue   Identifies the first value to be provided by the sequence being created.

IncrementValue   Identifies the interval that is to be used to calculate the next consecutive value for the sequence being created.

MinValue   Specifies the minimum value at which a descending sequence either cycles or stops generating values, or an ascending sequence cycles to after reaching the maximum value.

MaxValue   Specifies the maximum value at which an ascending sequence either cycles or stops generating values, or a descending sequence cycles to after reaching the minimum value. (It is possible for *MaxValue* to be equal to *MinValue*; if that is the case, the sequence will return a constant value.)

CacheSize   Identifies the number of values of the identity sequence that are to be pre-generated and kept in memory. (Pregenerating and storing values in the cache reduces synchronous I/O to the log when values are generated for the sequence. However, in the event of a system failure, all cached sequence values that have not been used in committed statements are lost; that is, they can never be used.)

Thus, if you wanted to create a sequence that generates numbers, starting with the number 100 and incrementing each subsequent number produced by 10, you could do so by executing a CREATE SEQUENCE SQL statement that looks something like this:

```
CREATE SEQUENCE emp_id START WITH 100 INCREMENT BY 10
```

Once this sequence is created, the first value returned by it will be 100. Subsequent values will be 110, 120, 130, 140, and so forth. Values are generated each time the sequence is queried (for example, by executing the statement VALUES NEXT VALUE FOR emp_id INTO :empid) regardless of which user/application performs the query.

On the other hand, if you wanted to create a sequence that generates numbers, starting with the number 5, incrementing each subsequent number produced by 5, and caching 5 numbers at a time, you could do so by executing a CREATE SEQUENCE SQL statement that looks something like this:

```
CREATE SEQUENCE dept_id START WITH 5 INCREMENT BY 5 CACHE 5
```

In this case, the numbers returned by the sequence can vary, depending upon how the sequence is used. For example, if three different transactions were to access the sequence, because five values are generated at a time, the first transaction would get the numbers 5, 10, 15, 20, and 25; the second transaction would get the numbers 30, 35, 40, 45, and 50; while the third transaction would get the numbers 55, 60, 65, 70, and 75. If any one of these transactions terminates without using the full set of numbers available, those numbers are lost. (Because sequences are persistent across transaction boundaries, their behavior is not affected by commit or rollback operations.)

Triggers

A trigger is used to define a set of actions that are to be executed whenever an insert, update, or delete operation is performed against a table or updatable view. Triggers are often used to enforce *data integrity rules* and *business rules*. (A data integrity rule might be that whenever the record for an employee is deleted from the table that holds employee information, the corresponding record will be deleted from the table that holds payroll information; a business rule might be that an employee's salary cannot be increased by more than 10 percent.) Triggers can also be used to update other tables, automatically generate or transform values for inserted or updated rows, and invoke functions to perform such tasks as issuing alerts.

[handwritten margin note: Can we use a trigger to copy a deleted pending SA row to the Cancel table?]

By using triggers, the logic needed to enforce business rules can be placed directly in the database, and applications that work with the database can concentrate solely on data storage, management, and retrieval. And by storing the logic needed to enforce data integrity and business rules directly in the database, it can be modified as those rules change without requiring applications to be recoded and recompiled.

Before a trigger can be created, the following components must be identified:

Subject table/view: The table or view with which the trigger is to interact.

Trigger event: An SQL operation that causes the trigger to be activated whenever the event is performed against the subject table/view. This operation can be an insert operation, an update operation, or a delete operation.

Trigger activation time: Indicates whether the trigger should be activated before, after, or instead of the trigger event. A BEFORE trigger will be activated before the trigger event occurs; therefore, it will be able to see new data values before they are inserted into the subject table. An AFTER trigger will be activated after the trigger event occurs; therefore, it can see only data values that have already been inserted into the subject table. An INSTEAD OF trigger will replace the trigger event made against the subject view. (A BEFORE trigger might be used to trap and process unwanted values, while an AFTER trigger could be used to copy data values entered to other tables or views.)

Set of affected rows: The rows of the subject table/view that are being inserted, updated, or deleted.

Trigger granularity: Specifies whether the actions the trigger will perform are to be performed once for the entire insert, update, or delete operation or once for every row affected by the insert, update, or delete operation.

Triggered action: An optional search condition and a set of SQL statements that are to be executed whenever the trigger is activated. (If a search condition is specified, the SQL statements will only be executed if the search condition evaluates to TRUE.) If the trigger is a BEFORE trigger, the triggered action can include statements that retrieve data, set transition variables, or signal SQL states. If the trigger is an AFTER trigger, the triggered action can include statements that retrieve data, insert records, update records, delete records, or signal SQL states.

Triggered actions can refer to the values in the set of affected rows using what are known as *transition variables*. Transition variables use the names of the columns in the subject table, qualified by a specified name that indicates whether the reference is to the original value (before the insert, update, or delete operation is performed) or the new value (after the insert, update, or delete operation is performed). Another means of referring to values in the set of affected rows is through the use of *transition tables*. Transition tables also use the names of the columns in the subject table, but they allow the complete set of affected rows to be treated as a table. Transition tables can only be used in after triggers.

Once the appropriate trigger components have been identified, a trigger can be created by executing the CREATE TRIGGER SQL statement. The basic syntax for this statement is:

```
CREATE TRIGGER [TriggerName]
[<NO CASCADE> BEFORE | AFTER | INSTEAD OF]
[INSERT | UPDATE | DELETE <OF [ColumnName], ... >]
ON [TableName | ViewName]
<REFERENCING [Reference]>
[FOR EACH ROW | FOR EACH STATEMENT]
<WHEN ( [SearchCondition] )>
[TriggeredAction]
```

where:

TriggerName   Identifies the name to be assigned to the trigger to be created.

ColumnName   Identifies one or more columns in the subject table or view of the trigger whose values must be updated before the trigger's triggered action (*TriggeredAction*) will be executed.

TableName   Identifies, by name, the subject table of the BEFORE or AFTER trigger to be created.

ViewName   Identifies, by name, the subject view of the INSTEAD OF trigger to be created.

Reference   Identifies one or more transition variables and/or transition tables that are to be used by the trigger's triggered action (*TriggeredAction*). The syntax used to create transition variables and/or transition tables that are to be used by the trigger's triggered action is:

```
<OLD <AS> [CorrelationName]>
<NEW <AS> [CorrelationName]>
<OLD TABLE <AS> [Identifier]>
<NEW TABLE <AS> [Identifier]>
```

where:

CorrelationName   Identifies a name to be used to identify a specific row in the subject table of the trigger, either before it was modified by the trigger's triggered action (OLD <AS>) or after it has been modified by the trigger's triggered action (NEW <AS>).

Identifier   Identifies a name that is to be used to identify a temporary table that contains a set of rows found in the subject table of the trigger, either before they were modified by the trigger's triggered action (OLD TABLE <AS>) or after they have been modified by the trigger's triggered action (NEW TABLE <AS>).

Each column affected by an activation event (insert, update, or delete operation) can be made available to the trigger's triggered action by qualifying the column's name with the appropriate correlation name or table identifier.

SearchCondition   Specifies a search condition that, when evaluated, will return either TRUE, FALSE, or Unknown. This condition is used to determine whether the trigger's triggered action (*TriggeredAction*) is to be performed.

TriggeredAction   Identifies the action to be performed when the trigger is activated. The triggered action must consist of one or more SQL statements; when multiple statements are specified, the first statement must be preceded by the keywords BEGIN ATOMIC, the last statement must be followed by the keyword END, and every statement between these keywords must be terminated with a semicolon (;).

Thus, suppose you have a base table named EMPLOYEES that has the following characteristics:

Column Name ...	Data Type ...
EMPNO	INTEGER
FNAME	CHAR(20)
LNAME	CHAR(30)
TITLE	CHAR(10)
DEPARTMENT	CHAR(20)
SALARY	DECIMAL(6,2)

If you wanted to create a trigger for EMPLOYEES that will cause the value for the column named EMPNO to be incremented each time a row is added to the table, you could do so by executing a CREATE TRIGGER statement that looks something like this:

```
CREATE TRIGGER empno_inc
AFTER INSERT ON employees
FOR EACH ROW
UPDATE empno SET empno = empno + 1
```

Triggers can also be created using the Create Trigger dialog, which can be activated by selecting the appropriate action from the Triggers menu found in the Control Center. Figure 4–23 shows the Control Center menu items that must be selected to activate the Create Trigger dialog; Figure 4–24 shows how the Create Trigger dialog might look when it is first activated.

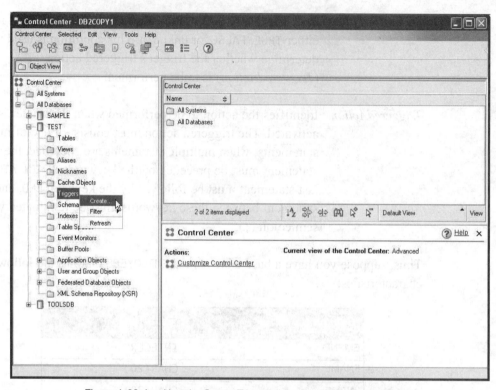

Figure 4–23: Invoking the Create Trigger dialog from the Control Center.

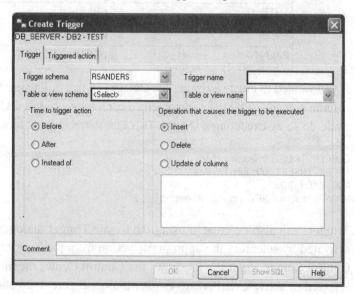

Figure 4–24: The Create Trigger dialog.

It is important to note that if you want a trigger to be fired whenever a Data Manipulation Language (DML) operation is performed against a table, you must create three separate triggers for that table: one that handles INSERT events, one that handles UPDATE events, and another that handles DELETE events.

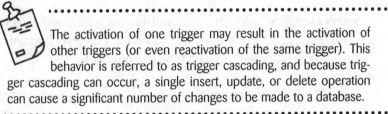

The activation of one trigger may result in the activation of other triggers (or even reactivation of the same trigger). This behavior is referred to as trigger cascading, and because trigger cascading can occur, a single insert, update, or delete operation can cause a significant number of changes to be made to a database.

User-Defined Data Types

As the name implies, user-defined data types (UDTs) are data types that are created (and named) by database users. With DB2 9, two types of UDTs are available: *distinct* and *structured*.

Distinct data types

A distinct data type is a user-defined data type that is derived from one of the built-in data types available with DB2. Although a distinct data type shares a common internal representation with a built-in data type, it is considered a separate data type that is distinct from any other data type (hence, the "distinct" in the name). And even though distinct data types share the same representation as other built-in types, the DB2 Database Manager guarantees that *strong data typing* exists, which means that the value of a user-defined data type is compatible only with values of that same type. As a result, user-defined data types cannot be used as arguments for most of the built-in functions available. (Similarly, a built-in data type cannot be used in arguments or operands designed to use a distinct data type.) Instead, user-defined functions (or methods) that provide similar functionality must be developed when that kind of capability is needed.

Distinct user-defined data types can be created by executing the CREATE DISTINCT TYPE SQL statement. The basic syntax for this statement is:

```
CREATE DISTINCT TYPE [TypeName]
AS [SourceDataType]
<WITH COMPARISONS>
```

where:

TypeName   Identifies the name that is to be assigned to the distinct data
                    type to be created.

SourceDataType   Identifies the built-in data type that the distinct data type to be
                    created is to be based on. (Table 4–2 contains a list of valid
                    built-in data type definitions.)

Thus, if you wanted to create a distinct data type named CURRENCY that can be
used to store numeric data, you could do so by executing a CREATE DISTINCT
TYPE SQL statement that looks something like this:

```
CREATE DISTINCT TYPE currency AS NUMERIC(7,2)
WITH COMPARISONS
```

Distinct data types can also be created using the Create Distinct Type dialog,
which can be activated by selecting the appropriate action from the User Defined
Distinct Datatypes menu found in the Control Center. Figure 4–25 shows the
Control Center menu items that must be selected to activate the Create Distinct
Type dialog; Figure 4–26 shows how the Create Distinct Type dialog might look
when it is first activated.

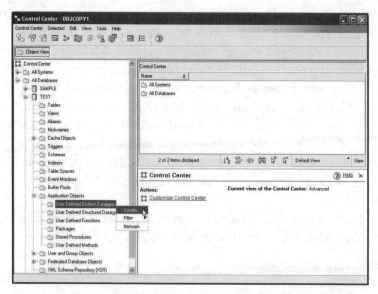

Figure 4–25: Invoking the Create Distinct Type dialog from the Control Center.

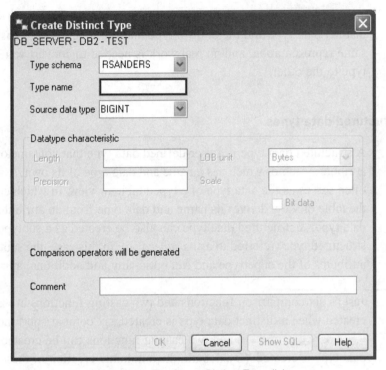

Figure 4–26: The Create Distinct Type dialog.

When a distinct data type is created, six comparison functions (named =, <>, <, <=, >, and >=) may also be created. (Because BLOB, CLOB, DBCLOB, LONG VARCHAR and LONG VARGRAPHIC data types cannot be compared, comparison functions cannot be created for distinct data types that are based on these data types.) These functions allow two instances of the distinct data type to be compared in the same manner as any two values of the same built-in data type can be compared. Thus, the ORDER BY, GROUP BY, and DISTINCT clauses of a SELECT SQL statement can be used with most columns that have been defined using a distinct data type.

Two casting functions are also generated when a distinct data type is created. These functions are used to convert data between the new distinct data type and the built-in data type on which the distinct data type is based. The name of the casting function that will convert a built-in data type value to a distinct data type value is the same as that of the distinct data type itself. Thus, if a distinct data type named EMPID that is based on an INTEGER built-in data type is created, the DB2 Database Manager automatically generates the casting functions EMPID(INTEGER) and INTEGER(EMPID). Both casting functions are extremely efficient because the distinct data type and the built-in type that the functions are based on share the same representation, and no real work is needed to convert values from one data type to the other.

Structured data types

A structured data type is a user-defined data type that contains one or more attributes, each of which has a name and data type of its own. A structured data type often serves as the data type of a typed table or view, in which case each column of the table or view derives its name and data type from an attribute of the structured data type. A structured data type can also be created as a subtype of another structured type (referred to as its *supertype*). In this case, the subtype inherits all the attributes of the supertype and can optionally add additional attributes of its own.

Just as six comparison functions and two casting functions are automatically created when a distinct data type is created, six comparison functions (also called =, <>, <, <=, >, and >=) and two casting functions can be created when a structured data type is created. (By default, the automatic creation of these functions is suppressed.) When created, these comparison functions are used to compare references to the structured data type, but not to the data type values themselves. Likewise, the two casting functions are used to cast between the generated reference type of the structured data type and the underlying data type that the structured data type uses as a reference type. Structured data types are created by executing the CREATE TYPE SQL statement.

User-Defined Functions (or Methods)

User-defined functions (UDFs) are special objects that are used to extend and enhance the support provided by the built-in functions available with DB2 9. Like user-defined data types, user-defined functions (or methods) are created and named by a database user. However, unlike DB2's built-in functions, user-defined functions can take advantage of system calls and DB2's administrative APIs, thereby providing more synergy between applications and databases.

Five types of user-defined functions can be created:

Sourced (or Template). A sourced function is constructed from a function that is already registered with a database (referred to as the *source function*). Sourced functions can be columnar, scalar, or table in nature or they can be designed to overload a specific operator such as +, -, *, and /. When a sourced function is invoked, all arguments passed to it are converted to the data types that are expected by the underlying source function, and the source function itself is invoked. Upon completion, the source function performs any conversions necessary on the results produced and returns them to the calling SQL statement. The most common use of sourced functions is to enable a user-defined distinct data type to inherit selectively some of the semantics of the built-in data type on which it is based.

SQL Scalar, Table, or Row. Although a sourced function is constructed from a function that already exists, an SQL function is constructed from the ground up, using only SQL statements. An SQL function can be scalar in nature (scalar functions return a single value and can be specified in an SQL statement wherever a regular expression can be used) or can return a single row or an entire table.

External Scalar. An external scalar function is a function that is written using a high-level programming language such as C, C++, or Java and returns a single value. The function itself resides in an external library and is registered in the database, along with any related attributes.

External Table. Like external scalar functions, external table functions are written using a high-level programming language. But where an external scalar function returns a single value, an external table function returns a result data set, in the form of a table, to the SQL statement that references it. External table functions are powerful because they enable you to make almost any source of data appear to be a DB2 base table; the result data set returned can be used in join operations, grouping operations, set operations (for example, UNIONs), or any other operation that can be applied to a read-only view. Again, the function itself resides in an external library and is registered in the database, along with any related attributes.

OLE DB External Table. Like external table functions, external Object Linking and Embedding (OLE) DB table functions are written using a high-level programming language and return a result data set, in the form of a table, to SQL statements that reference them. However, with OLE DB table functions, a generic built-in OLE DB consumer can be used to interface with any OLE DB provider to access data; you need only to register an OLE DB table function and refer to the appropriate OLE DB provider as the data source. No additional programming is needed. OLE DB is designed to provide access to all types of data in an OLE Component Object Model (COM) environment. Again, the function resides in an external library and is registered in the database, along with any related attributes.

User-defined functions are created (or registered) by executing the CREATE FUNCTION SQL statement. Several flavors of this statement are available, and the appropriate form to use is determined by the type of user-defined function to be created.

Stored Procedures

In a basic DB2 client/server environment, each time an SQL statement is executed against a remote database, the statement itself is sent through a network from the client workstation to a database server. The database server then processes the statement, and the results are sent back, again through the network, to the client workstation. This means that two messages must go through the network for every SQL statement executed. Client/server application development focuses on breaking an application into two separate parts, storing those parts on two different platforms (the client and the server), and having them communicate with each other as the application executes. This allows the code that interacts directly with a database to reside on a database server, where computing power and centralized control can be used to provide quick, coordinated data access. At the same time, the application logic can reside on one or more client workstations so that it can make effective use of all the resources that a workstation has to offer without causing a bottleneck at the server.

If you have an application that contains one or more transactions that perform a relatively large amount of database activity with little or no user interaction, those transactions can be stored on the database server as a *stored procedure*. When a stored procedure is used, all database processing done by the transaction can be performed directly at the database server. And, because a stored procedure is invoked by a single SQL statement, fewer messages have to be transmitted across the network—only the data that is actually needed at the client workstation has to be sent across. It is important to note that a stored procedure can be invoked by a user-defined function, and a user-defined function can be invoked as part of a stored procedure.

Just as there are different types of user-defined functions available, there are different types of stored procedures available. They are *SQL* and *external*.

User-defined functions and stored procedures are the only "executable" database objects available. For this reason, both are often referred to as "routines" or "routine objects."

SQL stored procedures

As the name implies, an SQL stored procedure is composed entirely of SQL statements. SQL stored procedures are created by executing one form of the CREATE PROCEDURE SQL statement. (Two forms of this statement are available; we'll look at the other form a little later.) The basic syntax for the form of the CREATE PROCEDURE statement that is used to create an SQL stored procedure looks something like this:

```
CREATE PROCEDURE [ProcedureName]
( [ParamType] [ParamName] [DataType], ...)
<SPECIFIC [SpecificName]>
<DYNAMIC RESULT SETS [NumResultSets]>
<MODIFIES SQL DATA | CONTAINS SQL | READS SQL DATA>
<DETERMINISTIC | NOT DETERMINISTIC>
<CALLED ON NULL INPUT>
<INHERIT SPECIAL REGISTERS>
<[OLD | NEW] SAVEPOINT LEVEL>
<LANGUAGE SQL>
<<NO> EXTERNAL ACTION>
[SQLStatements]
```

where:

ProcedureName   Identifies the name that is to be assigned to the procedure to be created.

ParamType   Indicates whether the parameter identified by *ParamName* is an input parameter (IN), an output parameter (OUT), or both an input and an output parameter (INOUT).

ParamName   Identifies the name to be assigned to a procedure parameter.

DataType Identifies the type of data the procedure expects to receive or send for the parameter identified by *ParamName*.

SpecificName Identifies the specific name to be assigned to the procedure. This name can be used later to comment on the procedure or drop the procedure; however, it cannot be used to invoke the procedure.

NumResultSets Specifies whether the procedure being created will return one or more result data sets and if so, how many. (The default value is 0.)

SQLStatement Specifies an SQL statement or a compound SQL statement (i.e., two or more SQL statements enclosed with the keywords BEGIN ATOMIC and END and terminated with a semicolon) that is to be executed when the procedure is invoked.

• •

When a specific name is assigned to a procedure, the procedure can be dropped by referencing the specific name in a special form of the DROP SQL statement (DROP SPECIFIC PROCEDURE [SpecificName]). However, if no specific name is assigned to a procedure, both the procedure name and the procedure's signature (a list of the data types used by each of the procedure's parameters) must be provided as input to the DROP PROCEDURE statement.

• •

Thus, a simple SQL stored procedure could be created by executing a CREATE PROCEDURE statement that looks something like this:

```
CREATE PROCEDURE get_sales
    (IN quota INTEGER, OUT retcode CHAR(5))
    DYNAMIC RESULT SETS 1
    LANGUAGE SQL
    BEGIN
        DECLARE sqlstate CHAR(5);
        DECLARE sales_results CURSOR WITH RETURN FOR
            SELECT sales_person, SUM(sales) AS total_sales
            FROM sales
            GROUP BY sales_person
            HAVING SUM(sales) > quota;
        DECLARE EXIT HANDLER FOR SQLEXCEPTION
            SET retcode = sqlstate;
        OPEN sales_results;
        SET retcode = sqlstate;
    END
```

The resulting SQL stored procedure, called GET_SALES, accepts an integer input value (in an input parameter called QUOTA) and returns a character value (in an output parameter called RETCODE) that reports the procedure's success or failure. The procedure body consists of a compound SQL statement that returns a result data set (i.e., an open cursor) containing the name and total sales figures for each salesperson whose total sales exceed the quota specified. This is done by:

1. Indicating the SQL procedure is to return a result data set by specifying the DYNAMIC RESULT SETS clause of the CREATE PROCEDURE statement and assigning it the value 1.

2. Declaring a cursor within the procedure body (using the WITH RETURN FOR clause) for the result data set that is to be returned. (A cursor is a named control structure that points to a specific row within a result data set and is used to retrieve values for each row in the set.)

3. Opening the cursor (which produces the result data set that is to be returned).

4. Leaving the cursor open when the SQL procedure ends.

It is important to note that when an SQL stored procedure is used to implement a business rule, the logic used to apply that business rule can be incorporated into any application simply by invoking the stored procedure. Thus, the same business rule logic is guaranteed to be enforced across all applications. When business rules change, only the logic in the SQL stored procedure needs to be changed; applications that call the procedure do not have to be modified. (The same can be said for external stored procedures, but the steps required to change the business logic coded in an external stored procedure are a little more complex.)

External stored procedures

An external stored procedure is a stored procedure that is written using a high-level programming language such as C, C++, Java, or COBOL. Whereas SQL procedures offer rapid application development and considerable flexibility, external stored procedures can be much more powerful than SQL stored procedures because they can take advantage of system calls and administrative APIs, as well as execute SQL statements. However, this increase in functionality makes them more difficult to create; to create any external procedure, the following steps must be performed:

1. Construct the body of the procedure, using a supported high-level programming language.

2. Compile the procedure.

3. Link the procedure to create a library (or dynamic-link library).

4. Debug the procedure and repeat steps 2 through 4 until all problems have been resolved.

5. Physically store the library containing the procedure on the database server. By default, the DB2 Database Manager looks for external user-defined functions in the *.../sqllib/function* and *.../sqllib/function/unfenced* subdirectories *(...\sqllib\function* and *...\sqllib\function\unfenced* subdirectories on Windows). Additionally, the system permissions for the library file containing the procedure must be modified so that all users can execute it. For example, in a UNIX environment, the chmod command is used to make a file executable; in a Windows environment, the attrib command is used for the same purpose.

6. Register the procedure with a DB2 database using the appropriate form of the CREATE PROCEDURE SQL statement.

The basic syntax for the form of the CREATE PROCEDURE statement that is used to register an external stored procedure (once it has been created as outlined above) looks something like this:

```
CREATE PROCEDURE [ProcedureName]
( [ParamType] [ParamName] [DataType], ...)
<SPECIFIC [SpecificName]>
<DYNAMIC RESULT SETS [NumResultSets]>
<NO SQL | CONTAINS SQL | READS SQL DATA | MODIFIES SQL DATA >
<DETERMINISTIC | NOT DETERMINISTIC>
<CALLED ON NULL INPUT>
<[OLD | NEW] SAVEPOINT LEVEL>
LANGUAGE [C | JAVA | COBOL | CLR | OLE]
EXTERNAL <NAME [ExternalName] | [Identifier]>
<FENCED <THREADSAFE | NOT THREADSAFE> | NOT FENCED <THREADSAFE>>
PARAMETER STYLE [DB2GENERAL | DB2SQL | GENERAL |
    GENERAL WITH NULLS | JAVA | SQL]
<PROGRAM TYPE [SUB | MAIN]>
<DBINFO | NO DBINFO>
```

where:

ProcedureName   Identifies the name to be assigned to the procedure to be registered.

ParamType   Indicates whether the parameter identified by *ParamName* is an input parameter (IN), an output parameter (OUT), or both an input parameter and an output parameter (INOUT).

ParamName   Identifies the name to be assigned to a procedure parameter.

DataType   Identifies the type of data the procedure expects to receive or send for the parameter identified by *ParamName*.

SpecificName   Identifies the specific name to be assigned to the procedure. This name can be used later to comment on or drop the procedure; however, it cannot be used to invoke the procedure.

NumResultSets   Specifies whether the procedure being registered will return one or more result data sets and if so, how many. (The default value is 0.)

SQLStatements   Specifies one or more SQL statements that are to be executed when the procedure is invoked. These statements make up the body of the procedure.

ExternalName   Identifies the name of the library, along with the name of the function in the library, that contains the executable code for the procedure being registered.

Identifier   Identifies the name of the library that contains the executable code of the procedure being registered, but only if the procedure was written using C or C++. The DB2 Database Manager will look for a function that has the same name as the library name specified.

Many of the clauses used with this form of the CREATE PROCEDURE SQL statement are similar to those used by the form of the CREATE PROCEDURE SQL statement that is used to create an SQL procedure; others are new. The meaning of these clauses are as follows:

<NO SQL | CONTAINS SQL | READS SQL DATA | MODIFIES SQL DATA>:This clause is used to identify which types of SQL statements have been coded in the body of the external stored procedure. Four different values are available:

NO SQL. The body of the stored procedure either does not contain any SQL or contains only nonexecutable SQL statements. (Examples of nonexecutable SQL statements are the INCLUDE and WHENEVER statements.)

CONTAINS SQL. The body of the stored procedure contains executable SQL statements that neither read nor modify data.

READS SQL DATA. The body of the stored procedure contains executable SQL statements that read but do not modify data.

MODIFIES SQL DATA. The body of the stored procedure contains executable SQL statements that both read and modify data.

<DETERMINISTIC | NOT DETERMINISTIC>: This clause is used to identify whether the procedure will always return the same results when passed the same parameter values (DETERMINISTIC) or not (NOT DETERMINISTIC). (A stored procedure that applies a 15% increase to any value passed to it would be considered DETERMINISTIC, whereas a stored procedure that generates a unique ID using the TIMESTAMP_ISO() function would be considered NOT DETERMINISTIC.)

<CALLED ON NULL INPUT>: When this clause is used, the stored procedure will always be invoked, even if a null value is passed for one or more of its input parameters.

<[OLD | NEW] SAVEPOINT LEVEL>: This clause is used to indicate whether or not the procedure is to establish a new "save point" within the transaction that invoked it. (Savepoints are used to shorten rollback recovery windows.)

EXTERNAL <NAME [*ExternalName*] | [*Identifier*]>: This clause is used to identify two things: the name of the library and, optionally, the name of the function within the library that contains the executable code for the procedure being registered. The high-level programming language used to construct the body of any external stored procedure determines how these names are provided. For example, if an external stored procedure is developed using the C or C++ programming language, the names of the library and function within the library that contains the body of the function can be specified in four different ways:

- ' LibraryName '
- ' LibraryName ! FunctionName '
- ' AbsolutePath '
- ' AbsolutePath ! FunctionName '

If a library name is provided instead of an absolute path, the DB2 Database Manager will look in the *.../sqllib/function* and *.../sqllib/function/unfenced* subdirectories (*...\sqllib\function* and *...\sqllib\function\unfenced* subdirectories on Windows) for the library name specified. On the other hand, if an absolute path is provided, the name of the library must be appended to the path, and the DB2 Database Manager will look in the location specified for the appropriate library. (If neither a library name nor an absolute path is provided, the DB2 Database Manager will look in the default subdirectories shown earlier for a library and function that have the same name as the name that is to be assigned to the user-defined function being registered.) If a function name is provided, the DB2 Database Manager will look for a function that has the name specified within the library specified; if no function name is provided, the DB2 Database Manager will look for a function that has the same name as the library name specified.

<FENCED | NOT FENCED>: This clause is used to identify whether the external stored procedure is considered "safe" enough to be run in the DB2 Database Manager operating environment's process/address space (NOT FENCED), or not (FENCED). If the FENCED clause is specified (or if neither clause is specified), the DB2 Database Manager will not allow the procedure to access its internal resources.

PARAMETER STYLE [DB2GENERAL | DB2SQL | GENERAL | GENERAL WITH NULLS | JAVA | SQL]>: This clause is used to identify the parameter-passing style that the procedure expects the calling application to use when passing values to it. As you can see, there are six parameter-passing styles available:

DB2GENERAL. Values are passed and returned using the calling conventions that are used to call a method in a Java class. (This style can only be used when the procedure is written using Java.)

DB2SQL. Values are passed and returned using calling conventions that are defined in the SQL/Persistent Stored Modules ISO working draft; along with the arguments identified, the following are passed to the procedure when it is called: a null indicator for each parameter passed, a placeholder for the SQLSTATE to be returned in, the qualified name of the procedure, the specific name of the procedure, and a placeholder for the SQL diagnostic string to be returned in. (This style can only be used when the procedure is written using C/C++, COBOL, or OLE.)

GENERAL. Values are passed and returned exactly as they are specified when the procedure is invoked. (This style can only be used when the procedure is written using C/C++ or COBOL.)

GENERAL WITH NULLS. Same as GENERAL, with one major difference— an additional argument containing a vector of null indicators is also passed to and returned from the procedure. (This style can only be used when the procedure is written using C/C++ or COBOL.)

JAVA. Values are passed and returned using calling conventions that conform to the Java language and SQLJ specifications. (This style can only be used when the procedure is written using Java.)

SQL. Same as DB2SQL.

<PROGRAM TYPE [SUB | MAIN]>: This clause is used to identify whether the procedure was defined as a main routine (MAIN) or as a subroutine (SUB). If the PROGRAM TYPE SUB clause is specified, the DB2 Database Manager will pass all parameter values to the stored procedure as separate arguments. In this case, the stored procedure can be assigned any name that conforms to the function-naming conventions allowed by the high-level programming language used. On the other hand, if the PROGRAM TYPE MAIN clause is specified, the DB2 Database Manager will pass all parameter values to the stored procedure as a combination of an argument counter and an array of argument values. In this case, the DB2 Database Manager expects the name of the stored procedure to be "main."

<DBINFO | NO DBINFO>: This clause is used to identify whether information known by DB2 is to be passed to the stored procedure as an additional argument when it is invoked (DBINFO) or not (NO DBINFO). If the DB2INFO clause is used, the DB2 Database Manager will pass a data structure that contains the following information to the stored procedure at the time it is invoked:

- The name of the currently connected database

- The unique application ID that is established for each connection to the database

- The application run-time authorization ID

- The database code page

- The version, release, and modification level of the database server invoking the stored procedure

- The operating system being used by the server

Thus, if you wanted to register an external stored procedure named EXTRACT_RESUME that is stored as a function (written in C) named ExResume in a library named *SProc* that resides in the directory *C:\StoredProcs*, you could do so by executing a CREATE PROCEDURE SQL statement that looks something like this:

```
EXEC SQL CREATE PROCEDURE extract_resume
    (IN filename  VARCHAR(255),
     IN empno     CHAR(6))
SPECIFIC extract_resume
DYNAMIC RESULT SETS 0
EXTERNAL NAME 'C:\StoredProcs\SProc!ExResume'
LANGUAGE C
PARAMETER STYLE GENERAL
DETERMINISTIC
FENCED
CALLED ON NULL INPUT
PROGRAM TYPE SUB;
```

When this particular CREATE PROCEDURE SQL statement is executed, an external stored procedure will be registered that:

- Has been assigned the name EXTRACT_RESUME

- Has one input parameter called FILENAME that expects a VARCHAR(255) data value and another input parameter called EMPNO that expects a CHAR(6) data value

- Has been assigned the specific name EXTRACT_RESUME

- Does not return a result data set

- Was constructed using the C or C++ programming language

- Expects calling applications to use the GENERAL style when passing parameters

- Will always return the same results if called with the same parameter values

- Is to be run outside the DB2 Database Manager operating environment's address space

- Is to be called, even if a null value has been provided for one of its parameters

- Was written as a subroutine

Packages

A package is an object that contains the information needed to process SQL statements associated with a source code file of an application program. High-level programming language compilers do not recognize, and therefore cannot interpret, SQL statements. Therefore, when SQL statements are embedded in a high-level programming language source code file, they must be converted to source code that a high-level programming language compiler can understand; this conversion process is performed by a tool known as the *SQL precompiler.* (An SQL precompiler is included with the DB2 Software Development Kit and is normally invoked from the Command Line Processor or a batch/make utility file.)

During the precompile process, a source code file containing embedded SQL statements is converted into a source code file that is made up entirely of high-level programming language statements. At the same time, a corresponding package that contains, among other things, the access plans that will be used to process each SQL statement embedded in the source code file is also produced. (Access plans contain optimized information that the DB2 Database Manager uses to execute SQL statements.) This package must reside in a DB2 database that contains the data objects referenced by the package before the corresponding application can be executed against that database.

The process of creating and storing a package in a DB2 database is known as *binding*, and by default, packages are automatically bound to a database during the precompile process. However, by specifying the appropriate precompiler options, you can elect to store the steps needed to create a package in a file and complete the binding process at a later point in time, using a tool known as the *SQL Binder* (or simply the Binder). This approach is known as *deferred binding*.

Deleting Database (Data) Objects

Just as it is important to be able to create and modify objects, it is important to be able to delete existing objects when they are no longer needed. Most existing objects can be removed from a database by executing some form of the DROP SQL statement. The basic syntax for this statement is:

```
DROP [ObjectType] [ObjectName]
```

where:

ObjectType   Identifies the type of object that is to be deleted (dropped).

ObjectName   Identifies the name that has been assigned to the object that is to be deleted.

Thus, if you wanted to delete a table that has been assigned the name SALES and resides in a schema named CORP, you could do so by executing a DROP SQL statement that looks something like this:

```
DROP TABLE corp.salses
```

Database objects can also be dropped from the Control Center by highlighting the appropriate object and selecting the appropriate action from any object menu found. Figure 4–27 shows the Control Center menu items that must be selected in order to drop a particular object (in this case, a table).

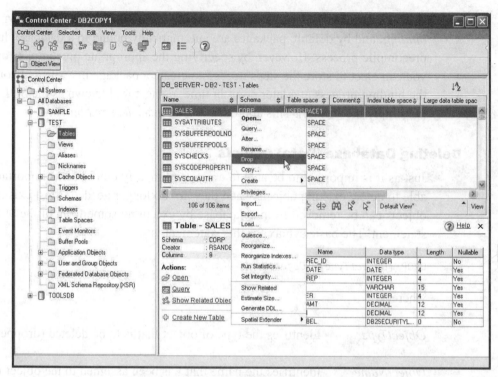

Figure 4–27: Dropping a table from the Control Center.

It is important to keep in mind that when an object is dropped, its removal may affect other objects that depend upon its existence. In some cases, when an object is dropped, all objects dependent upon that object are dropped as well (for example, if a table space containing one or more tables is dropped, all tables that resided in that table space, along with their corresponding data, are also dropped). In other cases, an object cannot be dropped if other objects are dependent upon its existence (for example, a schema can only be dropped after all objects in that schema have been dropped). And it goes without saying that built-in objects, such as system catalog tables and views, cannot be dropped.

> The rules that govern how objects can be dropped as well as the rules that determine how dependent objects are affected when an object is dropped can be found in the IBM DB2 SQL Reference, Volume 2 product documentation.

Practice Questions

Question 1

While attempting to connect to a database stored on an iSeries server from a Windows client, the following message was displayed:

SQL1013N The database alias name or database name "TEST_DB" could not be found.

Which of the following actions can be used to help determine why this message was displayed?

○ A. Execute the LIST REMOTE DATABASES command on the server; look for an entry for the TEST_DB database

○ B. Execute the LIST DCS DIRECTORY command on the server; look for an entry for the TEST_DB database

○ C. Execute the LIST REMOTE DATABASES command on the client; look for an entry for the TEST_DB database

○ D. Execute the LIST DCS DIRECTORY command on the client; look for an entry for the TEST_DB database

Question 2

A database named TEST_DB resides on a z/OS system and listens on port 446. The TCP/IP address for this system is 192.168.10.20 and the TCP/IP host name is MYHOST. Which of the following commands is required to make this database accessible to a Linux client?

○ A. CATALOG TCPIP NODE zos_srvr REMOTE myhost SERVER 192.168.10.20; CATALOG DATABASE zos_db AS test_db AT NODE zos_srvr; CATALOG DCS DATABASE zos_db AS test_db;

○ B. CATALOG TCPIP NODE zos_srvr REMOTE myhost SERVER 192.168.10.20; CATALOG DCS DATABASE zos_db AS test_db AT NODE zos_srvr;

○ C. CATALOG TCPIP NODE zos_srvr REMOTE myhost SERVER 446; CATALOG DCS DATABASE zos_db AS test_db AT NODE zos_srvr;

○ D. CATALOG TCPIP NODE zos_srvr REMOTE myhost SERVER 446; CATALOG DATABASE zos_db AS test_db AT NODE zos_srvr; CATALOG DCS DATABASE zos_db AS test_db;

Question 3

In which of the following scenarios would a stored procedure be beneficial?

○ A. An application running on a remote client needs to be able to convert degrees Celsius to degrees Fahrenheit and vice versa

○ B. An application running on a remote client needs to collect three input values, perform a calculation using the values provided, and store the input data, along with the results of the calculation in two different base tables

○ C. An application running on a remote client needs to track every modification made to a table that contains sensitive data

○ D. An application running on a remote client needs to ensure that every new employee that joins the company is assigned a unique, sequential employee number

Question 4

If the following SQL statements are executed in the order shown:

```
CREATE TABLE orders
    (order_num    INTEGER NOT NULL,
     Buyer_name   VARCHAR(35),
     Amount       NUMERIC(5,2));

CREATE UNIQUE INDEX idx_orderno ON orders(order_num);
```

Which of the following describes the resulting behavior?

○ A. Every ORDER_NUM value entered must be unique; whenever the ORDERS table is queried rows should be displayed in order of increasing ORDER_NUM values

○ B. Every ORDER_NUM value entered must be unique; whenever the ORDERS table is queried rows will be displayed in no particular order

○ C. Duplicate ORDER_NUM values are allowed; no other index can be created for the ORDERS table that reference the ORDER_NUM column

○ D. Every ORDER_NUM value entered must be unique; no other index can be created for the ORDERS table that reference the ORDER_NUM column

Question 5

An alias can be an alternate name for which two of the following DB2 objects?

❑ A. Sequence

❑ B. Trigger

❑ C. View

❑ D. Schema

❑ E. Table

Question 6

Which of the following DB2 objects can be referenced by an INSERT statement to generate values for a column?

○ A. Sequence

○ B. Identity column

○ C. Trigger

○ D. Table function

Question 7

Which of the following is NOT an attribute of Declared Global Temporary Tables (DGTTs)?

○ A. Each application that defines a DGTT has its own instance of the DGTT

○ B. Two different applications cannot create DGTTs that have the same name

○ C. DGTTs can only be used by the application that creates them, and only for the life of the application

○ D. Data stored in a DGTT can exist across transaction boundaries

Question 8

Which of the following is an accurate statement about packages?

○ A. Packages provide a logical grouping of database objects.

○ B. Packages contain control structures that are considered the bound form for SQL statements

○ C. Packages describe the objects in a DB2 database and their relationship to each other

○ D. Packages may be used during query optimization to improve the performance for a subset of SELECT queries

Question 9

Which of the following events will NOT cause a trigger to be activated?

○ A. A select operation

○ B. An insert operation

○ C. An update operation

○ D. A delete operation

Question 10

Which of the following DB2 objects is NOT considered executable using SQL?

○ A. Routine

○ B. Function

○ C. Procedure

○ D. Trigger

Question 11

Which of the following is NOT an accurate statement about views?

○ A. Views are publicly referenced names and no special authority or privilege is needed to use them.

○ B. Views can be used to restrict access to columns in a base table that contain sensitive data

○ C. Views can be used to store queries that multiple applications execute on a regular basis in a database

○ D. Views support INSTEAD OF triggers

Question 12

Which of the following SQL statements can be used to create a DB2 object to store numerical data as EURO data?

○ A. CREATE NICKNAME euro FOR DECIMAL (9,3)

○ B. CREATE ALIAS euro FOR DECIMAL (9,3)

○ C. CREATE DISTINCT TYPE euro AS DECIMAL (9,3)

○ D. CREATE DATA TYPE euro AS DECIMAL (9,3)

Question 13

A sequence was created with the DDL statement shown below:

```
CREATE SEQUENCE my_seq START WITH 10 INCREMENT BY 10 CACHE 10
```

User USER1 successfully executes the following statements in the order shown:

```
VALUES NEXT VALUE FOR my_seq INTO :hvar;
VALUES NEXT VALUE FOR my_seq INTO :hvar;
```

User USER2 successfully executes the following statements in the order shown:

```
ALTER SEQUENCE my_seq RESTART WITH 5 INCREMENT BY 5 CACHE 5;
VALUES NEXT VALUE FOR my_seq INTO :hvar;
```

After users USER1 and USER2 are finished, user USER3 executes the following query:

```
SELECT NEXT VALUE FOR my_seq FROM sysibm.sysdummy1
```

What value will be returned by the query?

○ A. 5

○ B. 10

○ C. 20

○ D. 30

Question 14

Given the following statements:

```
CREATE TABLE tab1 (c1 INTEGER, c2 CHAR(5));
CREATE VIEW view1 AS SELECT c1, c2 FROM tab1 WHERE c1 < 100;
CREATE VIEW view2 AS SELECT c1, c2 FROM view1
        WITH CASCADED CHECK OPTION;
```

Which of the following INSERT statements will fail to execute?

- ○ A. INSERT INTO view2 VALUES(50, 'abc')
- ○ B. INSERT INTO view1 VALUES (100, 'abc')
- ○ C. INSERT INTO view2 VALUES(150, 'abc')
- ○ D. INSERT INTO view1 VALUES(100, 'abc')

Question 15

Given the following statements:

```
CREATE TABLE t1 (c1 INTEGER, c2 CHAR(5));
CREATE TABLE t1audit (user VARCHAR(20), date DATE,
            action VARCHAR(20));

CREATE TRIGGER trig1 AFTER INSERT ON t1
    FOR EACH ROW
    MODE DB2SQL
    INSERT INTO t1audit VALUES (CURRENT USER, CURRENT DATE,
        'Insert');
```

If user USER1 executes the following statements:

```
INSERT INTO t1 VALUES (1, 'abc');
INSERT INTO t1 (c1) VALUES (2);
UPDATE t1 SET c2 = 'ghi' WHERE c1 = 1;
```

How many new records will be written to the database?

- ○ A. 0
- ○ B. 2
- ○ C. 3
- ○ D. 4

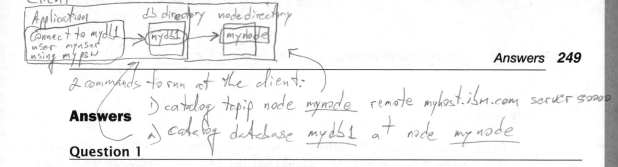

Handwritten annotations at top of page:

Client
Application
Connect to mydb1
user myuser
using mypsw

db directory → mydb1
node directory → mynode

2 commands to run at the client:
1) catalog tcpip node mynode remote myhost.ibm.com server 50000
2) catalog database mydb1 at node mynode

Answers

Question 1

The correct answer is **D**. In order to access a remote database from a client workstation, the database must be cataloged in the system database directory of both the client and the server *and* the server workstation must be cataloged in the client's node directory. (The entry in the node directory tells the DB2 Database Manager how to connect to the server to get access to the database stored there.) Because the information needed to connect to DRDA host databases is different from the information used to connect to LAN-based databases, information about remote host or iSeries databases is kept in a special directory known as the Database Connection Services (DCS) directory. If an entry in the DCS directory has a database name that corresponds to the name of a database stored in the system database directory, the specified Application Requester (which in most cases is DB2 Connect) can forward SQL requests to the database that resides on a remote DRDA server. The contents of the DCS directory file can be viewed by executing the `LIST DCS DIRECTORY` command. If there is no record for a zSeries or iSeries database in the DCS directory, no database connection can be established.

Question 2

The correct answer is **D**. In order to access a remote database on a z/OS server, the database must be cataloged in the system database directory of the client, the server must be cataloged in the client's node directory, and an entry for the database must exist in the DCS directory. Answer D illustrates the proper way to catalog the server, the DCS database, and create a corresponding entry for the DCS database in the system database directory.

Question 3

The correct answer is **B**. A scalar user-defined function would be the best option for the requirements outlined in answer A; an `UPDATE` trigger and a `DELETE` trigger that inserts records into an activity table every time update and delete operations are performed on a table containing sensitive data would be the best way to accomplish the requirements outlined in answer C; and an identity column or sequence could be used to address the requirements shown in answer D.

Question 4

The correct answer is **A**. If the UNIQUE clause is specified when the CREATE INDEX statement is executed, rows in the table associated with the index will not have two or more occurrences of the same values in the set of columns that make up the index key. Furthermore, the creation of an index provides a logical ordering of the rows of a table so in this example, rows inserted into the ORDERS table will be ordered ORDER_NUM values, in ascending order.

Question 5

The correct answers are **C** and **E**. An alias is simply an alternate name for a table or view. (Aliases can also be created for nicknames that refer to tables or views found on federated systems.) Once created, an alias can be referenced the same way the table or view the alias refers to can be referenced.

Question 6

The correct answer is **A**. Sequences, identity columns, and triggers can be used to automatically generate values for columns. However, only sequences can be referenced in an INSERT statement.

Question 7

The correct answer is **B**. Unlike base tables, whose descriptions and constraints are stored in the system catalog tables of the database to which they belong, declared temporary tables are not persistent and can only be used by the application that creates them—and only for the life of the application. When the application that creates a declared temporary table terminates, the rows of the table are deleted, and the description of the table is dropped. (However, data stored in a temporary table can exist across transaction boundaries.) Another significant difference focuses on naming conventions: base table names must be unique within a schema, but because each application that defines a declared temporary table has its own instance of that table, it is possible for many applications to create declared temporary tables that have the same name.

Question 8

The correct answer is **B**. A package is an object that contains the information needed to process SQL statements associated with a source code file of an application program. When an Embedded SQL source code file is precompiled, a corresponding package that contains, among other things, the access plans that will be used to process each SQL statement embedded in the source code file is produced. (Access plans contain optimized information that the DB2 Database Manager uses to execute SQL statements.) This package must reside in a DB2 database that contains the data objects referenced by the package before the corresponding application can be executed against that database. The process of creating and storing a package in a DB2 database is known as "binding," and by default, packages are automatically bound to a database during the precompile process.

Schemas provide a logical grouping of database objects; the system catalog describes the objects in a DB2 database and their relationship to each other; and Multi-dimensional Clustering Tables (MDCs) may be used during query optimization to improve the performance for a subset of SELECT queries.

Question 9

The correct answer is **A**. A trigger can be activated whenever an insert, update, or delete operation is performed against the subject table that is associated with the trigger.

Question 10

The correct answer is **D**. Routines are a type of database object that you can use to encapsulate logic that can be invoked like a programming sub-routine. There are many different types of routines available; routines can be grouped in different ways, but are primarily grouped by their system or user definitions, by their functionality, and by their implementation. The supported routine definitions are:

- System-defined routines
- User-defined routines

The supported functional types of routines are:

- Procedures (also called stored procedures)
- Functions
- Methods

The supported routine implementations are:

- Built-in routines
- Sourced routines
- SQL routines
- External routines

Question 11

The correct answer is **A**. Views can be used to restrict access to columns in a base table that contain sensitive data, views can be used to store queries that multiple applications execute on a regular basis in a database, and views support INSTEAD OF triggers. Aliases are publicly referenced names that require no special authority or privilege to use.

Question 12

The correct answer is **C**. A distinct data type is a user-defined data type that is derived from one of the built-in data types available with DB2. Although a distinct data type shares a common internal representation with a built-in data type, it is considered a separate data type that is distinct from any other data type (hence, the "distinct" in the name). Distinct user-defined data types can be created by executing the CREATE DISTINCT TYPE SQL statement. The basic syntax for this statement is:

```
CREATE DISTINCT TYPE [TypeName]
AS [SourceDataType]
<WITH COMPARISONS>
```

where:

TypeName   Identifies the name that is to be assigned to the distinct data type to be created.

SourceDataType Identifies the built-in data type that the distinct data type to be created is to be based on.

Thus, if you wanted to create a distinct data type to store EURO data, you could do so by executing an SQL statement like that in answer C.

Question 13

The correct answer is **D**. The first VALUES statement executed by user USER1 will return the value 10; the second will return the value 20. The ALTER statement changes the behavior of the sequence and the VALUES statement executed by user USER2 will return the value 5. When user USER3 executes queries the database to obtain the next sequence number, the value 30 is returned. Why? Because when user USER2 obtained a value from the sequence, four more values were generated and cached since a cache value of 5 was specified for the sequence.

Since an increment value of 5 was also used, the numbers cached were: 10, 15, 20, and 25. But none of the cached values were used – they were discarded when user USER2 terminated their database connection. Then, when user USER3 queries the sequence for the next number available, it received the number 30 because that was, in fact, the next number in the sequence.

Question 14

The correct answer is **C**. The statement "INSERT INTO view2 VALUES(150, 'abc')" will fail because the value 150 is greater than 100; because view VIEW2 was created with the WITH CASCADED CHECK OPTION specified, the "WHERE c1 < 100" clause used to create view VIEW1 became a constraint that is used to validate insert and update operations that are performed against view VIEW2 to ensure that all rows inserted into or updated in the base table the view refers to conform to the view's definition.

Question 15

The correct answer is **D**. Each time a record is inserted into table T1, trigger TRIG1 is fired and a record is written to the table T1AUDIT. If both tables were queried after the update operation completes, the results would look something like this:

```
SELECT * FROM t1

C1            C2
--------------
1             ghi
2             -
   2 record(s) selected.

SELECT * FROM t1audit

USER            DATE            ACTION
----------------------------------------
RSANDERS        01/20/2007      Insert
RSANDERS        01/20/2007      Insert
   2 record(s) selected.
```

In order to track update and delete operations performed against table T1, similar UPDATE and DELETE triggers would need to be created.

CHAPTER 5

Working with DB2 Data Using SQL and XQuery

Twenty-three and one-half percent (23.5%) of the DB2 9 Fundamentals certification exam (Exam 730) is designed to test your knowledge of the various Structured Query Language (SQL) statements and XQuery expressions that are commonly used to manipulate and retrieve data. The questions that make up this portion of the exam are intended to evaluate the following:

- Your ability to identify the Data Manipulation Language (DML) statements available with DB2

- Your ability to perform insert, update, and delete operations against a database

- Your ability to retrieve and format data using various forms of the SELECT statement

- Your ability to sort and group data retrieved by a query

- Your knowledge of what transactions are, as well as how transactions are initiated and terminated

- Your ability to invoke a user-defined function and call a stored procedure

- Your ability to access Extensible Markup Language (XML) data using XQuery expressions and the SQL/XML functions available with DB2

This chapter is designed to introduce you to the SQL statements and XQuery expressions that you need to be familiar with in order to access and manipulate data. In this chapter you will also learn what transactions are and how to terminate a transaction in such a way that all operations performed within that transaction are either applied to the database and made permanent (committed) or backed out (rolled back).

Structured Query Language (SQL)

Structured Query Language (SQL) is a standardized language used to work with database objects and the data they contain. Using SQL, you can define, alter, and delete database objects, as well as insert, update, delete, and retrieve data values stored in database tables. One of the strengths of SQL is that it can be used in a variety of ways: SQL statements can be executed interactively using tools such as the Command Editor and the Command Line Processor, they can be placed directly in UNIX shell scripts or Windows batch files, and they can be embedded in high-level programming language source code files. (Because SQL is nonprocedural by design, it is not an actual programming language; therefore, most embedded SQL applications are built by combining the decision and sequence control of a high-level programming language with the data storage, manipulation, and retrieval capabilities of SQL.)

Like most other languages, SQL has a defined syntax and a set of language elements. Most SQL statements can be categorized according to the function they have been designed to perform; SQL statements typically fall under one of the following categories:

Embedded SQL Application Construct Statements are SQL statements used for the sole purpose of constructing embedded SQL applications.

Data Control Language (DCL) Statements are SQL statements used to grant and revoke authorities and privileges.

Data Definition Language (DDL) Statements are SQL statements used to create, alter, and delete database objects.

Data Manipulation Language (DML) Statements are SQL statements used to store data in, manipulate data in, retrieve data from, and remove data from select database objects.

Transaction Management Statements are SQL statements used to establish and terminate database connections and active transactions.

In Chapter 3, "Security," we examined the DCL statements available when we looked at the GRANT and REVOKE statements. In Chapter 4, "Working with Databases and Database Objects," we encountered several DDL statements as we explored the various database objects to be had and examined how they are created and destroyed. In this chapter, we'll start out by examining the DML statements that are available; then we'll turn our attention to transactions and to the SQL statements that are designed to support them. You do not have to be familiar with the Embedded SQL Application Construct Statements to pass the DB2 9 Fundamentals certification exam (Exam 730), so they are not covered.

> Although basic syntax is presented for most of the SQL statements covered in this chapter, the actual syntax supported may be much more complex. To view the complete syntax for a specific SQL statement or to obtain more information about a particular statement, refer to the IBM DB2 SQL Reference, Volume 1 and IBM DB2 SQL Reference, Volume 2 product documentation.

SQL Data Manipulation Language (DML) Statements

In Chapter 4, "Working with Databases and Database Objects," we looked at several of the database objects that are available with DB2 and we saw two ways in which each object can be created. After one or more table objects have been defined, the next step toward creating a functioning database is to populate those table objects with data. And once a table is populated, at some point, its data may need to be retrieved, modified, or removed. That's where the Data Manipulation Language (DML) statements come in. DML statements are used exclusively to store data in, manipulate data in, retrieve data from, and remove data from tables and updatable views. There are four Data Manipulation Language statements available: the INSERT statement, the UPDATE statement, the DELETE statement, and the SELECT statement. We'll take a close look at each of these statements in the following sections.

The INSERT Statement

When a table is first created, it is nothing more than a definition of how a set of data values are to be stored; there is no data associated with it. But after it has been created, a table can be populated in a variety of ways. It can be bulk-loaded using the DB2 Load utility, it can be bulk-loaded using the DB2 Import utility, or rows can be added to it, one at a time, by executing the INSERT SQL statement. Of the three, the INSERT statement is the method that is used the most. Moreover, the INSERT statement can work directly with the table to be populated, or it can work with an updatable view that references the table to be populated. The basic syntax for the INSERT statement is:

```
INSERT INTO [TableName | ViewName]
< ( [ColumnName], ... ) >
VALUES ( [Value], ...)
```

or

```
INSERT INTO [TableName | ViewName]
< ( [ColumnName], ... ) >
[SELECTStatement]
```

where:

TableName   Identifies the name assigned to the table to which data is to be added.

ViewName   Identifies the name assigned to the updatable view to which data is to be added.

ColumnName   Identifies the name of one or more columns in the table or updatable view to which data values are to be assigned. Each name provided must identify an existing column in the table or updatable view specified.

Value   Identifies one or more data values that are to be added to the column(s) in the table or updatable view specified.

SELECTStatement   Identifies a SELECT SQL statement that, when executed, will produce the data values to be added to the column(s) in the table or updatable view specified (by retrieving data from other tables and/or views).

Thus, suppose you wanted to add a record to a base table named DEPARTMENT that has the following characteristics:

Column Name	Data Type
DEPTNO	INTEGER
DEPTNAME	CHAR(20)
MGRID	INTEGER

You could do so by executing an INSERT statement that looks something like this:

```
INSERT INTO department (deptno, deptname, mgrid)
   VALUES (1, 'SALES', 1001)
```

It is important to note that the number of values provided in the VALUES clause must be equal to the number of column names provided in the column name list. Furthermore, the values provided will be assigned to the columns specified based upon the order in which they appear—in other words, the first value provided will be assigned to the first column identified in the column name list, the second value provided will be assigned to the second column identified, and so on. Finally, each value provided must be compatible with the data type of the column to which the value is to be assigned.

If values are provided with the VALUES clause for every column found in the table, the column name list can be omitted. In this case, the first value provided will be assigned to the first column found in the table, the second value provided will be assigned to the second column found, and so on. Thus, the row of data that was added to the DEPARTMENT table in the previous example could just as well have been added by executing the following INSERT statement:

```
INSERT INTO department VALUES (1, 'SALES', 1001)
```

Along with literal values, two special tokens can be used to designate values that are to be assigned to base table columns. The first of these is the DEFAULT token, which is used to assign a system or user-supplied default value to an identity column or a column defined with the WITH DEFAULT constraint. The second is the NULL token, which is used to assign a NULL value to any column that was not defined with the NOT NULL constraint. (Identity columns, the WITH DEFAULT constraint, and the NOT NULL constraint are covered in detail in Chapter 6, "Working with DB2 Tables, Views, and Indexes.") Thus, you could add a record that contains a NULL value for the MGRID column to the DEPARTMENT table we looked at earlier by executing an INSERT statement that looks something like this:

```
INSERT INTO department VALUES (001, 'SALES', NULL)
```

By using a different form of the INSERT SQL statement, the results of a query can also be used to provide values for one or more columns in a base table. With this form of the INSERT statement, a SELECT statement (known as a *subselect*) is provided in place of the VALUES clause (we'll look at the SELECT statement shortly), and the results of the subselect are assigned to the appropriate columns. This form of the INSERT statement creates a type of "cut and paste" action in which values are retrieved from one base table or view and copied into another. As you might imagine, the number of values returned by the subselect must match the number of columns provided in the column name list (or the number of columns found in the table if no column name list is provided), and the order of assignment is the same as that used when literal values are provided in a VALUES clause. Thus, you could add a record to the DEPARTMENT table we looked at earlier, using the results of a query, by executing an INSERT statement that looks something like this:

```
INSERT INTO department (deptno, deptname)
SELECT deptno, deptname FROM sales_depts
```

You may have noticed that the INSERT statement used in the previous example did not provide values for every column found in the DEPARTMENT table. Just as there are times you may want to insert complete records into a table, there may be times when you only want to insert partial records into a table. Such operations can be performed by listing just the columns you have data values for in the column names list and providing corresponding values using either the VALUES clause or a subselect. However, in order for such an INSERT statement to execute correctly, all columns in the table the record is being inserted into that do not appear in the column name list provided must either accept NULL values or have a default value associated with them. Otherwise the INSERT statement will fail and an error will be generated.

The UPDATE statement

Data residing in a database is rarely static. Over time, the need to change, or even remove, one or more values stored in a table can, and will, arise. In such situations, specific data values can be altered by executing the UPDATE SQL statement. The basic syntax for this statement is:

```
UPDATE [TableName | ViewName]
SET [[ColumnName] = [Value] | NULL | DEFAULT, ... ]
<WHERE [Condition]>
```

or

```
UPDATE [TableName | ViewName]
SET ([ColumnName], ... ) = ([Value] | NULL | DEFAULT, ... )
<WHERE [Condition]>
```

or

```
UPDATE [TableName | ViewName]
SET ([ColumnName], ... ) = ( [SELECTStatement] )
<WHERE [Condition]>
```

where:

TableName   Identifies the name assigned to the table that contains the data to be modified.

ViewName   Identifies the name assigned to the updatable view that references the table that contains the data to be modified.

ColumnName   Identifies the name of one or more columns that contain data values to be modified. Each name provided must identify an existing column in the table or updatable view specified.

Value   Identifies one or more data values that are to be used to replace existing values found in the column(s) specified.

SELECTStatement	Identifies a SELECT SQL statement that, when executed, will produce the data values to be used to replace existing values found in the column(s) specified (by retrieving data from other tables and/or views).
Condition	Identifies the search criterion that is to be used to locate one or more specific rows whose data values are to be modified. (This condition is coded like the WHERE clause that can be used with a SELECT SQL statement; we will look at the WHERE clause and its predicates later.) If no condition is specified, the update operation will be performed on every row found in the table or updatable view specified.

It is very important that you provide a proper WHERE clause whenever the UPDATE statement is used. Failure to do so will cause an update operation to be performed on every row found in the table or updatable view specified.

Therefore, suppose you have a base table named EMPLOYEES that has the following characteristics:

Column Name	Data Type
EMPNO	INTEGER
FNAME	CHAR(20)
LNAME	CHAR(30)
TITLE	CHAR(10)
DEPARTMENT	CHAR(20)
SALARY	DECIMAL(6,2)

If you wanted to modify the records stored in EMPLOYEES such that the salary of every employee who has the title of DBA is increased by 10%, you could do so by executing an UPDATE statement that looks something like this:

```
UPDATE employees SET salary = salary * 1.10
WHERE title = 'DBA'
```

The UPDATE statement can also be used to remove values from nullable columns. This is done by changing the column's current value to NULL. Thus, the value assigned to the DEPARTMENT column of the EMPLOYEES table shown in the previous example could be removed by executing an UPDATE statement that looks like this:

```
UPDATE employees SET salary = NULL
```

Like the INSERT statement, the UPDATE statement can either work directly with the table that contains the values to be modified, or work with an updatable view that references the table containing the values to be modified. Similarly, the results of a query, or subselect, can be used to provide values for one or more columns identified in the column name list provided. As with the INSERT statement, this form of the UPDATE statement creates a type of "cut and paste" action in which values retrieved from one base table or view are used to modify values stored in another. And also like the INSERT statement, the number of values returned by the subselect must match the number of columns specified in the column name list provided. Thus, you could change the value assigned to the DEPT column of each record found in the EMPLOYEES table we looked at earlier, using the results of a query, by executing an UPDATE statement that looks something like this:

```
UPDATE employees SET (dept) = (SELECT deptname
FROM department WHERE deptno = 1)
```

It is important to note that update operations can be conducted in one of two ways: by performing a *searched update* operation or by performing a *positioned update* operation. So far, all of the examples we have looked at have been searched update operations. To perform a positioned update, a cursor must first be created, opened, and positioned on the row that is to be updated. Then the UPDATE statement that is to be used to modify one or more data values must contain a WHERE CURRENT OF [*CursorName*] clause (*CursorName* identifies the cursor being used—we'll look at cursors shortly). Because of their added complexity, positioned update operations are typically performed by embedded SQL applications.

The DELETE Statement

Although the UPDATE statement can be used to delete individual values from a base table or updatable view (by setting those values to NULL), it cannot be used to remove entire rows. When one or more complete rows of data need to be removed from a base table, the DELETE SQL statement must be used instead. As with the INSERT statement and the UPDATE statement, the DELETE statement can either work directly with the table that rows are to be removed from or work with an updatable view that references the table that rows are to be removed from. The basic syntax for the DELETE statement is:

```
DELETE FROM [TableName | ViewName]
<WHERE [Condition]>
```

where:

TableName	Identifies the name assigned to the table rows of data are to be removed from.
ViewName	Identifies the name assigned to the updatable view rows of data are to be removed from.
Condition	Identifies the search criterion to be used to locate one or more specific rows that are to be deleted. (This condition is coded as in the WHERE clause used with a SELECT SQL statement; we will look at the WHERE clause and its predicates later.) If no condition is specified, the delete operation will be performed on every row found in the table or updatable view specified.

• •

Because omitting the WHERE clause in a DELETE SQL statement causes the delete operation to be applied to all rows in the table or view specified, it is important to always provide a WHERE clause with a DELETE statement unless you explicitly want to erase all data stored in a table.

• •

Thus, suppose you wanted to remove every record for company XYZ from a base table named SALES that has the following characteristics:

Column Name	Data Type
PO_NUMBER	CHAR(10)
COMPANY	CHAR(20)
PURCHASEDATE	DATE
SALESPERSON	INTEGER

You could do so by executing a DELETE statement that looks something like this:

```
DELETE FROM sales
WHERE company = 'XYZ'
```

On the other hand, if you wanted to remove every record for which no sales person was assigned from a base table named SALES, you could do so by executing a DELETE statement that looks something like this:

```
DELETE FROM sales
WHERE salesperson IS NULL
```

Like update operations, delete operations can be conducted in one of two ways: as *searched delete* operations or as *positioned delete* operations. To perform a positioned delete, a cursor must first be created, opened, and positioned on the row to be deleted. Then, the DELETE statement used to remove the row must contain a WHERE CURRENT OF [*CursorName*] clause (*CursorName* identifies the cursor being used). Because of their added complexity, positioned delete operations are typically performed by embedded SQL applications.

The SELECT Statement

Sooner or later, almost all database users and/or applications have the need to retrieve specific pieces of information (data) from the database they are interacting with. The operation used to retrieve data from a database is called a *query* (because it searches the database to find the answer to some question), and the results returned by a query are typically expressed in one of two forms: either as a single row of data values or as a set of rows of data values, otherwise known as a *result data set* (or *result set*). If no data values that correspond to the query specification provided can be found in the database, an empty result data set will be returned.

All queries begin with the SELECT SQL statement, which is an extremely powerful statement that is used to construct a wide variety of queries containing an infinite number of variations (using a finite set of rules). And because the SELECT statement is recursive, a single SELECT statement can derive its output from a successive number of nested SELECT statements (which are known as subqueries). (Earlier, we saw how SELECT statements can be used to provide input to INSERT and UPDATE statements; SELECT statements can be used to provide input to other SELECT statements in a similar manner.)

In its simplest form, the syntax for the SELECT statement is:

```
SELECT * FROM [ [TableName] | [ViewName] ]
```

where:

TableName Identifies the name assigned to the table from which data is to be retrieved.

ViewName Identifies the name assigned to the view from which data is to be retrieved.

Consequently, if you wanted to retrieve all values stored in a base table named DEPARTMENT, you could do so by executing a SELECT statement that looks something like this:

```
SELECT * FROM department
```

If you executed this query against the SAMPLE database provided with DB2, you would get a result data set that looks something like this:

```
DEPTNO  DEPTNAME                MGRNO   ADMRDEPT  LOCATION
------  ----------------------  ------  --------  --------
A00     COMPUTER SERVICE DIV.    000010  A00        -
B01     PLANNING                 000020  A00        -
C01     INFORMATION CENTER       000030  A00        -
D01     DEVELOPMENT CENTER         -     A00        -
D11     MANUFACTURING SYSTEMS    000060  D01        -
D21     ADMINISTRATION SYSTEMS   000070  D01        -
E01     SUPPORT SERVICES         000050  A00        -
E11     OPERATIONS               000090  E01        -
E21     SOFTWARE SUPPORT         000100  E01        -
F22     BRANCH OFFICE F2           -     E01        -
G22     BRANCH OFFICE G2           -     E01        -
H22     BRANCH OFFICE H2           -     E01        -
I22     BRANCH OFFICE I2           -     E01        -
J22     BRANCH OFFICE J2           -     E01        -

  14 record(s) selected.
```

A Closer Look at the SELECT Statement and Its Clauses

We just saw that you can retrieve every value stored in a base table by executing a simple query that looks something like this:

```
SELECT * FROM [TableName]
```

But what if you wanted to see only the values stored in two columns of a table? Or what if you wanted the data retrieved to be ordered alphabetically in ascending order? (Data is stored in a table in no particular order, and unless otherwise specified, a query only returns data in the order in which it is found.) How do you construct a query that retrieves only certain data values and returns those values in a very specific format? You do so by using a more advanced form of the SELECT SQL statement to construct your query. The syntax for the form of the SELECT statement that is used to construct more advanced queries is:

```
SELECT <DISTINCT>
[* | [Expression] <<AS> [NewColumnName]>, ...]
FROM [[TableName] | [ViewName]
  <<AS> [CorrelationName]>, ...]
<WhereClause>
<GroupByClause>
<HavingClause>
<OrderByClause>
<FetchFirstClause>
```

where:

Expression	Identifies one or more columns values that are to be returned when the SELECT statement is executed. The value specified for this option can be any valid SQL language element; however, corresponding table or view column names are the most common elements used.
NewColumnName	Specifies a new column name to be used in place of the table or view column name specified in the result data set returned by the query.
TableName	Identifies the name(s) assigned to one or more tables from which data is to be retrieved.

ViewName	Identifies the name(s) assigned to one or more views from which data is to be retrieved.
CorrelationName	Identifies a shorthand name that can be used when referencing the table or view the correlation name is associated with in any of the SELECT statement clauses.
WhereClause	Identifies a WHERE clause that is to be used with the SELECT statement.
GroupByClause	Identifies a GROUP BY clause that is to be used with the SELECT statement.
HavingClause	Identifies a HAVING clause that is to be used with the SELECT statement.
OrderByClause	Identifies an ORDER BY clause that is to be used with the SELECT statement.
FetchFirstClause	Identifies a FETCH FIRST clause that is to be used with the SELECT statement.

Thus, if you wanted to retrieve all values for the columns named WORKDEPT and JOB from a table named EMPLOYEE, you could do so by executing a SELECT statement that looks something like this:

```
SELECT workdept, job FROM employee
```

And if you executed this query against the SAMPLE database provided with DB2, you would get a result data set that looks something like this:

```
WORKDEPT   JOB
---------  -------
A00        PRES
B01        MANAGER
C01        MANAGER
E01        MANAGER
D11        MANAGER
D21        MANAGER
E11        MANAGER
E21        MANAGER
A00        SALESREP
A00        CLERK
C01        ANALYST
C01        ANALYST
D11        DESIGNER
D11        DESIGNER
D11        DESIGNER
D11        DESIGNER
D11        DESIGNER
D11        DESIGNER
D11        DESIGNER
D11        DESIGNER
D21        CLERK
D21        CLERK
D21        CLERK
D21        CLERK
D21        CLERK
E11        OPERATOR
E11        OPERATOR
E11        OPERATOR
E11        OPERATOR
E21        FIELDREP
E21        FIELDREPE
21         FIELDREP
A00        SALESREP
A00        CLERK
C01        ANALYST
D11        DESIGNER
D11        DESIGNER
D21        CLERK
E11        OPERATOR
E11        OPERATOR
E21        FIELDREP
E21        FIELDREP
42 record(s) selected.
```

If the DISTINCT clause is specified with a SELECT statement, duplicate rows are removed from the final result data set returned. Two rows are considered to be duplicates of one another if the value of every column of the first row is identical to the value of the corresponding column of the second row. For the purpose of determining whether or not two rows are identical, null values are considered equal. However, the DISTINCT clause cannot be used if the result data set produced contains LONG VARCHAR, LONG VARGRAPHIC, BLOB, CLOB, DBCLOB, or XML data.

Thus, if you were to execute the same SELECT statement that was executed earlier with the DISTINCT clause specified, the resulting statement would look something like this:

```
SELECT DISTINCT workdept, job FROM employee
```

This time, when the query is executed, you should see a result data set that looks something like this:

```
WORKDEPT  JOB
———       ———————
C01       ANALYST
A00       CLERK
D21       CLERK
D11       DESIGNER
E21       FIELDREP
B01       MANAGER
C01       MANAGER
D11       MANAGER
D21       MANAGER
E01       MANAGER
E11       MANAGER
E21       MANAGER
E11       OPERATOR
A00       PRES
A00       SALESREP
15 record(s) selected.
```

Now suppose you wanted to retrieve every unique value (no duplicates) for a column named JOB in a table named EMPLOYEE, and you wanted to change the name of the JOB column in the result data set produced to TITLE. You could do so by executing a SELECT statement that looks something like this:

```
SELECT DISTINCT job AS title FROM employee
```

This time, when the query is executed, you should see a result data set that looks something like this:.

```
TITLE
──────
ANALYST
CLERK
DESIGNER
FIELDREP
MANAGER
OPERATOR
PRES
SALESREP
 8 record(s) selected.
```

You could also produce this result data set by executing the same query and using the correlation name E for the table named EMPLOYEE. The only difference is that, this time, the SELECT statement would look like this:

```
SELECT DISTINCT e.job AS title FROM employee AS e
```

Notice that the column named JOB is qualified with the correlation name E that was assigned to the table named EMPLOYEE. In this example, the use of a correlation name is not really necessary, because data is being retrieved from only one table and no two columns in a table can have the same name. However, if data was being retrieved from two or more tables and if some of the columns in those tables had the same name, a qualifier would be needed to tell the DB2 Database Manager which table to retrieve data from for a particular column.

If you were counting when we examined the syntax for the SELECT statement earlier, you may have noticed that a single SELECT statement can contain up to seven different clauses. These clauses are:

- The DISTINCT clause
- The FROM clause
- The WHERE clause
- The GROUP BY clause
- The HAVING clause
- The ORDER BY clause
- The FETCH FIRST clause

(Incidentally, these clauses are processed in the order shown.) We just saw how the DISTINCT clause and the FROM clause are used. Now let's turn our attention to the other clauses the SELECT statement recognizes.

The WHERE Clause

The WHERE clause is used to tell the DB2 Database Manager how to select the rows that are to be returned in the result data set produced in response to a query. When specified, the WHERE clause is followed by a *search condition,* which is nothing more than a simple test that, when applied to a row of data, will evaluate to TRUE, FALSE, or Unknown. If this test evaluates to TRUE, the row is returned in the result data set produced; if the test evaluates to FALSE or Unknown, the row is ignored.

The search condition of a WHERE clause is made up of one or more predicates that are used to make comparisons. Six common types of WHERE clause predicates are recognized by DB2. They are:

- Relational predicates
- BETWEEN
- LIKE
- IN
- EXISTS
- IS NULL

Each of these predicates can be used alone, or they can be combined using parentheses or Boolean operators such as AND and OR.

Relational predicates

The *relational predicates* (or *comparison operators*) consist of a set of special operators that are used to define a comparison relationship between the contents of a column and a constant value, the contents of two columns from the same table, or the contents of a column in one table with the contents of a column in another table. The following comparison operators are available:

- < (Less than)
- > (Greater than)
- <= (Less than or equal to)
- >= (Greater than or equal to)
- = (Equal to)
- <> (Not equal to)

Typically, relational predicates are used to include or exclude specific rows from the final result data set produced in response to a query. Thus, if you wanted to retrieve values from columns named EMPNO and SALARY in a table named EMPLOYEE where the value for the SALARY column is greater than or equal to $70,000.00, you could do so by executing a SELECT statement that looks something like this:

```
SELECT empno, salary
FROM employee
WHERE salary >= 70000.00
```

And if you executed this query against the SAMPLE database provided with DB2, you would get a result data set that looks something like this:

```
EMPNO    SALARY
_____    _____
000010   152750.00
000020   94250.00
000030   98250.00
000050   80175.00
000060   72250.00
000070   96170.00
000090   89750.00
000100   86150.00
000130   73800.00
 9 record(s) selected.
```

It is important to note that the data types of all items involved in a relational predicate comparison must be compatible, or the comparison will fail. If necessary, the built-in functions provided with DB2 can be used to make any conversions required. For example, if you wanted to retrieve values from columns named LASTNAME and HIREDATE in a table named EMPLOYEE for every employee who was hired in December, you could do so by executing a SELECT statement that looks something like this:

```
SELECT lastname, hiredate
FROM employee
WHERE MONTHNAME(hiredate) = 'December'
```

In this example, the built-in function MONTHNAME() is used to produce a mixed-case character string containing the name of the month for the month portion of the date value stored in the HIREDATE column. This string value is then compared with the string 'December' to determine which rows are to be returned in a result data set. If you executed this query against the SAMPLE database provided with DB2, you should get a result data set that looks something like this:

```
LASTNAME        HIREDATE
----------      ----------
O'CONNELL       12/05/1993
NICHOLLS        12/15/2006
MARINO          12/05/2004
NATZ            12/15/2006
MONTEVERDE      12/05/2004
   5 record(s) selected.
```

The BETWEEN predicate

The BETWEEN predicate is used to define a comparison relationship in which the contents of a column are checked to see whether they fall within a specified range of values. As with relational predicates, the BETWEEN predicate is used to include or exclude specific rows from the result data set produced in response to a query.

Therefore, if you wanted to retrieve values for columns named EMPNO and SALARY in a table named EMPLOYEE where the value for the SALARY column is greater than or equal to $60,000.00 and less than or equal to $70,000.00, you could do so by executing a SELECT statement that looks something like this:

```
SELECT empno, salary
FROM employee
WHERE salary BETWEEN 60000.00 AND 70000.00
```

And if you executed this query against the SAMPLE database provided with DB2, you would get a result data set that looks something like this:

```
EMPNO     SALARY
------    --------
000110    66500.00
000140    68420.00
000160    62250.00
000210    68270.00
200140    68420.00
200170    64680.00
200220    69840.00
   7 record(s) selected.
```

If the NOT (negation) operator is used in conjunction with the BETWEEN predicate (or with any other predicate, for that matter), the meaning of the predicate is reversed. In this case, contents of a column are checked, and only values that fall outside the range of values specified are returned to the final result data set produced. Thus, if you wanted to retrieve values for columns named EMPNO and

SALARY in a table named EMPLOYEE where the value for the SALARY column is less than $20,000.00 or more than $90,000.00, you could do so by executing a SELECT statement that looks something like this:

```
SELECT empno, salary
FROM employee
WHERE salary NOT BETWEEN 20000.00 AND 90000.00
```

When this query is executed, you should see a result data set that looks something like this:

```
EMPNO      SALARY
_____    _____
000010     152750.00
000020     94250.00
000030     98250.00
000070     96170.00
 4 record(s) selected.
```

The LIKE predicate

The LIKE predicate is used to define a comparison relationship in which a character string value is checked to see whether it contains a specific pattern of characters. The pattern of characters specified can consist of regular alphanumeric characters and/or special metacharacters that are interpreted as follows:

- The underscore character (_) is treated as a wildcard character that stands for any single alphanumeric character.

- The percent character (%) is treated as a wildcard character that stands for any sequence of alphanumeric characters.

Thus, if you wanted to retrieve values for columns named EMPNO and LASTNAME in a table named EMPLOYEE where the value for the LASTNAME column begins with the letter S, you could do so by executing a SELECT statement that looks something like this:

```
SELECT empno, lastname
FROM employee
WHERE lastname LIKE 'S%'
```

If you executed this query against the SAMPLE database provided with DB2, you should get a result data set that looks something like this:

```
EMPNO     LASTNAME
------    --------
000060    STERN
000100    SPENSER
000180    SCOUTTEN
000250    SMITH
000280    SCHNEIDER
000300    SMITH
000310    SETRIGHT
200280    SCHWARTZ
200310    SPRINGER
  9 record(s) selected.
```

When using wildcard characters, you must take care to ensure that they are placed in the appropriate location in the pattern string specified. Note that in the previous example, when the character string pattern 'S%' was specified, only records for employees whose last name begins with the letter S were returned. If the character string pattern used had been '%S%', records for employees whose last name *contains* the character S (anywhere in the name) would have been returned, and the result data set produced would have looked like this instead:

```
EMPNO     LASTNAME
------    --------
000010    HAAS
000020    THOMPSON
000060    STERN
000070    PULASKI
000090    HENDERSON
000100    SPENSER
000110    LUCCHESSI
000140    NICHOLLS
000150    ADAMSON
000170    YOSHIMURA
000180    SCOUTTEN
000210    JONES
000230    JEFFERSON
000250    SMITH
000260    JOHNSON
000280    SCHNEIDER
000300    SMITH
000310    SETRIGHT
200280    SCHWARTZ
200310    SPRINGER
  20 record(s) selected.
```

Likewise, you must also be careful about using uppercase and lowercase characters in pattern strings; if the data being examined is stored in a case-sensitive manner, the characters used in a pattern string must match the case that was used to store the value in the column being searched, or no matching records will be found.

Although the LIKE predicate provides a relatively easy way to search for data values, it should be used with caution; the overhead involved in processing a LIKE predicate is very high and can be extremely resource-intensive.

The IN predicate

The IN predicate is used to define a comparison relationship in which a value is checked to see whether it matches a value in a finite set of values. This finite set of values can consist of one or more literal values that are coded directly in the IN predicate, or it can be composed of the non-null values found in a result data set produced by a subquery.

A subquery may include search conditions of its own, and these search conditions may in turn include their own sub-queries. When such "nested" subqueries are processed, the DB2 Database Manager executes the innermost query first and uses the results to execute the next outer query, and so on until all nested queries have been processed.

Thus, if you wanted to retrieve values for columns named EMPNO and WORKDEPT in a table named EMPLOYEE where the value for the WORKDEPT column matches a value in a list of predefined department code values, you could do so by executing a SELECT statement that looks something like this:

```
SELECT lastname, workdept
FROM employee
WHERE workdept IN ('E11', 'E21')
```

And if you executed this query against the SAMPLE database provided with DB2, you would get a result data set that looks something like this:

```
LASTNAME       WORKDEPT
---------      --------
HENDERSON      E11
SCHNEIDER      E11
PARKER         E11
SMITH          E11
SETRIGHT       E11
SCHWARTZ       E11
SPRINGER       E11
SPENSER        E21
MEHTA          E21
LEE            E21
GOUNOT         E21
WONG           E21
ALONZO         E21
  13 record(s) selected.
```

On the other hand, if you wanted to retrieve values for columns named LASTNAME and WORKDEPT in a table named EMPLOYEE where the value for the WORKDEPT column matches a value in a list of department codes for departments that are managed by department A00, you could do so by executing a SELECT statement that looks something like this:

```
SELECT lastname, workdept
FROM employee
WHERE workdept IN
 (SELECT deptno FROM department WHERE admrdept = 'A00')
```

When this query is executed, you should see a result data set that looks something like this:

```
LASTNAME       WORKDEPT
---------      --------
HAAS           A00
THOMPSON       B01
KWAN           C01
GEYER          E01
LUCCHESSI      A00
O'CONNELL      A00
QUINTANA       C01
NICHOLLS       C01
HEMMINGER      A00
ORLANDO        A00
NATZ           C01
  11 record(s) selected.
```

In this case, the subquery SELECT deptno FROM department WHERE admrdept = 'A00' produces a result data set containing the values A00, B01, C01, D01, and E01, and the main query evaluates each value found in the WORKDEPT column of the EMPLOYEE table to determine whether it matches one of the values in the result data set produced by the subquery. If there is a match, the record is returned.

The EXISTS predicate

The EXISTS predicate is used to determine whether a particular value exists in a given result data set. The EXISTS predicate is always followed by a subquery, and it returns either TRUE or FALSE to indicate whether a specific value is found in the result data set produced by the subquery. Thus, if you wanted to find out which values found in the column named DEPTNO in a table named DEPARTMENT are used in the column named WORKDEPT in a table named EMPLOYEE, you could do so by executing a SELECT statement that looks something like this:

```
SELECT deptno, deptname
FROM department
WHERE EXISTS
  (SELECT workdept FROM employee WHERE workdept = deptno)
```

And if you executed this query against the SAMPLE database provided with DB2, you should get a result data set that looks something like this:

```
DEPTNO    DEPTNAME
----      ----------------------------
A00       SPIFFY COMPUTER SERVICE DIV.
B01       PLANNING
C01       INFORMATION CENTER
D11       MANUFACTURING SYSTEMS
D21       ADMINISTRATION SYSTEMS
E01       SUPPORT SERVICES
E11       OPERATIONS
E21       SOFTWARE SUPPORT
  8 record(s) selected.
```

In most situations, the EXISTS predicate is ANDed with other predicates to determine final row selection.

The NULL predicate

The NULL predicate is used to determine whether or not a particular value is a NULL value. So, if you wanted to retrieve values for columns named DEPTNO and DEPTNAME in a table named DEPARTMENT where the value for the MGRNO column is a NULL value, you could do so by executing a SELECT statement that looks something like this:

```
SELECT deptno, deptname
FROM department
WHERE mgrno IS NULL
```

If you executed this query against the SAMPLE database provided with DB2, you would get a result data set that looks something like this:

```
DEPTNO    DEPTNAME
-----     ------------
D01       DEVELOPMENT CENTER
F22       BRANCH OFFICE F2
G22       BRANCH OFFICE G2
H22       BRANCH OFFICE H2
I22       BRANCH OFFICE I2
J22       BRANCH OFFICE J2
  6 record(s) selected.
```

When using the NULL predicate, it is important to keep in mind that NULL, zero (0), and blank ("") are three different values. NULL is a special marker that is used to represent missing information, while zero and blank (empty string) are actual values that may be stored in a column to indicate a specific value or lack thereof. Moreover, some columns accept NULL values, while other columns do not, depending upon their definition. So, before writing WHERE clauses that check for NULL values, make sure that the NULL value is supported by the column(s) being queried.

The GROUP BY Clause

The GROUP BY clause is used to tell the DB2 Database Manager how to organize rows of data returned in the result data set produced in response to a query. In its simplest form, the GROUP BY clause is followed by a grouping expression that is usually one or more column names that identify columns found in the result data set to be organized. The GROUP BY clause can also be used to specify what columns are to be grouped together to provide input to aggregate functions such as SUM() and AVG().

Thus, if you wanted to obtain the average salary for all departments found in a column named WORKDEPT, using salary information stored in a column named SALARY in a table named EMPLOYEE, and you wanted to round the salary information retrieved to two decimal points and organize it by department, you could do so by executing a SELECT statement that looks something like this:

```
SELECT workdept, DECIMAL(AVG(salary), 9, 2) AS avg_salary
FROM
employee
GROUP BY workdept
```

If you executed this query against the SAMPLE database provided with DB2, you would get a result data set that looks something like this:

```
WORKDEPT    AVG_SALARY
____        _____
A00         70850.00
B01         94250.00
C01         77222.50
D11         58783.63
D21         51240.00
E01         80175.00
E11         45305.71
E21         47086.66
8 record(s) selected.
```

In this example, each row returned in the result data set produced contains the department code, along with the average salary for individuals who work in that department.

•••

A common mistake that is often made when using the GROUP BY clause is the addition of nonaggregate columns to the list of columns that follow the GROUP BY clause. Since grouping is performed by combining all of the nonaggregate columns together into a single concatenated key and breaking whenever that key value changes, extraneous columns can cause unexpected breaks to occur.

•••

The GROUP BY ROLLUP clause

The GROUP BY ROLLUP clause is used to analyze a collection of data in a single dimension but at more than one level of detail. For example, you could group data by successively larger organizational units, such as team, department, and division, or by successively larger geographical units, such as city, county, state or province, country, and continent. Thus, if you were to change the GROUP BY clause in the previous SELECT statement to a GROUP BY ROLLUP clause, you would end up with a SELECT statement that looks something like this:

```
SELECT workdept, DECIMAL(AVG(salary), 9, 2) AS avg_salary
FROM employee
GROUP BY ROLLUP (workdept)
```

And if you executed this query against the SAMPLE database provided with DB2, you should get a result data set that looks something like this:

```
WORKDEPT     AVG_SALARY
--------     ----------
-            58155.35
A00          70850.00
B01          94250.00
C01          77222.50
D11          58783.63
D21          51240.00
E01          80175.00
E11          45305.71
E21          47086.66
 9 record(s) selected.
```

This result data set contains average salary information for all employees found in the table named EMPLOYEES regardless of which department they work in (the line in the result data set returned that has a null value assigned to the WORKDEPT column), as well as average salary information for each department available (the remaining lines in the result data set returned).

In this example, only one expression (known as the *grouping expression*) is specified in the GROUP BY ROLLUP clause (in this case, the grouping expression is WORKDEPT). However, one or more grouping expressions can be specified in a single GROUP BY ROLLUP clause (for example, GROUP BY ROLLUP (workdept, division)). When multiple grouping expressions are specified, the DB2 Database Manager groups the data by all grouping expressions used, then by all but the last grouping expression used, and so on. Then, it makes one final grouping that consists of the entire contents of the specified table. Therefore, when specifying multiple grouping expressions, it is important to ensure that they are listed in the appropriate order—if one kind of group is logically contained inside another (for example departments within a division), then that group should be listed after the group it is contained in (i.e., GROUP BY ROLLUP (department, division)), never before.

The GROUP BY CUBE clause

The GROUP BY CUBE clause is used to analyze a collection of data by organizing it into groups in multiple dimensions. Thus, if you were to execute a SELECT statement that looks something like this:

```
SELECT workdept, sex, DECIMAL(AVG(salary), 9, 2) AS avg_salary
FROM employee
GROUP BY CUBE (workdept, sex)
```

You might see a result data set that looks something like this:

WORKDEPT	SEX	AVG_SALARY
-	F	63243.68
-	M	53951.95
-	-	58155.35
A00	-	70850.00
B01	-	94250.00
C01	-	77222.50
D11	-	58783.63
D21	-	51240.00
E01	-	80175.00
E11	-	45305.71
E21	-	47086.66
A00	F	99625.00
A00	M	51666.66
B01	M	94250.00
C01	F	77222.50
D11	F	58317.50
D11	M	59050.00
D21	F	60266.66
D21	M	44470.00
E01	M	80175.00
E11	F	48810.00
E11	M	36545.00
E21	F	35370.00
E21	M	49430.00

24 record(s) selected.

This result set contains average salary information for each department found in the table named EMPLOYEE (the lines that contain a null value in the SEX column and a value in the WORKDEPT column of the result data set returned), average salary information for all employees found in the table named EMPLOYEE regardless of which department they work in (the line that contains a null value for both the SEX and the WORKDEPT column of the result data set returned), average salary information for each gender (the lines that contain values in the SEX column and a null value in the WORKDEPT column of the result data set returned), and average salary information for each gender in each department available (the remaining lines in the result data set returned).

In other words, the data in the result data set produced is grouped:

- By department only
- By gender only
- By gender and department
- As a single group that contains all genders and all departments.

The term CUBE is intended to suggest that data is being analyzed in more than one dimension, and as you can see in the previous example, data analysis was actually performed in two dimensions, which resulted in four types of groupings. Suppose the following SELECT statement had been used instead:

```
SELECT workdept, sex, job,
  DECIMAL(AVG(salary), 9, 2) AS avg_salary
FROM employee
GROUP BY CUBE (workdept, sex, job)
```

Data analysis would have been performed in three dimensions, and the data would have been broken into eight types of groupings. Thus, the number of types of groups produced by a GROUP BY CUBE operation can be determined by the formula: 2^n where n is the number of expressions used in the GROUP BY CUBE clause.

The HAVING Clause

The HAVING clause is used to apply further selection criteria to columns referenced in a GROUP BY clause. This clause behaves like the WHERE clause, except that it refers to data that has already been grouped (the HAVING clause is used to tell the DB2 Database Manager how to select the rows to be returned in a result data set from rows that have already been grouped). And, like the WHERE clause, the HAVING clause is followed by a search condition that acts as a simple test that, when applied to a row of data, will evaluate to TRUE, FALSE, or Unknown. If this test evaluates to TRUE, the row is returned in the result data set produced; if the test evaluates to FALSE or Unknown, the row is skipped. Because it behaves like a WHERE clause, the search condition of a HAVING clause can consist of the same predicates that are recognized by the WHERE clause.

Thus, if you wanted to obtain the average salary for all departments found in a column named WORKDEPT, using salary information stored in a column named SALARY in a table named EMPLOYEE, and you wanted to organize the data retrieved by department, but you are interested only in departments whose average salary is greater than $60,000.00, you could obtain this information by executing a SELECT statement that looks something like this:

```
SELECT workdept, DECIMAL(AVG(salary), 9, 2)
 AS avg_salary FROM employee GROUP BY work
dept HAVING AVG(salary) > 60000
```

And if you executed this query against the SAMPLE database provided with DB2, you would get a result data set that looks something like this:

```
WORKDEPT        AVG_SALARY
---------       ----------
A00             70850.00
B01             94250.00
C01             77222.50
E01             80175.00
  4 record(s) selected.
```

As you can see from the output provided, each row in the result data set produced contains the department ID for every department whose average salary for individuals working in that department is greater than $60,000.00, along with the average salary found for each department.

The ORDER BY Clause

The ORDER BY clause is used to tell the DB2 Database Manager how to sort and order the rows that are to be returned in a result data set produced in response to a query. When specified, the ORDER BY clause is followed by the name of one or more column(s) whose data values are to be sorted and a keyword that indicates the desired sort order. If the keyword ASC follows the column's name, ascending order is used, and if the keyword DESC follows the column name, descending order is used. Multiple columns can be used for sorting, and each column used can be ordered in either ascending or descending order. Furthermore, when more than one column is identified in an ORDER BY clause, the corresponding result data set is sorted by the first column specified (the primary sort), then the sorted data is sorted again by the next column specified, and so on until the data has been sorted by each column specified.

Thus, if you wanted to retrieve values for columns named EMPNO, LASTNAME, and WORKDEPT in a table named EMPLOYEE and you wanted the information sorted by WORKDEPT in ascending order, followed by LASTNAME in descending order, you could do so by executing a SELECT statement that looks something like this:

```
SELECT empno, lastname, workdept
FROM employee
ORDER BY workdept ASC, lastname DESC
```

And if you executed this query against the SAMPLE database provided with DB2, you would get a result data set that looks something like this:

```
EMPNO      LASTNAME      WORKDEPT
-------    ---------     --------
200120     ORLANDO       A00
000120     O'CONNELL     A00
000110     LUCCHESSI     A00
200010     HEMMINGER     A00
000010     HAAS          A00
000020     THOMPSON      B01
000130     QUINTANA      C01
000140     NICHOLLS      C01
200140     NATZ          C01
000030     KWAN          C01
000170     YOSHIMURA     D11
200170     YAMAMOTO      D11
000190     WALKER        D11
000060     STERN         D11
000180     SCOUTTEN      D11
000160     PIANKA        D11
000220     LUTZ          D11
000210     JONES         D11
200220     JOHN          D11
000200     BROWN         D11
000150     ADAMSON       D11
000250     SMITH         D21
000070     PULASKI       D21
000270     PEREZ         D21
200240     MONTEVERDE    D21
000240     MARINO        D21
000260     JOHNSON       D21
000230     JEFFERSON     D21
000050     GEYER         E01
200310     SPRINGER      E11
000300     SMITH         E11
000310     SETRIGHT      E11
200280     SCHWARTZ      E11
000280     SCHNEIDER     E11
000290     PARKER        E11
000090     HENDERSON     E11
```

```
EMPNO       LASTNAME     WORKDEPT
------      --------     --------
200330      WONG         E21
000100      SPENSER      E21
000320      MEHTA        E21
000330      LEE          E21
000340      GOUNOT       E21
200340      ALONZO       E21
  42 record(s) selected.
```

Using the ORDER BY clause is easy if the result data set consists only of named columns. But what happens if the result data set produced needs to be ordered by a summary column or a result column that cannot be specified by name? Because these situations can exist, the ORDER BY clause allows an integer value that corresponds to a particular column's number to be used in place of the column name. When integer values are used, the first or leftmost column in the result data set produced is treated as column 1, the next is column 2, and so on. Therefore, the result data set produced by the previous query could have also been produced by executing a SELECT statement that looks like this:

```
SELECT empno, lastname, workdept
FROM employee
ORDER BY 1 ASC, 2 DESC
         3 ASC
```

It is important to note that even though integer values are primarily used in the ORDER BY clause to specify columns that cannot be specified by name, they can be used in place of any column name.

The FETCH FIRST Clause

The FETCH FIRST clause is used to limit the number of rows returned to the result data set produced in response to a query. When used, the FETCH FIRST clause is followed by a positive integer value and the words ROWS ONLY. This tells the DB2 Database Manager that the user/application executing the query does not want to see more than *n* number of rows, regardless of how many rows might exist in the result data set produced were the FETCH FIRST clause not specified.

Thus, if you wanted to retrieve just the first 10 values for columns named EMPNO, LASTNAME, and WORKDEPT from a table named EMPLOYEE, you could do so by executing a SELECT statement that looks something like this:

```
SELECT empno, lastname, workdept
FROM employee
FETCH FIRST 10 ROWS ONLY
```

If you executed this query against the SAMPLE database provided with DB2, you would get a result data set that looks something like this:

```
EMPNO        LASTNAME        WORKDEPT
------       --------        --------
000010       HAAS            A00
000020       THOMPSON        B01
000030       KWAN            C01
000050       GEYER           E01
000060       STERN           D11
000070       PULASKI         D21
000090       HENDERSON       E11
000100       SPENSER         E21
000110       LUCCHESSI       A00
000120       O'CONNELL       A00
  10 record(s) selected.
```

It is important to note that if you use other clauses to format the data before returning a specified number of rows, the actual values returned can be different. For example, suppose the previous SELECT statement was modified to include an ORDER BY clause like this:

```
SELECT empno, lastname, workdept FROM employee
ORDER BY lastname FETCH FIRST 10 ROWS ONLY
```

The result data set produced when the query is executed might look something like this:

```
EMPNO        LASTNAME        WORKDEPT
------       --------        --------
000150       ADAMSON         D11
200340       ALONZO          E21
000200       BROWN           D11
000050       GEYER           E01
000340       GOUNOT          E21
000010       HAAS            A00
200010       HEMMINGER       A00
000090       HENDERSON       E11
000230       JEFFERSON       D21
200220       JOHN            D11
  10 record(s) selected.
```

A Word About Common Table Expressions

Common table expressions are mechanisms that are used to construct local temporary tables that reside in memory and exist only for the life of the SQL statement that defines them. (In fact, the table that is created in response to a common table expression can only be referenced by the SQL statement that created it.) Common table expressions are typically used:

- In place of a view (when the creation of a view is undesirable, when general use of a view is not required, and when positioned update or delete operations are not used)

- To enable grouping by a column that is derived from a subquery or a scalar function that performs some external action

- When the desired result table is based on host variables

- When the same result table needs to be used by several different queries

- When the results of a query need to be derived using recursion

The syntax used to construct a common table expression is:

```
WITH [TableName] <( [ColumnName], ...] )>
AS ( [SELECTStatement] )
```

where:

TableName Specifies the name that is to be assigned to the temporary table to be created.

ColumnName Specifies the name(s) to be assigned to one or more columns that are to be included in the temporary table to be created. Each column name specified must be unique and unqualified; if no column names are specified, the names derived from the result data set produced by the *SELECTStatement* specified will be used. If a list of column names is specified, the number of column names provided must match the number of columns that will be returned by the SELECT statement used to create the temporary table. If a common table expression

recursive, or if the result data set produced by the
SELECT statement specified contains duplicate column
names, column names must be specified.

SELECTStatement   Identifies a SELECT SQL statement that, when executed,
will produce the data values to be added to the
column(s) in the temporary table to be created.

Thus, if you wanted to retrieve all values for the columns named EMPNO, LASTNAME,
HIREDATE, and SEX from a table named EMPLOYEE and store them in a common table
that is then referenced in a query that is designed to obtain employee number and
hire date information for all female employees working for the company, you
could do so by executing an SQL statement that looks something like this:

```
WITH
 emp_info (empno, lastname, hiredate, sex) AS
   (SELECT empno, lastname, hiredate, sex FROM employee)
SELECT empno, hiredate FROM emp_info WHERE sex = 'F'
```

And if you executed this statement against the SAMPLE database provided with DB2,
you would get a result data set that looks something like this:

```
EMPNO     HIREDATE
------    ----------
000010    01/01/1995
000030    04/05/2005
000070    09/30/2005
000090    08/15/2000
000130    07/28/2001
000140    12/15/2006
000160    10/11/2006
000180    07/07/2003
000220    08/29/1998
000260    09/11/2005
000270    09/30/2006
000280    03/24/1997
000310    09/12/1994
200010    01/01/1995
200140    12/15/2006
200220    08/29/2005
200280    03/24/1997
200310    09/12/1994
200330    02/23/2006
  19 record(s) selected.
```

Multiple common table expressions can be specified following a single WITH keyword, and each common table expression specified can be referenced, by name, in the FROM clause of subsequent common table expressions. However, if multiple common table expressions are defined within the same WITH keyword, the table name assigned to each temporary table created must be unique from all other table names used in the SELECT statement that creates them. It is also important to note that the table name assigned to the temporary table created by a common table expression will take precedence over any existing table, view, or alias (in the system catalog) that has the same qualified name; if the SELECT SQL statement -references the original table, view, or alias, it will actually be working with the temporary table created. (Existing tables, views, and aliases whose names match that of the temporary table are not altered but are simply no longer accessible.)

A Word About CASE Expressions

One efficient and concise way to display compared values in a readable format is to use one or more CASE expressions in the selection list of a query. Each CASE operation evaluates a specified expression and supplies a different value, depending on whether a certain condition is met. A CASE expression can take one of two forms: *simple* or *searched*. The basic syntax used to create a simple CASE expression is:

```
CASE [Expression1]
    [WHEN [Expression2] THEN [Result1], ...]
ELSE [Result2]
<END>
```

where:

Expression1 Identifies an expression or value that is to be compared to one or more *Expression2* expressions or values.

Expression2 Identifies one or more expressions or values that, when compared to *Expression1*, evaluate to TRUE or FALSE.

Result1 Identifies a value to be used when a search condition evaluates to TRUE.

Result2 Identifies a value to be used when a search condition evaluates to FALSE.

Thus, if you wanted to retrieve values for columns named EMPNO, LASTNAME, and DIVISION from a table named EMPLOYEE, and you knew that the first character of the work department code associated with an employee represents a division within the company, you could use a simple CASE expression to translate the codes and provide a complete division name to which each employee belongs by executing an SQL statement that looks something like this:

```
SELECT empno, lastname,
  CASE SUBSTR(workdept, 1, 1)
    WHEN 'A' THEN 'ADMINISTRATION'
    WHEN 'B' THEN 'HUMAN RESOURCES'
    WHEN 'C' THEN 'DESIGN'
    WHEN 'D' THEN 'OPERATIONS'
    ELSE 'UNKNOWN DEPARTMENT'
  END AS division
FROM employee
```

} 3rd column

If you executed this statement against the SAMPLE database provided with DB2, you would get a result data set that looks something like this:

EMPNO	LASTNAME	DIVISION
000010	HAAS	ADMINISTRATION
000020	THOMPSON	HUMAN RESOURCES
000030	KWAN	DESIGN
000050	GEYER	UNKNOWN DEPARTMENT
000060	STERN	OPERATIONS
000070	PULASKI	OPERATIONS
000090	HENDERSON	UNKNOWN DEPARTMENT
000100	SPENSER	UNKNOWN DEPARTMENT
000110	LUCCHESSI	ADMINISTRATION
000120	O'CONNELL	ADMINISTRATION
000130	QUINTANA	DESIGN
000140	NICHOLLS	DESIGN
000150	ADAMSON	OPERATIONS
000160	PIANKA	OPERATIONS
000170	YOSHIMURA	OPERATIONS
000180	SCOUTTEN	OPERATIONS
000190	WALKER	OPERATIONS
000200	BROWN	OPERATIONS
000210	JONES	OPERATIONS
000220	LUTZ	OPERATIONS
000230	JEFFERSON	OPERATIONS
000240	MARINO	OPERATIONS
000250	SMITH	OPERATIONS
000260	JOHNSON	OPERATIONS
000270	PEREZ	OPERATIONS
000280	SCHNEIDER	UNKNOWN DEPARTMENT

```
EMPNO     LASTNAME    DIVISION
-------   ----------  --------------------
000290    PARKER      UNKNOWN DEPARTMENT
000300    SMITH       UNKNOWN DEPARTMENT
000310    SETRIGHT    UNKNOWN DEPARTMENT
000320    MEHTA       UNKNOWN DEPARTMENT
000330    LEE         UNKNOWN DEPARTMENT
000340    GOUNOT      UNKNOWN DEPARTMENT
200010    HEMMINGER   ADMINISTRATION
200120    ORLANDO     ADMINISTRATION
200140    NATZ        DESIGN
200170    YAMAMOTO    OPERATIONS
200220    JOHN        OPERATIONS
200240    MONTEVERDE  OPERATIONS
200280    SCHWARTZ    UNKNOWN DEPARTMENT
200310    SPRINGER    UNKNOWN DEPARTMENT
200330    WONG        UNKNOWN DEPARTMENT
200340    ALONZO      UNKNOWN DEPARTMENT
  42 record(s) selected.
```

The syntax used to create a searched CASE expression is:

```
CASE
  [WHEN [SearchCondition] THEN [Result1], ...]
   ELSE [Result2]
<END>
```

where:

SearchCondition   Identifies one or more logical conditions that evaluate to TRUE or FALSE.

Result1   Identifies a value to be used when a search condition evaluates to TRUE.

Result2   Identifies a value to be used when a search condition evaluates to FALSE.

Thus, if you wanted to retrieve values for columns named EMPNO, LASTNAME, JOB, and SALARY from a table named EMPLOYEE, and you wanted to calculate salary increases based on the job each employee performs, you could use a searched CASE expression to provide new salary values based on the job held by executing an SQL statement that looks something like this:

```
SELECT empno, lastname, job, salary,
  CASE
    WHEN job IN ('MANAGER', 'SUPRVSR') THEN salary * 1.10
    WHEN job IN ('DBA', 'SYS PROG') THEN salary * 1.08
    WHEN job = 'PRGRMR' THEN salary * 1.05
    ELSE salary * 1.035
  END as new_salary
FROM employee
```

} 5th column

And if you executed this statement, you should get a result data set that looks something like this:

EMPNO	LASTNAME	JOB	SALARY	NEW_SALARY
000010	HAAS	PRES	152750.00	158096.25000
000020	THOMPSON	MANAGER	94250.00	103675.00000
000030	KWAN	MANAGER	98250.00	108075.00000
000050	GEYER	MANAGER	80175.00	88192.50000
000060	STERN	MANAGER	72250.00	79475.00000
000070	PULASKI	MANAGER	96170.00	105787.00000
000090	HENDERSON	MANAGER	89750.00	98725.00000
000100	SPENSER	MANAGER	86150.00	94765.00000
000110	LUCCHESSI	SALESREP	66500.00	68827.50000
000120	O'CONNELL	CLERK	49250.00	50973.75000
000130	QUINTANA	ANALYST	73800.00	76383.00000
000140	NICHOLLS	ANALYST	68420.00	70814.70000
000150	ADAMSON	DESIGNER	55280.00	57214.80000
000160	PIANKA	DESIGNER	62250.00	64428.75000
000170	YOSHIMURA	DESIGNER	44680.00	46243.80000
000180	SCOUTTEN	DESIGNER	51340.00	53136.90000
000190	WALKER	DESIGNER	50450.00	52215.75000
000200	BROWN	DESIGNER	57740.00	59760.90000
000210	JONES	DESIGNER	68270.00	70659.45000
000220	LUTZ	DESIGNER	49840.00	51584.40000
000230	JEFFERSON	CLERK	42180.00	43656.30000
000240	MARINO	CLERK	48760.00	50466.60000
000250	SMITH	CLERK	49180.00	50901.30000
000260	JOHNSON	CLERK	47250.00	48903.75000
000270	PEREZ	CLERK	37380.00	38688.30000
000280	SCHNEIDER	OPERATOR	36250.00	37518.75000
000290	PARKER	OPERATOR	35340.00	36576.90000
000300	SMITH	OPERATOR	37750.00	39071.25000
000310	SETRIGHT	OPERATOR	35900.00	37156.50000
000320	MEHTA	FIELDREP	39950.00	41348.25000
000330	LEE	FIELDREP	45370.00	46957.95000
000340	GOUNOT	FIELDREP	43840.00	45374.40000
200010	HEMMINGER	SALESREP	46500.00	48127.50000
200120	ORLANDO	CLERK	39250.00	40623.75000
200140	NATZ	ANALYST	68420.00	70814.70000
200170	YAMAMOTO	DESIGNER	64680.00	66943.80000

```
EMPNO     LASTNAME     JOB          SALARY     NEW_SALARY
------    ---------    --------- -  -----      ----------
200220    JOHN         DESIGNER     69840.00   72284.40000
200240    MONTEVERDE   CLERK        37760.00   39081.60000
200280    SCHWARTZ     OPERATOR     46250.00   47868.75000
200310    SPRINGER     OPERATOR     35900.00   37156.50000
200330    WONG         FIELDREP     35370.00   36607.95000
200340    ALONZO       FIELDREP     31840.00   32954.40000
  42 record(s) selected.
```

As you can see from these examples, the value provided by a CASE expression is the value of the result-expression (*Result1*) that follows the first (leftmost) case that evaluates to TRUE. If no case evaluates to TRUE and the ELSE keyword is present, then the result is the value of the second result-expression (*Result2*). If no case evaluates to TRUE and the ELSE keyword is not present, then the result is null. It is important to note that when a case evaluates to Unknown (because of null values), the case is not true and is treated the same as a case that evaluates to FALSE. And it goes without saying that the data type of the search condition specified must be comparable to the data type of each result-expression used.

Joining Tables

So far, all the examples we have looked at have involved only one table. However, one of the more powerful features of the SELECT statement (and the element that makes data normalization possible) is the ability to retrieve data from two or more tables by performing what is known as a *join operation*. In its simplest form, the syntax for a SELECT statement that performs a join operation is:

```
SELECT * FROM [ [TableName] | [ViewName], ...]
```

where:

TableName   Identifies the name assigned to each of two or more tables from which data is to be retrieved.

ViewName   Identifies the name assigned to each of two or more views from which data is to be retrieved.

Consequently, if you wanted to retrieve all values stored in two base tables named CL_SCHED and ORG, you could do so by executing a SELECT statement that looks something like this:

```
SELECT * FROM cl_sched, org
```

When such a SELECT statement is executed, the result data set produced will contain all possible combinations of the rows found in each table specified (otherwise known as a *Cartesian product*). Every row in the result data set produced is a row from the first table referenced concatenated with a row from the second table referenced, concatenated in turn with a row from the third table referenced, and so on. The total number of rows found in the result data set produced is the product of the number of rows in all the individual table references. Thus, if the table named CL_SCHED in our previous example contains five rows and the table named ORG contains eight rows, the result data set produced by the statement "SELECT * FROM cl_sched, org" will consist of 40 rows (5 × 8 = 40).

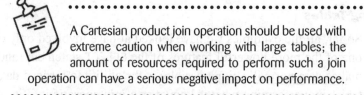

A Cartesian product join operation should be used with extreme caution when working with large tables; the amount of resources required to perform such a join operation can have a serious negative impact on performance.

A more common join operation involves collecting data from two or more tables that have one specific column in common and combining the results to create a result data set. The syntax for a SELECT statement that performs this type of join operation is:

```
SELECT
[* | [Expression] <<AS> [NewColumnName]>, ...]
 FROM [[TableName] <<AS> [CorrelationName]>, ...]
[JoinCondition]
```

where:

Expression   Identifies one or more columns whose values are to be returned when the SELECT statement is executed. The value specified for this option can be any valid SQL language element; however, corresponding table or view column names are commonly used.

NewColumnName	Identifies a new column name that is to be used in place of the corresponding table or view column name specified in the result data set returned by the SELECT statement.
TableName	Identifies the name(s) assigned to one or more tables from which data is to be retrieved.
CorrelationName	Identifies a shorthand name that can be used when referencing the table name specified in the *TableName* parameter.
JoinCondition	Identifies the condition to be used to join the tables specified. Typically, this is a WHERE clause in which the values of a column in one table are compared with the values of a similar column in another table.

Thus, a simple join operation could be conducted by executing a SELECT statement that looks something like this:

```
SELECT lastname, deptname
FROM employee e, department d
WHERE e.workdept = d.deptno
```

= *FROM employee e INNER JOIN department d ON e.workdept = d.deptno*

If you executed this query against the SAMPLE database provided with DB2, you would get a result data set that looks like this:

```
LASTNAME          DEPTNAME
---------         ----------------------------
HAAS              SPIFFY COMPUTER SERVICE DIV.
THOMPSON          PLANNING
KWAN              INFORMATION CENTER
GEYER             SUPPORT SERVICES
STERN             MANUFACTURING SYSTEMS
PULASKI           ADMINISTRATION SYSTEMS
HENDERSON         OPERATIONS
SPENSER           SOFTWARE SUPPORT
LUCCHESSI         SPIFFY COMPUTER SERVICE DIV.
O'CONNELL         SPIFFY COMPUTER SERVICE DIV.
```

LASTNAME	DEPTNAME
QUINTANA	INFORMATION CENTER
NICHOLLS	INFORMATION CENTER
ADAMSON	MANUFACTURING SYSTEMS
PIANKA	MANUFACTURING SYSTEMS
YOSHIMURA	MANUFACTURING SYSTEMS
SCOUTTEN	MANUFACTURING SYSTEMS
WALKER	MANUFACTURING SYSTEMS
BROWN	MANUFACTURING SYSTEMS
JONES	MANUFACTURING SYSTEMS
LUTZ	MANUFACTURING SYSTEMS
EFFERSON	ADMINISTRATION SYSTEMS
MARINO	ADMINISTRATION SYSTEMS
SMITH	ADMINISTRATION SYSTEMS
JOHNSON	ADMINISTRATION SYSTEMS
PEREZ	ADMINISTRATION SYSTEMS
SCHNEIDER	OPERATIONS
PARKER	OPERATIONS
SMITH	OPERATIONS
SETRIGHT	OPERATIONS
MEHTA	SOFTWARE SUPPORT
LEE	SOFTWARE SUPPORT
GOUNOT	SOFTWARE SUPPORT
HEMMINGER	SPIFFY COMPUTER SERVICE DIV.
ORLANDO	SPIFFY COMPUTER SERVICE DIV.
NATZ	INFORMATION CENTER
YAMAMOTO	MANUFACTURING SYSTEMS
JOHN	MANUFACTURING SYSTEMS
MONTEVERDE	ADMINISTRATION SYSTEMS
SCHWARTZ	OPERATIONS
SPRINGER	OPERATIONS
WONG	SOFTWARE SUPPORT
ALONZO	SOFTWARE SUPPORT

```
  42 record(s) selected.
```

This type of join is referred to as an *inner join*. Aside from a Cartesian product, only two types of joins can exist: inner joins and *outer joins*. And as you might imagine, there is a significant difference between the two.

Inner joins

After a Cartesian product, an inner join is the simplest type of join operation that can be performed. An inner join can be thought of as the cross product of two tables, in which every row in one table that has a corresponding row in another table is combined with that row to produce a new record. This type of join works well as long as every row in the first table has a corresponding row in the second table. However, if this is not the case, the result table produced may be missing rows found in either or both of the tables that were joined. In the last example, we saw the SELECT statement syntax that is commonly used to perform inner join operations. However, the following syntax can also be used to create a SELECT statement that performs an inner join operation:

```
SELECT
[* | [Expression] <<AS> [NewColumnName]> ,...]
FROM [[TableName1] <<AS> [CorrelationName1]>]
<INNER> JOIN [[TableName2] <<AS> [CorrelationName2]>]
ON [JoinCondition]
```

where:

Expression	Identifies one or more columns whose values are to be returned when the SELECT statement is executed. The value specified for this option can be any valid SQL language element; however, corresponding table or view column names are commonly used.
NewColumnName	Identifies a new column name to be used in place of the corresponding table or view column name specified in the result data set returned by the SELECT statement.
TableName1	Identifies the name assigned to the first table from which data is to be retrieved.
CorrelationName1	Identifies a shorthand name that can be used when referencing the leftmost table of the join operation.
TableName2	Identifies the name assigned to the second table from which data is to be retrieved.
CorrelationName2	Identifies a shorthand name that can be used when referencing the rightmost table of the join operation.
JoinCondition	Identifies the condition to be used to join the two tables specified.

Consequently, the same inner join operation we looked at earlier could be conducted by executing a SELECT statement that looks something like this:

```
SELECT lastname, deptname
FROM employee e INNER JOIN department d
ON e.workdept = d.deptno
```

Figure 5-1 illustrates how such an inner join operation would work.

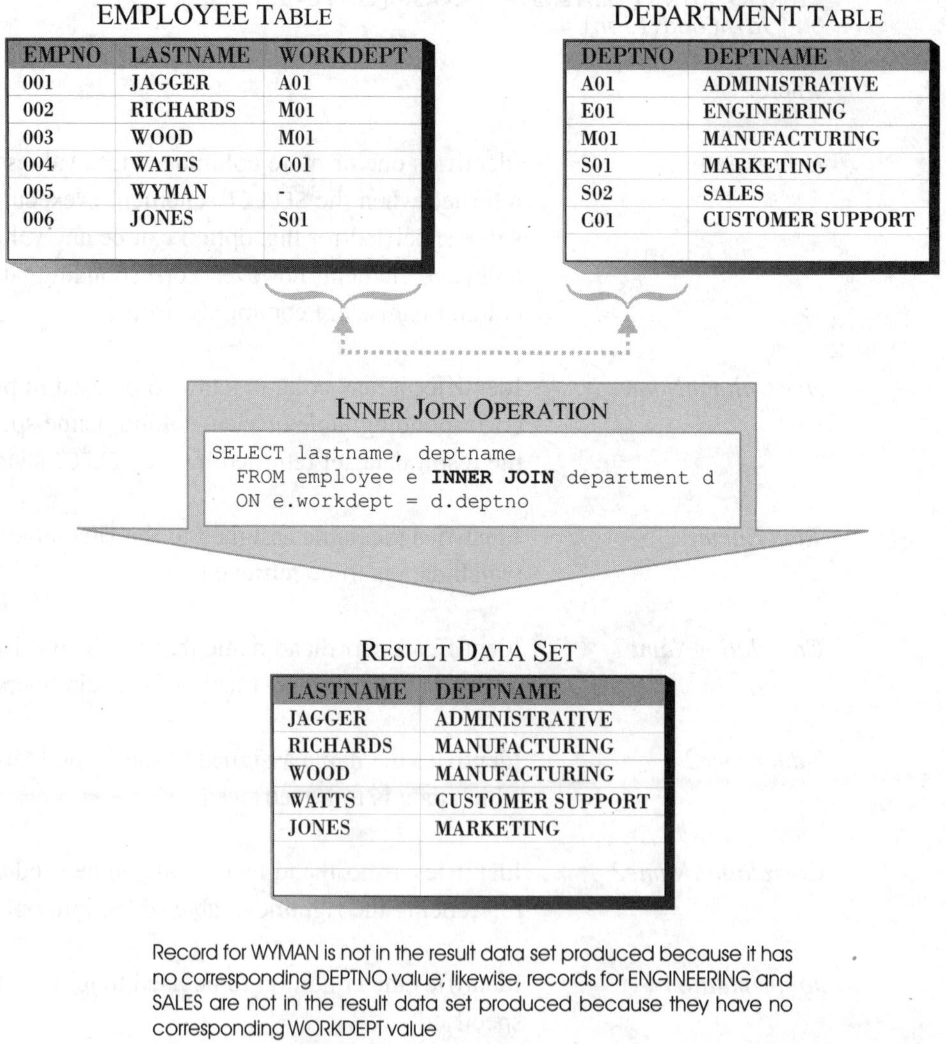

EMPLOYEE TABLE

EMPNO	LASTNAME	WORKDEPT
001	JAGGER	A01
002	RICHARDS	M01
003	WOOD	M01
004	WATTS	C01
005	WYMAN	-
006	JONES	S01

DEPARTMENT TABLE

DEPTNO	DEPTNAME
A01	ADMINISTRATIVE
E01	ENGINEERING
M01	MANUFACTURING
S01	MARKETING
S02	SALES
C01	CUSTOMER SUPPORT

INNER JOIN OPERATION

```
SELECT lastname, deptname
  FROM employee e INNER JOIN department d
  ON e.workdept = d.deptno
```

RESULT DATA SET

LASTNAME	DEPTNAME
JAGGER	ADMINISTRATIVE
RICHARDS	MANUFACTURING
WOOD	MANUFACTURING
WATTS	CUSTOMER SUPPORT
JONES	MARKETING

Record for WYMAN is not in the result data set produced because it has no corresponding DEPTNO value; likewise, records for ENGINEERING and SALES are not in the result data set produced because they have no corresponding WORKDEPT value

Figure 5–1: A simple inner join operation.

Outer joins

Outer join operations are used when a join operation is required and any rows that would normally be eliminated by an inner join operation need to be preserved. With DB2, three types of outer joins are available:

Left outer join. When a left outer join operation is performed, rows that would have been returned by an inner join operation, together with all rows stored in the leftmost table of the join operation (i.e., the table listed first in the OUTER JOIN clause) that would have been eliminated by the inner join operation, are returned in the result data set produced.

Right outer join. When a right outer join operation is performed, rows that would have been returned by an inner join operation, together with all rows stored in the rightmost table of the join operation (i.e., the table listed last in the OUTER JOIN clause) that would have been eliminated by the inner join operation, are returned in the result data set produced.

Full outer join. When a full outer join operation is performed, rows that would have been returned by an inner join operation, together with all rows stored in both tables of the join operation that would have been eliminated by the inner join operation, are returned in the result data set produced.

To understand the basic principles behind an outer join operation, it helps to look at an example. Suppose Table A and Table B are joined by an ordinary inner join operation. Any row in either Table A or Table B that does not have a matching row in the other table (according to the rules of the join condition) is eliminated from the final result data set produced. By contrast, if Table A and Table B are joined by an outer join, any row in either Table A or Table B that does not contain a matching row in the other table is included in the result data set (exactly once), and columns in that row that would have contained matching values from the other table are empty. Thus, an outer join operation adds nonmatching rows to the final result data set produced whereas an inner join operation excludes them. A left outer join of Table A with Table B preserves all nonmatching rows found in Table A, a right outer join of Table A with Table B preserves all nonmatching rows found in Table B, and a full outer join preserves nonmatching rows found in both Table A and Table B.

Figure 5–2 illustrates how a left outer join operation works; Figure 5–3 illustrates how a right outer join operation works; and Figure 5–4 illustrates how a full join operation works.

EMPLOYEE TABLE

EMPNO	LASTNAME	WORKDEPT
001	JAGGER	A01
002	RICHARDS	M01
003	WOOD	M01
004	WATTS	C01
005	WYMAN	-
006	JONES	S01

(Left Table)

DEPARTMENT TABLE

DEPTNO	DEPTNAME
A01	ADMINISTRATIVE
E01	ENGINEERING
M01	MANUFACTURING
S01	MARKETING
S02	SALES
C01	CUSTOMER SUPPORT

(Right Table)

LEFT OUTER JOIN OPERATION

```
SELECT lastname, deptname
  FROM employee e LEFT OUTER JOIN department d
  ON e.workdept = d.deptno
```

RESULT DATA SET

LASTNAME	DEPTNAME
JAGGER	ADMINISTRATIVE
RICHARDS	MANUFACTURING
WOOD	MANUFACTURING
WATTS	CUSTOMER SUPPORT
WYMAN	-
JONES	MARKETING

Record for WYMAN is included in the result data set produced even though it has no corresponding DEPTNO value; however, records for ENGINEERING and SALES are not in the result data set produced because they have no corresponding WORKDEPT value

Figure 5–2: A simple left outer join operation.

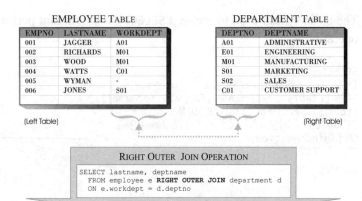

RIGHT OUTER JOIN OPERATION

```
SELECT lastname, deptname
  FROM employee e RIGHT OUTER JOIN department d
  ON e.workdept = d.deptno
```

RESULT DATA SET

LASTNAME	DEPTNAME
JAGGER	ADMINISTRATIVE
-	ENGINEERING
RICHARDS	MANUFACTURING
WOOD	MANUFACTURING
JONES	MARKETING
-	SALES
WATTS	CUSTOMER SUPPORT

Record for WYMAN is not in the result data set produced because it has no corresponding DEPTNO value; however, records for ENGINEERING and SALES are included in the result data set produced even though they have no corresponding WORKDEPT value

Figure 5–3: A simple right outer join operation.

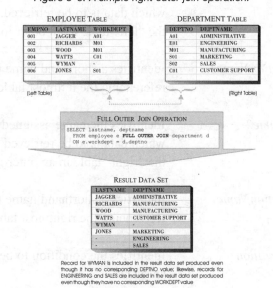

FULL OUTER JOIN OPERATION

```
SELECT lastname, deptname
  FROM employee e FULL OUTER JOIN department d
  ON e.workdept = d.deptno
```

RESULT DATA SET

LASTNAME	DEPTNAME
JAGGER	ADMINISTRATIVE
RICHARDS	MANUFACTURING
WOOD	MANUFACTURING
WATTS	CUSTOMER SUPPORT
WYMAN	-
JONES	MARKETING
-	ENGINEERING
-	SALES

Record for WYMAN is included in the result data set produced even though it has no corresponding DEPTNO value; likewise, records for ENGINEERING and SALES are included in the result data set produced even though they have no corresponding WORKDEPT value

Figure 5–4: A simple full outer join operation.

The basic syntax used to create a SELECT statement that performs an outer join operation is:

```
SELECT
[* | [Expression] <<AS> [NewColumnName]>, ...]
FROM [[TableName1] <<AS> [CorrelationName1]>]
[LEFT | RIGHT | FULL] OUTER JOIN
[[TableName2] <<AS> [CorrelationName2]>]
ON [JoinCondition]
```

where:

Expression	Identifies one or more columns whose values are to be returned when the SELECT statement is executed. The value specified for this option can be any valid SQL language element; however, corresponding table or view column names are commonly used.
NewColumnName	Identifies a new column name that is to be used in place of the corresponding table or view column name specified in the result data set returned by the SELECT statement.
TableName1	Identifies the name assigned to the first table from which data is to be retrieved. This table is considered the "left" table in an outer join.
CorrelationName1	Identifies a shorthand name that can be used when referencing the leftmost table of the join operation.
TableName2	Identifies the name assigned to the second table from which data is to be retrieved. This table is considered the "right" table in an outer join.
CorrelationName2	Identifies a shorthand name that can be used when referencing the rightmost table of the join operation.
JoinCondition	Identifies the condition to be used to join the two tables specified.

Thus, a simple left outer join operation could be conducted by executing a SELECT statement that looks something like this:

```
SELECT lastname, deptname
FROM employee e LEFT OUTER JOIN department d
ON e.workdept = d.deptno
```

A simple right outer join operation could be conducted by executing a SELECT statement that looks something like this:

```
SELECT lastname, deptname
FROM employee e RIGHT OUTER JOIN department d
ON e.workdept = d.deptno
```

And finally, a simple full outer join operation could be conducted by executing a SELECT statement that looks something like this:

```
SELECT lastname, deptname
FROM employee e FULL OUTER JOIN department d
ON e.workdept = d.deptno
```

If you executed this query against the SAMPLE database provided with DB2, you would get a result data set that looks something like this:

```
LASTNAME          DEPTNAME
---------         ------------------------------
HAAS              SPIFFY COMPUTER SERVICE DIV.
THOMPSON          PLANNING
KWAN              INFORMATION CENTER
GEYER             SUPPORT SERVICES
STERN             MANUFACTURING SYSTEMS
PULASKI           ADMINISTRATION SYSTEMS
HENDERSON         OPERATIONS
SPENSER           SOFTWARE SUPPORT
LUCCHESSI         SPIFFY COMPUTER SERVICE DIV.
O'CONNELL         SPIFFY COMPUTER SERVICE DIV.
QUINTANA          INFORMATION CENTER
NICHOLLS          INFORMATION CENTER
ADAMSON           MANUFACTURING SYSTEMS
PIANKA            MANUFACTURING SYSTEMS
YOSHIMURA         MANUFACTURING SYSTEMS
SCOUTTEN          MANUFACTURING SYSTEMS
WALKER            MANUFACTURING SYSTEMS
BROWN             MANUFACTURING SYSTEMS
JONES             MANUFACTURING SYSTEMS
LUTZ              MANUFACTURING SYSTEMS
JEFFERSON         ADMINISTRATION SYSTEMS
```

```
LASTNAME          DEPTNAME
---------         ------------------------
MARINO            ADMINISTRATION SYSTEMS
SMITH             ADMINISTRATION SYSTEMS
JOHNSON           ADMINISTRATION SYSTEMS
PEREZ             ADMINISTRATION SYSTEMS
SCHNEIDER         OPERATIONS
PARKER            OPERATIONS
SMITH             OPERATIONS
SETRIGHT          OPERATIONS
MEHTA             SOFTWARE SUPPORT
LEE               SOFTWARE SUPPORT
GOUNOT            SOFTWARE SUPPORT
HEMMINGER         SPIFFY COMPUTER SERVICE DIV.
ORLANDO           SPIFFY COMPUTER SERVICE DIV.
NATZ              INFORMATION CENTER
YAMAMOTO          MANUFACTURING SYSTEMS
JOHN              MANUFACTURING SYSTEMS
MONTEVERDE        ADMINISTRATION SYSTEMS
SCHWARTZ          OPERATIONS
SPRINGER          OPERATIONS
WONG              SOFTWARE SUPPORT
ALONZO            SOFTWARE SUPPORT
-                 BRANCH OFFICE H2
-                 RANCH OFFICE I2
-                 BRANCH OFFICE G2
-                 DEVELOPMENT CENTER
-                 BRANCH OFFICE F2
-                 BRANCH OFFICE J2
  48 record(s) selected.
```

Records that have a null value assigned to one of the columns are records that did not have a matching value in the two tables.

Combining the Results of Two or More Queries Using a Set Operator

With DB2, it is possible to combine two or more queries into a single query by using a special operator known as a *set operator*. When a set operator is used, the results of each query executed are combined in a specific manner to produce a single result data set. The following set operators are available:

UNION. When the UNION set operator is used, the result data sets produced by each individual query are combined and all duplicate rows are eliminated. Figure 5–5 illustrates how a simple UNION operation works.

EMP_INST_USA TABLE

EMPNO	LASTNAME	INSTRUMENT
001	JAGGER	HARMONICA
001	JAGGER	HARMONICA
002	RICHARDS	GUITAR
002	RICHARDS	GUITAR
003	WOOD	GUITAR

EMP_INST_UK TABLE

EMPNO	LASTNAME	INSTRUMENT
001	JAGGER	HARMONICA
001	JAGGER	HARMONICA
004	WYMAN	BASS GUITAR
005	WATTS	DRUMS

UNION SET OPERATION

```
SELECT * FROM emp_inst_usa
UNION
SELECT * FROM emp_inst_uk
ORDER BY empno, instrument
```

RESULT DATA SET

EMPNO	LASTNAME	INSTRUMENT
001	JAGGER	HARMONICA
002	RICHARDS	GUITAR
003	WOOD	GUITAR
004	WYMAN	BASS GUITAR
005	WATTS	DRUMS

Even though there are two identical occurrences of the record for JAGGER in each table, only one record appears in the result data set produced; the same is true for the two occurrences of the record for RICHARDS found in the first table.

Figure 5–5: A simple UNION set operation.

UNION ALL. When the UNION ALL set operator is used, the result data sets produced by each individual query are combined; all duplicate rows found are retained. Figure 5–6 illustrates how a simple UNION ALL operation would work.

EMP_INST_USA TABLE

EMPNO	LASTNAME	INSTRUMENT
001	JAGGER	HARMONICA
001	JAGGER	HARMONICA
002	RICHARDS	GUITAR
002	RICHARDS	GUITAR
003	WOOD	GUITAR

EMP_INST_UK TABLE

EMPNO	LASTNAME	INSTRUMENT
001	JAGGER	HARMONICA
001	JAGGER	HARMONICA
004	WYMAN	BASS GUITAR
005	WATTS	DRUMS

UNION ALL SET OPERATION

```
SELECT * FROM emp_inst_usa
UNION ALL
SELECT * FROM emp_inst_uk
ORDER BY empno, instrument
```

RESULT DATA SET

EMPNO	LASTNAME	INSTRUMENT
001	JAGGER	HARMONICA
001	JAGGER	HARMONICA
001	JAGGER	HARMONICA
001	JAGGER	HARMONICA
002	RICHARDS	GUITAR
002	RICHARDS	GUITAR
003	WOOD	GUITAR
004	WYMAN	BASS GUITAR
005	WATTS	DRUMS

Every occurrence of every record found in each table appears in the result data set produced.

Figure 5–6: A simple UNION ALL set operation.

INTERSECT. When the INTERSECT set operator is used, the result data sets produced by each individual query are combined, all duplicate rows found are eliminated, and all records found in the first result data set that do not have a corresponding record in the second result data set are eliminated, leaving just the records that are found in both result data sets. Figure 5–7 illustrates how a simple INTERSECT operation would work.

EMP_INST_USA TABLE

EMPNO	LASTNAME	INSTRUMENT
001	JAGGER	HARMONICA
001	JAGGER	HARMONICA
002	RICHARDS	GUITAR
002	RICHARDS	GUITAR
003	WOOD	GUITAR

EMP_INST_UK TABLE

EMPNO	LASTNAME	INSTRUMENT
001	JAGGER	HARMONICA
001	JAGGER	HARMONICA
004	WYMAN	BASS GUITAR
005	WATTS	DRUMS

INTERSECT SET OPERATION

```
SELECT * FROM emp_inst_usa
INTERSECT
SELECT * FROM emp_inst_uk
ORDER BY empno, instrument
```

RESULT DATA SET

EMPNO	LASTNAME	INSTRUMENT
001	JAGGER	HARMONICA

Because the record for JAGGER is the only record that is identical in both tables, it is the only record that appears in the result data set produced. And even though there are multiple occurrences of the record for JAGGER in both tables, only one record appears in the result data set produced.

Figure 5–7: A simple INTERSECT set operation.

INTERSECT ALL: When the INTERSECT ALL set operator is used, the result data sets produced by each individual query are combined and all records found in the first result data set that do not have a corresponding record in the second result data set are eliminated, leaving just the records that are found in both result data sets; all duplicate rows found are retained. Figure 5–8 illustrates how a simple INTERSECT ALL operation would work.

EMP_INST_USA TABLE

EMPNO	LASTNAME	INSTRUMENT
001	JAGGER	HARMONICA
001	JAGGER	HARMONICA
002	RICHARDS	GUITAR
002	RICHARDS	GUITAR
003	WOOD	GUITAR

EMP_INST_UK TABLE

EMPNO	LASTNAME	INSTRUMENT
001	JAGGER	HARMONICA
001	JAGGER	HARMONICA
004	WYMAN	BASS GUITAR
005	WATTS	DRUMS

INTERSECT ALL SET OPERATION

```
SELECT * FROM emp_inst_usa
INTERSECT ALL
SELECT * FROM emp_inst_uk
ORDER BY empno, instrument
```

RESULT DATA SET

EMPNO	LASTNAME	INSTRUMENT
001	JAGGER	HARMONICA
001	JAGGER	HARMONICA

Because the record for JAGGER is the only record that is identical in both tables, it is the only record that appears in the result data set produced. And since there are two occurrences of the record for JAGGER in each table, both records appear in the result data set produced.

Figure 5–8: A simple INTERSECT ALL set operation.

EXCEPT: When the EXCEPT set operator is used, the result data sets produced by each individual query are combined, all duplicate rows found are eliminated, and all records found in the first result data set that have a corresponding record in the second result data set are eliminated, leaving just the records that are not found in both result data sets. Figure 5–9 illustrates how a simple EXCEPT operation would work.

EMP_INST_USA TABLE

EMPNO	LASTNAME	INSTRUMENT
001	JAGGER	HARMONICA
001	JAGGER	HARMONICA
002	RICHARDS	GUITAR
002	RICHARDS	GUITAR
003	WOOD	GUITAR

EMP_INST_UK TABLE

EMPNO	LASTNAME	INSTRUMENT
001	JAGGER	HARMONICA
001	JAGGER	HARMONICA
004	WYMAN	BASS GUITAR
005	WATTS	DRUMS

EXCEPT SET OPERATION

```
SELECT * FROM emp_inst_usa
EXCEPT
SELECT * FROM emp_inst_uk
ORDER BY empno, instrument
```

RESULT DATA SET

EMPNO	LASTNAME	INSTRUMENT
002	RICHARDS	GUITAR
003	WOOD	GUITAR

Because the records for RICHARDS and WOODS are the only records in the first table that do not have identical records in the second table, they are the only records that appear in the result data set produced.

Figure 5–9: A simple EXCEPT set operation.

It is important to note that, in contrast to the UNION, UNION ALL, INTERSECT, and INTERSECT ALL set operators, if the queries used with the EXCEPT and EXCEPT ALL set operators are reversed, a different result data set will be produced. Figure 5–10 illustrates how the same EXCEPT operation would work if the order of the queries specified were reversed.

EMP_INST_UK TABLE

EMPNO	LASTNAME	INSTRUMENT
001	JAGGER	HARMONICA
001	JAGGER	HARMONICA
004	WYMAN	BASS GUITAR
005	WATTS	DRUMS

EMP_INST_USA TABLE

EMPNO	LASTNAME	INSTRUMENT
001	JAGGER	HARMONICA
001	JAGGER	HARMONICA
002	RICHARDS	GUITAR
002	RICHARDS	GUITAR
003	WOOD	GUITAR

EXCEPT SET OPERATION

```
SELECT * FROM emp_inst_uk
EXCEPT
SELECT * FROM emp_inst_usa
ORDER BY empno, instrument
```

RESULT DATA SET

EMPNO	LASTNAME	INSTRUMENT
004	WYMAN	BASS GUITAR
005	WATTS	DRUMS

Now, because the records for WYMAN and WATTS are the only records in the first table that do not have identical records in the second table, they are the only records that appear in the result data set produced.

Figure 5–10: A simple EXCEPT set operation with the queries reversed.

EXCEPT ALL: When the EXCEPT ALL set operator is used, the result data sets produced by each individual query are combined and all records found in the first result data set that have a corresponding record in the second result data set are eliminated, leaving just the records that are not found in both result data sets; all duplicate rows found are retained. Figure 5–11 illustrates how a simple EXCEPT ALL operation would work.

EMP_INST_USA TABLE

EMPNO	LASTNAME	INSTRUMENT
001	JAGGER	HARMONICA
001	JAGGER	HARMONICA
002	RICHARDS	GUITAR
002	RICHARDS	GUITAR
003	WOOD	GUITAR

EMP_INST_UK TABLE

EMPNO	LASTNAME	INSTRUMENT
001	JAGGER	HARMONICA
001	JAGGER	HARMONICA
004	WYMAN	BASS GUITAR
005	WATTS	DRUMS

EXCEPT ALL SET OPERATION

```
SELECT * FROM emp_inst_usa
EXCEPT ALL
SELECT * FROM emp_inst_uk
ORDER BY empno, instrument
```

RESULT DATA SET

EMPNO	LASTNAME	INSTRUMENT
002	RICHARDS	GUITAR
002	RICHARDS	GUITAR
003	WOOD	GUITAR

Because the records for RICHARDS and WOODS are the only records in the first table that do not have identical records in the second table, they are the only records that appear in the result data set produced. And since there are two occurrences of the record for RICHARDS in the first table, both records appear in the result data set produced.

Figure 5–11: A simple EXCEPT ALL set operation.

In order for two result data sets to be combined with a set operator, both must have the same number of columns, and each of those columns must have the same data types assigned to it. So when would you want to combine the results of two queries using a set operator? Suppose your company keeps individual employee expense account information in a table whose contents are archived at the end of each fiscal year. When a new fiscal year begins, expenditures for that year are essentially recorded in a new table. Now suppose, for tax purposes, you need a record of all employees' expenses for the last two years. To obtain this information, each archived table must be queried, and the results must then be combined. Rather than do this by running individual queries against the archived tables and storing the results in some kind of temporary table, this operation could be performed simply by using the UNION set operator, along with two SELECT SQL statements. Such a set of SELECT statements might look something like this:

```
SELECT * FROM emp_exp_02
UNION
SELECT * FROM emp_exp_01
```

Obtaining Results from a Result Data Set Using a Cursor

So far, we have looked at a variety of ways in which a query can be constructed using the SELECT SQL statement. We have also seen how the results of a query can be returned to the user when an SQL statement is executed from the Command Editor or the Command Line Processor. However, we have not seen how the results of a query can be obtained when a SELECT statement is executed from an application program.

When a query is executed from within an application, DB2 uses a mechanism known as a *cursor* to retrieve data values from the result data set produced. The name "cursor" probably originated from the blinking cursor found on early computer screens, and just as that cursor indicated the current position on the screen and identified where typed words would appear next, a DB2 cursor indicates the current position in the result data set (i.e., the current row) and identifies which row of data will be returned to the application next. Depending upon how it has been defined, a cursor can be categorized as follows:

Read-only: Read-only cursors are cursors that have been constructed in such a way that rows in their corresponding result data set can be read but not modified or deleted. A cursor is considered read-only if it is based on a read-only SELECT statement. (For example, the statement "SELECT deptname FROM department" is a read-only SELECT statement.)

Updatable: Updatable cursors are cursors that have been constructed in such a way that rows in their corresponding result data set can be modified or deleted. A cursor is considered updatable if the FOR UPDATE clause was specified when the cursor was created. (Only one table can be referenced in the SELECT statement that is used to create an updatable cursor.)

Ambiguous: Ambiguous cursors are cursors that have been constructed in such a way that it is impossible to tell if they are meant to be read-only or updatable. (Ambiguous cursors are treated as read-only cursors if the BLOCKING ALL option was specified during precompiling or binding. Otherwise, they are considered updatable.)

Regardless of which type of cursor used, the following steps must be performed in order for a cursor is to be incorporated into an application program:

1. Declare (define) the cursor along with its type and associate it with the desired query (SELECT or VALUES SQL statement).

2. Open the cursor. This action will cause the corresponding query to be executed and a result data set to be produced.

3. Retrieve (fetch) each row in the result data set, one by one, until an "End of data" condition occurs—each time a row is retrieved from the result data set, the cursor is automatically moved to the next row.

4. If appropriate, alter or delete the current row by executing an UPDATE ... WHERE CURRENT OF or a DELETE ... WHERE CURRENT OF SQL statement (only if the cursor is updatable).

5. Close the cursor. This action will cause the result data set that was produced when the corresponding query was executed to be deleted.

With DB2 (as with most other relational database management systems), the following SQL statements are used to carry out the preceding steps:

```
DECLARE CURSOR
OPEN
FETCH
CLOSE
```

The DECLARE CURSOR Statement

Before a cursor can be used in an application program, it must be created and associated with the SELECT statement that will be used to generate its corresponding result data set. This is done by executing the DECLARE CURSOR SQL statement. The basic syntax for this statement is:

```
DECLARE CURSOR [CursorName]
<WITH HOLD>
<WITH RETURN <TO CLIENT | TO CALLER>>
FOR [[SELECTStatement] | [StatementName]]
<FOR READ ONLY | FOR FETCH ONLY |
  FOR UPDATE <OF [ColumnName, ...]>>
```

where:

CursorName	Identifies the name that is to be assigned to the cursor to be created.
SELECTStatement	Identifies a SELECT SQL statement that, when executed, will produce a result data set that is to be associated with the cursor to be created.
StatementName	Identifies a prepared SELECT SQL statement that, when executed, will produce a result data set that is to be associated with the cursor to be created. (This SELECT statement must be prepared with the PREPARE SQL statement before it is used to create a cursor; this statement can contain parameter markers.)
ColumnName	Identifies the name of one or more columns in the result data set to be produced whose values can be modified by performing a positioned update or a positioned delete operation. (Each name provided must identify an existing column in the result data set produced.)

If the WITH HOLD option is specified when the DECLARE CURSOR statement is executed, the cursor created will remain open (once it has been opened) across transaction boundaries and must be explicitly closed. (If this option is not used, the scope of the cursor is limited to the transaction in which it is defined, and the cursor will be closed automatically when the transaction that declares and opens it is terminated.) If the WITH RETURN option is specified when the DECLARE CURSOR statement is executed, it is assumed that the cursor has been created from within a stored procedure and that once opened, the cursor is to remain open when control is passed back to either the calling application or the client application, depending on how the WITH RETURN option was specified.

The clauses FOR READ ONLY, FOR FETCH ONLY, and FOR UPDATE <OF [*ColumnName*, ...]> are actually part of the SELECT statement used to build the result data set associated with the cursor and are not part of the DECLARE CURSOR statement's syntax. As you might imagine, the use (or lack) of these clauses determine whether the cursor to be created will be a read-only, updatable, or ambiguous cursor.

Thus, if you wanted to define a read-only cursor named MY_CURSOR that is associated with a result data set that contains values obtained from the WORKDEPT and JOB columns found in a table named EMPLOYEE, you could do so by executing a DECLARE CURSOR statement that looks something like this:

```
DECLARE my_cursor CURSOR
  FOR SELECT workdept, job FROM employee
  FOR READ ONLY
```

Multiple cursors can be created within a single application; however, each cursor created (within the same source code file) must be assigned a unique name.

The OPEN Statement

Although a cursor is defined when the DECLARE CURSOR SQL statement is executed, the result data set associated with the cursor is not actually produced until the cursor is opened; when a cursor is opened, all rows that satisfy the query associated with the cursor's definition are retrieved and copied to a result data set. Cursors are opened by executing the OPEN SQL statement. The basic syntax for this statement is:

```
OPEN [CursorName]
<USING [HostVariable], ... |
  USING DESCRIPTOR [DescriptorName]>
```

where:

CursorName   Identifies the name to be assigned to the cursor to be opened.

HostVariable   Identifies one or more host variables that are to be used to provide values for any parameter markers that were coded in the SELECT statement used to create the cursor to be opened. (Host variables and parameter markers are used to provide dynamic information to the DB2 Optimizer when an SQL statement is prepared for execution.)

DescriptorName Identifies an SQL Descriptor Area (SQLDA) data structure variable that contains descriptions of each host variable that is to be used to provide values for parameter markers coded in the SELECT statement used to create the cursor to be opened. (The SQLDA data structure variable is another way to provide dynamic information to the DB2 Optimizer when an SQL statement is prepared for execution.)

Thus, if you wanted to open a cursor named MY_CURSOR (which, in turn, would cause the corresponding result data set to be produced), you could do so by executing an OPEN statement that looks like this:

```
OPEN my_cursor
```

On the other hand, if you wanted to open a cursor named MY_CURSOR and associate two host variables (named LASTNAME and FIRSTNAME) with parameter markers that were coded in the SELECT statement that was used to create the cursor to be opened, you could do so by executing an OPEN statement that looks like this:

```
OPEN MY_CURSOR USING :lastname, :firstname
```

It is important to note that the rows of the result data set associated with a query may be derived during the execution of the OPEN statement (in which case a temporary table may be created to hold them); or they may be derived during the execution of each subsequent FETCH statement. In either case, when a cursor is opened, it is placed in the "Open" state, and the cursor pointer is positioned before the first row of data in the result data set produced; if the result data set is empty, the position of the cursor is effectively "after the last row," and any subsequent FETCH operations performed will generate a NOT FOUND (+100) condition.

It is important to note that once a cursor has been opened, it can be in one of three possible positions: "Before a Row of Data," "On a Row of Data," or "After the Last Row of Data." If a cursor is positioned "Before a Row of Data," it will be moved just before the first row of the result data set, and the data values stored in that row will be assigned to the appropriate host variables when the FETCH statement is executed. If a cursor is positioned "On a Row of Data" when the FETCH statement is executed, it will be moved to the next row in the result data set (if one exists), and the data values stored in that row will be assigned to the appropriate host variables. If a cursor is positioned on the last row of the result data set when the FETCH statement is executed, it will be moved to the "After the Last Row of Data" position, the value +100 will be assigned to the sqlcode field of the current SQLCA data structure variable, and the value "02000" will be assigned to the sqlstate field of the current SQLCA data structure variable. (In this case, no data is copied to the host variables specified.)

The FETCH Statement

Once a cursor has been opened, data is retrieved from its associated result data set by calling the FETCH statement repeatedly until all records have been processed. The basic syntax for the FETCH statement is:

FETCH <FROM> [*CursorName*] INTO [*HostVariable, ...*]

or

FETCH <FROM> [*CursorName*] USING DESCRIPTOR [*DescriptorName*]

where

CursorName   Identifies the name assigned to the cursor that data is to be retrieved from.

HostVariable   Identifies one or more host variables to which values obtained from the result data set associated with the specified cursor are to be copied.

DescriptorName   Identifies an SQL Descriptor Area (SQLDA) data structure variable that contains descriptions of each host variable to which values obtained from the result data set associated with the specified cursor are to be copied.

Thus, if you wanted to retrieve a record from the result data set associated with a cursor named MY_CURSOR and copy the values obtained to two host variables named DEPTNUMBER and DEPTNAME, you could do so by executing a FETCH statement that looks something like this:

```
FETCH FROM my_cursor CURSOR INTO :deptnumber, :deptname
```

The CLOSE Statement

When all records stored in the result data set associated with a cursor have been retrieved (and copied to host variables) or when the result data set associated with a cursor is no longer needed, it can be destroyed by executing the CLOSE SQL statement. The syntax for this statement is:

```
CLOSE [CursorName]
<WITH RELEASE>
```

where:

CursorName   Identifies the name assigned to the cursor to be closed.

If the WITH RELEASE option is specified when the CLOSE statement is executed, an attempt will be made to release all locks that were acquired on behalf of the cursor. (It is important to note that not all of the locks acquired are necessarily released; some locks may be held for other operations or activities.)

Therefore, if you wanted to close a cursor named MY_CURSOR and destroy its associated result data set, you could do so by executing a CLOSE statement that looks like this:

```
CLOSE my_cursor
```

Putting It All Together

Now that we have seen how each of the cursor-processing statements available are used, let's examine how they are typically coded in an application. An application written in the C programming language that uses a cursor to obtain and print employee identification numbers and last names for all employees who have the job title DESIGNER might look something like this:

```c
#include <stdio.h>
#include <stdlib.h>
#include <sql.h>
void main()
{
  /* Include The SQLCA Data Structure Variable */
  EXEC SQL INCLUDE SQLCA;

  /* Declare The SQL Host Memory Variables */
  EXEC SQL BEGIN DECLARE SECTION;
    char    EmployeeNo[7];
    char    LastName[16];
  EXEC SQL END DECLARE SECTION;

   /* Connect To The SAMPLE Database */
  EXEC SQL CONNECT TO sample USER db2admin USING ibmdb2;

    /* Declare A Cursor */
  EXEC SQL DECLARE c1 CURSOR FOR
    SELECT empno, lastname
    FROM employee
    WHERE job = 'DESIGNER';

  /* Open The Cursor */
  EXEC SQL OPEN c1;

  /* Fetch The Records */
  while (sqlca.sqlcode == SQL_RC_OK)
  {
    /* Retrieve A Record */
    EXEC SQL FETCH c1
      INTO :EmployeeNo, :LastName

    /* Print The Information Retrieved */
    if (sqlca.sqlcode == SQL_RC_OK)
      printf("%s, %s\n", EmployeeNo, LastName);
  }

  /* Close The Cursor */
  EXEC SQL CLOSE c1;

  /* Issue A COMMIT To Free All Locks */
  EXEC SQL COMMIT;

  /* Disconnect From The SAMPLE Database */
  EXEC SQL DISCONNECT CURRENT;
}
```

Remember, an application can use several cursors concurrently; however, each cursor must have its own unique name and its own set of DECLARE CURSOR, OPEN, FETCH, and CLOSE SQL statements.

Transactions and Transaction Boundaries

A *transaction* (also known as a *unit of work*) is a sequence of one or more SQL operations grouped together as a single unit, usually within an application process. Such a unit is called *atomic* (from the Greek word meaning "not able to be cut," because it is indivisible—either all of its work is carried out, or none of its work is carried out. A given transaction can perform any number of SQL operations— from a single operation to many hundreds or even thousands, depending on what is considered a "single step" within your business logic. (It is important to note that the longer a transaction is, the more database concurrency decreases and the more resource locks are acquired; this is usually considered a sign of a poorly written application.)

The initiation and termination of a single transaction defines points of data consistency within a database (we'll take a closer look at data consistency in Chapter 7, "Data Concurrency"); either the effects of all operations performed within a transaction are applied to the database and made permanent (committed), or the effects of all operations performed are backed out (rolled back) and the database is returned to the state it was in before the transaction was initiated. (Any data pages that were copied to a buffer pool on behalf of a transaction will remain in the buffer pool until their storage space is needed—at that time, they will be removed.)

In most cases, transactions are initiated the first time an executable SQL statement is executed after a connection to a database has been made or immediately after a pre-existing transaction has been terminated. Once initiated, transactions can be implicitly terminated using a feature known as "automatic commit" (in this case, each executable SQL statement is treated as a single transaction, and any changes made by that statement are applied to the database if the statement executes successfully or discarded if the statement fails), or they can be explicitly terminated by executing the COMMIT or the ROLLBACK SQL statement. The basic syntax for these two statements is:

COMMIT <WORK>

and

ROLLBACK <WORK>

When the COMMIT statement is used to terminate a transaction, all changes made to the database since the transaction began are made permanent. On the other hand, when the ROLLBACK statement is used, all changes made are backed out and the database is returned to the state it was in just before the transaction began. Figure 5–12 shows the effects of a transaction that was terminated with a COMMIT statement; Figure 5–13 shows the effects of a transaction that was terminated with a ROLLBACK statement.

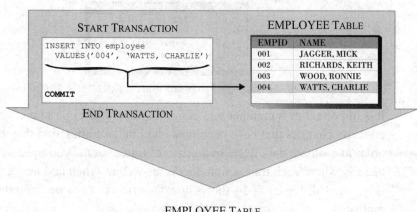

EMPLOYEE TABLE
(BEFORE TRANSACTION)

EMPID	NAME
001	JAGGER, MICK
002	RICHARDS, KEITH
003	WOOD, RONNIE

START TRANSACTION

```
INSERT INTO employee
  VALUES('004', 'WATTS, CHARLIE')


COMMIT
```

END TRANSACTION

EMPLOYEE TABLE

EMPID	NAME
001	JAGGER, MICK
002	RICHARDS, KEITH
003	WOOD, RONNIE
004	WATTS, CHARLIE

EMPLOYEE TABLE
(AFTER TRANSACTION)

EMPID	NAME
001	JAGGER, MICK
002	RICHARDS, KEITH
003	WOOD, RONNIE
004	WATTS, CHARLIE

Figure 5–12: Terminating a transaction with the COMMIT SQL statement.

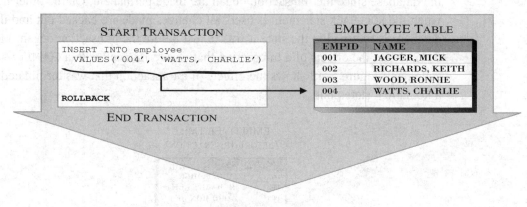

EMPLOYEE TABLE
(BEFORE TRANSACTION)

EMPID	NAME
001	JAGGER, MICK
002	RICHARDS, KEITH
003	WOOD, RONNIE

START TRANSACTION

```
INSERT INTO employee
  VALUES('004', 'WATTS, CHARLIE')


ROLLBACK
```

END TRANSACTION

EMPLOYEE TABLE

EMPID	NAME
001	JAGGER, MICK
002	RICHARDS, KEITH
003	WOOD, RONNIE
004	WATTS, CHARLIE

EMPLOYEE TABLE
(AFTER TRANSACTION)

EMPID	NAME
001	JAGGER, MICK
002	RICHARDS, KEITH
003	WOOD, RONNIE

Figure 5–13: Terminating a transaction with the ROLLBACK SQL statement.

It is important to remember that commit and rollback operations only have an effect on changes that have been made within the transaction they terminate. So in order to evaluate the effects of a series of transactions, you must be able to identify where each transaction begins, as well as when and how each transaction is terminated. Figure 5–14 shows how the effects of a series of transactions can be evaluated.

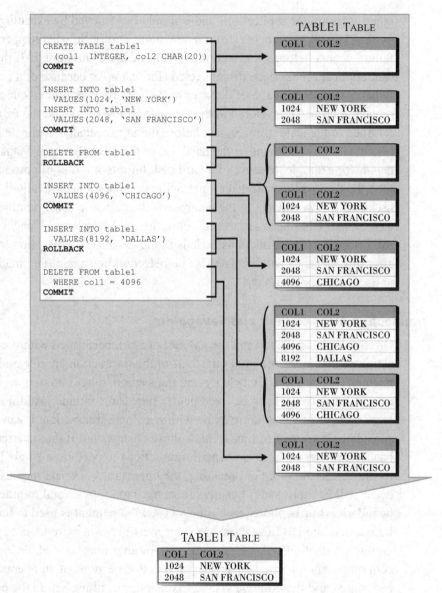

Figure 5–14: Evaluating the effects of a series of transactions.

Changes made by a transaction that have not been committed are usually inaccessible to other users and applications (there are exceptions, which we will look at in Chapter 7, "Data Concurrency," when we look at the Uncommitted Read isolation level), and can be backed out with a rollback operation. However, once changes made by a transaction have been committed, they become accessible to all other users and/or applications and can only be removed by executing new UPDATE or DELETE SQL statements (from a new transaction). So what happens if a system failure occurs before a transaction's changes can be committed? If the user/application has been disconnected (for example, because of a network failure), the DB2 Database Manager backs out all uncommitted changes (by replaying information stored in the transaction log files), and the database is returned to the state it was in just before the unexpectedly terminated transaction began. On the other hand, if the database or the DB2 Database Manager is terminated (for example, because of a hard disk failure or a loss of power), the next time the database is restarted (which will take place automatically the next time a user attempts to connect to the database if the database configuration parameter autorestart has been set accordingly), the DB2 Database Manager will try to roll back all open transactions it finds in the database's transaction log files. Only after this succeeds will the database be placed online again (i.e., made accessible to users and applications).

Transaction Management and Savepoints

Often, it is desirable to limit the amount of work performed within a single transaction so that locks acquired on behalf of the transaction are released in a timely manner. (When locks are held by one transaction, other transactions may be forced to wait for those locks to be freed before they can continue.) Additionally, if a large number of changes are made within a single transaction, it can take a considerable amount of time to back those changes out if the transaction is rolled back. However, using several small transactions to perform a single large task has its drawbacks as well. For one thing, the opportunity for data inconsistency to occur will be increased if business rules have to cross several transaction boundaries. Furthermore, each time a COMMIT statement is used to terminate a transaction, the DB2 Database Manager must perform extra work to commit the current transaction and start a new one. (Another drawback of having multiple commit points for a particular operation is that portions of an operation might be committed and therefore be visible to other applications before the operation is completed.)

To get around these issues, DB2 uses a mechanism known as a *savepoint* to allow an application to break the work being performed by a single large transaction into one or more subsets. By using savepoints, an application avoids the exposure to "dirty data" that might occur when multiple commits are performed, yet it provides granular control over an operation—you can use as many savepoints as you want within a single transaction as long as the savepoints used are not nested.

Savepoints are created by executing the SAVEPOINT SQL statement. The basic syntax for this statement is:

```
SAVEPOINT [SavepointName]
<UNIQUE>
ON ROLLBACK RETAIN CURSORS
<ON ROLLBACK RETAIN LOCKS>
```

where:

SavepointName   Identifies the name that is to be assigned to the savepoint to be created.

If the UNIQUE option is specified when the SAVEPOINT statement is executed, the name assigned to the savepoint created will be unique and cannot be reused by the application that created it as long as the savepoint is active.

Thus, if you wanted to create a savepoint named MY_SP, you could do so by executing a SAVEPOINT statement that looks like this:

```
SAVEPOINT my_sp ON ROLLBACK RETAIN CURSORS
```

Once created, a savepoint can be used in conjunction with a special form of the ROLLBACK SQL statement to return a database to the state it was in at the point in time a particular savepoint was created. The syntax for this form of the ROLLBACK statement is:

```
ROLLBACK <WORK> TO SAVEPOINT <[SavepointName]>
```

where:

SavepointName   Identifies the name assigned to the savepoint that indicates the point in time that operations performed against the database are to be rolled back (backed out) to.

When a savepoint is no longer needed, it can be released by executing the RELEASE SAVEPOINT SQL statement. The syntax for this statement is:

```
RELEASE <TO> SAVEPOINT <[SavepointName]>
```

where:

SavepointName   Identifies the name assigned to the savepoint that is to be released.

Thus, suppose a table named EMPLOYEES has the following characteristics:

Column Name	Data Type
EMPID	INTEGER
NAME	CHAR(20)
AGE	INTEGER

Now, suppose it was populated as follows:

EMPID	NAME	AGE
1	MICK JAGGER	63
2	KEITH RICHARDS	63
3	RONNIE WOOD	59
4	CHARLIE WATTS	65

If the following sequence of SQL operations were to be performed within a single transaction, in the order shown:

```
UPDATE employees SET empid = 3 WHERE empid = 2;
SAVEPOINT s1 ON ROLLBACK RETAIN CURSORS;
UPDATE employees SET empid = 5 WHERE empid = 3;
SAVEPOINT s2 ON ROLLBACK RETAIN CURSORS;
INSERT INTO employees VALUES (6, 'BILL WYMAN', 70);
ROLLBACK TO SAVEPOINT s1;
UPDATE employees SET empid = 2 WHERE empid = 4;
```

Then the records stored in the EMPLOYEES table would look like this:

EMPID	NAME	AGE
1	MICK JAGGER	63
3	KEITH RICHARDS	63
3	RONNIE WOOD	59
2	CHARLIE WATTS	65

In this example, only the effects of the first and last update operation were retained; all other changes were removed when the ROLLBACK TO SAVEPOINT SQL statement was executed.

Once a savepoint is created, all subsequent SQL statements executed are associated with that savepoint until it is released – either explicitly by calling the RELEASE SAVEPOINT statement or implicitly by ending the transaction or unit of work that the savepoint was created in. In addition, when you issue a ROLLBACK TO SAVEPOINT SQL statement, the corresponding savepoint is not automatically released as soon as the rollback operation is completed. Instead, you can issue multiple ROLLBACK TO SAVEPOINT statements for a given transaction, and each time a ROLLBACK TO SAVEPOINT statement is executed, the database will be returned to the state it was in at the time the savepoint was created. (If multiple savepoints have been created, it is possible to rollback to any savepoint available; you are not required to rollback successively to every savepoint, in the opposite order in which they were created, to return the database to the state it was in when an earlier savepoint was created.)

Invoking User-Defined Functions

In Chapter 4, "Working with Databases and Database Objects," we saw that user-defined functions (UDFs) are special objects that are used to extend and enhance the support provided by the built-in functions available with DB2 9. Like user-defined data types, user-defined functions (or methods) are created and named by a database user. However, unlike DB2's built-in functions, user-defined functions can take advantage of system calls and DB2's administrative APIs, thereby providing more synergy between applications and databases.

Five types of user-defined functions can be created:

1. **Sourced (or Template).** A sourced function is constructed from a function that is already registered with a database (referred to as the source function). Sourced functions can be columnar, scalar, or table in nature or they can be designed to overload a specific operator such as +, –, *, and /. When a sourced function is invoked, all arguments passed to it are converted to the data types that are expected by the underlying source function, and the source function itself is invoked. Upon completion, the source function performs any conversions necessary on the results produced and returns them to the calling SQL statement. The most common use of sourced functions is to enable a user-defined distinct data type to selectively inherit some of the semantics of the built-in data type on which it is based.

2. **SQL Scalar, Table, or Row.** Whereas a sourced function is constructed from a function that already exists, an SQL function is constructed from the ground up, using only SQL statements. An SQL function can be scalar in nature (scalar functions return a single value and can be specified in an SQL statement wherever a regular expression can be used) or can return a single row or an entire table.

3. **External Scalar.** An external scalar function is a function that is written using a high-level programming language such as C, C++, or Java that returns a single value. The function itself resides in an external library and is registered in the database, along with any related attributes.

4. **External Table.** Like external scalar functions, external table functions are written using a high-level programming language. But where an external scalar function returns a single value, an external table function returns a result data set, in the form of a table, to the SQL statement that references it. External table functions are powerful because they enable you to make almost any source of data appear to be a DB2 base table; the result data set returned can be used in join operations, grouping operations, set operations (for example, UNIONs), or any other operation that can be applied to a read-only view. Again, the function itself resides in an external library and is registered in the database, along with any related attributes.

5. **OLE DB External Table.** OLE DB is designed to provide access to all types of data in an OLE Component Object Model (COM) environment. Like external table functions, external OLE DB table functions are written using a high-level programming language and return a result data set, in the form of

a table, to SQL statements that references them. However, with OLE DB table functions, a generic built-in OLE DB consumer can be used to interface with any OLE DB provider to access data; you need only to register an OLE DB table function and refer to the appropriate OLE DB provider as the data source. No additional programming is needed. Again, the function resides in an external library and is registered in the database, along with any related attributes.

How a user-defined function is invoked depends a lot on what it has been designed to do; scalar user-defined functions can be invoked as an expression in the select list of a query, whereas table and row functions must be referenced by the FROM clause. For example, you could invoke a scalar user-defined function named CONVERT_TEMP that is designed to convert temperatures in degrees Fahrenheit to degrees Celsius by executing a SELECT statement that looks something like this:

```
SELECT temp AS tempf, convert_temp(temp, 'F') AS tempc
FROM climate_info
```

On the other hand, if you wanted to obtain records from a user-defined function named MGR_LIST that is designed to produce a list of managers and their contact information be examining records stored in a table named EMPLOYEE, you would so by executing a SELECT statement that looks something like this:

```
SELECT firstname, lastname, phone
FROM TABLE(MGR_LIST())
```

Calling a Stored Procedure

In Chapter 4, "Working with Databases and Database Objects," we also saw that workloads in a client/server environment can be moved from the client to the sever by creating one or more stored procedures. Once a stored procedure has been created and registered with a database (by executing the CREATE PROCEDURE SQL statement), that procedure can be invoked, either interactively, using a utility such as the Command Line Processor, or from a client application. Stored procedures are invoked by executing the CALL SQL statement. The basic syntax for this statement is:

```
CALL [ProcedureName] ( <[InputParameter] |
  [OutputParameter] | NULL>, ...)
```

where:

ProcedureName   Identifies the name assigned to the procedure to be invoked.

InputValue   Identifies one or more parameter values that are to be passed to the procedure being invoked.

OutputParameter Identifies one or more parameter markers or host variables that are to receive return values from the procedure being invoked.

Suppose an SQL stored procedure named GET_SALES was created by executing a CREATE PROCEDURE statement that looks like this:

```
CREATE PROCEDURE get_sales
  (IN quota INTEGER, OUT retcode CHAR(5))
  DYNAMIC RESULT SETS 1
  LANGUAGE SQL
  BEGIN
    DECLARE sqlstate CHAR(5);
    DECLARE sales_results CURSOR WITH RETURN FOR
     SELECT sales_person, SUM(sales) AS total_sales
     FROM sales
     GROUP BY sales_person
     HAVING SUM(sales) > quota;
    DECLARE EXIT HANDLER FOR SQLEXCEPTION
     SET retcode = sqlstate;
    OPEN sales_results;
    SET retcode = sqlstate;
  END
```

This procedure could be invoked from the Command Line Processor by connecting to the appropriate database and executing a CALL statement that looks like this:

```
CALL get_sales (25, ?)
```

If you created this procedure and executed this statement after connecting to the SAMPLE database provided with DB2, the value 25 would be passed to the input parameter named QUOTA, and a question mark (?) would be used as a place-holder for the value that will be returned in the output parameter named RETCODE. The procedure would then execute the SQL statements contained in it and return information that looks something like this:

```
Value of output parameters
--------------------------
Parameter Name  : RETCODE
Parameter Value : 00000
Result set 1
-----------
SALES_PERSON    TOTAL_SALES
------------    -----------
GOUNOT          50
LEE             91
2 record(s) selected.
Return Status = 0
```

Working with XML Data

Like traditional data, XML documents can be added to a database table, altered, removed, and retrieved using SQL Data Manipulation Language statements (INSERT, UPDATE, DELETE, and SELECT statements). Typically, XML documents (as defined in the XML 1.0 specification) are manipulated by application programs; when performing DML operations from an application program, IBM recommends that XML data be manipulated through host variables, rather than literals, so DB2 can use the host variable data type to determine some of the encoding information needed for processing. And although you can manipulate XML data using XML, binary, or character types, IBM recommends that you use XML or binary types to avoid code page conversion issues.

XML data used in an application is often in a serialized string format; when this data is inserted into an XML column or when data in an XML column is updated, it must be converted to its XML hierarchical format. If the application data type used is an XML data type, DB2 performs this operation implicitly. However, if the application data type is a character or binary data type, the XMLPARSE() function must be used to convert the data explicitly from its serialized string format to the XML hierarchical format during insert and update operations. A simple INSERT statement that uses the XMLPARSE() function to insert a string value into an XML column named CUSTINFO in a table named CUSTOMERS might look something like this:

```
INSERT INTO customers (custinfo) VALUES
  (XMLPARSE(DOCUMENT '<name>John Doe</name>'
   PRESERVE WHITESPACE))
```

When the Command Line Processor is used to manipulate XML documents stored in XML columns, string data can be directly assigned to XML columns without an explicit call to the XMLPARSE() function if insert, update, and delete operationsare performed. For example, let's say you want to add a record containing XML data to a table named CUSTOMER that has the following characteristics:

Column Name	Data Type
CUSTID	INTEGER
INFO	XML

You could do so by executing an INSERT statement from the Command Line Processor that looks something like this:

```
INSERT INTO customer VALUES (1000,
'<customerinfo xmlns="http://custrecord.dat" custid="1000">
<name>John Doe</name>
<addr country="United States">
 <street>25 East Creek Drive</street>
 <city>Raleigh</city>
 <state-prov>North Carolina</state-prov>
 <zip-pcode>27603</zip-pcode>
</addr>
<phone type="work">919-555-1212</phone>
<email>john.doe@xyz.com</email>
</customerinfo>')
```

And if you wanted to update the XML data portion of this record from the Command Line Processor, you could do so by executing an UPDATE statement that looks something like this:

```
UPDATE customer SET custinfo =
'<customerinfo xmlns="http://custrecord.dat" custid="1000">
<name>Jane Doe</name>
<addr country="Canada">
 <street>25 East Creek Drive</street>
 <city>Raleigh</city>
 <state-prov>North Carolina</state-prov>
 <zip-pcode>27603</zip-pcode>
</addr>
<phone type="work">919-555-1212</phone>
<email>jane.doe@xyz.com</email>
</customerinfo>'
WHERE XMLEXISTS ('declare default element namespace "http://custrecord.dat";
$info/customerinfo[name/text()="John Doe"]' PASSING custinfo AS "info")
```

Finally, if you wanted to delete the record from the CUSTOMER table, you could do so by executing a DELETE statement from the Command Line Processor that looks something like this:

```
DELETE FROM customer
WHERE XMLEXISTS ('declare default element namespace "http://custrecord.dat";
$info/customerinfo[name/text()="John Doe"]' PASSING custinfo AS "info")
```

So how do you retrieve XML data once it has been stored in a table? With DB2 9, XML data can be retrieved using an SQL query or one of the SQL/XML query functions available. When querying XML data using SQL, you can only retrieve data at the column level—in other words, an entire XML document must be retrieved. It is not possible to return fragments of a document using SQL; to query within XML documents, you need to use *XQuery*.

XQuery is a functional programming language that was designed by the World Wide Web Consortium (W3C) to meet specific requirements for querying XML data. Unlike relational data, which is predictable and has a regular structure, XML data is often unpredictable, highly variable, sparse, and self-describing. Because the structure of XML data is unpredictable, the queries that are performed on XML data often differ from typical relational queries. For example, you might need to create XML queries that perform the following operations:

- Search XML data for objects that are at unknown levels of the hierarchy.

- Perform structural transformations on the data (for example, you might want to invert a hierarchy).

- Return results that have mixed types.

In XQuery, expressions are the main building blocks of a query. Expressions can be nested and form the body of a query. A query can also have a prolog that contains a series of declarations that define the processing environment for the query. Thus, if you wanted to retrieve customer names for all customers who reside in North Carolina from XML documents stored in the CUSTINFO column of a table named CUSTOMER (assuming this table has been populated with the INSERT statement we looked at earlier), you could do so by executing an XQuery expression that looks something like this:

```
XQUERY declare default element namespace "http://custrecord.dat"; FOR $info
IN db2-fn:xmlcolumn('CUSTOMER.CUSTINFO')/customerinfo WHERE
$info/addr/state-prov="North Carolina" RETURN $info/name
```

When this XQuery expression is executed from the Command Line Processor, it should return information that looks like this (again, assuming the CUSTOMER table has been populated with the INSERT statement we looked at earlier):

```
1
-----------------------------------------------------
<name xmlns="http://custrecord.dat">John Doe</name>
```

If you wanted to remove the XML tags and just return the customer name, you could do so by executing an XQuery expression that looks like this instead:

```
XQUERY declare default element namespace "http://custrecord.dat"; for $info
in db2-fn:xmlcolumn('CUSTOMER.CUSTINFO')/customerinfo where
$info/addr/state-prov="North Carolina" return $info/name/text()
```

Now, when the XQuery expression is executed from the Command Line Processor, it should return information that looks like this:

```
1
---------
John Doe
```

As mentioned earlier, XQuery expressions can be invoked from SQL using any of the following SQL/XML functions or predicates:

XMLQUERY(). XMLQUERY() is an SQL scalar function that enables you to execute an XQuery expression from within an SQL context. XMLQUERY() returns an XML value, which is an XML sequence. This sequence can be empty or it can contain one or more items. You can also pass variables to the XQuery expression specified in XMLQUERY().

XMLTABLE(). XMLTABLE() is an SQL table function that returns a table from the evaluation of XQuery expressions; XQuery expressions normally return values as a sequence, however, XMLTABLE() allows you to execute an XQuery expression and return values as a table instead. The table that is returned can contain columns of any SQL data type, including XML. The structure of the resulting table is defined by the COLUMNS clause of XMLTABLE().

XMLEXISTS. The XMLEXISTS predicate determines whether an XQuery expression returns a sequence of one or more items. If the XQuery expression specified in this predicate returns an empty sequence, XMLEXISTS returns FALSE; otherwise, TRUE is returned. The XMLEXISTS predicate can be used in the WHERE clauses of UPDATE, DELETE, and SELECT statements. This usage means that values from stored XML documents can be used to restrict the set of rows that a DML statement operates on.

By executing XQuery expressions from within the SQL context, you can:

- Operate on parts of stored XML documents instead of entire XML documents (only XQuery can query within an XML document; SQL alone queries at the whole document level)

- Enable XML data to participate in SQL queries

- Operate on both relational and XML data

- Apply further SQL processing to the returned XML values (for example, ordering results with the ORDER BY clause of a subselect)

Thus, suppose you wanted to retrieve customer IDs and customer names a table named CUSTOMER that has the following characteristics:

Column Name	Data Type
CUSTID	INTEGER
INFO	XML

You could do so (assuming this table has been populated with the INSERT statement we looked at earlier) by executing a SELECT statement from the Command Line Processor that looks something like this:

```
SELECT custid, XMLQUERY ('declare default element namespace "http://
custrecord.dat"; $d/customerinfo/name' PASSING custinfo AS "d") AS address
FROM customer;
```

And when this query is executed, it should return information that looks something like this:

```
CUSTID    ADDRESS
------    --------------------------
 1000     <name xmlns="http://custrecord.dat">John Doe</name>
```

Practice Questions

Question 1

Given the following two tables:

```
                    NAMES
    ---------------------------
    NAME                 NUMBER
    _____           _____

    Wayne Gretzky        99
    Jaromir Jagr         68
    Bobby Orr            4
    Bobby Hull           23
    Mario Lemieux        66


                    POINTS
    ---------------------------
    NAME                 POINTS
    _____           _____

    Wayne Gretzky        244
    Bobby Orr            129
    Brett Hull           121
    Mario Lemieux        189
    Joe Sakic            94
```

How many rows would be returned using the following statement?

```
SELECT name FROM names, points
```

○ A. 0

○ B. 5

○ C. 10

○ D. 25

Question 2

Given the following two tables:

```
        TAB1
-------------------------
COL_1           COL_2
-----           -----
A               10
B               12
C               14


        TAB2
-------------------------
COL_A           COL_B
-----           -----
A               21
C               23
D               25
```

Assuming the following results are desired:

COL_1	COL_2	COL_A	COL_B
A	10	A	21
B	12	–	–
C	14	C	23
–	–	D	25

Which of the following joins will produce the desired results?

○ A. SELECT * FROM tab1 INNER JOIN tab2 ON col_1 = col_a

○ B. SELECT * FROM tab1 LEFT OUTER JOIN tab2 ON col_1 = col_a

○ C. SELECT * FROM tab1 RIGHT OUTER JOIN tab2 ON col_1 = col_a

○ D. SELECT * FROM tab1 FULL OUTER JOIN tab2 ON col_1 = col_a

Question 3

Given the following table:

```
          TAB1
---------------------
COL1          COL2
-----         -----
A             10
B             20
C             30
A             10
D             40
C             30
```

Assuming the following results are desired:

```
          TAB1
---------------------
COL1          COL2
-----         -----
A             10
B             20
C             30
D             40
```

Which of the following statements will produce the desired results?

○ A. SELECT UNIQUE * FROM tab1

○ B. SELECT DISTINCT * FROM tab1

○ C. SELECT UNIQUE(*) FROM tab1

○ D. SELECT DISTINCT(*) FROM tab1

Question 4

Given the following two tables:

```
EMPLOYEE

ID NAME             DEPTID
-- --------------   -------
01 Mick Jagger       10
02 Keith Richards    20
03 Ronnie Wood       20
04 Charlie Watts     20
05 Bill Wyman        30
06 Brian Jones       -


DEPARTMENT

ID  DEPTNAME
--  ----------------
10 Executive Staff
20 Sales
30 Marketing
40 Engineering
50 Human Resources
```

Which two of the following queries will display the employee name and department name for all employees that are in Sales?

❏ A. SELECT e.name, d.deptname
      FROM employee e, department d
      WHERE e.deptid = d.id AND d.id = '20'

❏ B. SELECT e.name, d.deptname
      FROM employee e FULL OUTER JOIN department d
      ON e.deptid = d.id
      WHERE d.id = '20'

❏ C. SELECT e.name, d.deptname
      FROM employee e RIGHT OUTER JOIN department d
      ON e.deptid = d.id
      WHERE d.id = '20'

❏ D. SELECT e.name, d.deptname
      FROM employee e LEFT OUTER JOIN department d
      ON e.deptid = d.id
      WHERE d.id = '20'

❏ E. SELECT e.name, d.deptname
      FROM employee e INNER JOIN department d
      ON e.deptid = d.id
      WHERE d.id = '20'

Try these

Question 5

Given the following queries:

```
SELECT c1 FROM tab1;
SELECT c1 FROM tab2;
```

Which of the following set operators can be used to produce a result data set that contains only records that are not found in the result data set produced by each query after duplicate rows have been eliminated?

○ A. UNION

○ B. INTERSECT

○ C. EXCEPT

○ D. MERGE

Question 6

Given the following two tables:

```
                 NAMES
         -----------------------------
NAME                     NUMBER
----------               -------
Wayne Gretzky            99
Jaromir Jagr             68
Bobby Orr                4
Bobby Hull               23
Brett Hull               16
Mario Lemieux            66
Mark Messier             11

                 POINTS
         -----------------------------
NAME                     POINTS
----------               -------
Wayne Gretzky            244
Jaromir Jagr             168
Bobby Orr                129
Brett Hull               121
Mario Lemieux            189
Joe Sakic                94
```

Which of the following statements will display the player name, number, and points for all players that have scored points?

○ A. SELECT p.name, n.number, p.points FROM names n
       INNER JOIN points p ON n.name = p.name

○ B. SELECT p.name, n.number, p.points FROM names n
       LEFT OUTER JOIN points p ON n.name = p.name

○ C. SELECT p.name, n.number, p.points FROM names n
       RIGHT OUTER JOIN points p ON n.name = p.name

○ D. SELECT p.name, n.number, p.points FROM names n
       FULL OUTER JOIN points p ON n.name = p.name

Question 7

Given the following tables:

YEAR_2007

```
EMPID   NAME
-----   -----------
1       Jagger, Mick
2       Richards, Keith
3       Wood, Ronnie
4       Watts, Charlie
5       Jones, Darryl
6       Leavell, Chuck
```

YEAR_1962

```
EMPID   NAME
-----   -----------
1       Jagger, Mick
2       Richards, Keith
3       Jones, Brian
4       Wyman, Bill
5       Watts, Charlie
6       Stewart, Ian
```

If the following SQL statement is executed, how many rows will be returned?

```
SELECT name FROM year_2007
UNION ALL
SELECT name FROM year_1962
```

○ A. 6

○ B. 9

○ C. 10

○ D. 12

Question 8

Given the following table:

```
EMPLOYEE

EMPID  NAME              INSTRUMENT
---    ---------  -----
1          Jagger, Mick         01
2          Richards, Keith      02
3          Wood, Ronnie         02
4          Watts, Charlie       03
5          Jones, Darryl        04
6          Leavell, Chuck       05
```

If the following query is executed:

```
SELECT name,
    CASE WHEN instrument = '01' THEN 'HARMONICA'
         WHEN instrument = '02' THEN 'GUITAR'
         WHEN instrument = '03' THEN 'DRUMS'
         ELSE 'UNKNOWN'
    END AS instrument
FROM employee
```

What will be the results?

○ A.
```
NAME                 INSTRUMENT
----------------  --------------
Jagger, Mick         HARMONICA
Richards, Keith      GUITAR
Wood, Ronnie         GUITAR
Watts, Charlie       DRUMS
Jones, Darryl        ERROR
Leavell, Chuck       ERROR
```

○ B.
```
NAME                 INSTRUMENT
----------------  --------------
Jagger, Mick         HARMONICA
Richards, Keith      GUITAR
Wood, Ronnie         GUITAR
Watts, Charlie       DRUMS
Jones, Darryl        04
Leavell, Chuck       05
```

○ C.
```
NAME                 INSTRUMENT
----------------  --------------
Jagger, Mick         HARMONICA
Richards, Keith      GUITAR
Wood, Ronnie         GUITAR
Watts, Charlie       DRUMS
Jones, Darryl        UNKNOWN
Leavell, Chuck       UNKNOWN
```

○ D.
```
NAME                 INSTRUMENT
----------------  --------------
Jagger, Mick         HARMONICA
Richards, Keith      GUITAR
Wood, Ronnie         GUITAR
Watts, Charlie       DRUMS
Jones, Darryl        -
Leavell, Chuck       -
```

Question 9

Given the following table definition:

```
                    SALES
-----------------------------------------
INVOICE_NO           CHAR(20) NOT NULL
SALES_DATE           DATE
SALES_PERSON         VARCHAR(25)
REGION               CHAR(20)
SALES_AMT            DECIMAL(9,2)
```

Which of the following queries will return SALES information, sorted by SALES_PERSON, from A to Z, and SALES_DATE, from most recent to earliest?

- A. SELECT invoice_no, sales_person, sales_date, sales_amt FROM sales SORT BY sales_person, sales_date DESC
- B. SELECT invoice_no, sales_person, sales_date, sales_amt FROM sales SORT BY sales_person DESC, sales_date
- C. SELECT invoice_no, sales_person, sales_date, sales_amt FROM sales ORDER BY sales_person, sales_date DESC
- D. SELECT invoice_no, sales_person, sales_date, sales_amt FROM sales ORDER BY sales_person DESC, sales_date

Question 10

Given the following statement:

```
SELECT hyear, AVG(salary)
FROM SELECT YEAR(hiredate) AS hyear, salary
    FROM employee WHERE salary > 30000
GROUP BY hyear
```

Which of the following describes the result if this statement is executed?

- A. The statement will return the year and average salary for all employees that have a salary greater than $30,000, sorted by year.
- B. The statement will return the year and average salary for all employees hired within a given year that have a salary greater than $30,000.
- C. The statement will return the year and average salary for all years that every employee hired had a salary greater than $30,000.
- D. The statement will return the year and average salary for all years that any employee had a salary greater than $30,000.

Question 11

Which two of the following statements are true about the HAVING clause?

❑   A.   The HAVING clause is used in place of the WHERE clause.

❑   B.   The HAVING clause uses the same syntax as the WHERE clause.

❑   C.   The HAVING clause can only be used with the GROUP BY clause.

❑   D.   The HAVING clause accepts wildcards.

❑   E.   The HAVING clause uses the same syntax as the IN clause.

Question 12

Given the following table:

```
CURRENT_EMPLOYEES
----------------------------
EMPID          INTEGER NOT NULL
NAME           CHAR(20)
SALARY         DECIMAL(10,2)


PAST_EMPLOYEES
----------------------------
EMPID          INTEGER NOT NULL
NAME           CHAR(20)
SALARY         DECIMAL(10,2)
```

Assuming both tables contain data, which of the following statements will NOT successfully add data to table CURRENT_EMPLOYEES?

○   A.   INSERT INTO current_employees (empid) VALUES (10)

○   B.   INSERT INTO current_employees VALUES (10, 'JAGGER', 85000.00)

○   C.   INSERT INTO current_employees SELECT empid, name, salary
        FROM past_employees WHERE empid = 20

○   D.   INSERT INTO current_employees (name, salary) VALUES
        (SELECT name, salary FROM past_employees WHERE empid = 20)

Question 13

Given the following UPDATE statement:

```
UPDATE employees SET workdept =
    (SELECT deptno FROM department WHERE deptno = 'A01')
    WHERE workdept IS NULL
```

Which of the following describes the result if this statement is executed?

- O A. The statement will fail because an UPDATE statement cannot contain a subquery.
- O B. The statement will only succeed if the data retrieved by the subquery does not contain multiple records.
- O C. The statement will succeed; if the data retrieved by the subquery contains multiple records, only the first record will be used to perform the update.
- O D. The statement will only succeed if every record in the EMPLOYEES table has a null value in the WORKDEPT column.

Question 14

Given the following table definition:

```
SALES
--------------------------------
SALES_DATE          DATE
SALES_PERSON        CHAR(20)
REGION              CHAR(20)
SALES               INTEGER
```

Which of the following SQL statements will remove all rows that had a SALES_DATE in the year 1995?

- O A. DELETE * FROM sales WHERE YEAR(sales_date) = 1995
- O B. DELETE FROM sales WHERE YEAR(sales_date) = 1995
- O C. DROP * FROM sales WHERE YEAR(sales_date) = 1995
- O D. DROP FROM sales WHERE YEAR(sales_date) = 1995

Question 15

The following SQL statement:

```
DELETE FROM tab1 WHERE CURRENT OF csr1 WITH RR
```

Is used to perform which type of delete operation?

- ○ A. Positioned
- ○ B. Searched
- ○ C. Embedded
- ○ D. Dynamic

Question 16

Given the following data:

```
TAB1

C1   C2
--   ---
200  abc
250  abc
150  def
300  ghi
175  def
```

If the following query is executed:

```
WITH subset (col1, col2) AS
    (SELECT c1, c2 FROM tab1 WHERE c1 > 150)
SELECT col2, SUM(col1) AS col1_sum
  FROM subset
  GROUP BY col2
  ORDER BY col2
```

Which of the following result data sets will be produced?

- ○ A.
  ```
  COL2       COL1_SUM
  ----       --------
  abc        200
  abc        250
  def        175
  ghi        300
  4 record(s) selected.
  ```

- ○ B.
  ```
  COL2       COL1_SUM
  ----       --------
  abc        450
  def        175
  ghi        300
  3 record(s) selected.
  ```

Question 16 *continued*

```
○ C.  COL2        COL1_SUM
      ----        --------
      abc         450
      def         325
      ghi         300
      3 record(s) selected.


○ D.  COL2        COL1_SUM
      ----        --------
      abc         450
      abc         450
      def         175
      def         175
      ghi         300
      5 record(s) selected.
```

Question 17

Which of the following best describes a unit of work?

○ A. It is a recoverable sequence of operations whose point of consistency is established when a connection to a database has been established or when a mechanism known as a savepoint is created.

○ B. It is a recoverable sequence of operations whose current point of consistency can be determined by querying the system catalog tables.

○ C. It is a recoverable sequence of operations whose point of consistency is established when an executable SQL statement is processed after a connection to a database has been established or a previous transaction has been terminated.

○ D. It is a recoverable sequence of operations whose point of consistency is only established if a mechanism known as a savepoint is created.

Question 18

Given the following set of statements:

```
CREATE TABLE tab1 (col1 INTEGER, col2 CHAR(20));
COMMIT;
INSERT INTO tab1 VALUES (123, 'Red');
INSERT INTO tab1 VALUES (456, 'Yellow');
SAVEPOINT s1 ON ROLLBACK RETAIN CURSORS;
DELETE FROM tab1 WHERE col1 = 123;
INSERT INTO tab1 VALUES (789, 'Blue');
ROLLBACK TO SAVEPOINT s1;
INSERT INTO tab1 VALUES (789, 'Green');
UPDATE tab1 SET col2 = NULL WHERE col1 = 789;
COMMIT;
```

Which of the following records would be returned by the following statement?

```
SELECT * FROM tab1
```

○ A. COL1   COL2
       ----   -------
       123   Red
       456   Yellow
       2 record(s) selected.

○ B. COL1   COL2
       ----   -------
       456   Yellow
       1 record(s) selected.

○ C. COL1   COL2
       ----   -----
       123   Red
       456   Yellow
       789   -
       3 record(s) selected.

○ D. COL1   COL2
       ----   -------
       123   Red
       456   Yellow
       789   Green
       3 record(s) selected.

Question 19

Given the following table:

TAB1

COL1	COL2
A	10
B	20
C	30
D	40
E	50

And the following SQL statements:

```
DECLARE c1 CURSOR WITH HOLD FOR
    SELECT * FROM tab1 ORDER BY col_1;
OPEN c1;
FETCH c1;
FETCH c1;
FETCH c1;
COMMIT;
FETCH c1;
CLOSE c1;
FETCH c1;
```

Which of the following is the last value obtained for COL_2?

- ○ A. 20
- ○ B. 30
- ○ C. 40
- ○ D. 50

Question 20

A stored procedure has been created with the following statement:

```
CREATE PROCEDURE proc1 (IN var1 VARCHAR(10), OUT rc INTEGER)
SPECIFIC myproc LANGUAGE SQL ...
```

What is the correct way to invoke this procedure from the command line processor (CLP)?

- ○ A. CALL proc1 ('SALES', ?)
- ○ B. CALL myproc ('SALES', ?)
- ○ C. CALL proc1 (SALES, ?)
- ○ D. RUN proc1 (SALES, ?)

Question 21

Given the following table:

```
TEMP_DATA

TEMP        DATE
_____       _____
45          12/25/2006
51          12/26/2006
67          12/27/2006
72          12/28/2006
34          12/29/2006
42          12/30/2006
```

And the following SQL statement:

```
CREATE FUNCTION degf_to_c (temp INTEGER)
    RETURNS INTEGER
    LANGUAGE SQL
    CONTAINS SQL
    NO EXTERNAL ACTION
    DETERMINISTIC
    BEGIN ATOMIC
        DECLARE newtemp INTEGER;
        SET newtemp = temp - 32;
        SET newtemp = newtemp * 5;
        RETURN newtemp / 9;
    END
```

Which two of the following SQL statements illustrate the proper way to invoke the scalar function DEGF_TO_C?

❑ A. VALUES degf_to_c(32)

❑ B. SELECT date, degf_to_c(temp) AS temp_c FROM temp_data

❑ C. CALL degf_to_c(32)

❑ D. SELECT * FROM TABLE(degf_to_c(temp)) AS temp_c

❑ E. VALUES degf_to_c(32) AS temp_c

Question 22

Given the following CREATE TABLE statement:

```
CREATE TABLE customer(custid INTEGER, info XML)
```

And the following INSERT statements:

```
INSERT INTO customer VALUES (1000,
'<customerinfo xmlns="http://custrecord.dat" custid="1000">
  <name>John Doe</name>
  <addr country="United States">
    <street>25 East Creek Drive</street>
    <city>Raleigh</city>
    <state-prov>North Carolina</state-prov>
    <zip-pcode>27603</zip-pcode>
  </addr>
  <phone type="work">919-555-1212</phone>
  <email>john.doe@abc.com</email>
</customerinfo>');

INSERT INTO customer VALUES (1000,
'<customerinfo xmlns="http://custrecord.dat" custid="1001">
  <name>Paul Smith</name>
  <addr country="Canada">
    <street>412 Stewart Drive</street>
    <city>Toronto</city>
    <state-prov>Ontario</state-prov>
    <zip-pcode>M8X-3T6</zip-pcode>
  </addr>
  <phone type="work">919-555-4444</phone>
  <email>psmith@xyz.com</email>
</customerinfo>');
```

What is the result of the following XQuery expression?

```
XQUERY declare default element namespace "http://custrecord.dat"; for
$info in db2-fn:xmlcolumn('CUSTOMER.INFO')/customerinfo where
$info/addr/state-prov="Ontario" return $info/name/text();
```

○ A. Paul Smith

○ B. <name xmlns="http://custrecord.dat">Paul Smith</name>

○ C. <customerinfo xmlns="http://custrecord.dat"
   custid="1001"><name xmlns="http://custrecord.dat">Paul
   Smith</name>

○ D. <customerinfo xmlns="http://custrecord.dat"
   custid="1001">Paul Smith</customerinfo>

Answers

Question 1

The correct answer is **D**. When a SELECT statement such as the one shown is executed, the result data set produced will contain all possible combinations of the rows found in each table specified (otherwise known as the Cartesian product). Every row in the result data set produced is a row from the first table referenced concatenated with a row from the second table referenced, concatenated in turn with a row from the third table referenced, and so on. The total number of rows found in the result data set produced is the product of the number of rows in all the individual table-references; in this case, 5 x 5 = 25.

Question 2

The correct answer is **D**. When a full outer join operation is performed, rows that would have been returned by an inner join operation, together with all rows stored in both tables of the join operation that would have been eliminated by the inner join operation are returned in the result data set produced. An inner join can be thought of as the cross product of two tables, in which every row in one table that has a corresponding row in another table is combined with that row to produce a new record. When a left outer join operation is performed, rows that would have been returned by an inner join operation, together with all rows stored in the leftmost table of the join operation (i.e., the table listed first in the OUTER JOIN clause) that would have been eliminated by the inner join operation, are returned in the result data set produced. When a right outer join operation is performed, rows that would have been returned by an inner join operation, together with all rows stored in the rightmost table of the join operation (i.e., the table listed last in the OUTER JOIN clause) that would have been eliminated by the inner join operation, are returned in the result data set produced.

Question 3

The correct answer is **B**. If the DISTINCT clause is specified with a SELECT statement, duplicate rows are removed from the final result data set returned. Two rows are considered to be duplicates of one another if the value of every column of the first row is identical to the value of the corresponding column of the second row.

Question 4

The correct answers are **A** and **E**. An inner join can be thought of as the cross product of two tables, in which every row in one table that has a corresponding row in another table is combined with that row to produce a new record. The syntax for a SELECT statement that performs an inner join operation is:

```
SELECT
[* | [Expression] <<AS> [NewColumnName]> ,...]
FROM [[TableName] <<AS> [CorrelationName]> ,...]
[JoinCondition]
```

where:

Expression   Identifies one or more columns whose values are to be
                           returned when the SELECT statement is executed. The
                           value specified for this option can be any valid SQL
                           language element; however, corresponding table or view
                           column names are commonly used.

NewColumnName   Identifies a new column name that is to be used in place
                           of the corresponding table or view column name
                           specified in the result data set returned by the SELECT
                           statement.

TableName   Identifies the name(s) assigned to one or more tables
                           that data is to be retrieved from.

CorrelationName   Identifies a shorthand name that can be used when
                           referencing the table name specified in the *TableName*
                           parameter.

JoinCondition   Identifies the condition to be used to join the tables
                           specified. Typically, this is a WHERE clause in which the
                           values of a column in one table are compared with the
                           values of a similar column in another table.

The following syntax can also be used to create a SELECT statement that performs an inner join operation:

```
SELECT
[* | [Expression] <<AS> [NewColumnName]> ,...]
FROM [[TableName1] <<AS> [CorrelationName1]>]
<INNER> JOIN
[[TableName2] <<AS> [CorrelationName2]>]
ON [JoinCondition]
```

where:

Expression	Identifies one or more columns whose values are to be returned when the SELECT statement is executed. The value specified for this option can be any valid SQL language element; however, corresponding table or view column names are commonly used.
NewColumnName	Identifies a new column name to be used in place of the corresponding table or view column name specified in the result data set returned by the SELECT statement.
TableName1	Identifies the name assigned to the first table data is to be retrieved from.
CorrelationName1	Identifies a shorthand name that can be used when referencing the leftmost table of the join operation.
TableName2	Identifies the name assigned to the second table data is to be retrieved from.
CorrelationName2	Identifies a shorthand name that can be used when referencing the rightmost table of the join operation.
JoinCondition	Identifies the condition to be used to join the two tables specified.

Question 5

The correct answer is **C**. When the EXCEPT set operator is used, the result data sets produced by each individual query are combined, all duplicate rows found are eliminated, and all records found in the first result data set that have a corresponding record in the second result data set are eliminated, leaving just the records that are not found in both result data sets. When the UNION set operator is used, the result data sets produced by each individual query are combined and all duplicate rows are eliminated; when the INTERSECT set operator is used, the result data sets produced by each individual query are combined, all duplicate rows found are eliminated, and all records found in the first result data set that do not have a corresponding record in the second result data set are eliminated, leaving just the records that are found in both result data sets; MERGE is not a set operator.

Question 6

The correct answer is **C**. When a right outer join operation is performed, rows that would have been returned by an inner join operation, together with all rows stored in the rightmost table of the join operation (i.e., the table listed last in the OUTER JOIN clause) that would have been eliminated by the inner join operation are returned in the result data set produced. In this case, we want to see *all* records found in the POINTS table, along with any corresponding records found in the NAMES table, so a right outer join is the appropriate join operation to use.

Question 7

The correct answer is **D**. When the UNION ALL set operator is used, the result data sets produced by each individual query are combined; all duplicate rows found are retained. Thus with this example, the results of both tables are combined (6 rows + 6 rows = 12 rows) and the duplicate rows for "Jagger, Mick", "Richards, Keith", and "Watts, Charlie" are retained. Had the UNION set operator been used instead, the result data sets produced by each individual query would have been combined and all duplicate rows would have been eliminated and the answer would have been 9 (12 – 3 = 9 rows).

Question 8

The correct answer is **C**. One efficient and concise way to display coded values in a readable format is to use one or more CASE expressions in the selection list of a query. Each CASE operation evaluates a specified expression and supplies a different value, depending on whether a certain condition is met. A CASE expression can take one of two forms: *simple* or *searched*. The CASE statement presented in the question is a searched CASE expression; in this example, if the INSTRUMENT column contains the value '01', the word 'HARMONICA' is returned, if the INSTRUMENT column contains the value '02', the word 'GUITAR' is returned, if the INSTRUMENT column contains the value '03', the word 'DRUMS' is returned, and if the INSTRUMENT column contains any other value, the word 'UNKNOWN' is returned.

Question 9

The correct answer is **C**. Data is stored in a table in no particular order, and unless otherwise specified, a query only returns data in the order in which it is found. The ORDER BY clause is used to tell the DB2 Database Manager how to sort and order the rows that are to be returned in a result data set produced in response to a query. When specified, the ORDER BY clause is followed by the name of one or more column(s) whose data values are to be sorted and a keyword that indicates the desired sort order. If the keyword ASC follows the column's name, ascending order is used, and if the keyword DESC follows the column name, descending order is used. If no keyword is specified, ascending order is used by default.

Question 10

The correct answer is **B**. The subselect produces a result data set that contains hire year and salary information for each employee whose salary is greater than $30,000.00. The GROUP BY clause is used to tell the DB2 Database Manager how to organize rows of data returned in the result data set produced in response to a query. (The GROUP BY clause specifies an intermediate result table consisting of a group of rows.) In this example, the GROUP BY clause tells the outer SELECT to calculate and group average salary information by hire year.

Question 11

The correct answers are **B** and **C**. The HAVING clause is used to apply further selection criteria to columns that are referenced in a GROUP BY clause. This clause behaves like the WHERE clause, except that it refers to data that has already been grouped by a GROUP BY clause (the HAVING clause is used to tell the DB2 Database Manager how to select the rows that are to be returned in a result data set from rows that have already been grouped). And like the WHERE clause, the HAVING clause is followed by a search condition that acts as a simple test that, when applied to a row of data, will evaluate to TRUE, FALSE, or Unknown.

Question 12

The correct answer is **D**. Because the EMPID column in each table was defined in such a way that it does not allow null values, a non-null value must be provided for this column any time data is inserted into either table. The INSERT statement shown in answer D does not provide a value for the EMPID column of the CURRENT_EMPLOYEES table, so the statement will fail.

Question 13

The correct answer is **B**. When the results of a query, or subselect, are used to provide values for one or more columns identified in the column name list provided for an UPDATE statement, the values retrieved from one base table or view are used to modify values stored in another. The number of values returned by the subselect must match the number of columns provided in the column name list specified, and only one record can be returned.

Question 14

The correct answer is **B**. The DELETE statement is used to remove specific records from a table (the DROP statement completely destroys the table object), and the correct syntax for the DELETE statement is DELETE FROM [*TableName*] ...

Question 15

The correct answer is **A**. Delete operations can be conducted in one of two ways: as *searched delete* operations or as *positioned delete* operations. To perform a positioned delete, a cursor must first be created, opened, and positioned on the row to be deleted. Then, the DELETE statement used to remove the row must contain a WHERE CURRENT OF [*CursorName*] clause (*CursorName* identifies the cursor being used). Because of their added complexity, positioned delete operations are typically performed by embedded SQL applications.

Question 16

The correct answer is **B**. Common table expressions are mechanisms that are used to construct local temporary tables that reside in memory and only exist for the life of the SQL statement that defines them. The syntax used to construct a common table expression is:

```
WITH [TableName] <( [ColumnName] ,...] )>
AS ( [SELECTStatement] )
```

where:

TableName   Specifies the name that is to be assigned to the temporary table to be created.

ColumnName   Specifies the name(s) to be assigned to one or more columns that are to be included in the temporary table to be created. Each column name specified must be unique and unqualified; if no column names are specified, the names derived from the result data set produced by the SELECT statement specified will be used. If a list of column names is specified, the number of column names provided must match the number of columns that will be returned by the SELECT statement used to create the temporary table. If a common table expression is recursive, or if the result data set produced by the SELECT statement specified contains duplicate column names, column names must be specified.

SELECTStatement   Identifies a SELECT SQL statement that, when executed, will produce the data values to be added to the column(s) in the temporary table to be created.

So in this example, all of the data stored in table TAB1, with the exception of the record "150 - def" is copied to a common table named SUBSET, and then a query is run against this common table.

Question 17

The correct answer is **C**. A *transaction* (also known as a *unit of work*) is a sequence of one or more SQL operations grouped together as a single unit, usually within an application process. A given transaction can perform any number of SQL operations—from a single operation to many hundreds or even thousands, depending on what is considered a "single step" within your business logic. The initiation and termination of a single transaction defines points of data consistency within a database; either the effects of all operations performed within a transaction are applied to the database and made permanent (committed), or the effects of all operations performed are backed out (rolled back) and the database is returned to the state it was in before the transaction was initiated. In most cases, transactions are initiated the first time an executable SQL statement is executed after a connection to a database has been made or immediately after a preexisting transaction has been terminated. Once initiated, transactions can be implicitly terminated using a feature known as "automatic commit" (in this case, each executable SQL statement is treated as a single transaction, and any changes made by that statement are applied to the database if the statement executes successfully or discarded if the statement fails) or they can be explicitly terminated by executing the COMMIT or the ROLLBACK SQL statement.

Question 18

The correct answer is **C**. DB2 uses a mechanism known as a *savepoint* to allow an application to break the work being performed by a single large transaction into one or more subsets. Once created, a savepoint can be used in conjunction with a special form of the ROLLBACK SQL statement to return a database to the state it was in at the point in time a particular savepoint was created. The syntax for this form of the ROLLBACK statement is:

```
ROLLBACK <WORK> TO SAVEPOINT <[SavepointName]>
```

where:

SavepointName   Identifies the name assigned to the savepoint that indicates the point in time that operations performed against the database are to be rolled back (backed out) to.

So, in this example, every operation performed between the time savepoint S1 was created and the ROLLBACK TO SAVEPOINT statement was executed was undone.

Question 19

The correct answer is **C**. When a cursor that has been declared with the WITH HOLD option specified (as in the example shown) is opened, it will remain open across transaction boundaries until it is explicitly closed; otherwise, it will be implicitly closed when the transaction that opens it is terminated. In this example, the cursor is opened, the first three rows are fetched from it, the transaction is committed (but the cursor is not closed), another row is fetched from it, and then the cursor is closed. Thus, the last value obtained will be:

```
       TAB1
-----------------
COL1      COL2
----      ---
D         40
```

Question 20

The correct answer is **A**. The CALL statement is used to invoke a stored procedure, so answer D is wrong; because a stored procedure cannot be invoked using its specific name, answer B is wrong; and since SALES is a character string value that is being passed to the procedure, it must be enclosed in single quotes. Therefore, answer C is wrong.

Question 21

The correct answers are **A** and **B**. How a user-defined function is invoked depends a lot on what it has been designed to do; scalar user-defined functions can be invoked as an expression in the select list of a query while table and row functions must be referenced by the FROM clause. In because the user-defined function used in this example is a scalar function that only returns a single value, answer B is the correct way to call it. A scalar function can also be invoked by executing a VALUES statement that looks something like the one shown in answer A.

Question 22

The correct answer is **A**. In XQuery, expressions are the main building blocks of a query. Expressions can be nested and form the body of a query. A query can also have a prolog that contains a series of declarations that define the processing environment for the query. Thus, if you wanted to retrieve customer names for all customers who reside in North Carolina from XML documents stored in the CUSTINFO column of a table named CUSTOMER (assuming this table has been populated with the INSERT statement we looked at earlier), you could do so by executing an XQuery expression that looks something like this:

```
XQUERY declare default element namespace "http://custrecord.dat";
for $info in db2-fn:xmlcolumn('CUSTOMER.CUSTINFO')/customerinfo
where $info/addr/state-prov="North Carolina" return $info/name
```

And when this XQuery expression is executed from the Command Line Processor, it should return information that looks like this (again, assuming this table has been populated with the INSERT statement we looked at earlier):

```
1
---------------------------------
<name xmlns="http://custrecord.dat">John Doe</name>
```

If you wanted to remove the XML tags and just return the customer name, you could do so by executing an XQuery expression that looks like this instead:

```
XQUERY declare default element namespace "http://custrecord.dat";
 for $info in db2-fn:xmlcolumn('CUSTOMER.CUSTINFO')/customerinfo
where $info/addr/state-prov="North Carolina" return
$info/name/text()
```

Now, when the XQuery expression is executed from the Command Line Processor, it should return information that looks like this:

```
1
-------
John Doe
```

6

Working with DB2 Tables, Views, and Indexes

Twenty-three and one-half percent (23.5%) of the DB2 9 Fundamentals certification exam (Exam 730) is designed to test your ability to identify the data types and constraints that are available with DB2 9, as well as to test your knowledge of how and when each one should be used in a table definition. The questions that make up this portion of the exam are intended to evaluate the following:

- Your knowledge of the DB2 data types available and your ability to demonstrate when and how each data type available should be used

- Your knowledge of the constraints available and your ability to identify when and how NOT NULL constraints, default constraints, CHECK constraints, UNIQUE constraints, and referential integrity constraints should be used

- Your ability to create a database table, using data types and constraints

- Your ability to identify characteristics of a table, view, or index

- Your ability to identify how operations performed on the parent table of a referential integrity constraint are reflected in the child table of the constraint

- Your ability to identify when triggers should be used

This chapter is designed to introduce you to the data types and constraints that are available with DB2 and to show you how to construct base tables using any combination of each. This chapter is also designed to show you how triggers can be used to supplement constraints.

DB2 9's Data Types

If you stop and think about it, most of the "data" you encounter on a day-to-day basis falls into distinct categories. The money you buy coffee with and the change you get back are numerical in nature; the email messages you read and the replies you send are composed of character strings; and many of the things you do, such as waking up, going to the office, returning home, and going to bed revolve around time. Much of the data that gets stored in a DB2 database can be categorized in a similar manner. To ensure that all data is stored as efficiently as possible, DB2 comes equipped with a rich assortment of built-in data types. And in case none of those meet your needs, DB2 also provides the capability to create an infinite number of user-defined data types, which can in turn be used to store complex, nontraditional data that might be found in an intricate computing environment.

The built-in data types available with DB2 9 are classified according to the kind of data they have been designed to hold:

- Numeric data
- Character string data
- Date/time data
- Large object data
- Extensible Markup Language (XML) documents

In addition to these more common data types, special data types designed to be used with the DB2 Extenders are also available.

Numeric Data Types

As the name suggests, numeric data types are used to store numeric values—specifically, numeric values that have a *sign* and a *precision*. The sign is considered positive if the value is greater than or equal to zero and negative if the value is less than zero, while the precision is the actual number of digits used to present the value. Numeric data is stored using a fixed amount of storage space, and the amount of space required increases as the precision of the number goes up. Numeric data types include:

Small integer: The small integer data type is used to store numeric values that have a precision of 5 digits or less. The range for small integer values is

–32,768 to 32,767, and 2 bytes of storage space are required for every small integer value stored. (Positive numbers have one less value in their range because they start at the value 0, while negative numbers start at –1.) The keyword SMALLINT is used to denote the small integer data type.

Integer: The integer data type is used to store numeric values that have a precision of 10 digits. The range for integer values is –2,147,483,648 to 2,147,483,647, and 4 bytes of storage space are required for every integer value stored. The keywords INTEGER and INT are used to denote the integer data type.

Big integer: The big integer data type is used to store numeric values that have a precision of 19 digits. The range for big integer values is –9,223,372,036,854,775,808 to 9,223,372,036,854,775,807, and 8 bytes of storage space are required for every big integer value stored. The keyword BIGINT is used to denote the big integer data type. (This data type is typically used on systems that provide native support for 64-bit integers; on such systems, processing large numbers that have been stored as big integers is much more efficient, and any calculations performed are more precise.)

Decimal: The decimal data type is used to store numeric values that contain both whole and fractional parts, separated by a decimal point. The exact location of the decimal point is determined by the precision and the scale of the value (the scale is the number of digits used by the fractional part). The maximum precision allowed for decimal values is 31 digits, and the corresponding scale must be a positive number less than the precision of the number. The amount of storage space needed to store a decimal value can be determined by solving the following equation: *Precision* ÷ 2 (truncated) + 1 = *Bytes required*. (For example, the value 67.12345 has precision of 7, 7 ÷ 2 is 3, + 1 makes 4; therefore, 4 bytes are required to store the value 67.12345.) The keywords DECIMAL, DEC, NUMERIC, and NUM are used to denote the decimal data type. If no precision or scale is specified, a scale of 5 and a precision of 0 are used by default: DECIMAL(5,0).

Single-precision floating-point: The single-precision floating-point data type is used to store a 32-bit *approximation* of a real number. This number can be zero, or it can fall within the range –3.402E+38 to –1.175E–37 or the range 1.175E–37 to 3.402E+38. Each single-precision floating-point value can be up to 24 digits in length, and 4 bytes of storage space are required for every value stored. The keywords REAL and FLOAT are used to denote the single-precision floating-point data type.

Double-precision floating-point: The double-precision floating-point data type is used to store a 64-bit *approximation* of a real number. This number can be zero, or it can fall within the range $-1.79769E+308$ to $-2.225E-307$ or $2.225E-307$ to $1.79769E+308$. Each double-precision floating-point value can be up to 53 digits in length, and 8 bytes of storage space is required for every value stored. The terms DOUBLE, DOUBLE PRECISION, and FLOAT are used to denote the double-precision floating-point data type.

Character String Data Types

Character string data types are used to store values composed of one or more alphanumeric characters. Together, these characters may form a word, a sentence, a paragraph, or a complete document. A variety of character string data types are available. Deciding on which one to use for a given situation primarily depends on the storage requirements of the data value to be stored. Character string data types include:

Fixed-length character string: The fixed-length character string data type is used to store character string values that are between 1 and 254 characters in length. The amount of storage space needed to store a fixed-length character string value can be determined by solving the following equation: (*Number of characters* × 1) = *Bytes required*. (A fixed amount of storage space is allocated, even if all of the space allocated is not needed—short strings are padded with blanks.) The keywords CHARACTER and CHAR are used to denote the fixed-length character string data type.

Varying-length character string: The varying-length character string data type is used to store character string values that are up to 32,672 characters in length. However, the actual length allowed is governed by the table space page size used. For tables that reside in table spaces that use 4K pages, varying-length character string values cannot be more than 4,092 characters in length; for tables that reside in a table spaces that use 8K pages, varying-length character string values cannot be more than 8,188 characters in length, and so on. The amount of storage space needed to store a varying-length character string value can be determined by solving the following equation: (*Number of characters* × 1) + 4 = *Bytes required*. (Only the amount of storage space actually needed, plus 4 bytes for an "end-of-string" marker, is allocated—strings are not blank padded.) The keywords CHARACTER VARYING, CHAR VARYING, and VARCHAR are used to denote the varying-length character string data type.

Long varying-length character string: The long varying-length character string data type is used to store character string values that are up to 32,672 characters in length, regardless of the table space page size used. The amount of storage space needed to store a long varying-length character string value can be determined by solving the following equation: (*Number of characters* × 1) + 24 = *Bytes required*. The keyword LONG VARCHAR is used to denote the long varying-length character string data type.

Fixed-length double-byte character string: The fixed-length double-byte character string data type is used to store DBCS (double-byte character set) character string values that are up to 127 characters in length. (Most Asian character sets are double-byte character sets.) The amount of storage space needed to store a fixed-length double-byte character string value can be determined by solving the following equation: (*Number of characters* × 2) = *Bytes required*. The term GRAPHIC is used to denote the fixed-length double-byte character string data type.

Varying-length double-byte character string: The varying-length double-byte character string data type is used to store DBCS character string values that are up to 16,336 characters in length. Again, the actual length allowed is governed by the table space page size used. For tables that reside in table spaces that use 4K pages, varying-length double-byte character string values cannot be more than 2,046 characters in length; for tables that reside in table spaces that use 8K pages, varying-length double-byte character string values cannot be more than 4,094 characters in length; and so on. The amount of storage space needed to store a varying-length double-byte character string value can be determined by solving the following equation: (*Number of characters* × 2) + 4 = *Bytes required*. The keyword VARGRAPHIC is used to denote the varying-length double-byte character string data type.

Long varying-length double-byte character string: The long varying-length double-byte character string data type is used to store DBCS character string values that are up to 16,350 characters in length, regardless of the table space page size used. The amount of storage space needed to store a long varying-length double-byte character string value can be determined by solving the following equation: (*Number of characters* × 2) + 24 = *Bytes required*. The keyword LONG VARGRAPHIC is used to denote the long varying-length character string data type.

Date/Time Data Types

Data/time data types are used to store values that represent dates and times. From a user perspective, these values appear to be character strings; however, they are physically stored as binary packed strings. Date/time data types include:

Date: The date data type is used to store three-part values (year, month, and day) that represent calendar dates. The range for the year portion is 0001 to 9999; the range for the month portion is 1 to 12; and the range for the day portion is 1 to 28, 29, 30, or 31, depending upon the month value specified and whether or not the year specified is a leap year. Externally, date values appear to be fixed-length character string values 10 characters in length. However, only 4 bytes of storage space are required for every date value stored. The keyword DATE is used to denote the date data type.

Time: The time data type is used to store three-part values (hours, minutes, and seconds) that represent time, using a 24-hour clock. The range for the hours portion is 0 to 24; the range for the minutes portion is 0 to 59; and the range for the seconds portion is 0 to 59. Externally, time values appear to be fixed-length character string values 8 characters in length. However, only 3 bytes of storage space are required for every time value stored. The keyword TIME is used to denote the time data type.

Timestamp: The timestamp data type is used to store seven-part values (year, month, day, hours, minutes, seconds, and microseconds) that represent a specific calendar date and time (using a 24-hour clock). The range for the year portion is 0001 to 9999; the range for the month portion is 1 to 12; the range for the day portion is 1 to 28, 29, 30, or 31, depending upon the month value specified and whether or not the year specified is a leap year; the range for the hours portion is 0 to 24; the range for the minutes portion is 0 to 59; and the range for the seconds portion is 0 to 59; and the range for the microseconds portion is 0 to 999,999. Externally, timestamp values appear to be fixed-length character string values 26 characters in length (this string is displayed in the form *YYYY-MM-DD-HH.MM.SS.NNNNNN*, which translates to Year-Month-Day-Hour.Minute.Second.Microseconds). However, only 10 bytes of storage space are required for every timestamp value stored. The keyword TIMESTAMP is used to denote the timestamp data type.

Because the representation of date and time values varies throughout the world, the actual string format used to present a date or a time value is dependent upon the territory code assigned to the database being used. Table 6–1 shows the date and time string formats that are available with DB2 9.

Table 6-1 DB2 9 Date and Time Formats

Format Name	Abbreviation	Date String Format	Time String Format
International Organization for Standardization	ISO	YYYY-MM-DD	HH.MM.SS
IBM USA Standard	USA	MM/DD/YYYY	HH:MM AM or PM
IBM European Standard	EUR	DD.MM.YYYY	HH.MM.SS
Japanese Industrial Standard	JIS	YYYY-MM-DD	HH:MM:SS
Site Specific	LOC	Based on database territory and country code	Based on database territory and country code
For date formats, YYYY = Year, MM = Month, and DD = Day; for time formats, HH = Hour, MM = Minute, and SS = Seconds			
Adapted from Tables 3 and 4 on page 89 of the *DB2 SQL Reference - Volume 1* manual.			

Large Object (LOB) Data Types

Large object (LOB) data types are used to store large amounts of unstructured data. Large object data types include the following:

Binary large object: The binary large object data type is used to store binary data values (such as documents, graphic images, pictures, audio, and video) that are up to 2 gigabytes in size. The keywords BINARY LARGE OBJECT and BLOB are used to denote the binary large object data type. The amount of storage space set aside to store a binary large object value is determined by the length specification provided when a binary large object data type is defined. For example, 800 bytes of storage space would be set aside for a BLOB(800) definition.

Character large object: The character large object data type is used to store SBCS (single-byte character set) or MBCS (multibyte character set) character string values that are between 32,700 and 2,147,483,647 characters in length. The keywords CHARACTER LARGE OBJECT, CHAR LARGE OBJECT, and CLOB are used to denote the character large object data type. The amount of storage space set aside to store a character large object value is determined by the length specification provided when a character large object data type is defined. For example, 800 bytes of storage space would be set aside for a CLOB(800) definition.

Double-byte character large object: The double-byte character large object data type is used to store DBCS (double-byte character set) character string values that are between 16,350 and 1,073,741,823 characters in length. The keyword DBCLOB is used to denote the double-byte character large object data type. The amount of storage space set aside to store a double-byte character large object value is determined by the length specification provided when a double-byte character large object data type is defined. For example, 800 bytes of storage space would be set aside for a DBCLOB(400) definition.

The Extensible Markup Language (XML) Document Data Type

Extensible Markup Language (XML) is a simple, very flexible text format that provides a neutral way to exchange data between different devices, systems, and applications; data is maintained in a self-describing format that is hierarchical in nature. The *Extensible Markup Language Document* data type is used to store XML documents in their native format. (An XML value that is stored in a column defined with the Extensible Markup Language data type must be a well-formed XML document.) XML values are processed in an internal representation that is not comparable to any string value; however, an XML value can be transformed into a serialized string value representing the XML document using the XMLSERIALIZE() function. Similarly, a string value that represents an XML document can be transformed into an XML value using the XMLPARSE() function. The keyword XML is used to denote the XML data type. The amount of storage space set aside to store an XML document varies and is determined, in part, by the size and characteristics of the XML document being stored.

XML documents can only be stored in single-partition databases that have been defined using the UTF-8 code set. Furthermore, using the XML data type prevents future use of the Database Partitioning Feature that is available for DB2 Enterprise Server Edition.

Extenders

The extender products that are available with DB2 9 consist of unique sets of user-defined data types and user-defined functions that can be used to store and manipulate nontraditional data such as graphical images and audio/video clips. Since many of the data types provided by the DB2 Extenders are based on built-in data types, the size limits and storage requirements of an extender data type often match those of their built-in data type counterparts—provided extender data is actually stored in the database. Some of the DB2 Extenders allow their data to be stored in external files that reside outside the database, while the location of the files themselves is stored in a database table. When this is the case, the storage requirements for an extender data type can be much lower than for its built-in data type equivalent.

User-Defined Data Types

In Chapter 4, "Working with Databases and Database Objects," we saw that user-defined data types (UDTs) are data types that are explicitly created by a database user. A user-defined data type can be a distinct data type that shares a common representation with one of the built-in data types provided with DB2 (created by executing the CREATE DISTINCT TYPE SQL statement), or it can be a structured type that consists of a sequence of named attributes, each of which have their own data type (created by executing the CREATE TYPE SQL statement). Structured data types can also be created as subtypes of other structured types, thereby defining a type hierarchy.

User-defined data types are subject to strong data typing, which means that even though they may share the same representation as other built-in or user-defined data types, the value of one user-defined data type is only compatible with values of that same type (or of other user-defined data types within the same data type hierarchy). As a result, user-defined data types cannot be used as arguments for most built-in functions. However, user-defined functions and operators that duplicate the functionality provided by the built-in functions can be created.

Understanding Constraints

Within most businesses, data often must adhere to a certain set of rules and restrictions. For example, companies typically have a specific format and numbering sequence they use when generating purchase orders. Constraints allow you to place the logic needed to enforce such business rules directly in the database rather than in applications that work with the database. Essentially, constraints are rules that govern how data values can be added to a table, as well as how those values can be modified once they have been added. The following types of constraints are available:

- NOT NULL constraints
- Default constraints
- CHECK constraints
- UNIQUE constraints
- Referential integrity constraints
- Informational constraints

Constraints are usually defined during table creation; however, constraints can also be added to existing tables using the ALTER TABLE SQL statement.

NOT NULL Constraints

With DB2, null values (not to be confused with empty strings) are used to represent missing or unknown data and/or states. By default, every column in a table will accept a null value. This allows you to add records to a table when not all of the values that pertain to the record are known. However, there may be times when this behavior is unacceptable (for example, a tax identification number might be required for every employee who works for a company). When such a situation arises, the NOT NULL constraint can be used to ensure that a particular column in a base table is never assigned a null value; once the NOT NULL constraint has been defined for a column, any operation that attempts to place a null value in that column will fail. Figure 6–1 illustrates how the NOT NULL constraint is used.

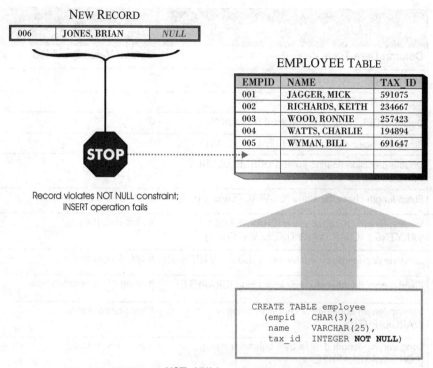

Figure 6–1: How the NOT NULL *constraint prevents null values.*

Because NOT NULL constraints are associated with a specific column in a base table, they are usually defined during the table creation process.

Default Constraints

Just as there are times when it is objectionable to accept a null value, there may be times when it is desirable to have the system provide a specific value for you (for example, you might want to automatically assign the current date to a particular column whenever a new record is added to a table). In these situations, the default constraint can be used to ensure that a particular column in a base table is assigned a predefined value (unless that value is overridden) each time a record is added to the table. The predefined value provided could be null (if the NOT NULL constraint has not been defined for the column), a user-supplied value compatible with the column's data type, or a value furnished by the DB2 Database Manager. Table 6–2 shows the default values that can be provided by the DB2 Database Manager for the various DB2 9 data types available.

Table 6-2 DB2 Database Manager-Supplied Default Values

Column Data Type	Default Value Provided
Small integer (SMALLINT)	0
Integer (INTEGER or INT)	0
Decimal (DECIMAL, DEC, NUMERIC, or NUM)	0
Single-precision floating-point (REAL or FLOAT)	0
Double-precision floating-point (DOUBLE, DOUBLE PRECISION, or FLOAT)	0
Fixed-length character string (CHARACTER or CHAR)	A string of blank characters
Varying-length character string (CHARACTER VARYING, CHAR VARYING, or VARCHAR)	A zero-length string
Long varying-length character string (LONG VARCHAR)	A zero-length string
Fixed-length double-byte character string (GRAPHIC)	A string of blank characters
Varying-length double-byte character string (VARGRAPHIC)	A zero-length string
Long varying-length double-byte character string (LONG VARGRAPHIC)	A zero-length string
Date (DATE)	The system date at the time the record is added to the table. (When a date column is added to an existing table, existing rows are assigned the date January 01, 0001.)
Time (TIME)	The system time at the time the record is added to the table. (When a time column is added to an existing table, existing rows are assigned the time 00:00:00.)
Timestamp (TIMESTAMP)	The system date and time (including microseconds) at the time the record is added to the table. (When a timestamp column is added to an existing table, existing rows are assigned a timestamp that corresponds to January 01, 0001, 00:00:00.000000)
Binary large object (BLOB)	A zero-length string
Character large object (CLOB)	A zero-length string
Double-byte character large object (DBCLOB)	A zero-length string

Table 6-2 DB2 Database Manager-Supplied Default Values (continued)	
Column Data Type	**Default Value Provided**
Double-byte character large object (DBCLOB)	A zero-length string
XML document (XML)	Not applicable
Any distinct user-defined data type	The default value provided for the built-in data type the distinct user-defined data type is based on (typecast to the distinct user-defined data type)
Adapted from Table 11 on page 67 of the *DB2 SQL Reference - Volume 2* manual	

Figure 6–2 illustrates how the default constraint is used.

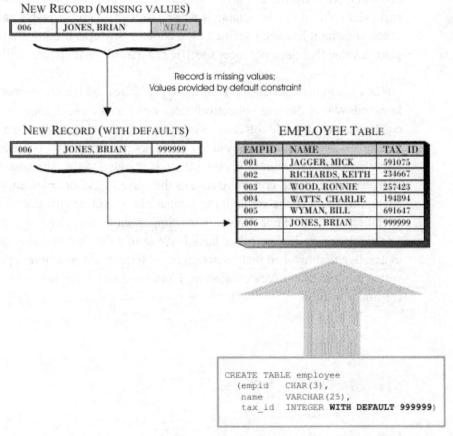

Figure 6–2: How the default constraint is used to provide data values.

Like NOT NULL constraints, default constraints are associated with a specific column in a base table and are usually defined during the table creation process.

CHECK Constraints

Sometimes, it is desirable to control what values will be accepted for a particular item and what values will not (for example, a company might decide that all nonexempt employees must be paid, at a minimum, the federal minimum wage). When this is the case, the logic needed to determine whether a value is acceptable can be incorporated directly into the data entry program being used to collect the data. A better way to achieve the same objective is by defining a CHECK constraint for the column in the base table that is to receive the data value. A CHECK constraint (also known as a *table check constraint*) can be used to ensure that a particular column in a base table is never assigned an unacceptable value—once a check constraint has been defined for a column, any operation that attempts to place a value that does not meet specific criteria into that column will fail.

CHECK constraints consist of one or more predicates (which are connected by the keywords AND or OR) that collectively are known as the *check condition*. This check condition is compared with data values provided, and the result of this comparison is returned as the value TRUE, FALSE, or Unknown. If the CHECK constraint returns the value TRUE, the value is acceptable, so it is added to the database. If, on the other hand, the CHECK constraint returns the value FALSE or Unknown, the operation attempting to place the value in the database fails, and all changes made by that operation are backed out. However, it is important to note that when the results of a particular operation are rolled back because of a CHECK constraint violation, the transaction that invoked that operation is not terminated, and other operations within that transaction are unaffected. Figure 6–3 illustrates how a simple CHECK constraint is used.

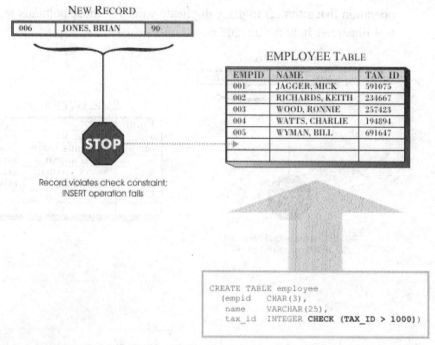

Figure 6–3: How a CHECK constraint is used to control what values are accepted by a column.

Like NOT NULL constraints and default constraints, CHECK constraints are associated with a specific column in a base table and are usually defined during the table creation process.

UNIQUE Constraints

By default, records that are added to a base table can have the same values assigned to any of the columns available any number of times. As long as the records stored in the table do not contain information that should not be duplicated, this kind of behavior is acceptable. However, there are times when certain pieces of information that make up a record should be unique (for example, if an employee identification number is assigned to each individual who works for a particular company, each number used should be unique—two employees should never be assigned the same employee identification number). In these situations, the UNIQUE constraint can be used to ensure that the value(s) assigned to one or more columns when a record is added to a base table are always unique. Once a UNIQUE constraint has been defined for one or more columns, any operation that attempts to place duplicate values in those columns will fail. Figure 6–4 illustrates how the UNIQUE constraint is used.

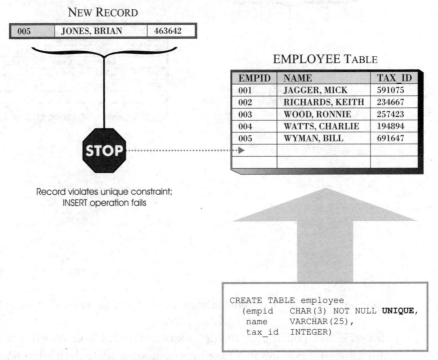

Figure 6–4: How the UNIQUE constraint prevents the duplication of data values.

Unlike NOT NULL constraints, default constraints, and CHECK constraints, which can only be associated with a single column in a base table, UNIQUE constraints can be associated with an individual column or a group of columns. However, each column in a base table can only participate in one UNIQUE constraint, regardless of how the columns are grouped. Like the other constraints, UNIQUE constraints are usually defined during the table creation process.

Regardless of when a UNIQUE constraint is defined, when it is created, the DB2 Database Manager looks to see whether an index for the columns to which the UNIQUE constraint refers already exists. If so, that index is marked as being unique and system-required. If not, an appropriate index is created and marked as being unique and system-required. This index is then used to enforce uniqueness whenever new records are added to the column(s) for which the UNIQUE constraint was defined for.

> Although a unique, system-required index is used to enforce a UNIQUE constraint, there is a distinction between defining a UNIQUE constraint and creating a unique index. Even though both enforce uniqueness, a unique index allows NULL values and generally cannot be used in a referential constraint. A UNIQUE constraint, on the other hand, does not allow NULL values, and can be referenced in a foreign key specification. (The value NULL means a column's value is undefined *and* distinct from any other value, *including* other NULL values.)

A *primary key*, which we will look at next, is a special form of UNIQUE constraint. Only one primary key is allowed per table, and every column that is used to define a primary key must be assigned the NOT NULL constraint. In addition to ensuring that every record added to a table has some unique characteristic, primary keys allow tables to participate in referential constraints.

A table can have any number of UNIQUE constraints; however, a table cannot have more than one UNIQUE constraint defined on the same set of columns. And because UNIQUE constraints are enforced by indexes, all the limitations that apply to indexes (for example, a maximum of 16 columns with a combined length of 255 bytes is allowed, and none of the columns used can have a large object or long character string data type) apply to UNIQUE constraints.

Referential Integrity Constraints

If you've worked with a relational database management system for any length of time, you are probably aware that data normalization is a technique used to ensure that there is only one way to get to a single fact. Data normalization is possible because two or more individual base tables can have some type of relationship with one another, and information stored in related base tables can be combined if necessary, using a join operation. This is where referential integrity constraints come into play. Referential integrity constraints (also known as referential constraints and foreign key constraints) are used to define required relationships between two base tables.

To understand how referential constraints work, it helps to look at an example. Suppose you own a small auto parts store, and you use a database to keep track of the inventory you have on hand. Many of the parts you stock will only work with a specific "make" and "model" of an automobile; therefore, your database has one table named MAKE to hold make information and another table named MODEL to hold model information. Since these two tables are related (every model must belong to a make), a referential constraint can be used to ensure that every record that is stored in the MODEL table has a corresponding record in the MAKE table. The relationship between these two tables is established by comparing values that are to be added to the MAKE column of the MODEL table (known as the *foreign key* of the *child table*) with the values that currently exist for the set of columns that make up the primary key of the MAKE table (known as the *parent key* of the *parent table*). To create the referential constraint just described, you would define a primary key, using one or more columns, in the MAKE table; then, in the MODEL table, you would define a foreign key for one or more corresponding columns that reference the MAKE table's primary key. Assuming a column named MAKEID is used to create the primary key for the MAKE table and a column, also named MAKEID is used, to create the foreign key for the MODEL table, the referential constraint created would look something like the one shown in Figure 6–5.

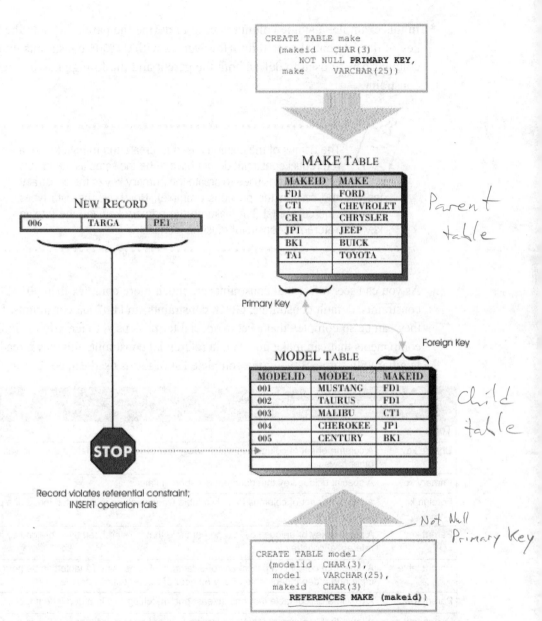

```
CREATE TABLE make
  (makeid   CHAR(3)
       NOT NULL PRIMARY KEY,
   make     VARCHAR(25))
```

MAKE TABLE

MAKEID	MAKE
FD1	FORD
CT1	CHEVROLET
CR1	CHRYSLER
JP1	JEEP
BK1	BUICK
TA1	TOYOTA

Parent table

Primary Key

Foreign Key

NEW RECORD

006	TARGA	PE1

MODEL TABLE

MODELID	MODEL	MAKEID
001	MUSTANG	FD1
002	TAURUS	FD1
003	MALIBU	CT1
004	CHEROKEE	JP1
005	CENTURY	BK1

Child table

STOP

Record violates referential constraint;
INSERT operation fails

Not Null Primary Key

```
CREATE TABLE model
  (modelid  CHAR(3),
   model    VARCHAR(25),
   makeid   CHAR(3)
       REFERENCES MAKE (makeid))
```

Figure 6–5: How a referential constraint is used to define a relationship between two tables.

In this example, a single column is used to define the parent key and the foreign key of the referential constraint. However, as with UNIQUE constraints, multiple columns can be used to define both the parent and the foreign key of a referential constraint.

> The names of the columns used to create the foreign key of a referential constraint do not have to be the same as the names of the columns used to create the primary key of the constraint (as was the case in the previous example). However, the data types used for the column(s) that make up the primary key and the foreign key of a referential constraint must be identical.

As you can see, referential constraints are much more complex than NOT NULL constraints, default constraints, CHECK constraints, and UNIQUE constraints. In fact, they can be so complex that a set of special terms is used to identify the individual components that can make up a single referential constraint. You may already be familiar with some of them; the complete list of terms used can be seen in Table 6–3.

Table 6-3: Referential Integrity Constraint Terminology

Term	Meaning
Unique key	A column or set of columns in which every row of values is different from the values of all other rows
Primary key	A special unique key that does not accept null values
Foreign key	A column or set of columns in a child table whose values must match those of a parent key in a parent table
Parent key	A primary key or unique key in a parent table that is referenced by a foreign key in a referential constraint
Parent table	A table that contains a parent key of a referential constraint. (A table can be both a parent table and a dependent table of any number of referential constraints.)
Parent row	A row in a parent table that has at least one matching row in a dependent table.
Dependent or child table	A table that contains at least one foreign key that references a parent key in a referential constraint. (A table can be both a dependent table and a parent table of any number of referential constraints.)
Dependent or child row	A row in a dependent table that has at least one matching row in a parent table.
Descendent table	A dependent table or a descendent of a dependent table.

Table 6-3: Referential Integrity Constraint Terminology (continued)	
Term	**Meaning**
Descendent row	A dependent row or a descendent of a dependent row.
Referential cycle	A set of referential constraints defined in such a way that each table in the set is a descendent of itself.
Self-referencing table	A table that is both a parent table and a dependant table in the same referential constraint. (The constraint is known as a self-referencing constraint.)
Self-referencing row	A row that is a parent of itself.

The primary reason referential constraints are created is to guarantee that data integrity is maintained whenever one table object references another. As long as a referential constraint is in effect, the DB2 Database Manager guarantees that, for every row in a child table that has a value in any column that is part of a foreign key, there is a corresponding row in the parent table. So what happens when an SQL operation attempts to manipulate data in a way that would violate a referential constraint? To answer this question, let's look at what could compromise dataintegrity if the checks and balances provided by a referential constraint were not in place:

- An insert operation could add a row of data to a child table that does not have a matching value in the corresponding parent table. (For example, using our MAKE/MODEL scenario, a record could be added to the MODEL table that does not have a corresponding value in the MAKE table.)

- An update operation could change an existing value in a child table such that it no longer has a matching value in the corresponding parent table. (For example, a record could be changed in the MODEL table so that it no longer has a corresponding value in the MAKE table.)

- An update operation could change an existing value in a parent table, leaving rows in a child table with values that no longer match those in the parent table. (For example, a record could be changed in the MAKE table, leaving records in the MODEL table that no longer have a corresponding MAKE value.)

- A delete operation could remove a value from a parent table, leaving rows in a child table with values that no longer match those in the parent table. (For example, a record could be removed from the MAKE table, leaving records in the MODEL table that no longer have a corresponding MAKE value.)

The DB2 Database Manager can either prohibit (restrict) these types of operations from being performed on tables that are part of a referential constraint, or attempt to carry out these actions in a way that will safeguard data integrity. In either case, DB2 uses a set of rules to control the operation's behavior. Each referential constraint has its own set of rules (which consist of an Insert Rule, an Update Rule, and a Delete Rule), and the way each rule is to be enforced is specified as part of the referential constraint creation process.

The Insert Rule for referential constraints

The Insert Rule guarantees that a value can never be inserted into the foreign key of a child table unless a matching value can be found in the corresponding parent key of the associated parent table. Any attempt to insert records into a child table that violates this rule will result in an error, and the insert operation will fail. In contrast, no checking is performed when records are added to the parent key of the parent table.

The Insert Rule for a referential constraint is implicitly created when the referential constraint itself is created. Figure 6–6 illustrates how a row that conforms to the Insert Rule for a referential constraint is successfully added to a child table; Figure 6–7 illustrates how a row that violates the Insert Rule causes an insert operation to fail.

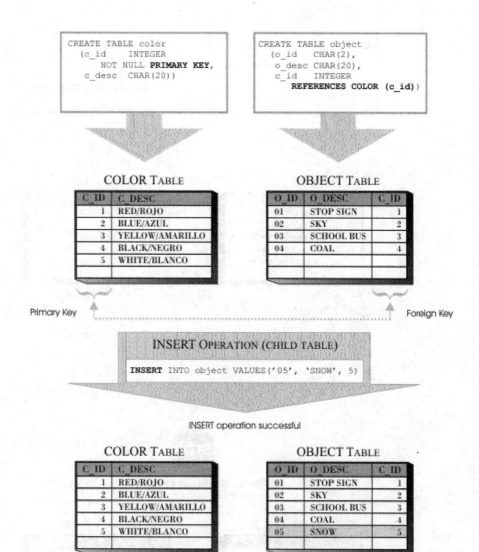

Figure 6–6: An insert operation that conforms to the Insert Rule of a referential constraint.

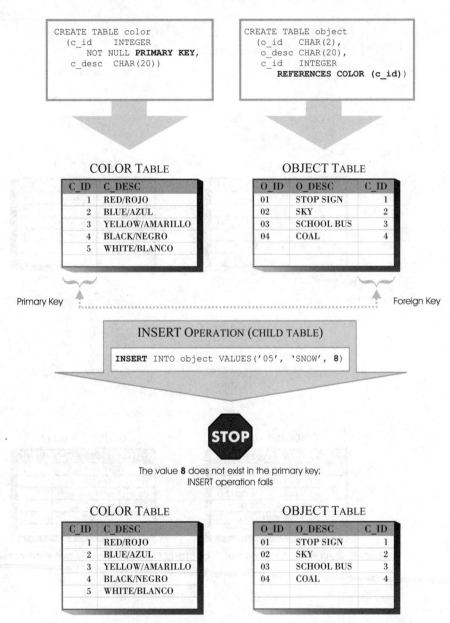

Figure 6–7: An insert operation that violates the Insert Rule of a referential constraint.

It is important to note that because the Insert Rule exists, records must be inserted in the parent key of the parent table before corresponding records can be inserted into the child table. (Going back to our MAKE/MODEL example, this means that a record for a new MAKE must be added to the MAKE table *before* a record that references the new MAKE can be added to the MODEL table.)

The Update Rule for referential constraints

The Update Rule controls how update operations performed against either table (child or parent) participating in a referential constraint are to be processed. The following two types of behaviors are possible, depending upon how the Update Rule is defined:

ON UPDATE RESTRICT: This definition ensures that whenever an update operation is performed on the parent table of a referential constraint, the value for the foreign key of each row in the child table will have the same matching value in the parent key of the parent table that it had before the update operation was performed.

ON UPDATE NO ACTION: This definition ensures that whenever an update operation is performed on either table in a referential constraint, the value for the foreign key of each row in the child table will have a matching value in the parent key of the corresponding parent table; however, the value may not be the same as it was before the update operation occurred.

Figure 6–8 illustrates how the Update Rule is enforced when the ON UPDATE RESTRICT definition is used; Figure 6–9 illustrates how the Update Rule is enforced when the ON UPDATE NO ACTION definition is used.

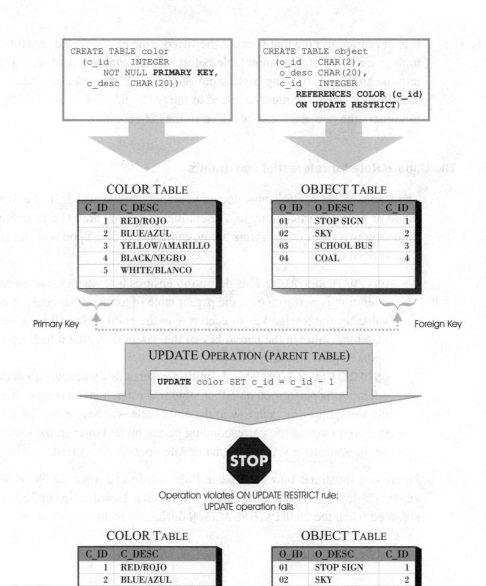

Figure 6–8: How the *ON UPDATE RESTRICT* Update Rule of a referential constraint is enforced.

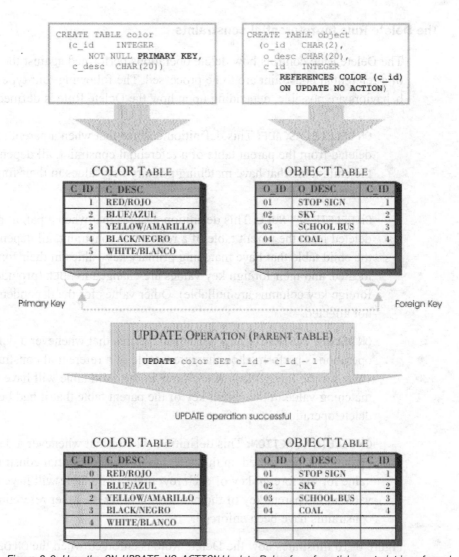

Figure 6–9: How the ON UPDATE NO ACTION Update Rule of a referential constraint is enforced.

Like the Insert Rule, the Update Rule for a referential constraint is implicitly created when the referential constraint itself is created. If no Update Rule definition is provided, the ON UPDATE NO ACTION definition is used by default. Regardless of which Update Rule definition is used, if the condition of the rule is not met, the update operation will fail, an error message will be displayed, and any changes made to the data in either table participating in the referential constraint will be backed out.

The Delete Rule for referential constraints

The Delete Rule controls how delete operations performed against the parent table of a referential constraint are to be processed. The following four types of behaviors are possible, depending upon how the Delete Rule is defined:

ON DELETE CASCADE: This definition ensures that when a parent row is deleted from the parent table of a referential constraint, all dependent rows in the child table that have matching primary key values in their foreign key are deleted as well.

ON DELETE SET NULL: This definition ensures that when a parent row is deleted from the parent table of a referential constraint, all dependent rows in the child table that have matching primary key values in their foreign key are located, and their foreign key values are changed to NULL (provided the foreign key columns are nullable). Other values for the dependent row are not affected.

ON DELETE RESTRICT: This definition ensures that whenever a delete operation is performed on the parent table of a referential constraint, the value for the foreign key of each row in the child table will have the same matching value in the parent key of the parent table that it had before the delete operation was performed.

ON DELETE NO ACTION: This definition ensures that whenever a delete operation is performed on the parent table of a referential constraint, the value for the foreign key of each row in the child table will have a matching value in the parent key of the parent table after the other referential constraints have been enforced.

Figure 6–10 illustrates how the Delete Rule is enforced when the ON DELETE CASCADE definition is used; Figure 6–11 illustrates how the Delete Rule is enforced when the ON DELETE SET NULL definition is used;

Figure 6–12 illustrates how the Delete Rule is enforced when the ON DELETE RESTRICT definition is used; and Figure 6–13 illustrates how the Delete Rule is enforced when the ON DELETE NO ACTION definition is used.

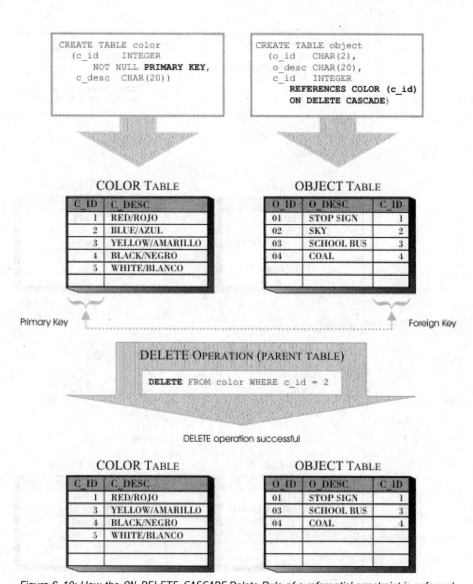

Figure 6–10: How the ON DELETE CASCADE Delete Rule of a referential constraint is enforced.

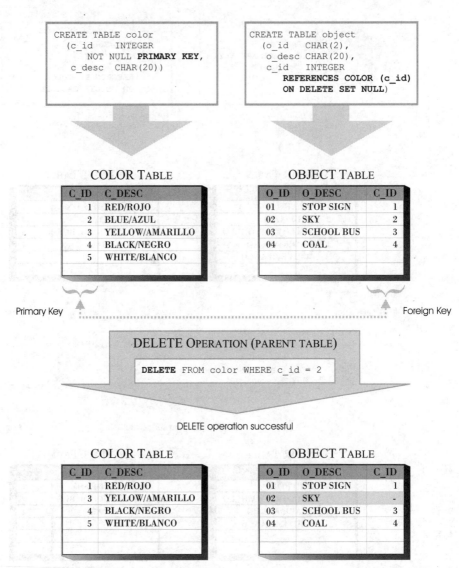

Figure 6–11: How the *ON DELETE SET NULL* Delete Rule of a referential constraint is enforced.

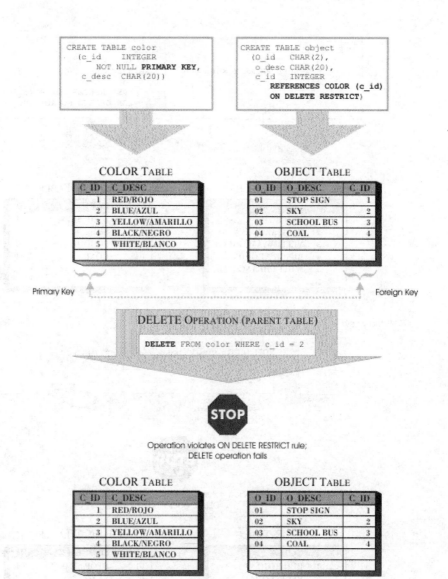

Figure 6–12: How the *ON DELETE RESTRICT* Delete Rule of a referential constraint is enforced.

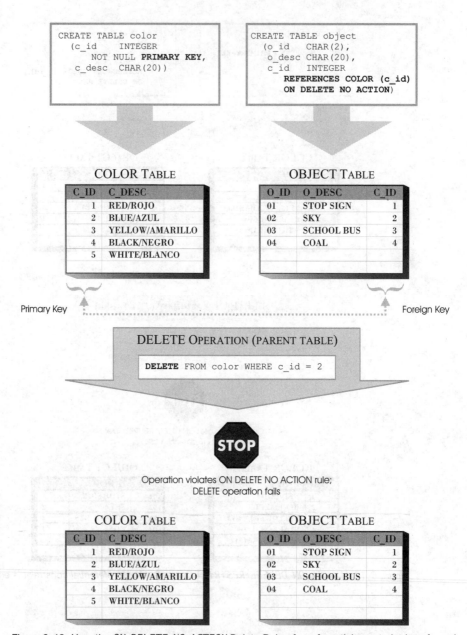

Figure 6–13: How the ON DELETE NO ACTION Delete Rule of a referential constraint is enforced.

Like the Insert Rule and the Update Rule, the Delete Rule for a referential constraint is implicitly created when the referential constraint itself is created. If no Delete Rule definition is provided, the ON DELETE NO ACTION definition is used by default. No matter which form of the Delete Rule is used, if the condition of the rule is not met, an error message will be displayed, and the delete operation will fail.

If the ON DELETE CASCADE Delete Rule is used and the deletion of a parent row in a parent table causes one or more dependent rows to be deleted from the corresponding child table, the delete operation is said to have been *propagated* to the child table. In such a situation, the child table is said to be *delete-connected* to the parent table. Because a delete-connected child table can also be the parent table in another referential constraint, a delete operation that is propagated to one child table can, in turn, be propagated to another child table, and so on. Thus, the deletion of one parent row from a single parent table can result in the deletion of several hundred rows from any number of tables, depending upon how tables are delete-connected. Therefore, the ON DELETE CASCADE Delete Rule should be used with extreme caution when a hierarchy of referential constraints permeates a database.

Informational Constraints

The DB2 Database Manager automatically enforces all of the constraints that we have looked at so far whenever new data values are added to a table or existing data values are modified or deleted. As you might imagine, if a large number of constraints have been defined, a large amount of system overhead can be required to enforce those constraints, particularly when large amounts of data are loaded into a table.

If an application is coded in such a way that it validates data before inserting it into a DB2 database, it may be more efficient to create one or more *informational constraints*, as opposed to creating any of the other constraints available. Unlike other constraints, informational constraints are not enforced during insert and update processing. However, the DB2 SQL Optimizer will evaluate information provided by an informational constraint when considering the best access plan to use to resolve a query. (Informational constraints are defined by appending the keywords NOT ENFORCED ENABLE QUERY OPTIMIZATION to a normal constraint definition.) As a result, an informational constraint may result in better query performance even though the constraint itself will not be used to validate data entry/modification. Figure 6–14 illustrates the behavior of a simple informational constraint.

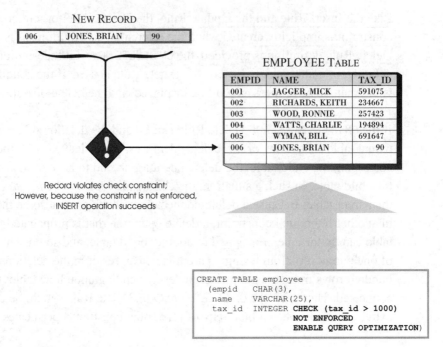

Figure 6–14: Behavior of a simple informational constraint.

It is important to note that because the DB2 Optimizer evaluates informational constraints when selecting the best data access plan to use to resolve a query, records that have been inserted into a table that violate one or more informational constraints may not be returned by some queries. For example, if the query "SELECT * FROM employee WHERE tax_id = 90" were to be executed against the EMPLOYEE table shown in Figure 6–14, no records would be returned because the access plan chosen would assume that no records with a TAX_ID value that is less than 1000 exist in the table.

Temporarily Suspending Constraint Checking with the SET INTEGRITY SQL Statement

Although constraints provide a means of ensuring that some level of integrity is maintained as data is manipulated within a base table, their enforcement can prevent some types of operations from executing successfully. For example, suppose you want to bulk-load 10,000 rows of data into a base table using the LOAD utility. If the data that is to be loaded contains values that will violate a constraint that has been defined for the table into which the data is to be loaded, the operation will fail. Or suppose you wish to add a new constraint to an existing table that already contains several hundred rows of data. If one or more rows in the table contain data values that violate the constraint you wish to add, any attempt to add the constraint will fail. In situations like these, it can be advantageous to suspend constraint checking just long enough to perform the desired operation. However when constraint checking is suspended, at some point it must be resumed, and at that time, rows in the table that cause a constraint to be violated must be located and dealt with.

Constraint checking for a table can be suspended temporarily by executing the SET INTEGRITY SQL statement. When used to suspend constraint checking, the syntax for the simplest form of this statement is:

```
SET INTEGRITY FOR [TableName, ...] OFF <AccessMode>
```

where:

TableName   Identifies the name of one or more base tables that constraint checking is to be temporarily suspended for.

AccessMode   Specifies whether or not the table(s) specified can be accessed in read-only mode while constraint checking is suspended. The following values are valid for this parameter: NO ACCESS and READ ACCESS—if no access mode is specified, NO ACCESS is used as the default.

Thus, if you wanted to suspend constraint checking for a table named EMPLOYEES temporarily and deny read-only access to that table while constraint checking is turned off, you could do so by executing a SET INTEGRITY statement that looks something like this:

```
SET INTEGRITY FOR employees OFF
```

When constraint checking is suspended for a particular table, that table is placed in "Check Pending" state to indicate that it contains data that has not been checked (and that it may not be free of constraint violations). While a table is in "Check Pending" state, it cannot be used in insert, update, or delete operations, nor can it be used by any DB2 utility that needs to perform these types of operations. Indexes cannot be created for a table while it is in "Check Pending" state, and data stored in the table can only be retrieved if the access mode specified when the SET INTEGRITY statement was used to place the table in "Check Pending" state allows read-only access.

Just as one form of the SET INTEGRITY statement is used to suspend constraint checking temporarily, another form is used to resume it. In this case, the syntax for the simplest form of the SET INTEGRITY statement is:

```
SET INTEGRITY FOR [TableName] IMMEDIATE CHECKED FOR EXCEPTION
[IN [TableName] USE [ExceptionTable], ...]
```

or

```
SET INTEGRITY FOR [[TableName] [ConstraintType], ...] IMMEDIATE UNCHECKED
```

where:

TableName　　　Identifies the name of one or more base tables for which suspended constraint checking is to be resumed. These are also the base tables from which all rows that are in violation of a referential constraint or a CHECK constraint are to be copied.

ExceptionTable　Identifies the name of a base table to which all rows that are in violation of a referential constraint or a CHECK constraint are to be copied.

ConstaintType　Identifies the type of constraint checking that is to be resumed. The following values are valid for this parameter: FOREIGN KEY, CHECK, MATERILIZED QUERY, GENERATED COLUMN, STAGING, and ALL.

Thus, if you wanted to resume constraint checking for the EMPLOYEES table that constraint checking was suspended for in the previous example, you could do so by executing a SET INTEGRITY statement that looks something like this:

```
SET INTEGRITY FOR employees
IMMEDIATE CHECKED
```

When this particular form of the SET INTEGRITY statement is executed, the table named EMPLOYEES is taken out of the "Check Pending" state, and each row of data stored in the table is checked for constraint violations. If an offensive row is found, constraint checking is stopped, and the EMPLOYEES table is returned to the "Check Pending" state.

If you want to be able to see the offending rows at a glance, the following form of the SET INTEGRITY statement can be executed:

```
SET INTEGRITY FOR employees
IMMEDIATE CHECKED
FOR EXCEPTION IN employees USE bad_rows
```

With this form, each row found that violates one or more of the constraints that have been defined for the EMPLOYEES table will be copied to a table named BAD_ROWS, where it can be corrected and copied back to the EMPLOYEES table if so desired.

And finally, if this form of the SET INTEGRITY statement is executed:

```
SET INTEGRITY FOR employees ALL
IMMEDIATE UNCHECKED
```

the table named EMPLOYEES is taken out of the "Check Pending" state, and no constraint checking is performed. However, this is a very hazardous thing to do and should be done only if you have some independent means of ensuring that the EMPLOYEES table does not contain data that violates one or more constraints defined for the EMPLOYEES table.

Creating Tables

In Chapter 4, "Working with Databases and Database Objects," we saw that tables present data as a collection of unordered rows with a fixed number of columns; each column contains values of the same data type or one of its subtypes, each row contains a set of values for each column available, and usually the columns in a table are logically related. Like many of the other database objects available, tables can be created using a GUI tool that is accessible from the Control Center. In this case, the tool is the Create Table Wizard, and it can be activated by selecting the appropriate action from the Tables menu.

Tables can also be created using the CREATE TABLE SQL statement. However, this statement is probably the most complex SQL statement available (in fact, over 60 pages of the *DB2 SQL Reference, Volume 2* manual are devoted to this statement alone). Because this statement is so complex, its syntax can be quite intimidating. Fortunately, you do not have to know all the nuances of the CREATE TABLE statement to pass the DB2 9 Fundamentals certification exam (Exam 730). Still, you do need to know the basics, and the remainder of this section is devoted to the CREATE TABLE statement and to the syntax you need to be familiar with. With that said, let's begin by taking a look at the simplest form of the CREATE TABLE SQL statement.

In its simplest form, the syntax for the CREATE TABLE SQL statement is:

```
CREATE TABLE [TableName] ( [Element], ...)
<IN [TablespaceName]>
<INDEX IN [TablespaceName]>
<LONG IN [TablespaceName]>
```

where:

TableName   Identifies the name that is to be assigned to the table to be created. (A table name must be unique within the schema the table is to be defined in.)

Element   Identifies one or more columns, UNIQUE and primary key constraints, referential constraints, CHECK constraints, and/or informational constraints to be included in the table definition. The syntax used for defining each of these elements varies according to the element being defined.

TablespaceName Identifies the table spaces in which the table and its regular data, indexes, and/or long data/large object data are to be stored.

The basic syntax used to define a column is:

```
[ColumnName] [DataType]
<NOT NULL>
<WITH DEFAULT <[DefaultValue] | CURRENT DATE |
CURRENT TIME | CURRENT TIMESTAMP | NULL>>
<UniqueConstraint>
<CheckConstraint>
<ReferentialConstraint>
```

where:

ColumnName   Identifies the unique name to be assigned to the column
                             that is to be created.

DataType   Identifies the data type (built-in or user-defined) that is
                             to be assigned to the column to be created; the data type
                             specified determines the kind of data values that can be
                             stored in the column. Table 6–4 contains a list of the
                             data type definitions that are valid.

DefaultValue   Identifies the value that is to be provided for the column
                             in the event no value is supplied when an insert or
                             update operation is performed against the table.

UniqueConstraint   Identifies a UNIQUE or primary key constraint that is to
                             be associated with the column.

CheckConsraint   Identifies a CHECK constraint that is to be associated
                             with the column.

ReferentialConstraint   Identifies a referential constraint that is to be associated
                             with the column.

Table 6-4: Data Type Definitions That Can Be Used with the CREATE TABLE Statement	
Data Type	**Definition(s)**
Small integer	SMALLINT
Integer	INTEGER INT
Big Integer	BIGINT
Decimal	DECIMAL(*Precision, Scale*) DEC(*Precision, Scale*) NUMERIC(*Precision, Scale*) NUM(*Precision, Scale*) where *Precision* is any number between 1 and 31; *Scale* is any number between 0 and *Precision*
Single-precision floating-point	REAL FLOAT (*Precision*) where *Precision* is any number between 1 and 24
Double-Precision Floating-Point	DOUBLE FLOAT(*Precision*) where *Precision* is any number between 25 and 53
Fixed-Length Character String	CHARACTER(*Length*) <FOR BIT DATA> CHAR(*Length*) <FOR BIT DATA> where *Length* is any number between 1 and 254. See footnote for the FOR BIT DATA phrase.
Varying-Length Character String	CHARACTER VARYING(*MaxLength*) <FOR BIT DATA> CHAR VARYING(*MaxLength*) <FOR BIT DATA> VARCHAR(*MaxLength*) <FOR BIT DATA> where *MaxLength* is any number between 1 and 32,672. See footnote for the FOR BIT DATA clause.
Long Varying-Length Character String	GRAPHIC(*Length*) where *Length* is any number between 1 and 127
Varying-Length Double-Byte Character String	VARGRAPHIC(*MaxLength*) where *MaxLength* is any number between 1 and 16,336

Table 6-4: Data Type Definitions That Can Be Used with the CREATE TABLE Statement (continued)	
Data Type	**Definition(s)**
Long Varying-Length Double-Byte Character String	`LONG VARGRAPHIC`
Date	`DATE`
Time	`TIME`
Timestamp	`TIMESTAMP`
Binary Large Object	`BINARY LARGE OBJECT(Length <K | M | G>)` `BLOB(Length <K | M | G>)` where *Length* is any number between 1 and 2,147,483,647; if K (for kilobyte) is specified, *Length* is any number between 1 and 2,097,152; if M (for megabyte) is specified, *Length* is any number between 1 and 2,048; if G (for gigabyte) is specified, *Length* is any number between 1 and 2.
Character Large Object	`CHARACTER LARGE OBJECT(Length <K | M | G>)` `CHAR LARGE OBJECT(Length <K | M | G>)` `CLOB(Length <K | M | G>)` where *Length* is any number between 1 and 2,147,483,647; if K (for kilobyte) is specified, *Length* is any number between 1 and 2,097,152; if M (for megabyte) is specified, *Length* is any number between 1 and 2,048; if G (for gigabyte) is specified, *Length* is any number between 1 and 2.
Double-Byte Character Large Object	`DBCLOB(Length <K | M | G>)` where *Length* is any number between 1 and 1,073,741,823; if K (for kilobyte) is specified, *Length* is any number between 1 and 1,048,576; if M (for megabyte) is specified, *Length* is any number between 1 and 1,024; if G (for gigabyte) is specified, *Length* is must be 1.
XML Document	`XML`
Label-Based Access Control (LBAC) Security Label	`DB2SECURITYLABEL`

Note: If the `FOR BIT DATA` option is used with any character string data type definition, the contents of the column to which the data type is assigned are treated as binary data. As a result, code page conversions are not performed if data is exchanged between other systems, and all comparisons made are done in binary, regardless of the collating sequence used by the database.

The syntax used to create a unique or primary key constraint as part of a column definition is:

```
<CONSTRAINT [ConstraintName]> [UNIQUE | PRIMARY KEY]
```

where:

ConstraintName   Identifies the unique name that is to be assigned to the constraint to be created.

The syntax used to create a check constraint as part of a column definition is:

```
<CONSTRAINT [ConstraintName]> CHECK ( [CheckCondition] )
<ENFORCED | NOT ENFORCED>
<ENABLE QUERY OPTIMIZATION | DISABLE QUERY OPTIMIZATION>
```

where:

ConstraintName   Identifies the unique name that is to be assigned to the constraint to be created.

CheckCondition   Identifies a condition or test that must evaluate to TRUE before a value can be stored in the column.

And finally, the syntax used to create a referential constraint as part of a column definition is:

```
<CONSTRAINT [ConstraintName]>
REFERENCES [PKTableName] < ( [PKColumnName], ...) >
<ON UPDATE [RESTRICT | NO ACTION]>
<ON DELETE [CASCADE | SET NULL | RESTRICT | NO ACTION]>
<ENFORCED | NOT ENFORCED>
<ENABLE QUERY OPTIMIZATION | DISABLE QUERY OPTIMIZATION>
```

where:

ConstraintName   Identifies the unique name that is to be assigned to the constraint to be created.

PKTableName   Identifies the name of the parent table that is to participate in the referential constraint.

PKColumnName Identifies the column(s) that make up the parent key of the parent table that is to participate in the referential constraint.

If the NOT ENFORCED clause is specified as part of a constraint's definition an informational constraint will be created and the constraint will not be enforced during insert and update processing. If the ENABLE QUERY OPTIMIZATION clause is specified, the DB2 optimizer will evaluate the information provided about the constraint when generating an access plan in response to a query. (When the ENABLE QUERY OPTIMIZATION is used, the constraint will be imposed when SELECT statements are issued against the table; and records stored in the table that do not conform to the constraint are not returned.)

Therefore, if you wanted to create a table that had three columns in it, two of which use an integer data type and another that uses a fixed-length character string data type, you could do so by executing a CREATE TABLE SQL statement that looks something like this:

```
CREATE TABLE employees
  (empid INTEGER,
   name  CHAR(50)
   dept  INTEGER)
```

If you wanted to create the same table such that the EMPID column had both the NOT NULL constraint and a primary key constraint associated with it, you could do so by executing a CREATE TABLE statement that looks something like this:

```
CREATE TABLE employees
  (empid INTEGER NOT NULL PRIMARY KEY,
   name  CHAR(50)
   dept  INTEGER)
```

If you wanted to create the same table such that the DEPT column participates in a referential constraint with a column named DEPTID that resides in a table named DEPARTMENT, you could do so by executing a CREATE TABLE statement that looks something like this:

```
CREATE TABLE employees
  (empid INTEGER,
   name  CHAR(50)
   dept  INTEGER REFERENCES department (deptid))
```

And finally, if you wanted to create the same table such that the EMPID column has an informational constraint associated with it, you could do so by executing a CREATE TABLE statement that looks something like this:

```
CREATE TABLE employees
  (empid INTEGER NOT NULL
    CONSTRAINT inf_cs CHECK (empid BETWEEN 1 AND 100)
    NOT ENFORCED
    ENABLE QUERY OPTIMIZATION,
  name CHAR(50)
  dept INTEGER)
```

As you can see from these examples, a UNIQUE constraint, a CHECK constraint, a referential constraint, and/or an informational constraint that involves a single column can be defined as part of that particular column's definition. But what if you needed to define a constraint that encompasses multiple columns in the table? Or what if you want to separate the constraint definitions from the column definitions? You do this by defining a constraint as another element, rather than as an extension to a single column's definition. The basic syntax used to define a UNIQUE constraint as an individual element is:

```
<CONSTRAINT [ConstraintName]> [UNIQUE | PRIMARY KEY]
( [ColumnName], ...)
```

where:

ConstraintName   Identifies the unique name that is to be assigned to the constraint to be created.

ColumName   Identifies one or more columns that are to be part of the UNIQUE or primary key constraint to be created.

The syntax used to create a CHECK constraint as an individual element is the same as the syntax used to create a CHECK constraint as part of a column definition:

```
<CONSTRAINT [ConstraintName]> CHECK ( [CheckCondition] )
<ENFORCED | NOT ENFORCED>
<ENABLE QUERY OPTIMIZATION | DISABLE QUERY OPTIMIZATION>
```

where:

ConstraintName Identifies the unique name that is to be assigned to the constraint to be created.

CheckCondition Identifies a condition or test that must evaluate to TRUE before a value can be stored in the column.

And finally, the syntax used to create a referential constraint as an individual element is:

```
<CONSTRAINT [ConstraintName]>
FOREIGN KEY ( [ColumnName] ,...)
REFERENCES [PKTableName] < ( [PKColumnName] ,...) >
<ON UPDATE [NO ACTION | RESTRICT]>
<ON DELETE [CASCADE | SET NULL | NO ACTION | RESTRICT]>
<ENFORCED | NOT ENFORCED>
<ENABLE QUERY OPTIMIZATION | DISABLE QUERY OPTIMIZATION>
```

where:

ConstraintName Identifies the unique name that is to be assigned to the constraint to be created.

ColumnName Identifies one or more columns that are to be part of the referential constraint to be created.

PKTableName Identifies the name of the parent table that is to participate in the referential constraint.

PKColumnName Identifies the column(s) that make up the parent key of the parent table that is to participate in the referential constraint.

Thus, a table that was created by executing a CREATE TABLE statement that looks something like this:

```
CREATE TABLE employees
  (empid INTEGER NOT NULL PRIMARY KEY,
   name  CHAR(50)
   dept  INTEGER REFERENCES department(deptid))
```

could also be created by executing a CREATE TABLE statement that looks something like this:

```
EATE TABLE employees
  (empid INTEGER NOT NULL,
   name  CHAR(50)
   dept  INTEGER,
   PRIMARY KEY (empid),
   FOREIGN KEY (dept) REFERENCES department(deptid))
```

Creating Tables with XML Columns

Earlier, we saw that the XML data type can be used to store well-formed XML documents in their native format. Although XML values are processed in an internal representation that is not a string and not directly comparable to string values, the process for defining an XML column is the same as that used to define a string column: You simply assign the XML data type to a column when you create a table definition using the CREATE TABLE statement.

For example, if you want to create a table that has two columns in it, one of which uses the integer data type and another that uses the XML data type, you can do so by executing a CREATE TABLE SQL statement that looks something like this:

```
CREATE TABLE emp_resume
  (empid  INTEGER NOT NULL PRIMARY KEY,
   resume XML)
```

A table can contain any number of XML columns; however, each XML column used has the following restrictions:

- It cannot be part of any index except an XML index.

- It cannot be included as a column of a primary key or UNIQUE constraint.

- It cannot be a foreign key of a referential constraint.

- It cannot have a specified default value or a WITH DEFAULT clause—if the column is nullable, the default value for the column is the null value.

- It cannot be used in a table with a distribution key. ?

- It cannot be used in range-clustered or range-partitioned tables. ?

In addition, XML columns can be referenced in a CHECK constraint only if the CHECK constraint contains the VALIDATED predicate. (The VALIDATED predicate checks to see whether an XML value has been validated using the XMLVALIDATE() function. The XMLVALIDATE() function returns a copy of the input XML value, augmented with information obtained from XML schema validation, including default values and type annotations. If the value of the column is null, the result of the VALIDATED predicate is unknown; otherwise, the result is either TRUE or FALSE.)

Therefore, if you wanted to add a check constraint that uses the VALIDATED predicate to the XML column in the table we created earlier, you could do so by executing a CREATE TABLE SQL statement that looks something like this:

```
CREATE TABLE emp_resume
  (empid  INTEGER NOT NULL PRIMARY KEY,
   resume XML,
   CONSTRAINT valid_check CHECK (resume IS VALIDATED))
```

Once this statement is executed, whenever an attempt is made to insert or update XML data in the EMP_RESUME table, a check is performed to ensure the data represents a valid, well-formed XML document. (If it does not, the insert/update operation fails and no changes are made to the table.)

Creating Tables with Identity Columns

Many times, base tables are designed such that a single column will be used to store a unique identifier that represents an individual record (or row). More often than not, this identifier is a number that is sequentially incremented each time a new record is added to the table. Numbers for such columns can be generated using a before trigger, or the DB2 Database Manager can automatically generate numbers for such a column if the column is defined as an *identity column*. Identity columns are created by specifying the GENERATED...AS IDENTITY clause along with one or more of the identity column attributes available, as part of the column definition. The syntax used to create an identity column is:

```
[ColumnName] [DataType]
GENERATED <ALWAYS | BY DEFAULT> AS IDENTITY
<(
  <START WITH [1 | StartingValue]>
  <INCREMENT BY [1 | IncrementValue]>
  <NO MINVALUE | MINVALUE [MinValue]>
  <NO MAXVALUE | MAXVALUE [MaxValue]>
  <NO CYCLE | CYCLE>
  <CACHE 20 | NO CACHE | CACHE [CacheSize]>
  <NO ORDER | ORDER>
)>
```

or

```
[ColumnName] [DataType]
GENERATED <ALWAYS | BY DEFAULT> AS (Expression)
```

where:

ColumnName	Identifies the unique name that is to be assigned to the identity column to be created.
DataType	Identifies the numeric data type that is to be assigned to the identity column to be created. The data type specified must be a numeric data type with a scale of 0; therefore, the following values are valid for this parameter: SMALLINT, INTEGER, BIGINT, DECIMAL or NUMERIC, or a user-defined data type that is based on any of these data types.
StartingValue	Identifies the first value that is to be assigned to the identity column to be created.
IncrementValue	Identifies the interval that is to be used to calculate each consecutive value that is to be assigned to the identity column to be created.
MinValue	Identifies the smallest value that can be assigned to the identity column to be created.
MaxValue	Identifies the largest value that can be assigned to the identity column to be created.
CacheSize	Identifies the number of values of the identity sequence that are to be generated at one time and kept in memory.
Expression	Identifies an expression or user-defined external function that is to be used to generate values for the identity column to be created.

If the CYCLE clause is specified as part of the identity column's definition, values will continue to be generated for the column after any minimum or maximum value specified has been reached: After an ascending identity column reaches the maximum value allowed, a new minimum value will be generated and the cycle will begin again; after a descending identity column reaches the minimum value allowed, a new maximum value will be generated and the cycle will repeat itself.

Thus, if you wanted to create a table that had a simple identity column in it for which the DB2 Database Manager will always generate a value, you could do so by executing a CREATE TABLE SQL statement that looks something like this:

```
CREATE TABLE employees
  (empid INTEGER GENERATED ALWAYS AS IDENTITY,
   name  CHAR(50)
   dept  INTEGER)
```

On the other hand, if you want to create a table that has a simple identity column in it for which the DB2 Database Manager will generate a value if no value is explicitly provided, you could do so by executing a CREATE TABLE SQL statement that looks something like this:

```
CREATE TABLE employees
  (empid INTEGER GENERATED BY DEFAULT AS IDENTITY,
   name  CHAR(50)
   dept  INTEGER)
```

In the first example, the SQL statement "INSERT INTO employees VALUES (1, 'SCHIEFER', 50)" would fail because the DB2 Database Manager is expected to provide values for the EMPID column. In the second example, the same SQL statement would succeed because the DB2 Database Manager is only expected to provide a value for the EMPID column if no value is explicitly provided.

It is important to note that a table can have only one identity column. All identity columns are implicitly assigned a NOT NULL constraint; identity columns cannot have a default constraint.

Creating Partitioned Tables

Table partitioning (also referred to as *range partitioning*) is a data organization scheme in which table data is divided across multiple storage objects called *data partitions* or *ranges* based on values in one or more columns. Each data partition is stored separately and the storage objects used can be in different table spaces, in the same table space, or a combination of the two. Table partitioning improves performance and eliminates the need to create a partitioned database using the Data Partitioning Feature.

Data from a given table is partitioned into multiple storage objects based on the specifications provided in the PARTITION BY clause of the CREATE TABLE statement. The syntax for the PARTITION BY clause is:

```
<PARTITION BY <RANGE>
 ([ColumnName] <NULLS LAST | NULLS FIRST> ,...)
 (STARTING <FROM>
    <(> [Start | MINVALUE | MAXVALUE] < ,...)>
    <INCLUSIVE | EXCLUSIVE>
  ENDING <AT>
    <(> [End | MINVALUE | MAXVALUE] < ,...)>
    <INCLUSIVE | EXCLUSIVE>
  EVERY <(>[Constant] <DurationLabel><)>
 )>
```

or

```
<PARTITION BY <RANGE>
 ([ColumnName] <NULLS LAST | NULLS FIRST> ,...)
 (<PARTITION [PartitionName]>
  STARTING <FROM>
    <(> [Start | MINVALUE | MAXVALUE] < ,...)>
    <INCLUSIVE | EXCLUSIVE>
  ENDING <AT>
    <(> [End | MINVALUE | MAXVALUE] < ,...)>
    <INCLUSIVE | EXCLUSIVE>
  <IN [TableSpaceName]>
 )>
```

where:

ColumnName   Identifies one or more columns, by name, whose values are to be used to determine which data partition a particular row is to be stored in. (The group of columns specified make up the partitioning key for the table.)

PartitionName   Identifies the unique name that is to be assigned to the data partition to be created.

Start   Specifies the low end of the range for each data partition.

End   Specifies the high end of the range for each data partition.

Constant   Specifies the width of each data partition range when the automatically generated form of the syntax is used. Data partitions will be created starting at the STARTING FROM value and will contain this number of values in the range. This form of the syntax is only supported if the partitioning key consists of a single column that has been assigned a numeric, date, time, or timestamp data type.

DurationLabel   Identifies the duration that is associated with the *Constant* value specified if the partitioning key column has been assigned a date, time, or timestamp data type. The following values are valid for this parameter: YEAR, YEARS, MONTH, MONTHS, DAY, DAYS, HOUR, HOURS, MINUTE, MINUTES, SECOND, SECONDS, MICROSECOND, and MICROSECONDS.

TableSpaceName Identifies the table space that each data partition is to be stored in.

Thus, if you wanted to create a table that is partitioned such that each quarter's data is stored in a different data partition, and each partition resides in a different table space, you could do so by executing a CREATE TABLE SQL statement that looks something like this:

```
CREATE TABLE part_table
  (col1    DATE,
  col2    NUMERIC(5,2))
  IN tbsp0, tbsp1, tbsp2, tbsp3
  PARTITION BY RANGE (col1 NULLS FIRST)
    (STARTING '1/1/2006' ENDING '12/31/2006'
    EVERY 3 MONTHS)
```

On the other hand, if you wanted to create a table that is partitioned such that rows with numerical values that fall in the range of 0 to 9 are stored in one partition that resides in one table space, rows with numerical values that fall in the range of 10 to 19 are stored in another partition that resides in another table space, and so on, you could do so by executing a CREATE TABLE SQL statement that looks something like this:

```
CREATE TABLE part_table
  (col1    INT
  col2    CHAR(3))
  PARTITION BY (col1 NULLS FIRST)
    (STARTING 0 ENDING 9 IN tbsp0,
    STARTING 10 ENDING 19 IN tbsp1,
    STARTING 20 ENDING 29 IN tbsp2,
    STARTING 30 ENDING 39 IN tbsp3)
```

Advantages of using table partitioning include:

Easy roll-in and roll-out of data: Rolling in partitioned table data allows a new range to be easily incorporated into a partitioned table as an additional data partition. Rolling out partitioned table data allows you to separate ranges of data from a partitioned table easily for subsequent purging or archiving. Data can be quickly rolled in and out by using the ATTACH PARTITION and DETACH PARTITION clauses of the ALTER TABLE statement.

Easier administration of large tables: Table level administration becomes more flexible because administrative tasks can be performed on individual data partitions. Such tasks include detaching and reattaching of a data partition, backing up and restoring individual data partitions, and reorganizing individual indexes. In addition, time-consuming maintenance operations can be shortened by breaking them down into a series of smaller operations. For example, backup operations can be performed at the data partition level when each data partition is placed in separate table spaces. Thus, it is possible to back up one data partition of a partitioned table at a time.

Flexible index placement: With table partitioning, indexes can be placed in different table spaces, allowing for more granular control of index placement.

Better query processing: When resolving queries, one or more data partitions may be automatically eliminated, based on the query predicates used. This functionality, known as Data Partition Elimination, improves the performance of many decision support queries because less data has to be analyzed before a result data set can be returned.

Creating Tables That Are Like Existing Tables

At times, it may be desirable to create a new table that has the same definition as an existing table. To perform such an operation, you could execute a CREATE TABLE statement that looks identical to the CREATE TABLE statement that was used to define the original table. Or better still, you could use a special form of the CREATE TABLE statement. The syntax for this form of the CREATE TABLE statement is:

```
CREATE TABLE [TableName] LIKE [SourceTable]
<[INCLUDING | EXCLUDING] COLUMN DEFAULTS>
<[INCLUDING | EXCLUDING] IDENTITY COLUMN ATTRIBUTES>
```

where:

TableName   Identifies the unique name that is to be assigned to the table to be created.

SourceTable   Identifies the name of an existing table whose structure is to be used to define the table to be created.

Thus, if you wanted to create an empty table named 2ND_QTR_SALES that has the same structure as an existing table named 1ST_QTR_SALES, you could do so by executing a CREATE TABLE SQL statement that looks something like this:

```
CREATE TABLE 2nd_qtr_sales LIKE 1st_qtr_sales
```

When this form of the CREATE TABLE is executed, the table that is created will have the same number of columns as the source table specified, and these columns will have the same names, data types, and nullability characteristics as those of the source table. Unless the EXCLUDING COLUMN DEFAULTS option is specified, any default constraints defined for columns in the source table will be copied to the new table as well. However, no other attributes of the source table will be duplicated. Thus, the table that is created will not contain UNIQUE constraints, referential constraints, triggers, or indexes that have been defined for the source table used. (If the target table needs these characteristics, they must be created separately after the target table is created.)

A Quick Review of Schemas

In Chapter 4, "Working with Databases and Database Objects," we saw that schemas are objects that are used to logically classify and group other objects in the database. Schemas also make it possible to create multiple objects in a database without encountering namespace collisions. Most objects in a DB2 database are named using a two-part naming convention. The first (leftmost) part of the name is called the *schema name* or *qualifier*, and the second (rightmost) part is called the *object name*. Syntactically, these two parts are concatenated and delimited with a period (for example, PAYROLL.STAFF). When any object that can be qualified by a schema name (such as a table, view, index, user-defined data type, user-defined function, nickname, package, or trigger) is first created, it is assigned to a particular schema based on the qualifier in its name. Figure 6–15 illustrates how a table named EMPLOYEES would be assigned to the HR schema during the table creation process.

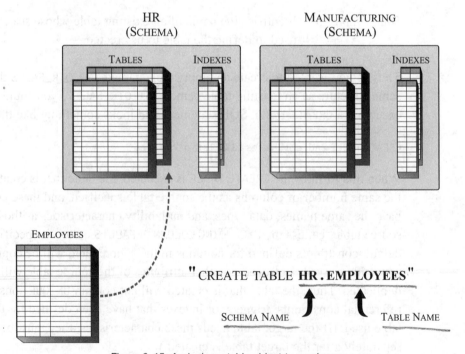

Figure 6–15: Assigning a table object to a schema.

The CURRENT SCHEMA (or CURRENT_SCHEMA) special register contains a value that identifies the schema name that is to be used to qualify references to database objects if no schema/qualifier name is specified. (With DB2 for z/OS, the CURRENT SQLID, or CURRENT_SQLID, special register is used instead.) The initial value of the CURRENT SCHEMA register is the authorization ID of the current session user. However, this value can be changed by executing the SET SCHEMA SQL statement. The syntax for the SET SCHEMA SQL statement is:

```
SET <CURRENT> SCHEMA <=>
  [['SchemaName'] |
  USER |
  SESSION_USER |
  SYSTEM_USER |
  CURRENT_USER]
```

where:

SchemaName   Identifies the name of an existing schema. (The name specified must be enclosed in single quotes and cannot exceed 30 characters in length.)

Thus, if you wanted to change the value of the CURRENT SCHEMA register from the authentication ID of the current user to "PAYROLL", you could do so by executing a SET SCHEMA SQL statement that looks something like this:

```
SET CURRENT SCHEMA = 'PAYROLL'
```

It is important to note that the value assigned to the CURRENT SCHEMA special register is not persistent across database restarts. Therefore, if you assign a value to the CURRENT SCHEMA special register, disconnect from the database, and reconnect, the CURRENT SCHEMA special register will contain your authentication ID, not the value you assigned it earlier.

Examples of the CREATE TABLE SQL Statement

Now that we've seen the basic syntax for the CREATE TABLE statement and have studied some simple examples of the CREATE TABLE statement's use, let's take a look at some more complex CREATE TABLE statement examples and examine the characteristics of the resulting tables that would be created if each statement shown were executed.

Example 1

Suppose the following CREATE TABLE statement is executed:

```
CREATE TABLE project
  (projno  CHAR(6) NOT NULL,
   projname VARCHAR(24) NOT NULL,
   deptno  SMALLINT,
   budget  DECIMAL(6,2),
   startdate DATE,
   enddate  DATE)
```

A table named PROJECT will be created that has the following characteristics:

- The first column will be assigned the name PROJNO and can be used to store fixed-length character string data that is six characters in length (for example, "PROJ01" or "PROJ02").

- The second column will be assigned the name PROJNAME and can be used to store variable-length character string data that can be up to 24 characters in length (for example, "DB2 Benchmarks Tool" or "Auto-Configuration Tool").

- The third column will be assigned the name DEPTNO and can be used to store numeric values in the range of −32,768 to +32,767.

- The fourth column will be assigned the name BUDGET and can be used to store numerical values that contain both whole and fractional parts. Up to six numbers can be specified—four for the whole number part and two for the fractional part (for example, 1500.00, 2000.50, etc.).

- The fifth column will be assigned the name STARTDATE and can be used to store date values.

- The sixth column will be assigned the name ENDDATE and can also be used to store date values.

- Whenever data is added to the PROJECT table, values must be provided for the PROJNO column and the PROJNAME column. (Null values are not allowed because the NOT NULL constraint was defined for both of these columns.)

- The PROJECT table will be created in the table space USERSPACE1 (because no table space was specified, this is the default table space used).

Example 2

Suppose the following CREATE TABLE statement is executed:

```
CREATE TABLE central.sales
  (po_number INTEGER NOT NULL CONSTRAINT uc1 UNIQUE,
   date    DATE NOT NULL WITH DEFAULT,
   office   CHAR(128) NOT NULL WITH DEFAULT 'Dallas',
   amt     DECIMAL(10,2) NOT NULL CHECK (amt > 99.99)
   IN my_space
```

A table named SALES will be created that has the following characteristics:

- The first column will be assigned the name PO_NUMBER (for Purchase Order Number) and can be used to store numeric values in the range of –2,147,483,648 to 2,147,483,647.

- The second column will be assigned the name DATE and can be used to store date values.

- The third column will be assigned the name OFFICE and can be used to store fixed-length character string data that can be up to 128 characters in length (for example, "Kansas City" or "Dallas").

- The fourth column will be assigned the name AMT (for Amount) and can be used to store numerical values that contain both whole and fractional parts. Up to 10 numbers can be specified—eight for the whole number part and two for the fractional part (for example, 20,000,000.50).

- Whenever data is added to the SALES table, values must be provided for the PO_NUMBER and the AMT columns. (Null values are not allowed in any column because the NOT NULL constraint was defined for each column; however, default values are provided for two columns.)

- Every value provided for the PO_NUMBER column must be unique. (Because a UNIQUE constraint named UC1 was created for the PO_NUMBER column.)

- An index was automatically created for the PO_NUMBER column. (Because a UNIQUE constraint named UC1 was created for the PO_NUMBER column.) As data is added to the table, the values provided for the PO_NUMBER column will be added to the index, and the index will be sorted in ascending order.

- If no value is provided for the DATE column when a row is inserted into the SALES table, the system date at the time the row is inserted will be written to the column by default (because a default constraint was created for the DATE column).

- If no value is provided for the OFFICE column, the value "Dallas" will be written to the column by default (because a default constraint was created for the OFFICE column).

- Every value provided for the AMT column must be greater than or equal to 100.00 (because a CHECK constraint was created for the AMT column).

- The SALES table will be created in a schema named CENTRAL.

- The SALES table will be created in a table space named MY_SPACE.

Example 3

Suppose the following CREATE TABLE statements are executed in the order shown:

```
CREATE TABLE payroll.employees
(empid    INTEGER NOT NULL PRIMARY KEY,
emp_fname CHAR(30),
emp_lname CHAR(30))

CREATE TABLE payroll.paychecks
(empid    INTEGER,
weeknumber CHAR(3),
pay_amt   DECIMAL(6,2),
CONSTRAINT fkconst FOREIGN KEY (empid)
REFERENCES employee(empid) ON DELETE CASCADE,
CONSTRAINT chk1 CHECK (pay_amt > 0 AND weeknumber
BETWEEN 1 AND 52))
```

First, a table named EMPLOYEES will be created that has the following characteristics:

- The first column will be assigned the name EMPID (for Employee ID) and can be used to store numeric values in the range of –2,147,483,648 to 2,147,483,647.

- The second column will be assigned the name EMP_FNAME (for Employee First Name) and can be used to store fixed-length character string data that can be up to 30 characters in length (for example, "Bob" or "Mark").

- The third column will be assigned the name EMP_LNAME (for Employee Last Name) and can be used to store fixed-length character string data that can be up to 30 characters in length (for example, "Jancer" or "Hayakawa").

- Whenever data is added to the EMPLOYEES table, values must be provided for the EMPID column. (Null values are not allowed because the NOT NULL constraint was defined for this column.)

- Every value provided for the EMPID column must be unique (because a primary key constraint was created for the EMPID column).

- An index was automatically created for the EMPID column. (Because a primary key constraint was created for the EMPID column.) As data is added to the table, the values provided for the EMPID column will be added to the index, and the index will be sorted in ascending order.

- The EMPLOYEES table will be created in a schema named PAYROLL.

- The EMPLOYEES table will be created in the table space USERSPACE1 (because no table space was specified, this is the default table space used).

Then a table named PAYCHECKS will be created that has the following characteristics:

- The first column will be assigned the name EMPID and can be used to store numeric values in the range of –2,147,483,648 to 2,147,483,647.

- The second column will be assigned the name WEEKNUMBER and can be used to store fixed-length character string data that can be up to three characters in length (for example, "1" or "35").

- The third column will be assigned the name PAY_AMT and can be used to store numerical values that contain both whole and fractional parts. Up to six numbers can be specified—four for the whole number part and two for the fractional part (for example, 2,000.50).

- Every value entered in the EMPID column must have a matching value in the EMPID column of the EMPLOYEES table created earlier (because a referential constraint has been created in which the EMPID column of the EMPLOYEES table is the parent key and the EMPID column of the PAYCHECKS table is the foreign key—this referential constraint is assigned the name FKCONST).

- Whenever a row is deleted from the EMPLOYEES table created earlier, all rows in the PAYCHECKS table that have a value in the EMPID column that matches the primary key of the row being deleted will also be deleted.

- Every value provided for the PAY_AMT column must be greater than 0 (because a CHECK constraint named CHK1 was created for the PAY_AMT and WEEKNUMBER columns).

- Every value provided for the WEEKNUMBER column must be greater than or equal to 1 and less than or equal to 52 (again, because a CHECK constraint named CHK1 was created for the PAY_AMT and WEEKNUMBER columns.)

- The PAYCHECKS table will be created in a schema named PAYROLL.

- The PAYCHECKS table will be created in the table space USERSPACE1 (because no table space was specified, this is the default table space used).

Example 4

Suppose the following CREATE TABLE statement is executed:

```
CREATE TABLE employee
  (empid    SMALLINT NOT NULL
        GENERATED BY DEFAULT AS IDENTITY,
   firstname VARCHAR(30) NOT NULL,
   lastname  VARCHAR(30) NOT NULL,
   deptid    CHAR(3),
   edlevel   CHAR(1) CHECK (edlevel IN ('C', 'H', 'N')),
   CONSTRAINT emp_pk PRIMARY KEY (empid),
   CONSTRAINT emp_dept_fk FOREIGN KEY (deptid)
     REFERENCES department (deptno))
```

A table named EMPLOYEE will be created that has the following characteristics:

- The first column will be assigned the name EMPID (for Employee ID) and can be used to store numeric values in the range of –32,768 to +32,767.

- The second column will be assigned the name FIRSTNAME and can be used to store variable length character string data that can be up to 30 characters in length (for example, "Mark" or "Antonio").

- The third column will be assigned the name LASTNAME and can be used to store variable length character string data that can be up to 30 characters in length (for example, "Hayakawa" or "Robinson").

- The fourth column will be assigned the name DEPTID and can be used to store fixed-length character string data that can be up to three characters in length (for example, "1", "35", etc.).

- The fifth column will be assigned the name EDLEVEL and can be used to store fixed-length character string data that can only be one character in length (for example, 'C', or 'H').

- The EMPID column is an identity column. Therefore a unique numeric value will automatically be assigned to this column whenever data is added to the EMPLOYEE table; this value can be overridden by specifying a value for the EMPID column in the INSERT statement used to add data. (Null values are not allowed because the NOT NULL constraint was defined for this column.)

- Whenever data is added to the EMPLOYEE table, values must be provided for the FIRSTNAME and the LASTNAME columns. (Null values are not allowed because the NOT NULL constraint was defined for these columns.)

- The only values that can be inserted into the EDLEVEL column are 'C', 'H', and 'N' (because a CHECK constraint was created for the EDLEVEL column).

- Every value provided for the EMPID column must be unique (because a primary key constraint named EMP_PK was created for the EMPID column).

- An index was automatically created for the EMPID column (again, because a primary key constraint named EMP_PK was created for the EMPID column). As data is added to the table, the values generated/provided for the EMPID column will be added to the index, and the index will be sorted in ascending order.

- Every value entered in the DEPTID column must have a matching value in the DEPTNO column of a table named DEPARTMENT (because a referential constraint has been created in which the DEPTNO column of the DEPARTMENT table is the parent key and the DEPTID column of the EMPLOYEE table is the foreign key—this referential constraint was assigned the name EMP_DEPT_FK).

- The EMPLOYEE table will be created in the table space USERSPACE1 (because no table space was specified, this is the default table space used).

Example 5

Suppose the following CREATE TABLE statement is executed:

```
CREATE TABLE stock.activity
  (activityno  SMALLINT NOT NULL
    GENERATED BY DEFAULT AS IDENTITY
    (START WITH 10 INCREMENT BY 10),
   actkwd    CHAR(6) NOT NULL,
   actdesc   VARCHAR(20) NOT NULL,
UNIQUE (activityno))
```

A table named ACTIVITY will be created that has the following characteristics:

- The first column will be assigned the name ACTIVITYNO (for Activity Number) and can be used to store numeric values in the range of –32,768 to +32,767.

- The second column will be assigned the name ACTKWD (for Activity Keyword) and can be used to store fixed-length character string data that can be up to 6 characters in length (for example, "Sale" or "Buy").

- The third column will be assigned the name ACTDESC (for Activity Description) and can be used to store variable-length character string data that can be up to 20 characters in length (for example, "Sale of 1000 shares of EMC" or "Buy 250 shares IBM").

- The ACTIVITYNO column is an identity column. Therefore a unique numeric value will automatically be assigned to this column whenever data is added to the ACTIVITY table; this value can be overridden by specifying a value for the ACTIVITY column in the INSERT statement used to add data. If no value is provided, the first value generated will be the number 10, and subsequent generated values will be incremented by 10. (Null values are not allowed because the NOT NULL constraint was defined for this column.)

- Whenever data is added to the ACTIVITY table, values must be provided for the ACTKWD and the ACTDESC columns. (Null values are not allowed because the NOT NULL constraint was defined for these columns.)

- Every value provided for the ACTIVITYNO column must be unique (because a UNIQUE constraint was created for the ACTIVITYNO column).

- An index was automatically created for the AVTIVITYNO column (again, because a UNIQUE constraint was created for the ACTIVITYNO column). As data is added to the table, the values generated/provided for the ACTIVITY *No* column will be added to the index, and the index will be sorted in ascending order.

- The ACTIVITY table will be created in a schema named STOCK.

- The ACTIVITY table will be created in the table space USERSPACE1 (because no table space was specified, this is the default table space used).

Example 6

Suppose the following CREATE TABLE statement is executed:

```
CREATE TABLE self_reference
  (idcol1 SMALLINT NOT NULL PRIMARY KEY,
   idcol2 SAMLLINT,
   CONSTRAINT fkconst FOREIGN KEY (idcol2)
   REFERENCES self_reference(idcol1))
```

A table named SELF_REFERENCE will be created that has the following characteristics:

- The first column will be assigned the name IDCOL1 and can be used to store numeric values in the range of −32,768 to +32,767.

- The second column will be assigned the name IDCOL2 and can be used to store numeric values in the range of −32,768 to +32,767.

- Every value entered in the IDCOL2 column must have a matching value in the IDCOL1 column of the same table (because a referential constraint has been created in which the IDCOL1 column of the table is the parent key and the IDCOL2 column of the same table is the foreign key—this referential constraint was assigned the name FKCONST). Every value provided for the IDCOL1 column must be unique (because a primary key constraint was created for the IDCOL1 column).

- An index was automatically created for the IDCOL1 column (again, because a primary key constraint was created for the IDCOL1 column). As data is added *Not an identity col* to the table, the values generated/provided for the IDCOL01 column will be added to the index, and the index will be sorted in ascending order.

- The SELF_REFERENCE table will be created in the table space USERSPACE1 (because no table space was specified, this is the default table space used).

A Closer Look At Declared Temporary Tables

In Chapter 4, "Working with Databases and Database Objects," we saw that
another type of table that is commonly used is a declared temporary table. Unlike
base tables, whose descriptions and constraints are stored in the system catalog
tables of the database to which they belong, declared temporary tables are not
persistent and can be used only by the application that creates them—and only for
the life of the application. When the application that creates a declared temporary
table terminates, the rows of the table are deleted, and the definition of the table is
dropped. (However, data stored in a temporary table can exist across transaction
boundaries.) Another significant difference between the two centers around
naming conventions: base table names must be unique within a schema, but
because each application that defines a declared temporary table has its own
instance of that table, it is possible for many applications to create declared
temporary tables that have the same name.

or

> Before a declared global temporary table can be defined and
> used, a user temporary table space must exist for the database
> the application that will be defining the declared global temporary
> table will be working with.

Whereas base tables are created with the CREATE TABLE SQL statement, declared
temporary tables are created with the DECLARE GLOBAL TEMPORARY TABLE
statement. The basic syntax for this statement is:

```
DECLARE GLOBAL TEMPORARY TABLE [TableName]
( [ColumnDefinition] ,...)

<ON COMMIT DELETE ROWS | ON COMMIT PRESERVE ROWS>
<NOT LOGGED <ON ROLLBACK DELETE ROWS |
  ON ROLLBACK PRESERVE ROWS>>
<WITH REPLACE>
<IN [TablespaceName]>
```

or

```
DECLARE GLOBAL TEMPORARY TABLE [TableName]
LIKE [SourceTable | SourceView]
<[INCLUDING | EXCLUDING] COLUMN DEFAULTS>
<[INCLUDING | EXCLUDING] IDENTITY COLUMN ATTRIBUTES>
<ON COMMIT DELETE ROWS | ON COMMIT PRESERVE ROWS>
<NOT LOGGED <ON ROLLBACK DELETE ROWS |
   ON ROLLBACK PRESERVE ROWS>>
<WITH REPLACE>
<IN [TablespaceName]>
```

or

```
DECLARE GLOBAL TEMPORARY TABLE [TableName]
AS ([SELECTStatement]) DEFINITION ONLY
<ON COMMIT DELETE ROWS | ON COMMIT PRESERVE ROWS>
<NOT LOGGED <ON ROLLBACK DELETE ROWS |
   ON ROLLBACK PRESERVE ROWS>>
<WITH REPLACE>
<IN [TablespaceName]>
```

where:

TableName   Identifies the name that is to be assigned to the global temporary table to be created.

ColumnDefinition Identifies one or more columns to be included in the global temporary table definition.

SourceTable   Identifies the name of an existing table whose structure is to be used to define the global temporary table to be created.

SourceView   Identifies the name of an existing view whose structure is to be used to define the global temporary table to be created.

SELECTStatement Identifies a SELECT SQL statement that, when executed, will produce column definition data that will be used to define the global temporary table to be created.

TablespaceName Identifies the user temporary table space in which the global temporary table is to be created.

The basic syntax used to define a column is:

```
[ColumnName] [DataType]
<NOT NULL>
<WITH DEFAULT <[DefaultValue] | CURRENT DATE |
CURRENT TIME | CURRENT TIMESTAMP | NULL>>
```

or

```
[ColumnName] [DataType]
GENERATED [ALWAYS | BY DEFAULT] AS IDENTITY
<(
  <START WITH [1 | StartingValue]>
  <INCREMENT BY [1 | IncrementValue]>
  <NO MINVALUE | MINVALUE [MinValue]>
  <NO MAXVALUE | MAXVALUE [MaxValue]>
  <NO CYCLE | CYCLE>
  <CACHE 20 | NO CACHE | CACHE [CacheSize]>
  <NO ORDER | ORDER>
)>
```

or

```
[ColumnName] [DataType]
GENERATED [ALWAYS | BY DEFAULT] AS (Expression)
```

where:

ColumnName   Identifies the unique name to be assigned to the column that is to be created.

DataType   Identifies the data type (built-in or user-defined) that is to be assigned to the column to be created. The data type specified determines the kind of data values that can be stored in the column. Table 6–4 contains a list of the data type definitions that are valid.

DefaultValue   Identifies the value that is to be provided for the column in the event no value is supplied when an insert or update operation is performed against the global temporary table.

StartingValue   Identifies the first value that is to be assigned to the identity column to be created.

IncrementValue   Identifies the interval that is to be used to calculate each consecutive value that is to be assigned to the identity column to be created.

MinValue   Identifies the smallest value that can be assigned to the identity column to be created.

MaxValue   Identifies the largest value that can be assigned to the identity column to be created.

CacheSize   Identifies the number of values of the identity sequence that are to be generated at one time and kept in memory.

Expression   Identifies an expression or user-defined external function that is to be used to generate values for the identity column to be created.

Thus, if an application needed to create a global temporary table named TEMP_EMP that had three columns in it, two of which use an integer data type and another that uses a fixed-length character string data type, it could do so by executing a DECLARE GLOBAL TEMPORARY TABLE SQL statement that looks something like this:

```
DECLARE GLOBAL TEMPORARY TABLE temp_emp
  (empid INTEGER,
   name  CHAR(50)
   dept  INTEGER)
```

On the other hand, if an application wanted to create a global temporary table named TEMP_EMP that had a simple identity column in it, it could do so by executing a DECLARE GLOBAL TEMPORARY TABLE SQL statement that looks something like this:

```
DECLARE GLOBAL TEMPORARY TABLE temp_emp
  (empid INTEGER GENERATED ALWAYS AS IDENTITY,
   name  CHAR(50)
   dept  INTEGER)
```

Or, if an application wanted to create a global temporary table named TEMP_EMP that has the same structure as a base table named EMPLOYEE and that, once populated, will retain its contents after transactions are committed, it could do so by executing a DECLARE GLOBAL TEMPORARY TABLE SQL statement that looks something like this:

```
DECLARE GLOBAL TEMPORARY TABLE temp_emp LIKE employee
   ON COMMIT PRESERVE ROWS
```

And finally, if an application wanted to create a global temporary table named TEMP_EMP and define its structure using two columns from a view named EMPLOYEES in such a way that, once populated, it will retain its contents after transactions are committed, it could do so by executing a DECLARE GLOBAL TEMPORARY TABLE SQL statement that looks something like this:

```
DECLARE GLOBAL TEMPORARY TABLE temp_emp
AS (SELECT empid, lastname FROM employees) DEFINITION ONLY
   ON COMMIT PRESERVE ROWS
```

All of these examples have one thing in common: Once the application that created the global temporary table is terminated, any records in the table are deleted and the table itself is destroyed.

Another Look At Views

In Chapter 4, "Working with Databases and Database Objects," we saw that views are used to provide a different way of looking at the data stored in one or more base tables. Essentially, a view is a named specification of a result table that is populated whenever the view is referenced in an SQL statement. (Each time a view is referenced, a query is executed and the results are retrieved from the underlying table and returned in a table-like format.) Like base tables, views can be thought of as having columns and rows. And in most cases, data can be retrieved from a view the same way it can be retrieved from a table.

Views can be created by executing the CREATE VIEW SQL statement. The basic syntax for this statement is:

```
CREATE VIEW [ViewName]
<( [ColumnName] ,... )>
AS [SELECTStatement]
<WITH <LOCAL | CASCADED> CHECK OPTION>
```

where:

ViewName	Identifies the name that is to be assigned to the view to be created.
ColumnName	Identifies the names of one or more columns that are to be included in the view to be created. If a list of column names is specified, the number of column names provided must match the number of columns that will be returned by the SELECT statement used to create the view. (If a list of column names is not provided, the columns of the view will inherit the names that are assigned to the columns returned by the SELECT statement used to create the view.)
SELECTStatement	Identifies a SELECT SQL statement that, when executed, will produce data that will populate the view.

Thus, if you wanted to create a view that references specific data values stored in a table named DEPARTMENT and assign it the name DEPT_VIEW, you could do so by executing a CREATE VIEW SQL statement that looks something like this:

```
CREATE VIEW dept_view
AS SELECT (dept_no, dept_name, dept_size)
 FROM department
 WHERE dept_size > 25
```

The view created by this statement would contain department number, department name, and department size information for each department that has more than 25 people in it.

If the WITH LOCAL CHECK OPTION clause of with the CREATE VIEW SQL statement is specified, insert and update operations performed against the view that is created are validated to ensure that all rows being inserted into or updated in the base table the view refers to conform to the view's definition (otherwise, the insert/update operation will fail). So what exactly does this mean? Suppose a view was created using the following CREATE VIEW statement:

```
CREATE VIEW priority_orders
AS SELECT * FROM orders WHERE response_time < 4
WITH LOCAL CHECK OPTION
```

Now, suppose a user tries to insert a record into this view that has a RESPONSE_TIME value of 6. The insert operation will fail because the record violates the view's definition. Had the view not been created with the WITH LOCAL CHECK OPTION clause, the insert operation would have been successful, even though the new record would not be visible to the view that was used to add it.

If the WITH CASCADED CHECK OPTION clause of the CREATE VIEW SQL statement is specified, the view created will inherit the search conditions of the *parent view* upon which the view is based and treat those conditions as one or more constraints that are used to validate insert and update operations that are performed against the view. Additionally, every view created that is a child of the view that was created with the WITH CASCADED CHECK OPTION clause specified will inherit those constraints; the search conditions of both parent and child views are ANDed together to form the constraints. To better understand what this means, let's look at an example. Suppose a view was created using the following CREATE VIEW statement:

```
CREATE VIEW priority_orders
AS SELECT * FROM orders WHERE response_time < 4
```

Now, suppose a second view was created using this CREATE VIEW statement:

```
CREATE VIEW special_orders
AS SELECT * FROM priority_orders
WITH CASCADED CHECK OPTION
```

If a user tries to insert a record into the SPECIAL_ORDERS view that has a RESPONSE_TIME value of 6, the insert operation will fail because the record violates the search condition of the PRIORITY_ORDERS view's definition (which is a constraint for the SPECIAL_ORDERS view).

A Closer Look At Indexes

In Chapter 4, "Working with Databases and Database Objects," we saw that an index is an object that contains an ordered set of pointers that refer to rows in a base table. Each index is based upon one or more columns in the base table they refer to (known as *keys*), yet they are stored as separate entities.

While some indexes are created implicitly to provide support for a table's definition (for example, to provide support for a primary key), indexes are typically created explicitly, using tools available with DB2. One way to explicitly create an index is by executing the CREATE INDEX SQL statement. The basic syntax for this statement is:

```
CREATE <UNIQUE> INDEX [IndexName]
ON [TableName] ( [PriColumnName] <ASC | DESC>, ... )
<INCLUDE ( [SecColumnName], ... )>
<CLUSTER>
<DISALLOW REVERSE SCANS | ALLOW REVERSE SCANS>
```

where:

IndexName Identifies the name that is to be assigned to the index to be created.

TableName Identifies the name assigned to the base table with which the index to be created is to be associated.

PriColumnName Identifies one or more primary columns that are to be part of the index's key. (The combined values of each primary column specified will be used to enforce data uniqueness in the associated base table.)

SecColumnName Identifies one or more secondary columns whose values are to be stored with the values of the primary columns specified, but are not to be used to enforce data uniqueness.

If the UNIQUE clause is specified when the CREATE INDEX statement is executed, rows in the table associated with the index to be created must not have two or more occurrences of the same values in the set of columns that make up the index key. If the base table for which the index is to be created contains data, this uniqueness is checked when the DB2 Database Manager attempts to create the index specified. If records with duplicate values for the index key are found, the index will not be created; if no duplicates are found, the index is created, and uniqueness is enforced each time an insert or update operation is performed against the table. Any time the uniqueness of the index key is compromised, the insert or update operation will fail and an error will be generated.

Therefore, if you wanted to create an index for a base table named EMPLOYEES such that the index key consists of a column named EMPNO and all employee numbers entered into the EMPNO column are guaranteed to be unique, you could do so by executing a CREATE INDEX statement that looks something like this:

```
CREATE UNIQUE INDEX empno_indx
ON employees (empno)
```

If an index is created for an empty table, that index will not have any entries stored in it until the table the index is associated with is populated. On the other hand, if an index is created for a table that already contains data, index entries will be generated for the existing data and added to the index as soon as it is created.

Any number of indexes can be created for a table, using a wide variety of combinations of columns. However, each index comes at a price in both storage requirements and performance: Each index replicates its key values, and this replication requires additional storage space. And because each modification to a table results in a similar modification to all indexes defined on the table, performance can decrease when insert, update, and delete operations are performed. In fact, if a large number of indexes are created for a table that is modified frequently, overall performance will decrease, rather than increase. Tables that are used for data mining, business intelligence, business warehousing, and other applications that execute many (and often complex) queries while rarely modifying data are prime targets for multiple indexes. On the other hand, tables that are used in on-line transactional processing (OLTP) environments, or other environments where data throughput is high, should use indexes sparingly.

Clustering Indexes

A clustering index is a special index that, when used, informs the DB2 Database Manager to always try to store records on a page that contains other records that have similar index key values. (If no space is available on that page, the DB2 Database Manager will attempt to store the record in a page that is nearby.) A clustering index usually increases performance by decreasing the amount of I/O required to access data: this results in fewer page fetches, since like data values are stored on the same physical page. (Only one index in a table can be a clustering index.)

When a logical set of rows are physically stored close together, a read operation on the set of rows will require less I/O, because adjacent rows are more likely to be found within the same extent (remember, data pages are written in batches called *extents*) instead of being widely distributed across multiple extents. And because similar key values are placed on the same data page whenever possible, often only a portion of a table will need to be read in response to a query. A clustering index is most useful for columns that have range predicates because it allows better sequential access of data in the base table.

A clustering index is created by specifying the CLUSTER option with the CREATE INDEX SQL statement. Thus, if you wanted to create a clustering index for a base table named EMPLOYEES such that the index key consists of a column named EMPNO and all employee numbers entered into the EMPNO column are guaranteed to be unique, you could do so by executing a CREATE INDEX statement that looks something like this:

```
CREATE UNIQUE INDEX empno_cindx
ON employees (empno)
  CLUSTER
```

When creating a clustering index, the PCTFREE option of the CREATE INDEX SQL statement can be used to control how much space is reserved for future insert and update operations. Specify a higher PCTFREE value (the default is 10 percent) at index creation time to reduce the likelihood of index page splits occurring when records are inserted into the index.

Over time, update operations can cause rows to change page locations, thereby reducing the degree of clustering that exists between an index and its data pages. Reorganizing a table (with the REORG utility) using the appropriate index will return the specified index to its original level of clustering.

Multidimensional Clustering (MDC) Indexes

Multidimensional clustering (MDC) provides a way to cluster data along multiple dimensions automatically. Such clustering results in significant improvement in query performance, as well as significant reduction in the overhead of data maintenance operations, such as table/index reorganization, and index maintenance operations during insert, update, and delete operations. Multidimensional clustering is primarily intended for data warehousing, OLTP, and large database environments.

Earlier, we saw that when a clustering index is used, the DB2 Database Manager maintains the physical order of data on pages in the key order of the index, as records are inserted and updated in the table. With good clustering, only a portion of the table needs to be accessed in response to a query, and when the pages are stored sequentially, more efficient prefetching can be performed. With MDC, these benefits are extended to multiple keys (or dimensions); MDC allows a table to be physically clustered on more than one key (or dimension) simultaneously. Not only will queries access only those pages that contain records with the correct dimension values, these qualifying pages will be grouped by extents. Furthermore, although a table with a clustering index can become unclustered over time as space fills up in the table, an MDC table is able to maintain its clustering over all dimensions automatically and continuously, thus eliminating the need to reorganize a table in order to restore the original level of clustering used.

Another Look at Triggers

In Chapter 4, "Working with Databases and Database Objects," we saw that a trigger is used to define a set of actions that are to be executed whenever an insert, update, or delete operation is performed against a table or updatable view. Like constraints, triggers are often used to enforce data integrity and business rules. Unlike constraints, triggers can also be used to update other tables, automatically generate or transform values for inserted or updated rows, and invoke functions to perform tasks such as issuing errors or alerts.

Before a trigger can be created, the following components must be identified:

Subject table/view: The table or view that the trigger is to interact with.

Trigger event: An SQL operation that causes the trigger to be activated whenever it is performed against the subject table/view. This operation can be an insert operation, an update operation, or a delete operation.

Trigger activation time: Indicates whether the trigger should be activated before, after, or instead of the trigger event. A BEFORE trigger will be activated before the trigger event occurs; therefore, it will be able to see new data values before they are inserted into the subject table. An AFTER trigger will be activated after the trigger event occurs; therefore, it can see only data values that have already been inserted into the subject table. An INSTEAD OF trigger will replace the trigger event made against the subject view. (A BEFORE trigger might be used to trap and process unwanted values, while an AFTER trigger could be used to copy data values entered to other tables or views.)

Set of affected rows: The rows of the subject table/view that are being inserted, updated, or deleted.

Trigger granularity: Specifies whether the actions the trigger will perform are to be performed once for the entire insert, update, or delete operation or once for every row affected by the insert, update, or delete operation.

Triggered action: An optional search condition and a set of SQL statements that are to be executed whenever the trigger is activated. (If a search condition is specified, the SQL statements will only be executed if the search condition evaluates to TRUE.) If the trigger is a BEFORE trigger, the triggered action can include statements that retrieve data, set transition variables, or signal SQL states. If the trigger is an AFTER trigger, the triggered action can include statements that retrieve data, insert records, update records, delete records, or signal SQL states.

Triggered actions can refer to the values in the set of affected rows using what are known as *transition variables*. Transition variables use the names of the columns in the subject table, qualified by a specified name that indicates whether the reference is to the original value (before the insert, update, or delete operation is performed) or the new value (after the insert, update, or delete operation is performed). Another means of referring to values in the set of affected rows is through the use of *transition tables*. Transition tables also use the names of the columns in the subject table, but they allow the complete set of affected rows to be treated as a table. Transition tables can only be used in after triggers.

Once the appropriate trigger components have been identified, a trigger can be created by executing the CREATE TRIGGER SQL statement. The basic syntax for this statement is:

```
CREATE TRIGGER [TriggerName]
[<NO CASCADE> BEFORE | AFTER | INSTEAD OF]
[INSERT | DELETE | UPDATE <OF [ColumnName], ... >]
ON [TableName | ViewName]
<REFERENCING [Reference]>
[FOR EACH ROW | FOR EACH STATEMENT]
<WHEN ( [SearchCondition] )>
[TriggeredAction]
```

where:

TriggerName	Identifies the name to be assigned to the trigger to be created.
ColumnName	Identifies one or more columns in the subject table or view of the trigger whose values must be updated before the trigger's triggered action (*TriggeredAction*) will be executed.
TableName	Identifies, by name, the subject table of the BEFORE or AFTER trigger to be created.
ViewName	Identifies, by name, the subject view of the INSTEAD OF trigger to be created.
Reference	Identifies one or more transition variables and/or transition tables that are to be used by the trigger's triggered action (*TriggeredAction*). The syntax used to create transition variables and/or transition tables that are to be used by the trigger's triggered action is:

```
<OLD <AS> [CorrelationName]>
<NEW <AS> [CorrelationName]>
<OLD TABLE <AS> [Identifier]>
<NEW TABLE <AS> [Identifier]>
```

where:

CorrelationName	Identifies a name to be used to identify a specific row in the subject table of the trigger, either before it was modified by the trigger's triggered action (OLD <AS>) or after it has been modified by the trigger's triggered action (NEW <AS>).
Identifier	Identifies a name that is to be used to identify a temporary table that

contains a set of rows found in the subject table of the trigger, either before they were modified by the trigger's triggered action (OLD TABLE <AS>) or after they have been modified by the trigger's triggered action (NEW TABLE <AS>).

Each column affected by an activation event (insert, update, or delete operation) can be made available to the trigger's triggered action by qualifying the column's name with the appropriate correlation name or table identifier.

SearchCondition   Specifies a search condition that, when evaluated, will return either TRUE, FALSE, or Unknown. This condition is used to determine whether the trigger's triggered action (*TriggeredAction*) is to be performed.

TriggeredAction   Identifies the action to be performed when the trigger is activated. The triggered action must consist of one or more SQL statements; when multiple statements are specified, the first statement must be preceded by the keywords BEGIN ATOMIC, the last statement must be followed by the keyword END, and every statement between these keywords must be terminated with a semicolon (;).

Thus, if you wanted to create a trigger for a table named EMPLOYEES that will increase the SALARY of the row being updated by 10%, you could do so by executing a CREATE TRIGGER statement that looks something like this:

```
CREATE TRIGGER pay_raise
NO CASCADE BEFORE UPDATE ON employees
FOR EACH ROW
SET new.salary = salary * 1.1
```

Or, if you wanted to allow users to add records to a table named ACTIVITY_HISTORY, but prevent them from updating or deleting records once they have been stored in the table, you could do so by executing two CREATE TRIGGER statements that look something like this:

```
CREATE TRIGGER block_updates
NO CASCADE BEFORE UPDATE ON activity_history
FOR EACH ROW
SIGNAL SQLSTATE '75001'
  SET MESSAGE_TEXT = 'Updates not allowed!'
CREATE TRIGGER block_deletes
NO CASCADE BEFORE DELETE ON activity_history
FOR EACH ROW
SIGNAL SQLSTATE '75002'
  SET MESSAGE_TEXT = 'Deletes not allowed!'
```

Why not Instead Of ?

Notice that in this case, two triggers had to be created: one that handles UPDATE events and another that handles DELETE events for the ACTIVITY_HISTORY table. If necessary, several different triggers can be created for a single table. For example, consider the following scenario: Suppose you have a table named SALES, which has the following characteristics:

Column Name	Data Type
INVOICE	INTEGER
SALE_DATE	DATE
SALE_AMT	DECIMAL(6,2)
SHIP_DATE	DATE
BILL_DATE	DATE

Business rules dictate that any time a record is inserted into this table, the current date is to be recorded as the sale date, a shipping date is to be scheduled three days out from the date of sale (i.e., the current date), and billing is to take place thirty days from the date of sale. To adhere to these business rules, you could create three different AFTER triggers by executing the following set of CREATE TRIGGER statements:

```
CREATE TRIGGER trigger_a
AFTER INSERT ON sales
REFERENCING NEW AS new
FOR EACH ROW
UPDATE sales SET sale_date = CURRENT DATE
  WHERE invoice = n.invoice
```

```
CREATE TRIGGER trigger_b
AFTER INSERT ON sales
REFERENCING NEW AS new
FOR EACH ROW
UPDATE sales SET ship_date = CURRENT DATE + 3 DAYS
  WHERE invoice = n.invoice

CREATE TRIGGER trigger_c
AFTER INSERT ON sales
REFERENCING NEW AS new
FOR EACH ROW
UPDATE sales SET bill_date = CURRENT DATE + 30 DAYS
  WHERE invoice = n.invoice
```

Can all 3 be combined into a single trigger?

Since triggers are executed in the order in which they have been created, each time a new record is inserted into the SALES table, trigger TRIGGER_A will fire, then trigger TRIGGER_B will fire, and finally, trigger TRIGGER_C will fire. If, for some reason, one trigger fails, the others will not be affected.

Practice Questions

Question 1

Which of the following is a valid DB2 data type?

○ A. NUMBER
○ B. INTERVAL
○ C. BYTE
○ D. NUM   *(Numeric)*

Question 2

Which of the following DB2 data types does NOT have a fixed length?

○ A. INT
○ B. CHAR
○ C. XML
○ D. DOUBLE

Question 3

Which of the following is the best statement to use to create a user-defined data type that can be used to store currency values?

○ A. CREATE DISTINCT TYPE currency AS NUMERIC(7,2)
○ B. CREATE DISTINCT TYPE currency AS SMALLINT
○ C. CREATE DISTINCT TYPE currency AS BIGINT
○ D. CREATE DISTINCT TYPE currency AS DOUBLE

Question 4

Which of the following DB2 data types can be used to store 1000 MB of single-byte character data?

○ A. BLOB
○ B. CLOB
○ C. DBCLOB
○ D. GRAPHIC

Question 5

Which of the following DB2 data types can NOT be used to create an identity column?

- ○ A. SMALLINT
- ○ B. INTEGER
- ○ C. NUMERIC
- ○ D. DOUBLE

Question 6

Which of the following strings can NOT be inserted into an XML column using XMLPARSE()?

- ○ A. "<employee />"
- ○ B. "<name>John Doe</name>"
- ○ C. "<?xml version='1.0' encoding='UTF-8' ?>"
- ○ D. "<p></p>"

Question 7

Which two of the following are optional and do not have to be specified when creating a table?

- ❑ A. Table name
- ❑ B. Column name
- ❑ C. Default constraint
- ❑ D. Column data type
- ❑ E. NOT NULL constraint

Question 8

Which of the following can NOT be used to restrict specific values from being inserted into a column in a particular table?

- ○ A. Index
- ○ B. Check constraint
- ○ C. Referential constraint
- ○ D. Default constraint

Question 9

Given the following CREATE TABLE statement:

```
CREATE TABLE table2 LIKE table1
```

Which two of the following will NOT occur when the statement is executed?

❑ A. TABLE2 will have the same column names and column data types as TABLE1

❑ B. TABLE2 will have the same column defaults as TABLE1

❑ C. TABLE2 will have the same nullability characteristics as TABLE1

❑ D. TABLE2 will have the same indexes as TABLE1.

❑ E. TABLE2 will have the same referential constraints as TABLE1

Question 10

If the following SQL statements are executed:

```
CREATE TABLE tab1 (id SMALLINT NOT NULL PRIMARY KEY,
                   name  VARCHAR(25));

CREATE TABLE tab2 (empid    SMALLINT,
                   weekno   SMALLINT,
                   payamt   DECIMAL(6,2),
       CONSTRAINT const1 FOREIGN KEY (empid)
           REFERENCES taba(id) ON UPDATE NO ACTION);
```

Which of the following statements is true?

○ A. Only values that exist in the ID column of table TAB1 are allowed to be inserted in the EMPID column of table TAB2

○ B. The updating of values in the ID column of table TAB1 is not allowed

○ C. Only values that do not already exist in the ID column of table TAB1 are allowed to be inserted in the EMPID column of table TAB2

○ D. When values that exist in the ID column of table TAB1 are updated, corresponding values in the EMPID column of table TAB2 are updated as well

Question 11

Which of the following is used to indicate a column will not accept NULL values and can be referenced in another table's foreign key specification?

○ A. Check constraint

○ B. Unique constraint

○ C. Default constraint

○ D. Informational constraint

Question 12

If table TAB1 is created using the following statement:

```
CREATE TABLE tab1 (col1  INTEGER NOT NULL,
                   col2  CHAR(5),
    CONSTRAINT cst1 CHECK (col1 in (1, 2, 3)))
```

Which of the following statements will successfully insert a record into table TAB1?

○ A. INSERT INTO tab1 VALUES (0, 'abc')

○ B. INSERT INTO tab1 VALUES (NULL, 'abc')

○ C. INSERT INTO tab1 VALUES (ABS(2), 'abc')

○ D. INSERT INTO tab1 VALUES (DEFAULT, 'abc')

Question 13

If the following SQL statements are executed:

```
CREATE TABLE make (makeid SMALLINT NOT NULL PRIMARY KEY,
                   make    VARCHAR(25));

CREATE TABLE model (modelid  SMALLINT,
                    model    VARCHAR(25),
                    makeid   SMALLINT,
      CONSTRAINT const1 FOREIGN KEY (makeid)
          REFERENCES make(makeid) ON DELETE RESTRICT);
```

And each table created is populated as follows:

```
MAKE

MAKEID  MAKE
------  --------
  1       Ford
  2       Chevrolet
  3       Toyota
```

Question 13 *continued*

```
MODEL

MODELID   MODEL        MAKEID
-------   -------      ------
1         Mustang      1 ⎫
2         Escort       1 ⎬
3         Malibu       2 ⎭
4         Camry        3
```

If the following SQL statement is executed:

```
DELETE FROM make WHERE makeid = 1
```

What is the total number of rows that will be deleted?

○ A. 0

○ B. 1

○ C. 2

○ D. 3

Question 14

Which of the following is NOT a characteristic of a unique index?

○ A. Each column in a base table can only participate in one unique index, regardless of how the columns are grouped (the same column cannot be used in multiple unique indexes)

○ B. In order for an index to be used to support a unique constraint, it must have been defined with the UNIQUE attribute

○ C. A unique index cannot be created for a populated table if the key column specified contains more than one NULL value

○ D. A unique index can only be created for a non-nullable column

Question 15

If the following statement is executed:

```
CREATE TABLE employee
    (empid      INT NOT NULL GENERATED BY DEFAULT
        AS IDENTITY (START WITH 1, INCREMENT BY 5),
    name        VARCHAR(20),
    dept        INT CHECK (dept BETWEEN 1 AND 20),
    hiredate    DATE WITH DEFAULT CURRENT DATE,
    salary      DECIMAL(7,2),
    PRIMARY KEY(empid),
      CONSTRAINT cst1 CHECK (YEAR(hiredate) > 2006 OR
          Salary > 60500));
```

Which of the following INSERT statements will fail?

○ A. INSERT INTO employee VALUES (15, 'Smith', 5, '01/22/2004', 92500.00)

○ B. INSERT INTO employee VALUES (DEFAULT, 'Smith', 2, '10/07/2002', 80250.00)

○ C. INSERT INTO employee VALUES (20, 'Smith', 5, NULL, 65000.00)

○ D. INSERT INTO employee VALUES (DEFAULT, 'Smith', 10, '11/18/2004', 60250.00)

Question 16

Which type of key is defined on the child table to implement a referential constraint?

○ A. Unique key

○ B. Primary key

○ C. Foreign key

○ D. Composite key

Question 17

Which of the following is NOT true about schemas?

○ A. If a schema name is not specified, either by qualifying a database object name or by executing the SET CURRENT SCHEMA statement, the authorization ID of the current session user is used as the schema name by default

○ B. The value assigned to the CURRENT SCHEMA special register is persistent across database restarts

○ C. A schema enables the creation of multiple objects in a database without encountering namespace collisions

○ D. When most database objects are created, they are either implicitly or explicitly assigned to a schema

Question 18

When does a view get populated?

○ A. When it is created

○ B. When it is referenced in an INSERT statement

○ C. The first time any executable SQL statement references it

○ D. Any time an executable SQL statement references it

Question 19

Given the following statements:

```
CREATE TABLE table1 (col1 INTEGER, col2 CHAR(3));
CREATE VIEW view1 AS
    SELECT col1, col2 FROM table1
    WHERE col1 < 100
    WITH LOCAL CHECK OPTION;
```

Which of the following INSERT statements will execute successfully?

○ A. INSERT INTO view1 VALUES (50, abc)

○ B. INSERT INTO view1 VALUES(100, abc)

○ C. INSERT INTO view1 VALUES(50, 'abc')

○ D. INSERT INTO view1 VALUES(100, 'abc')

Question 20

Which of the following actions will NOT cause a trigger to be fired?

○ A. INSERT

○ B. DELETE

○ C. ALTER

○ D. UPDATE

Question 21

The following triggers were defined for a table named SALES in the order shown:

```
CREATE TRIGGER trigger_a
NO CASCADE BEFORE INSERT ON sales
REFERENCING NEW AS new
FOR EACH ROW
SET new.commission = sale_amt * .05
    WHERE invoice = n.invoice;

CREATE TRIGGER trigger_b
AFTER INSERT ON sales
REFERENCING NEW AS new
FOR EACH ROW
UPDATE sales SET bill_date = CURRENT DATE + 30 DAYS
    WHERE invoice = n.invoice;

CREATE TRIGGER trigger_c
NO CASCADE BEFORE DELETE ON sales
FOR EACH ROW
SIGNAL SQLSTATE '75005'
    SET MESSAGE_TEXT = 'Deletes not allowed!';
```

Which of the following statements is NOT true?

○ A. Once a row has been added to the SALES table, it cannot be removed

○ B. Whenever a row is inserted into the SALES table, the value in the
BILL_DATE column is automatically set to 30 days from today

○ C. Each time a row is inserted into the SALES table, trigger TRIGGER_A is
fired first, followed by trigger TRIGGER_B

○ D. Whenever a row in the SALES table is updated, all three triggers are fired
but nothing happens because none of the triggers have been coded to trap
update operations

Question 22

Which of the following CREATE TABLE statements will NOT be successful?

○ A. CREATE TABLE t1 (c1 XML NOT NULL UNIQUE, c2 INT)

○ B. CREATE TABLE t1 (c1 XML NOT NULL, c2 CHAR(20))

○ C. CREATE TABLE t1 (c1 XML CHECK (c1 IS VALIDATED), c2 INT)

○ D. CREATE TABLE t1 (c1 XML, c2 XML)

Question 23

If the following SQL statement is executed:

```
CREATE TABLE sales                     ─── Data type ?
     (invoice_no   NOT NULL PRIMARY KEY,
      sales_date   DATE,
      sales_amt    NUMERIC(7,2))
     IN tbsp0, tbsp1, tbsp2, tbsp3
     PARTITION BY RANGE (sales_date NULLS FIRST)
         (STARTING '1/1/2007' ENDING '12/31/2007'
          EVERY 3 MONTHS)
```

Which of the following statements is true?

○ A. Administrative tasks such as backing up, restoring, and reorganizing data stored in the SALES table must be done at the table level; not at the partition level

○ B. Data can be quickly rolled in and out of the SALES table by using the ATTACH PARTITION and DETACH PARTITION clauses of the ALTER TABLE statement

○ C. If an index is created for the SALES table, its data must be stored in table space TBSP0

○ D. When resolving queries against the SALES table, each partition used is scanned asynchronously and the results of each partition scan are merged to produce the result data set returned

Question 24

Which of the following is NOT a characteristic of a declared temporary table?

O A. Declared temporary tables are not persistent and can only be used by the application that creates them

O B. It is possible for many applications to create declared temporary tables that have the same name

O C. Declared temporary tables are created by executing a CREATE TABLE statement with the DECLARED GLOBAL TEMPORARY clause specified

O D. Once the application that created a global temporary table is terminated, any records in the table are deleted and the table is automatically destroyed

Answers

Question 1

The correct answer is **D**. NUMBER, INTERVAL, and BYTE are not valid DB2 data types. The terms DECIMAL, DEC, NUMERIC, and NUM are used to denote the decimal data type. The decimal data type is used to store numeric values that contain both whole and fractional parts, separated by a decimal point. The exact location of the decimal point is determined by the precision and the scale of the value (the scale is the number of digits used by the fractional part). The maximum precision allowed for decimal values is 31 digits, and the corresponding scale must be a positive number less than the precision of the number. If no precision or scale is specified, a scale of 5 and a precision of 0 is used by default – DECIMAL(5,0).

Question 2

The correct answer is **C**. The XML data type is used to store XML documents in their native format. The amount of storage space set aside to store an XML document varies and is determined in part, by the size and characteristics of the XML document being stored.

The integer data type is used to store numeric values that have a precision of 10 digits. The range for integer values is –2,147,483,648 to 2,147,483,647, and 4 bytes of storage space is required for every integer value stored. The terms INTEGER and INT are used to denote the integer data type.

The fixed-length character string data type is used to store character string values that are between 1 and 254 characters in length. The amount of storage space needed to store a fixed-length character string value can be determined by solving the following equation: (*Number of characters* x 1) = *Bytes required*. (A fixed amount of storage space is allocated, even if all of the space allocated is not needed—short strings are padded with blanks.) The terms CHARACTER and CHAR are used to denote the fixed-length character string data type.

The double-precision floating-point data type is used to store a 64-bit *approximation* of a real number. This number can be zero, or it can fall within the range –1.79769E+308 to –2.225E–307 or 2.225E–307 to 1.79769E+308. Each double-precision floating-point value can be up to 53 digits in length, and 8 bytes of storage space is required for every value stored. The terms DOUBLE, DOUBLE PRECISION, and FLOAT are used to denote the double-precision floating-point data type.

Question 3

The correct answer is **A**. The decimal data type is used to store numeric values that contain both whole and fractional parts, separated by a decimal point. The terms DECIMAL, DEC, NUMERIC, and NUM are used to denote the decimal data type. Since currency values contain both whole and fractional parts, the decimal data type is the best choice to base a user-defined data type on. And to create a distinct data type named CURRENCY that can be used to store numeric data you would execute a CREATE DISTINCT TYPE SQL statement that looks like the one shown in Answer A.

Question 4

The correct answer is **B**. The character large object (CLOB) data type is used to store single-byte character data. The binary large object (BLOB) data type is used to store binary data; the double-byte character large object (DBCLOB) data type is used to store double-byte character data; and the fixed-length double-byte character string (GRAPHIC) data type is used to store double-byte character data strings.

Question 5

The correct answer is **D**. The data type assigned to an identity column must be a numeric data type with a scale of 0; therefore, the only data types that can be assigned to an identity column are: SMALLINT, INTEGER, BIGINT, DECIMAL/NUMERIC, or a user-defined data type that is based on one of these data types.

Question 6

The correct answer is **C**. The XMLPARSE function parses a character string and returns an XML value; the character string expression to be parsed must evaluate to a well-formed XML document that conforms to XML 1.0, as modified by the XML Namespaces recommendation. Answers A, B, and D are character strings that are comprised of a starting tag, an optional value, and a corresponding ending tag. As a result, these strings can be converted into a well-formed, but small, XML documents.

Question 7

The correct answers are **C** and **E**. At a minimum, when a new table is created, a table name, one or more column names, and corresponding column data types must be specified.

Primary keys, constraints (NOT NULL, default, check, unique, referential integrity, and informational), and table space information is optional and is not required.

Question 8

The correct answer is **D**. A unique index, a check constraint, and a referential constraint place restrictions on what can and cannot be stored in the column(s) they are associated with. A default constraint, however, is used to provide a default value for a particular column if no data is provided for that column when data is inserted into a table; if a value is provided for the column, the default value is ignored.

Question 9

The correct answers are **D** and **E**. When the CREATE TABLE ... LIKE ... statement is executed, each column of the table that is created will have exactly the same name, data type and nullability characteristic as the columns of the source table used to create the new table. Furthermore, if the EXCLUDING COLUMN DEFAULTS option is not specified (which is the case in this example), all column defaults will be copied as well. However, the new table will not contain any unique constraints, foreign key constraints, triggers, or indexes that exist in the original.

Question 10

The correct answer is **A**. The Insert Rule for a referential constraint guarantees that a value can never be inserted into the foreign key of a child table unless a matching value can be found in the corresponding parent key of the associated parent table. Any attempt to insert records into a child table that violates this rule will result in an error, and the insert operation will fail. The Insert Rule for a referential constraint is implicitly created when the referential constraint itself is created. In this example, the EMPID column of table TAB2 is a foreign key (in a child table) that references the ID column (the parent key) of table TAB1 (the parent table). Therefore, because of the Insert Rule, values cannot be added to the EMPID column of table TAB2 that do not already exist in the ID column of table TAB1.

Question 11

The correct answer is **B**. A unique constraint can be used to ensure that the value(s) assigned to one or more columns when a record is added to a base table are always unique; once a unique constraint has been defined for one or more columns, any operation that attempts to place duplicate values in those columns will fail. Although a unique, system-required index is used to enforce a unique constraint, there is a distinction between defining a unique constraint and creating a unique index; even though both enforce uniqueness, a unique index allows NULL values and generally cannot be used in a referential constraint. A unique constraint on the other hand, does not allow NULL values and can be referenced in a foreign key specification. (The value "NULL" means a column's value is undefined *and* distinct from any other value, *including* other NULL values).

A check constraint (also known as a *table check constraint*) can be used to ensure that a particular column in a base table is never assigned an unacceptable value—once a check constraint has been defined for a column, any operation that attempts to place a value in that column that does not meet specific criteria will fail. The default constraint can be used to ensure that a particular column in a base table is assigned a predefined value (unless that value is overridden) each time a record is added to the table. The predefined value provided could be null (if the NOT NULL constraint has not been defined for the column), a user-supplied value compatible with the column's data type, or a value furnished by the DB2 Database Manager. Unlike other constraints, informational constraints are not enforced during insert and update processing. However, the DB2 SQL optimizer will evaluate information provided by an informational constraint when considering the best access plan to use to resolve a query. As a result, an informational constraint may result in better query performance even though the constraint itself will not be used to validate data entry/modification.

Question 12

The correct answer is **C**. A check constraint is used to ensure that a particular column in a base table is never assigned an unacceptable value—once a check constraint has been defined for a column, any operation that attempts to place a value in that column that does not meet specific criteria will fail. Check constraints are comprised of one or more predicates that collectively are known as the *check condition*. This check condition is compared with the data value provided and the result of this comparison is returned as the value TRUE, FALSE, or Unknown. If the check constraint returns the value TRUE, the value is acceptable, so it is added to the database. If, on the other hand, the check constraint returns the value FALSE or Unknown, the operation attempting to place the value in the database fails, and all changes made by that operation are backed out.

In this example, the check constraint CST1 defined for table TAB1 only allows the values 1, 2, or 3 to be entered into column COL1. The INSERT statement shown in Answer C is the only INSERT statement that has a valid value specified for column COL1.

Question 13

The correct answer is **A**. The ON DELETE RESTRICT ensures that whenever a delete operation is performed on the parent table of a referential constraint, the value for the foreign key of each row in the child table will have the same matching value in the parent key of the parent table that it had before the delete operation was performed. Therefore, in this example no row will be deleted from the MAKE because two rows exists in the MODEL table that references the row the DELETE statement is trying to remove.

Had the ON DELETE CASCADE definition been used instead, the delete operation would have succeeded and the tables would have looked like this:

MAKE

MAKEID	MAKE
2	Chevrolet
3	Toyota

MODEL

MODELID	MODEL	MAKEID
3	Malibu	2
4	Camry	3

On the other hand, if the ON DELETE SET NULL definition had been used, the delete operation would have succeeded and the tables would have looked like this:

MAKE

MAKEID	MAKE
2	Chevrolet
3	Toyota

MODEL

MODELID	MODEL	MAKEID
1	Mustang	-
2	Escort	-
3	Malibu	2
4	Camry	3

Question 14

The correct answer is **D**. A unique index allows one and only one NULL value; the value "NULL" means a column's value is undefined and distinct from any other value. The remaining characteristics are true for unique indexes.

Question 15

The correct answer is **D**. In this example, the statement "INSERT INTO employee VALUES (DEFAULT, 'Smith', 10, '11/18/2004', 60250.00)" will fail because the hire date and the salary specified violates check constraint CST1 – YEAR(hiredate) > 2006 OR salary > 60500)

Question 16

The correct answer is C. To create a referential constraint, you define a primary key, using one or more columns in the parent table, and you define a *foreign key for one or more corresponding columns in the child table* that reference the parent table's primary key. (The list of column names in the foreign key clause must be identical to the list of column names specified in the primary key OR a unique constraint for the columns in the parent table that are referenced by the foreign key in the child must exist in order for a referential constraint to be successfully created.)

Question 17

The correct answer is **B**. The value assigned to the CURRENT SCHEMA special register is not persistent across database restarts. Therefore, if you assign a value to the CURRENT SCHEMA special register, disconnect from the database, and reconnect, the CURRENT SCHEMA special register will contain your authentication ID – not the value you assigned it earlier.

Question 18

The correct answer is **D**. A view is a named specification of a result table that is populated whenever the view is referenced in an SQL statement. (Each time a view is referenced, a query is executed and the results are retrieved from the underlying table and returned in a table-like format.) Like base tables, views can be thought of as having columns and rows. And in most cases, data can be retrieved from a view the same way it can be retrieved from a table.

Question 19

The correct answer is **C**. If the WITH LOCAL CHECK OPTION clause of with the CREATE VIEW SQL statement is specified, insert and update operations performed against the view that is created are validated to ensure that all rows being inserted into or updated in the base table the view refers to conform to the view's definition (otherwise, the insert/update operation will fail). So what exactly does this mean? Suppose a view was created using the following CREATE VIEW statement:

```
CREATE VIEW priority_orders
AS SELECT * FROM orders WHERE response_time < 4
WITH LOCAL CHECK OPTION
```

Now, suppose a user tries to insert a record into this view that has a RESPONSE_TIME value of 6. The insert operation will fail because the record violates the view's definition. Had the view not been created with the WITH LOCAL CHECK OPTION clause, the insert operation would have been successful, even though the new record would not be visible to the view that was used to add it.

Because VIEW1 was created using a SELECT statement that only references rows that have a value less than 100 in COL1 and because VIEW1 was created with the WITH LOCAL CHECK OPTION specified, each value inserted into COL1 (using VIEW1) must be less than 100. In addition, because COL2 was defined using a character data type, all values inserted into COL2 must be enclosed in single quotes. The INSERT statements shown in Answers B and D will fail because the value to be assigned to COL1 exceeds 100; the INSERT statement shown in Answer A will fail because the value "abc" is not enclosed in single quotation marks.

Question 20

The correct answer is **C**. Whenever an insert operation, an update operation, or a delete operation is performed against the subject table or view, a trigger can be activated (fired).

Question 21

The correct answer is **D**. Triggers are only fired if the trigger event they have been designed to watch for takes place against the subject table they are designed to interact with. In this example, no UPDATE trigger was defined; therefore, no triggers are fired when the sales table is updated.

Trigger TRIGGER_C will be fired anytime a delete operation is performed against the SALES table and triggers TRIGGER_A and TRIGGER_B will be fired *in the order they were created* whenever an insert operation is performed against the SALES table. Trigger TRIGGER_A is designed to calculate a sales commission for an invoice based on the sale amount; trigger TRIGGER_B is designed to assign a value to the BILL_DATE column that is 30 days from today; and trigger TRIGGER_C is designed to display an error message whenever anyone tries to delete records from the SALES table.

Question 22

The correct answer is **A**. The XML data type can be used to store well-formed XML documents in their native format. A table can contain any number of XML columns; however each XML column used has the following restrictions:

- It cannot be part of any index except an XML index.
- It cannot be included as a column of a primary key or unique constraint.
- It cannot be a foreign key of a referential constraint.
- It cannot have a specified default value or a WITH DEFAULT clause—if the column is nullable, the default value for the column is the null value.
- It cannot be used in a table with a distribution key.
- It cannot be used in range-clustered or range-partitioned tables.

In addition, XML columns can only be referenced in a check constraint if the check constraint contains the VALIDATED predicate. (The VALIDATED predicate checks to see if an XML value has been validated using the XMLVALIDATE() function. The XMLVALIDATE() function returns a copy of the input XML value, augmented with information obtained from XML schema validation, including default values and type annotations. If the value of the column is null, the result of the VALIDATED predicate is unknown; otherwise, the result is either TRUE or FALSE.)

Question 23

The correct answer is **B**. The SALES table in the example is partitioned such that each quarter's data is stored in a different data partition, and each partition resides in a different table space. Advantages of using table partitioning include:

Easy roll-in and roll-out of data. Rolling in partitioned table data allows a new range to be easily incorporated into a partitioned table as an additional data partition. Rolling out partitioned table data allows you to easily separate ranges of data from a partitioned table for subsequent purging or archiving. Data can be quickly rolled in and out by using the ATTACH PARTITION and DETACH PARTITION clauses of the ALTER TABLE statement.

Easier administration of large tables. Table level administration becomes more flexible because administrative tasks can be performed on individual data partitions. Such tasks include: detaching and reattaching of a data partition, backing up and restoring individual data partitions, and reorganizing individual indexes. In addition, time consuming maintenance operations can be shortened by breaking them down into a series of smaller operations. For example, backup operations can be performed at the data partition level when the each data partition is placed in separate table space. Thus, it is possible to backup one data partition of a partitioned table at a time.

Flexible index placement. With table partitioning, indexes can be placed in different table spaces allowing for more granular control of index placement.

Better query processing. When resolving queries, one or more data partitions may be automatically eliminated, based on the query predicates used. This functionality, known as Data Partition Elimination, improves the performance of many decision support queries because less data has to be analyzed before a result data set can be returned.

Question 24

The correct answer is **C**. Unlike base tables, whose descriptions and constraints are stored in the system catalog tables of the database to which they belong, declared temporary tables are not persistent and can only be used by the application that creates them—and only for the life of the application. (Once the application that created the global temporary table is terminated, any records in the table are deleted and the table itself is destroyed.) When the application that creates a declared temporary table terminates, the rows of the table are deleted, and the definition of the table is dropped. (However, data stored in a temporary table can exist across transaction boundaries.) Another significant difference between the two centers around naming conventions: base table names must be unique within a schema, but because each application that defines a declared temporary table has its own instance of that table, it is possible for many applications to create declared temporary tables that have the same name. And where base tables are created with the CREATE TABLE SQL statement, declared temporary tables are created with the DECLARE GLOBAL TEMPORARY TABLE statement.

Database Concurrency

E leven percent (11%) of the DB2 9 Fundamentals certification exam (Exam 730) is designed to test your knowledge of the mechanisms DB2 9 uses to allow multiple users and applications to interact with a database simultaneously without negatively affecting data consistency. The questions that make up this portion of the exam are intended to evaluate the following:

- Your ability to identify the appropriate isolation level to use for a given situation

- Your ability to identify the characteristics of locks

- Your ability to list objects for which locks can be acquired

- Your ability to identify factors that can influence locking

This chapter is designed to introduce you to the concept of data consistency and to isolation levels and locks—the mechanisms DB2 uses to maintain data consistency in both single- and multi-user database environments.

Understanding Data Consistency

In order to understand how DB2 9 attempts to maintain data consistency in both single- and multi-user environments, you must first understand what data consistency is, as well as be able to identify what can cause a database to be placed in an inconsistent state. The best way to define data consistency is by example.

Suppose your company owns a chain of hardware stores and uses a database to keep track of inventory at each store. By design, this database contains an inventory table for each hardware store in the chain; whenever supplies are received or sold by a particular store, its corresponding inventory table is updated. Now, suppose a case of hammers is physically transferred from one hardware store to another. The hammer count value stored in the receiving hardware store's table needs to be raised, and the hammer count value in the donating store's table needs to be lowered, to reflect this inventory move. If a user raises the hammer count value in the receiving hardware store's inventory table but fails to lower the hammer count value in the donating store's inventory table, the data will be *inconsistent*. The total hammer inventory for the entire chain is no longer accurate.

A database can become inconsistent if a user forgets to make all necessary changes (as in the previous example), if the system crashes while a user is in the middle of making changes (the hammer count is lowered in donating store's table, then a system crash occurs before the hammer count is raised in receiving store's table), or if, for some reason, a database application stops execution prematurely.

Inconsistency can also occur when several users attempt to access the same data at the same time. For example, using the same hardware store scenario, one user might query the database and discover that no more hammers are available when some really are, because the query read another user's changes before all tables affected by those changes had been properly updated. (Reacting to this misinformation, the user might then place an order for more hammers when none are needed.)

To ensure that users and applications accessing the same data at the same time do not inadvertently place that data in an inconsistent state, DB2 relies on two mechanisms: *isolation levels* and *locks*.

Isolation Levels

In Chapter 5, "Working with DB2 Data Using SQL and XQuery," we saw that a transaction (otherwise known as a unit of work) is a recoverable sequence of one or more SQL operations grouped together as a single unit, usually within an application process. The initiation and termination of a single transaction defines points of data consistency within a database—either the effects of all SQL operations performed within a transaction are applied to the database and made permanent (committed) or the effects of all SQL operations performed are completely "undone" and thrown away (rolled back).

In single-user, single-application environments, each transaction runs serially and does not have to contend with interference from other transactions. However in multi-user environments, transactions can execute simultaneously, and each transaction has the potential to interfere with any other transaction that has been started but not yet terminated. Transactions that have the potential of interfering with one another are said to be *interleaved*, or *parallel*, whereas transactions that run isolated from each other are said to be *serializable*, which means that the results of running them simultaneously will be no different from the results of running them one right after another (serially). Ideally, every transaction should be serializable.

Why is it important that transactions be serializable? Suppose a salesperson is entering orders into a database system at the same time an accountant is using the system to generate bills. Now, suppose the salesperson enters an order for Company X to get a price quote but does not commit the entry. While the salesperson is relaying the price quote information to an individual from Company X, the accountant queries the database for a list of all unpaid orders, sees an unpaid order for Company X, and generates a bill. Now, suppose the individual from Company X decides not to place the order because the quoted price is higher than anticipated. The salesperson rolls back the transaction because no order was placed, and the order information used to produce the price quote is removed from the database. However, a week later, Company X receives a bill for an order it never placed. If the salesperson's transaction and the accountant's transaction had been isolated from each other (serialized), this situation wouldn't have occurred—either the salesperson's transaction would have finished before the accountant's transaction started or the accountant's transaction would have finished before the salesperson's transaction started. In either case, Company X would not have received a bill.

When transactions are not serializable (which is often the case in multi-user environments), the following types of events (or phenomena) can occur:

Lost Updates: This event occurs when two transactions read the same data and both attempt to update that data, resulting in the loss of one of the updates. For example: Transaction 1 and Transaction 2 read the same row of data and calculate new values for that row based upon the original values read. If Transaction 1 updates the row with its new value and Transaction 2 then updates the same row, the update operation performed by Transaction 1 is lost.

Dirty Reads: This event occurs when a transaction reads data that has not yet been committed. For example: Transaction 1 changes a row of data, and Transaction 2 reads the changed row before Transaction 1 commits the change. If Transaction 1 rolls back the change, Transaction 2 will have read data that never really existed.

Nonrepeatable Reads: This event occurs when a transaction reads the same row of data twice and gets different results each time. For example: Transaction 1 reads a row of data, then Transaction 2 modifies or deletes that row and commits the change. When Transaction 1 attempts to reread the row, it will retrieve different data values (if the row was updated) or discover that the row no longer exists (if the row was deleted).

Phantoms: This event occurs when a row of data matches some search criteria but isn't seen initially. For example: Transaction 1 retrieves a set of rows that satisfy some search criteria, then Transaction 2 inserts a new row that contains matching search criteria for Transaction 1's query. If Transaction 1 re-executes the query that produced the original set of rows, a different set of rows will be returned (the new row added by Transaction 2 will now be included in the set of rows produced).

Because several different users can access and modify data stored in a DB2 database at the same time, the DB2 Database Manager must be able to allow users to make necessary changes while ensuring that data integrity is never compromised. The sharing of resources by multiple interactive users or application programs at the same time is known as *concurrency*. One of the ways DB2 enforces concurrency is through the use of *isolation levels*, which determine how data accessed and/or modified by one transaction is "isolated from" other transactions. DB2 9 recognizes and supports the following isolation levels:

- Repeatable Read

- Read Stability

- Cursor Stability

- Uncommitted Read

Table 7–1 shows the various phenomena that can occur when each of these isolation levels are used.

Table 7–1: DB2 9's Isolation Levels and the Phenomena That Can Occur When Each Is Used				
Isolation Level	**Phenomena**			
	Lost Updates	**Dirty Reads**	**Nonrepeatable Reads**	**Phantoms**
Repeatable Read	No	No	No	No
Read Stability	No	No	No	Yes
Cursor Stability	No	No	Yes	Yes
Uncommitted Read	No	Yes	Yes	Yes

Adapted from Table 2 on page 55 of the *IBM DB2 Version 9 for Linux, UNIX, and Windows Performance Guide.*

The Repeatable Read Isolation Level

The Repeatable Read isolation level is the most restrictive isolation level available. When it's used, the effects of one transaction are completely isolated from the effects of other concurrent transactions. Lost updates, dirty reads, nonrepeatable reads, and phantoms cannot occur.

When this isolation level is used, every row that's referenced *in any manner* by the owning transaction is locked for the duration of that transaction. As a result, if the same SELECT SQL statement is issued multiple times within the same transaction, the result data sets produced are guaranteed to be identical. In fact, transactions running under this isolation level can retrieve the same set of rows any number of times and perform any number of operations on them until terminated, either by a commit or a rollback operation. However, other transactions are prohibited from performing insert, update, or delete operations that would affect any row that has been accessed by the owning transaction as long as that transaction remains active.

To ensure that the data being accessed by a transaction running under the Repeatable Read isolation level is not adversely affected by other transactions, each row referenced by the isolating transaction is locked—not just the rows that are actually retrieved or modified. Thus, if a transaction scans 1,000 rows in order to retrieve 10, locks are acquired and held on all 1,000 rows scanned—not just on the 10 rows retrieved.

• •

If an entire table or view is scanned in response to a query, the entire table or all table rows referenced by the view are locked. This greatly reduces concurrency, especially when large tables are used.

• •

So how does this isolation level work in a real-world situation? Suppose you use a DB2 database to keep track of hotel records that consist of reservation and room rate information, and you have a Web-based application that allows individuals to book rooms on a first-come, first-served basis. If your reservation application runs under the Repeatable Read isolation level, a customer scanning the database for a list of rooms available for a given date range will prevent you (the manager) from changing the room rate for any of the room records that were scanned to resolve the customer's query. Similarly, other customers won't be able to make or cancel reservations that would cause the first customer's list of available rooms to change if the same query were to be run again (provided the first customer's transaction remained active). However, you would be allowed to change room rates for any room record that was not read when the first customer's list was produced; likewise, other customers would be able to make or cancel room reservations for any room whose record was not read in order to produce a response to the first customer's query. Figure 7–1 illustrates this behavior.

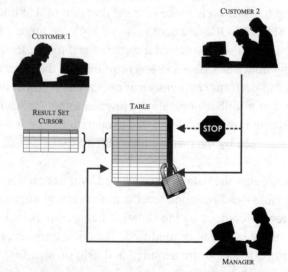

Figure 7–1: Example of how the Repeatable Read isolation level can affect application behavior.

The Read Stability Isolation Level

The Read Stability isolation level is not quite as restrictive as the Repeatable Read isolation level; therefore, it does not completely isolate one transaction from the effects of other, concurrent transactions. When this isolation level is used, lost updates, dirty reads, and nonrepeatable reads cannot occur; phantoms, however, can and may be seen. That's because when the Read Stability isolation level is used, only rows that are actually retrieved or modified by the owning transaction are locked. Thus, if a transaction scans 1,000 rows in order to retrieve 10, locks are only acquired and held on the 10 rows retrieved, not on the 1,000 rows scanned. Because fewer locks are acquired, more transactions can run concurrently. As a result, if the same SELECT SQL statement is issued two or more times within the same transaction, the result data set produced may not be the same each time.

As with the Repeatable Read isolation level, transactions running under the Read Stability isolation level can retrieve a set of rows and perform any number of operations on them until terminated. Other transactions are prohibited from performing update or delete operations that would affect the set of rows retrieved by the owning transaction as long as that transaction exists; however, other transactions can perform insert operations. (If rows inserted match the selection criteria of a query issued by the owning transaction, these rows may appear as phantoms in subsequent result data sets produced.)

So how does this isolation level change the way our hotel reservation application works? Now, when a customer scans the database to obtain a list of rooms available for a given date range, you (the manager) will be able to change the rate for any room that does not appear on the customer's list. Likewise, other customers will be able to make or cancel reservations that would cause the first customer's list of available rooms to change if the same query were to be run again. As a result, if the first customer queries the database for available rooms for the same date range again, the list produced may contain new room rates and/or rooms that were not available the first time the list was generated. Figure 7–2 illustrates this behavior.

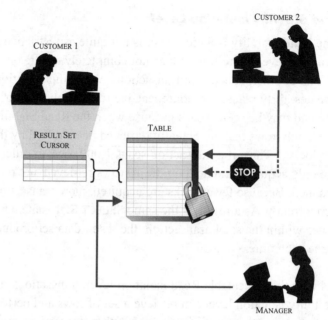

Figure 7–2: Example of how the Read Stability isolation level can affect application behavior.

The Cursor Stability Isolation Level

The Cursor Stability isolation level is even more relaxed than the Read Stability isolation level in the way it isolates one transaction from the effects of other concurrent transactions. When this isolation level is used, lost updates and dirty reads cannot occur; nonrepeatable reads and phantoms, on the other hand, can and may be seen. That's because in most cases, the cursor stability isolation level only locks the row that is currently referenced by a cursor that was declared and opened by the owning transaction. (The moment a record is retrieved from a result data set, a pointer—known as a *cursor*—will be positioned on the corresponding row in the underlying table, and that row will be locked. The lock acquired will remain in effect until the cursor is repositioned—more often than not by executing the FETCH SQL statement—or until the owning transaction terminates.) And because only one row-level lock is acquired, more transactions can run concurrently. The Cursor Stability isolation level is the isolation level used by default.

When a transaction using the Cursor Stability isolation level retrieves a row from a table via a cursor, no other transaction is allowed to update or delete that row while the cursor is positioned on it. Other transactions, however, can add new rows to the table as well as perform update and/or delete operations on rows positioned on either side of the locked row—provided the locked row itself wasn't accessed using an index. Once acquired, the lock remains in effect until the cursor is repositioned or until the owning transaction is terminated. (If the cursor is repositioned, the lock being held is released and a new lock is acquired for the row to which the cursor is moved.) Furthermore, if the owning transaction modifies any row it retrieves, no other transaction is allowed to update or delete that row until the owning transaction is terminated, even though the cursor may no longer be positioned on the modified row.

As you might imagine, when the Cursor Stability isolation level is used, if the same SELECT SQL statement is issued two or more times within the same transaction, the results returned may not always be the same. In addition, transactions using the Cursor Stability isolation level will not see changes made to other rows by other transactions until those changes have been committed.

Once again, let us see how this isolation level affects our hotel reservation application. Now, when a customer scans the database for a list of rooms available for a given date range and then views information about each room on the list produced (one room at a time), you (the manager) will be able to change the room rates for any room in the hotel *except* the room the customer is currently looking at (for the date range specified). Likewise, other customers will be able to make or cancel reservations for any room in the hotel *except* the room the customer is currently looking at (for the date range specified). However, neither you nor other customers will be able to do anything with the room record the first customer is currently looking at. When the first customer views information about another room in the list, you and other customers will be able to modify the room record the first customer was just looking at (provided the customer did not reserve it for himself). Again, neither you nor other customers will be able to do anything with the room record at which the first customer is currently looking. Figure 7–3 illustrates this behavior.

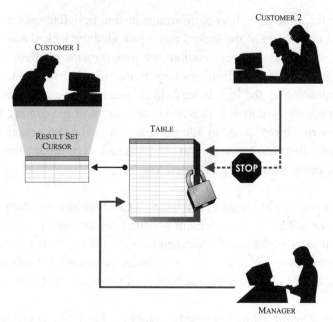

CUSTOMER 2

CUSTOMER 1

RESULT SET CURSOR

TABLE

STOP

MANAGER

Figure 7–3: Example of how the Cursor Stability isolation level can affect application behavior.

The Uncommitted Read Isolation Level

The Uncommitted Read isolation level is the least restrictive isolation level available. In fact, when the Uncommitted Read isolation level is used, rows retrieved by a transaction are only locked if the transaction modifies data associated with one or more rows retrieved or if another transaction attempts to drop or alter the table the rows were retrieved from. Because rows usually remain unlocked when this isolation level is used, dirty reads, nonrepeatable reads, and phantoms can occur. Thus, this isolation level is typically used for transactions that access read-only tables and views and for transactions that execute SELECT SQL statements for which uncommitted data from other transactions will have no adverse affect.

As the name implies, transactions running under the uncommitted read isolation level can see changes made to rows by other transactions before those changes have been committed. However, such transactions can neither see nor access tables, views, and indexes that are created by other transactions until those transactions themselves have been committed. The same applies to existing tables, views, or indexes that have been dropped; transactions using the uncommitted read will learn that these objects no longer exist only when the transaction that dropped them is committed. (It's important to note that when a transaction running under this isolation level uses an updatable cursor, the transaction will behave as if it is running under the Cursor Stability isolation level, and the constraints of the Cursor Stability isolation level will apply.)

So how does the Uncommitted Read isolation level affect our hotel reservation application? Now, when a customer scans the database to obtain a list of available rooms for a given date range, you (the manager) will be able to change the room rates for any room in the hotel over any date range. Likewise, other customers will be able to make or cancel reservations for any room in the hotel, including the room at which the customer is currently looking. In addition, the list of rooms produced for the first customer may contain records for rooms for which other customers are in the processing of reserving or canceling reservations. Figure 7–4 illustrates this behavior.

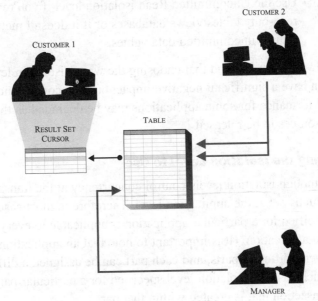

Figure 7–4: Example of how the Uncommitted Read isolation level can affect application behavior.

Choosing the Proper Isolation Level

In addition to controlling how well the DB2 Database Manager provides concurrency, the isolation level used determines how well applications running concurrently will perform. Typically, the more restrictive the isolation level used, the less concurrency is possible.

So how do you decide which isolation level to use? The best way is to identify which types of phenomena are unacceptable, and then select an isolation level that will prevent those phenomena from occurring. A good rule of thumb is:

- Use the Repeatable Read isolation level if you're executing large queries and you don't want concurrent transactions to have the ability to make changes that could cause the query to return different results if run more than once.

- Use the Read Stability isolation level when you want some level of concurrency between applications, yet you also want qualified rows to remain stable for the duration of an individual transaction.

- Use the Cursor Stability isolation level when you want maximum concurrency between applications, yet you don't want queries to see uncommitted data.

- Use the Uncommitted Read isolation level if you're executing queries on read-only tables/views/databases or if it doesn't matter whether a query returns uncommitted data values.

Always keep in mind that choosing the wrong isolation level for a given situation can have a significant negative impact on both concurrency and performance—performance for some applications may be degraded as they wait for locks on resources to be released.

Specifying the Isolation Level to Use

Although isolation levels control concurrency at the transaction level, they are actually set at the application level. Therefore in most cases, the isolation level specified for a particular application is applicable to every transaction initiated by that application. (It is important to note that an application can be constructed in several different parts, and each part can be assigned a different isolation level, in which case the isolation level specified for a particular part is applicable to every transaction that is created within that part.)

For embedded SQL applications, the isolation level is specified at precompile time or when the application is bound to a database (if deferred binding is used). In this case, the isolation level is set using the ISOLATION [RR | RS | CS | UR] option of the PRECOMPILE and BIND commands.

The isolation level for Call Level Interface (CLI) and Open Database Connectivity (ODBC) applications is set at application run time by calling the

`SQLSetConnectAttr()` function with the `SQL_ATTR_TXN_ISOLATION` connection attribute specified. (Alternatively, the isolation level for CLI/ODBC applications can be set by assigning a value to the `TXNISOLATION` keyword in the *db2cli.ini* configuration file; however, this approach does not provide the flexibility of changing isolation levels for different transactions within the application that the first approach does.)

Finally, the isolation level for Java Database Connectivity (JDBC) and SQLJ applications is set at application run time by calling the `setTransactionIsolation()` method that resides within DB2's *java.sql* connection interface.

When the isolation level for an application isn't explicitly set using one of these methods, the Cursor Stability isolation level is used as the default. This holds true for DB2 commands, SQL statements, and scripts executed from the Command Line Processor (CLP) as well as to Embedded SQL, CLI/ODBC, JDBC, and SQLJ applications. Therefore, it's also possible to specify the isolation level for operations that are to be performed from the DB2 Command Line Processor (as well as for scripts that are to be passed to the DB2 CLP for processing). In this case, the isolation level is set by executing the `CHANGE ISOLATION` command before a connection to a database is established.

DB2 Version 8.1 and later provides a `WITH` clause (`WITH [RR | RS | CS | UR]`) that can be appended to a `SELECT` statement to set a specific query's isolation level to Repeatable Read (`RR`), Read Stability (`RS`), Cursor Stability (`CS`), or Uncommitted Read (`UR`). A simple `SELECT` statement that uses this clause looks something like this:

```
SELECT * FROM employee WHERE empid = '001' WITH RR
```

If you have an application that needs to run in a less-restrictive isolation level the majority of the time (to support maximum concurrency), but contains one or two queries that must not see some phenomena, this clause provides an excellent way for you to meet your objective.

Locking

The one thing that all four of the isolation levels available have in common is that they all acquire one or more locks. But just what is a lock? A *lock* is a mechanism that is used to associate a data resource with a single transaction, for the sole purpose of controlling how other transactions interact with that resource while it is associated with the transaction that has it locked. (The transaction that has a data resource associated with it is said to "hold" or "own" the lock.) Essentially, locks in a database environment serve the same purpose as they do in a house or a car: They determine who can and cannot gain access to a particular resource—which can be one or more table spaces, tables, and/or rows. The DB2 Database Manager imposes locks to prohibit "owning" transactions from accessing uncommitted data that has been written by other transactions and to prevent other transactions from making data modifications that might adversely affect the owning transaction. When an owning transaction is terminated (by being committed or by being rolled back), any changes made to the resource that was locked are either made permanent or removed, and all locks on the resource that had been acquired by the owning transaction are released. Once unlocked, a resource can be locked again and manipulated by another active transaction. Figure 7–5 illustrates the principles of transaction/resource locking.

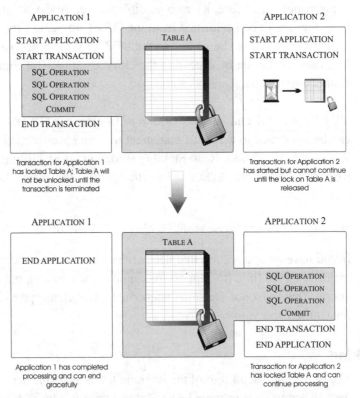

Figure 7–5: How DB2 9 prevents uncontrolled concurrent access to a resource through the use of locks.

Lock Attributes and Lock States

All locks used by DB2 have the following basic attributes:

Object: This attribute identifies the data resource that is being locked. The DB2 Database Manager implicitly acquires locks on data resources (specifically, table spaces, tables, and rows) whenever they are needed.

Size: This attribute identifies the physical size of the portion of the data resource that is being locked. A lock does not always have to control an entire data resource. For example, rather than giving an application exclusive control over an entire table, the DB2 Database Manager can elect to give an application exclusive control over one or more specific rows within a table.

Duration: This attribute identifies the length of time a lock is held. The isolation level used has a significant impact on the duration of a lock. (For example, the lock acquired for a Repeatable Read transaction that accesses 500 rows is likely to have a long duration if all 500 rows are to be updated; on the other hand, the lock acquired for a Cursor Stability transaction is likely to have a much shorter duration.)

State (or Mode): This attribute identifies the type of access allowed for the lock owner, as well as the type of access permitted for concurrent users of the locked data resource. Table 7–2 shows the various lock states available (along with their effects) in order of increasing control.

Table 7-2: Lock States

Lock State (Mode)	Applicable Objects	Lock Owner Access	Concurrent Transaction Access	Other Locks Acquired
Intent None (IN)	Table spaces, Tables	Lock owner can read all data, including uncommitted data, stored in the locked resource; however, lock owner cannot modify data stored in the locked resource. Intent None locks are typically acquired for read-only transactions that have no intention of modifying data (thus, additional locks will not be acquired on the transaction's behalf).	Other transactions can read and modify data stored in the locked resource, however, they cannot delete data stored in the locked resource.	None
Intent Share (IS)	Table spaces, Tables	Lock owner can read all data (excluding uncommitted data) stored in the locked resource; however, lock owner cannot modify data stored in the locked resource. Intent Share locks are typically acquired for transactions that do not convey the intent to modify data (transactions that execute SELECT FOR UPDATE, UPDATE WHERE, or INSERT statements convey the intent to modify data).	Other transactions can read and modify data stored in the locked resource.	If the lock is held on a table, a Share (S) or a Next Key Share (NS) lock is acquired on each row read from that table.
Next Key Share (NS)	Rows	Lock owner can read all data (excluding uncommitted data) stored in the locked resource; however, lock owner cannot modify data stored in the locked resource. Next Key Share locks are typically acquired in place of a Share (S) lock for transactions that are running under the Read Stability (RS) or Cursor Stability (CS) isolation level.	Other transactions can read all data (excluding uncommitted data) stored in the locked resource; however, they cannot modify data stored in the locked resource.	None
Share (S)	Tables, Rows	Lock owner can read all data (excluding uncommitted data) stored in the locked resource; however, lock owner cannot modify data stored in the locked resource. Share locks are typically acquired for transactions that do not convey the intent to modify data (transactions that execute SELECT FOR UPDATE, UPDATE WHERE, or INSERT statements convey the intent to modify data) that are running under the Repeatable Read (RR) isolation level.	Other transactions can read all data (excluding uncommitted data) stored in the locked resource; however, they cannot modify data stored in the locked resource.	Individual rows in a table can be Share (S) locked, provided the table itself is not Share (S) locked. (If the table is Share (S) locked, row-level locks cannot be acquired.)

Table 7-2: Lock States *(continued)*

Lock State (Mode)	Applicable Objects	Lock Owner Access	Concurrent Transaction Access	Other Locks Acquired
Intent Exclusive (IX)	Table spaces, Tables	Lock owner can read and modify data stored in the locked resource. Intent Exclusive locks are typically acquired for transactions that convey the intent to modify data (transactions that execute SELECT FOR UPDATE, UPDATE WHERE, or INSERT statements convey the intent to modify data).	Other transactions can read and modify data stored in the locked resource.	When the lock owner works with an Intent Exclusive (IX)-locked table, a Share (S) or a Next Key Share (NS) lock is acquired on every row read from that table, and both an Update (U) and an Exclusive (X) lock is acquired on every row to be modified.
Share With Intent Exclusive (SIX)	Tables	Lock owner can read and modify data stored in the locked resource. Share With Intent Exclusive locks are typically acquired when a transaction holding a Share (S) lock on a resource attempts to acquire an Intent Exclusive (IX) lock on the same resource (or vice versa).	Other transactions can read all data (excluding uncommitted data) stored in the locked resource; however, they cannot modify data stored in the locked resource.	When the lock owner works with a Share With Intent Exclusive (SIX) locked table, an Exclusive (X) lock is acquired on every row in that table that is to be modified.
Update (U)	Tables, Rows	Lock owner can modify all data (excluding uncommitted data) stored in the locked resource; however, lock owner cannot read data stored in the locked resource. Update locks are typically acquired for transactions that modify data with INSERT, UPDATE, or DELETE statements.	Uncommitted data) stored in the locked resource; however, they cannot modify data stored in the locked resource.	An Update (U) locked table, an Exclusive (X) lock is acquired on every row to be modified in that table.
Next Key Weak Exclusive (NW)	Rows	Lock owner can read all data (excluding uncommitted data) stored in the locked resource; however, lock owner cannot modify data stored in the locked resource. Next Key Weak Exclusive locks are typically acquired on the next available row in a table whenever a row is inserted into any index of a noncatalog table.	Other transactions can read all data (excluding uncommitted data) stored in the locked resource; however, they cannot modify data stored in the locked resource.	None

Table 7-2: Lock States (continued)

Lock State (Mode)	Applicable Objects	Lock Owner Access	Concurrent Transaction Access	Other Locks Acquired
Exclusive (X)	Tables, Rows	Lock owner can read and modify data stored in the locked resource. Exclusive locks are typically acquired for transactions that retrieve data with SELECT statements and then modify the data retrieved with INSERT, UPDATE, or DELETE statements.	Transactions using the Uncommitted Read isolation level can read all data, including uncommitted data, stored in the locked resource; however they cannot modify data stored in the locked resource. All other transactions can neither read, nor modify data stored in the locked resource.	Individual rows in a table can be Exclusive (X) locked, provided the table itself is not Exclusive (X) locked.
Weak Exclusive (WE)	Rows	Lock owner can read and modify data stored in the locked resource. Weak Exclusive locks are typically acquired on a row when it is inserted into a nonsystem catalog table.	Transactions using the Uncommitted Read isolation level can read all data, including uncommitted data, stored in the locked resource; however, they cannot modify data stored in the locked resource. All other transactions can neither read nor modify data stored in the locked resource.	None
Super Exclusive (Z)	Table spaces, Tables	Lock owner can read and modify data stored in the locked resource. Super Exclusive locks are typically acquired on a table whenever the lock owner attempts to alter that table, drop that table, create an index for that table, drop an index that has already been defined for that table, or reorganize the contents of the table (while the table is offline) by running the REORG utility.	Other transactions can neither read nor modify data stored in the locked resource.	None

Adapted from Table 4 on pages 60-61 of the *IBM DB2 Version 9 for Linux, UNIX, and Windows Performance Guide.*

How Locks Are Acquired

Except for occasions where the Uncommitted Read isolation level is used, it is never necessary for a transaction to request a lock explicitly. That's because the DB2 Database Manager implicitly acquires locks as they are needed; once acquired, these locks remain under the DB2 Database Manager's control until they are no longer needed. By default, the DB2 Database Manager always attempts to acquire row-level locks. However, it is possible to control whether the DB2 Database Manager will attempt to acquire row-level locks or table-level locks on a specific table resource by executing a special form of the ALTER TABLE SQL statement. The syntax for this form of the ALTER TABLE statement is:

```
ALTER TABLE [TableName] LOCKSIZE [ROW | TABLE]
```

where:

TableName　　　Identifies the name of an existing table for which the level of locking that all transactions are to use when accessing it is to be specified.

For example, when executed, the SQL statement

```
ALTER TABLE employee LOCKSIZE ROW
```

will force the DB2 Database Manager to acquire row-level locks for every transaction that accesses a table named EMPLOYEE. (This is the default behavior.) On the other hand, if the SQL statement

```
ALTER TABLE employee LOCKSIZE TABLE
```

is executed, the DB2 Database Manager will attempt to acquire table-level locks for every transaction that accesses the EMPLOYEE table.

But what if you don't want every transaction that works with a particular table to acquire table-level locks? What if, instead, you want one specific transaction to acquire table-level locks and all other transactions to acquire row-level locks when working with that particular table? In this case, you leave the default locking behavior alone (row-level locking) and use the LOCK TABLE SQL statement to acquire a table-level lock for the appropriate individual transaction. The syntax for the LOCK TABLE statement is:

```
LOCK TABLE [TableName] IN [SHARE | EXCLUSIVE] MODE
```

where:

TableName   Identifies the name of an existing table to be locked.

As you can see, the LOCK TABLE statement allows a transaction to acquire a table-level lock on a particular table in one of two modes: SHARE mode and EXCLUSIVE mode. If a table is locked using the SHARE mode, a table-level Share (S) lock is acquired on behalf of the requesting transaction, and other concurrent transactions are allowed to read, but not change, data stored in the locked table. On the other hand, if a table is locked using the EXCLUSIVE mode, a table-level Exclusive (X) lock is acquired, and other concurrent transactions can neither access nor modify data stored in the locked table.

For example, if executed, the SQL statement

```
LOCK TABLE employee IN SHARE MODE
```

would acquire a table-level Share (S) lock on the EMPLOYEE table on behalf of the current transaction (provided no other transaction holds a lock on this table), and other concurrent transactions would be allowed to read, but not change, the data stored in the table. On the other hand, if the statement

```
LOCK TABLE employee IN EXCLUSIVE MODE
```

were executed, a table-level Exclusive (X) lock would be acquired, and no other transaction would be allowed to read or modify data stored in the EMPLOYEE table until the owning transaction is terminated.

Lock granularity and concurrency

When it comes to deciding whether to use row-level locks or table-level locks, it is important to keep in mind that any time a transaction holds a lock on a particular resource, other transactions may be denied access to that resource until the owning transaction is terminated. Therefore, row-level locks are usually better than table-level locks, because they restrict access to a much smaller resource. However, because each lock acquired requires some amount of storage space (to hold) and some degree of processing time (to manage), often there is considerably less overhead involved when a single table-level lock is acquired, rather than several individual row-level locks.

To a certain extent, lock granularity (row-level locking versus table-level locking) can be controlled through the use of the ALTER TABLE and LOCK TABLE SQL statements—the ALTER TABLE statement controls granularity at a global level, while the LOCK TABLE statement controls granularity at an individual transaction level. So when is it more desirable to control granularity at the global level rather than at an individual transaction level? It all depends on the situation.

Suppose you have a read-only lookup table ~~table~~ that is to be accessed by multiple concurrent transactions. Forcing the DB2 Database Manager to acquire Share (S) table-level locks globally for every transaction that attempts to access this table might improve overall performance, since the locking overhead required would be greatly reduced. On the other hand, suppose you have a table that needs to be accessed frequently by read-only transactions and periodically by a single transaction designed to perform basic maintenance. Forcing the DB2 Database Manager to only acquire an Exclusive (X) table-level lock at the transaction level whenever the maintenance transaction executes makes more sense than forcing the DB2 Database Manager to acquire Exclusive (X) table-level locks globally for every transaction that needs to access the table. If this approach is used, the read-only transactions are locked out of the table only when the maintenance transaction runs; in all other situations, they can access the table concurrently while requiring very little locking overhead.

Which Locks Are Acquired?

Although it is possible to control whether the DB2 Database Manager will acquire row-level locks or table-level locks, it is not possible to control what type of lock will actually be acquired for a given transaction. Instead, the DB2 Database Manager implicitly makes that decision by analyzing the transaction to determine what type of processing it has been designed to perform. For the purpose of deciding which particular type of lock is needed for a given situation, the DB2 Database Manager places all transactions into one of the following categories:

- Read-Only
- Intent-to-Change
- Change
- Cursor-Controlled

The characteristics used to assign transactions to these categories, along with the types of locks that are acquired for each, are shown in Table 7–3.

Table 7–3: Types of Transactions Available and Their Associated Locks		
Type Of Transaction ...	**Description...**	**Locks Acquired ...**
Read-Only	Transactions that contain SELECT SQL statements (which are intrinsically read-only), SELECT SQL statements that have the FOR READ ONLY clause specified, or SQL statements that are ambiguous, but are presumed to be read-only because of the BLOCKING option specified as part of the precompile and/or bind process	Intent Share (IS) and/or Share (S) locks for table spaces, tables, and rows
Intent-to-Change	Transactions that contain SELECT SQL statements that have the FOR UPDATE clause specified or SQL statements that are ambiguous, but are presumed to be intended for change because of the way they are interpreted by the SQL pre-compiler	Share (S), Update (U), and Exclusive (X) locks for tables; Update (U), Intent Exclusive (IX), and Exclusive (X) locks for rows
Change	Transactions that contain INSERT, UPDATE, or DELETE SQL statements but not UPDATE WHERE CURRENT OF or DELETE WHERE CURRENT OF SQL statements	Intent Exclusive (IX) and/or Exclusive (X) locks for table spaces, tables, and rows
Cursor-Controlled	Transactions that contain UPDATE WHERE CURRENT OF or DELETE WHERE CURRENT OF SQL statements	Intent Exclusive (IX) and/or Exclusive (X) locks for table spaces, tables, and rows

It is important to keep in mind that in some cases, a single transaction will consist of multiple transaction types. For example, a transaction that contains an SQL statement that performs an insert operation against a table using the results of a subquery actually does two different types of processing: Read-Only and Change. Because of this, locks needed for the resources referenced in the subquery are determined using the rules for Read-Only transactions, while the locks needed for the target table of the insert operation are determined using the rules for Change transactions.

Locks and Performance

Although the DB2 Database Manager implicitly acquires locks as they are needed and, aside from using the ALTER TABLE and LOCK TABLE SQL statements to force the DB2 Database Manager to acquire table-level locks, locking is out of your control, there are several factors that can influence how locking affects performance. These factors include:

- Lock compatibility
- Lock conversion
- Lock escalation
- Lock waits and timeouts
- Deadlocks
- Concurrency and granularity

Knowing what these factors are and understanding how they can affect overall performance can assist you in designing database applications that work well in multi-user database environments and, indirectly, give you more control over how locks are used.

Lock compatibility

If the state of a lock placed on a data resource by one transaction is such that another lock can be placed on the same resource by another transaction before the first lock acquired is released, the locks are said to be *compatible*. Any time one transaction holds a lock on a data resource and another transaction attempts to acquire a lock on the same resource, the DB2 Database Manager will examine each lock's state and determine whether they are compatible. Table 7–4 contains a lock compatibility matrix that identifies which locks are compatible and which are not.

Table 7-4: Lock Compatibility Matrix

	Lock Requested by Second Transaction										
Lock State	**IN**	**IS**	**NS**	**S**	**IX**	**SIX**	**U**	**NW**	**X**	**WE**	**Z**
IN	Yes	Yes	Yes	Yes	Yes	Yes	Yes	Yes	Yes	Yes	No
IS	Yes	Yes	Yes	Yes	Yes	Yes	Yes	No	No	No	No
NS	Yes	Yes	Yes	Yes	No	No	Yes	Yes	No	No	No
S	Yes	Yes	Yes	Yes	No	No	Yes	No	No	No	No
IX	Yes	Yes	No	No	Yes	No	No	No	No	No	No
SIX	Yes	Yes	No	No	No	No	No	No	No	No	No
U	Yes	Yes	Yes	Yes	No	No	No	No	No	No	No
NW	Yes	No	Yes	No	No	No	No	No	No	Yes	No
X	Yes	No	No	No	No	No	No	No	No	No	No
WE	Yes	No	No	No	No	No	No	Yes	No	No	No
Z	No	o	No	No	No	No	No	No	No	No	No

(Left axis label: Lock Held by First Transaction)

Yes	Locks are compatible; therefore, the lock request is granted immediately.
No	Locks are not compatible; therefore, the requesting transaction must wait for the held lock to be released or for a lock timeout to occur before the lock request can be granted.

Lock States:

IN	Intent None	U	Update
IS	Intent Share	NW	Next Key Weak Exclusive
NS	Next Key Share	X	Exclusive
S	Share	WE	Weak Exclusive
IX	Intent Exclusive	Z	Super Exclusive
SIX	Share With Intent Exclusive		

Adapted from Table 5 on page 72 of the *IBM DB2 Version 9 for Linux, UNIX, and Windows Performance Guide.*

Lock conversion

If a transaction holding a lock on a resource needs to acquire a more restrictive lock on the same resource, the DB2 Database Manager will attempt to change the state of the existing lock to the more restrictive state. The action of changing the state of an existing lock to a more restrictive state is known as *lock conversion*. Lock conversion occurs because a transaction can hold only one lock on a specific data resource at any given time. Figure 7–6 illustrates a simple lock conversion process.

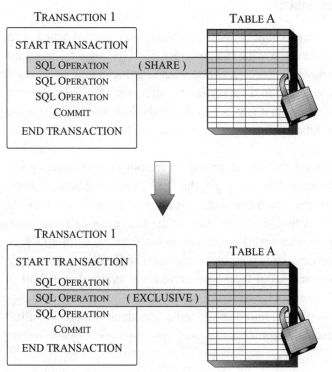

Figure 7–6: A simple lock conversion scenario—in this example, a Share (S) lock is converted to an Exclusive (X) lock.

In most cases, lock conversion is performed on row-level locks, and the conversion process is fairly straightforward. For example, if an Update (U) lock is held and an Exclusive (X) lock is needed, the Update (U) lock will be converted to an Exclusive (X) lock. However, Share (S) locks and Intent Exclusive (IX) locks are special cases, since neither lock is considered more restrictive than the other.

As a result, if one of these locks is held and the other is requested, the held lock is converted to a Share With Intent Exclusive (SIX) lock. With all other conversions, the lock state of the current lock is changed to the lock state being requested—provided the lock state being requested is a more restrictive state. (Lock conversion only occurs if the lock held can increase its restriction.) Once a lock has been converted, it stays at the highest level attained until the transaction holding the lock is terminated and the lock is released.

Lock escalation

When a connection to a database is first established, a specific amount of memory is set aside to hold a structure that DB2 uses to manage locks. This structure, known as the *lock list*, is where the locks held by every application concurrently connected to a database are stored after they are acquired. (The actual amount of memory that gets set aside for the lock list is determined by the `locklist` database configuration parameter.)

Because a limited amount of memory is available, and because this memory must be shared by everyone, the DB2 Database Manager imposes a limit on the amount of space each transaction is allowed to use in the lock list to store its own locks. (This limit is determined by the `maxlocks` database configuration parameter). To prevent a specific database agent from exceeding its lock list space limitations, a process known as *lock escalation* is performed whenever too many locks (regardless of their type) have been acquired on behalf of a single transaction. During lock escalation, space in the lock list is freed by converting several row-level locks into a single table-level lock. Figure 7–7 illustrates a simple lock escalation process.

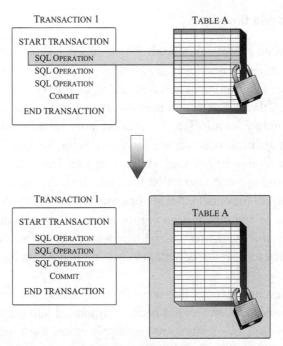

Figure 7–7: Lock escalation—several individual row-level locks are changed to a single table-level lock.

So just how does lock escalation work? When a transaction requests a lock and the database's lock list is full, one of the tables associated with the transaction is selected, a table-level lock is acquired on behalf of the transaction, and all row-level locks for that table are released to create space in the lock list. The table-level lock acquired is then added to the lock list. If this process does not free up the storage space needed to acquire the lock that was requested, another table is selected and the process is repeated until enough free space is made available—only then will the requested lock be acquired and the transaction be allowed to continue execution. If however, the lock list space needed is still unavailable after all of the transaction's row-level locks have been escalated, an SQL error code is generated, all changes that have been made to the database since the transaction was initiated are rolled back, and the transaction is gracefully terminated.

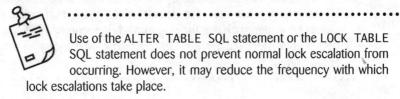

Use of the ALTER TABLE SQL statement or the LOCK TABLE SQL statement does not prevent normal lock escalation from occurring. However, it may reduce the frequency with which lock escalations take place.

Lock waits and timeouts

Any time a transaction holds a lock on a particular resource (table space, table, or row), other transactions may be denied access to that resource until the owning transaction terminates and frees all locks it has acquired. Thus, without some sort of lock timeout detection mechanism in place, a transaction might wait indefinitely for a lock to be released. For example, suppose a transaction in one user's application is waiting for a lock being held by a transaction in another user's application to be released. If the other user leaves his or her workstation without performing some interaction that will allow the application to terminate and release all locks held, the application waiting for the lock to be released will be unable to continue processing for an indeterminable amount of time. Unfortunately, it would also be impossible to terminate the application waiting for the lock to be released without compromising data consistency.

To prevent situations like these from occurring, an important feature known as *lock timeout detection* has been incorporated into the DB2 Database Manager. When used, this feature prevents applications from waiting indefinitely for a lock to be released. By assigning a value to the locktimeout configuration parameter in the appropriate database configuration file, you can control when lock timeout detection occurs. This parameter specifies the amount of time that any transaction will wait to obtain a requested lock; if the requested lock is not acquired before the time interval specified in the locktimeout configuration parameter has elapsed, the waiting application receives an error message, and the transaction requesting the lock is rolled back. Once the transaction has been rolled back, the waiting application will, by default, be terminated. (This behavior prevents data inconsistency from occurring.)

By default, the locktimeout configuration is set to −1, which means that applications will wait indefinitely to acquire the locks they need. In many cases, this value should be changed to something other than the default value. In addition, applications should be written such that they capture any timeout (or deadlock) SQL return code returned by the DB2 Database Manager and respond appropriately.

Deadlocks

In most cases, the problem of one transaction waiting indefinitely for a lock to be released can be resolved by establishing lock timeouts. However, that is not the case when lock contention creates a situation known as a *deadlock*. The best way to illustrate how a deadlock can occur is by example: Suppose Transaction 1 acquires an Exclusive (X) lock on Table A, and Transaction 2 acquires an Exclusive (X) lock on Table B. Now, suppose Transaction 1 attempts to acquire an Exclusive (X) lock on Table B, and Transaction 2 attempts to acquire an Exclusive (X) lock on Table A. We have already seen that processing by both transactions will be suspended until their second lock request is granted. However, because neither lock request can be granted until one of the owning transactions releases the lock it currently holds (by performing a commit or rollback operation), and because neither transaction can perform a commit or rollback operation because they both have been suspended (and are waiting on locks), a deadlock has occurred. Figure 7–8 illustrates this deadlock scenario.

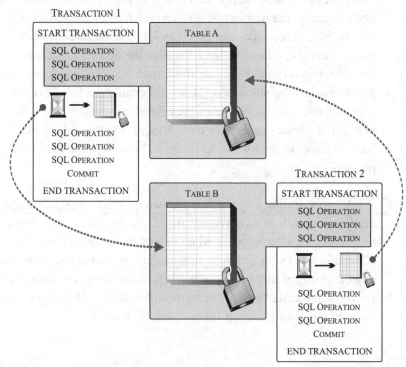

Figure 7–8: A deadlock scenario—Transaction 1 is waiting for Transaction 2 to release its lock on Table B, and Transaction 2 is waiting for Transaction 1 to release its lock on Table A; however, neither transaction can release their respective locks because they have been suspended and are waiting to acquire other locks.

A deadlock is more precisely referred to as a *deadlock cycle,* because the transactions involved form a circle of wait states; each transaction in the circle waits for a lock held by another transaction in the circle to be released (see Figure 7–8). When a deadlock cycle occurs, all transactions involved will wait indefinitely for a lock to be released unless some outside agent steps in and breaks the cycle. With DB2, this agent is a background process, known as the *deadlock detector*, and its sole responsibility is to locate and resolve any deadlocks found in the locking subsystem.

Each database has its own deadlock detector, which is activated as part of the database initialization process. Once activated, the deadlock detector stays "asleep" most of the time but "wakes up" at preset intervals and examines the locking subsystem to determine whether a deadlock situation exists. Normally, the deadlock detector wakes up, sees that there are no deadlocks in the locking subsystem, and goes back to sleep. If, however, the deadlock detector discovers a deadlock cycle, it randomly selects one of the transactions involved to roll back and terminate; the transaction chosen (referred to as the *victim process*) is then sent an SQL error code, and every lock it had acquired is released. The remaining transaction(s) can then proceed, because the deadlock cycle has been broken. It is possible, but very unlikely, that more than one deadlock cycle exists in a database's locking subsystem. If several deadlock cycles exist, the detector locates each one and terminates one of the offending transactions in the same manner, until all deadlock cycles have been broken. Eventually, the deadlock detector goes back to sleep, only to wake up again at the next predefined interval and repeat the process.

While most deadlock cycles involve two or more resources, a special type of deadlock, known as a *conversion deadlock*, can occur on one individual resource. Conversion deadlocks occur when two or more transactions that already hold compatible locks on an object request new, incompatible locks on that same object. This typically takes place when two or more concurrent transactions search for rows in a table by performing an index scan, and then try to modify one or more of the rows retrieved.

Practice Questions

Question 1

Application A holds an Exclusive lock on table TAB1 and needs to acquire an Exclusive lock on table TAB2. Application B holds an Exclusive lock on table TAB2 and needs to acquire an Exclusive lock on table TAB1. If lock timeout is set to -1 and both applications are using the Read Stability isolation level, which of the following will occur?

- ○ A. Applications A and B will cause a deadlock situation
- ○ B. Application B will read the copy of table TAB1 that was loaded into memory when Application A first read it
- ○ C. Application B will read the data in table TAB1 and see uncommitted changes made by Application A
- ○ D. Application B will be placed in a lock-wait state until Application A releases its lock

Question 2

Two applications have created a deadlock cycle in the locking subsystem. If lock timeout is set to 30 and both applications were started at the same time, what action will the deadlock detector take when it "wakes up" and discovers the deadlock?

- ○ A. It will randomly pick an application and rollback its current transaction
- ○ B. It will rollback the current transactions of both applications
- ○ C. It will wait 30 seconds, then rollback the current transactions of both applications if the deadlock has not been resolved
- ○ D. It will go back to sleep for 30 seconds, then if the deadlock still exists, it will randomly pick an application and rollback its current transaction

Question 3

Application A is running under the Repeatable Read isolation level and holds an Update lock on table TAB1. Application B wants to query table TAB1 and cannot wait for Application A to release its lock. Which isolation level should Application B run under to achieve this objective?

- ○ A. Repeatable Read
- ○ B. Read Stability
- ○ C. Cursor Stability
- ○ D. Uncommitted Read

Question 4

Application A holds a lock on a row in table TAB1. If lock timeout is set to 20, what will happen when Application B attempts to acquire a compatible lock on the same row?

- ○ A. Application B will acquire the lock it needs
- ○ B. Application A will be rolled back if it still holds its lock after 20 seconds have elapsed
- ○ C. Application B will be rolled back if Application A still holds its lock after 20 seconds have elapsed
- ○ D. Both applications will be rolled back if Application A still holds its lock after 20 seconds have elapsed

Question 5

To which of the following resources can a lock NOT be applied?

- ○ A. Tablespaces
- ○ B. Buffer pools
- ○ C. Tables
- ○ D. Rows

Question 6

Which of the following modes, when used with the LOCK TABLE statement, will cause the DB2 Database Manager to acquire a table-level lock that prevents other concurrent transactions from accessing data stored in the table while the owning transaction is active?

- ○ A. SHARE MODE
- ○ B. ISOLATED MODE
- ○ C. EXCLUSIVE MODE
- ○ D. RESTRICT MODE

Question 7

An application has acquired a Share lock on a row in a table and now wishes to update the row. Which of the following statements is true?

○ A. The application must release the row-level Share lock it holds and acquire an Update lock on the row

○ B. The application must release the row-level Share lock it holds and acquire an Update lock on the table

○ C. The row-level Share lock will automatically be converted to a row-level Update lock

○ D. The row-level Share lock will automatically be escalated to a table-level Update lock

Question 8

Application A wants to read a subset of rows from table TAB1 multiple times. Which of the following isolation levels should Application A use to prevent other users from making modifications and additions to table TAB1 that will affect the subset of rows read?

○ A. Repeatable Read

○ B. Read Stability

○ C. Cursor Stability

○ D. Uncommitted Read

Question 9

A transaction using the Read Stability isolation level scans the same table multiple times before it terminates. Which of the following can occur within this transaction's processing?

○ A. Uncommitted changes made by other transactions can be seen from one scan to the next.

○ B. Rows removed by other transactions that appeared in one scan will no longer appear in subsequent scans.

○ C. Rows added by other transactions that did not appear in one scan can be seen in subsequent scans.

○ D. Rows that have been updated can be changed by other transactions from one scan to the next.

Question 10

Application A issues the following SQL statements within a single transaction using the Uncommitted Read isolation level:

```
SELECT * FROM department WHERE deptno = 'A00';
UPDATE department SET mgrno = '000100' WHERE deptno = 'A00';
```

As long as the transaction is not committed, which of the following statements is FALSE?

O A. Other applications not running under the Uncommitted Read isolation level are prohibited from reading the updated row

O B. Application A is allowed to read data stored in another table, even if an Exclusive lock is held on that table

O C. Other applications running under the Uncommitted Read isolation level are allowed to read the updated row

O D. Application A is not allowed to insert new rows into the DEPARTMENT table as long as the current transaction remains active

Answers

Question 1

The correct answer is **A**. If Application B did not already have an Exclusive lock on table TAB2, Application B would be placed in a lock-wait state until Application A released its locks. However, because Application B holds an Exclusive lock on table TAB2, when Application A tries to acquire an Exclusive lock on table TAB2 and Application B tries to acquire an Exclusive lock on table TAB1, a deadlock will occur – processing by both transactions will be suspended until their second lock request is granted. Because neither lock request can be granted until one of the owning transactions releases the lock it currently holds (by performing a commit or rollback operation), and because neither transaction can perform a commit or rollback operation because they both have been suspended (and are waiting on locks), a deadlock has occurred.

Question 2

The correct answer is **A**. When a deadlock cycle occurs, all transactions involved will wait indefinitely for a lock to be released unless some outside agent steps in and breaks the cycle. With DB2, this agent is a background process, known as the *deadlock detector*, and its sole responsibility is to locate and resolve any deadlocks found in the locking subsystem. Each database has its own deadlock detector, which is activated as part of the database initialization process. Once activated, the deadlock detector stays "asleep" most of the time but "wakes up" at preset intervals and examines the locking subsystem to determine whether a deadlock situation exists. If the deadlock detector discovers a deadlock cycle, it randomly selects one of the transactions involved to roll back and terminate; the transaction chosen (referred to as the *victim process*) is then sent an SQL error code, and every lock it had acquired is released. The remaining transaction(s) can then proceed, because the deadlock cycle has been broken.

Question 3

The correct answer is **D**. Typically, locks are not acquired during processing when the Uncommitted Read isolation level is used. Therefore, if Application B runs under this isolation level, it will be able to retrieve data from table TAB1 immediately – lock compatibility is not an issue that will cause Application B to wait for a lock.

Question 4

The correct answer is **A**. Anytime one transaction holds a lock on a data resource and another transaction attempts to acquire a lock on the same resource, the DB2 Database Manager will examine each lock's state and determine whether they are *compatible*. If the state of a lock placed on a data resource by one transaction is such that another lock can be placed on the same resource by another transaction before the first lock acquired is released, the locks are said to be compatible and the second lock will be acquired. However, if the locks are not compatible, the transaction requesting the incompatible lock must wait until the transaction holding the first lock is terminated before it can acquire the lock it needs. If the requested lock is not acquired before the time interval specified in the *locktimeout* configuration parameter has elapsed, the waiting transaction receives an error message and is rolled back.

Question 5

The correct answer is **B**. Locks can only be acquired for tablespaces, tables, and rows.

Question 6

The correct answer is **C**. The LOCK TABLE statement allows a transaction to explicitly acquire a table-level lock on a particular table in one of two modes: SHARE and EXCLUSIVE. If a table is locked using the SHARE mode, a table-level Share (S) lock is acquired on behalf of the transaction, and other concurrent transactions are allowed to read, but not change, the data stored in the locked table. If a table is locked using the EXCLUSIVE mode, a table-level Exclusive (X) lock is acquired, and other concurrent transactions can neither access nor modify data stored in the locked table.

Question 7

The correct answer is **C**. If a transaction holding a lock on a resource needs to acquire a more restrictive lock on the same resource, the DB2 Database Manager will attempt to change the state of the existing lock to the more restrictive state. The action of changing the state of an existing lock to a more restrictive state is known as *lock conversion*. Lock conversion occurs because a transaction can hold only one lock on a specific data resource at any given time. In most cases, lock conversion is performed on row-level locks, and the conversion process is fairly straightforward. For example, if an Update (U) lock is held and an Exclusive (X) lock is needed, the Update (U) lock will be converted to an Exclusive (X) lock.

Question 8

The correct answer is **A**. When the Repeatable Read isolation level is used, the effects of one transaction are completely isolated from the effects of other concurrent transactions; when this isolation level is used, every row that's referenced in any manner by the owning transaction is locked for the duration of that transaction. As a result, if the same SELECT SQL statement is issued multiple times within the same transaction, the result data sets produced are guaranteed to be the identical. Other transaction are prohibited from performing insert, update, or delete operations that would affect any row that has been accessed by the owning transaction as long as that transaction remains active.

Question 9

The correct answer is **C**. When the Read Stability isolation level is used by a transaction that executes a query, locks are acquired on all rows returned to the result data set produced, and other transactions cannot modify or delete the locked rows; however, they can add new rows to the table that meet the query's search criteria. If that happens, and the query is run again, these new rows will appear in the new result data set produced.

Question 10

The correct answer is **D**. When the Uncommitted Read isolation level is used, rows retrieved by a transaction are only locked if the transaction modifies data associated with one or more rows retrieved or if another transaction attempts to drop or alter the table the rows were retrieved from. As the name implies, transactions running under the uncommitted read isolation level can see changes made to rows by other transactions before those changes have been committed. On the other hand, transactions running under the Repeatable Read, Read Stability, or Cursor Stability isolation level are prohibited from seeing uncommitted data. Therefore, applications running under the Uncommitted Read isolation level can read the row Application A updated while applications running under a different isolation level cannot. Because no locks are needed in order for Application A to read data stored in other tables, it can do so – even if a restrictive lock is held on that table. However, there is nothing that prohibits Application A from performing an insert operation from within the open transaction.

DB2 9 Fundamentals Exam (Exam 730) Objectives

The DB2 9 Fundamentals exam (Exam 730) consists of 64 questions, and candidates have 90 minutes to complete the exam. A score of 59% or higher is required to pass this exam.

The primary objectives the DB2 9 Fundamentals exam (Exam 730) is designed to cover are as follows:

Planning (14%)

- Knowledge of DB2 UDB products (client, server, etc.)
- Knowledge of the features and functions provided by DB2 tools such as the Control Center, the Configuration Advisor, the Configuration Assistant and the Command Line Processor
- Knowledge of database workloads (OLAP versus data warehousing)
- Knowledge of non-relational data concepts (extenders)
- Knowledge of XML data implications (non-shredding)

Security (11%)

- Knowledge of restricting data access
- Knowledge of different authorities and privileges available

- Knowledge of encryption options available (data and network)

- Given a DCL SQL statement, ability to identify results (GRANT, REVOKE, CONNECT statements)

Working with Databases and Database Objects (17%)

- Ability to identify and connect to DB2 servers and databases

- Ability to identify DB2 objects

- Knowledge of basic characteristics and properties of DB2 objects

- Given a DDL SQL statement, ability to identify results (ability to create DB2 objects)

Working with DB2 Data using SQL and XQuery (23.5%)

- Given a DML SQL statement, ability to identify results

- Ability to use SQL to SELECT data from tables

- Ability to use SQL to SORT or GROUP data

- Ability to use SQL to INSERT, UPDATE, or DELETE data

- Knowledge of transactions (i.e., COMMIT, ROLLBACK, and transaction boundaries)

- Ability to call a procedure or invoke a user defined function

- Given an XQuery statement, knowledge to identify results

Working with DB2 Tables, Views, and Indexes (23.5%)

- Ability to demonstrate proper usage of DB2 data types

- Given a situation, ability to create a table

- Ability to identify when referential integrity should be used

- Ability to identify methods of data constraint

- Ability to identify characteristics of a table, view or index

- Ability to identify when triggers should be used

- Knowledge of schemas

- Knowledge of data type options for storing XML data

Data Concurrency (11%)

- Ability to identify factors that influence locking

- Ability to list objects on which locks can be obtained

- Ability to identify characteristics of DB2 locks

- Given a situation, ability to identify the isolation level that should be used

APPENDIX

Sample Test

Welcome to the section that really makes this book unique. In my opinion, one of the best ways to prepare for the DB2 9 Fundamentals certification exam (Exam 730) is by answering sample questions that are presented in the same format that you will see when you take the certification exam. In this section you will find 150 sample questions, along with comprehensive answers for every question. (It's not enough to know which answer is correct; it's also important to know why the answer is correct and why the other choices are wrong!)

If you worked through the Practice Questions presented at the end of each chapter, many of these questions will be familiar; if you skipped that part, all of those questions can be found here, along with many new ones. All of the questions presented here were developed by analyzing the final set of questions that were chosen for the DB2 9 Fundamentals certification exam (Exam 730). (I was a member of the team that developed the DB2 9 Fundamentals certification exam so I had access to every question!) I hope you find this material helpful.

—Roger E. Sanders

Planning

Question 1

Which of the following is the lowest cost DB2 product that can be legally installed on a Windows server that has 2 CPUs?

- ○ A. DB2 Everyplace
- ○ B. DB2 Express Edition
- ○ C. DB2 Workgroup Server Edition
- ○ D. DB2 Enterprise Server Edition

Question 2

Which of the following products is allowed to access other DB2 servers, but cannot accept requests from other remote clients?

- ○ A. DB2 Personal Edition
- ○ B. DB2 Workgroup Server Edition
- ○ C. DB2 Enterprise Server Edition
- ○ D. DB2 Data Warehouse Edition

Question 3

A client application on z/OS must access a DB2 database on a Solaris Server. At a minimum, which of the following products must be installed on the Solaris workstation?

- ○ A. DB2 Connect Enterprise Edition
- ○ B. DB2 Workgroup Server Edition
- ○ C. DB2 Workgroup Server Edition and DB2 Connect Enterprise Edition
- ○ D. DB2 Enterprise Server Edition and DB2 Connect Enterprise Edition

Question 4

Which of the following is the lowest cost DB2 product that can be legally installed on an HP-UX server?

- ○ A. DB2 Express-C
- ○ B. DB2 Express
- ○ C. DB2 Personal Edition
- ○ D. DB2 Enterprise Server Edition

Question 5

Which of the following products must be installed on an AIX server in order to build an application for AIX that will access a DB2 for z/OS database?

○ A. DB2 Enterprise Server Edition

○ B. DB2 Personal Developer's Edition

○ C. DB2 Universal Developer's Edition

○ D. DB2 Universal Database Enterprise Edition and DB2 Connect Enterprise Edition

Question 6

Which of the following DB2 products can only be installed on a System i server?

○ A. DB2 for z/OS

○ B. DB2 for i5/OS

○ C. DB2 Data Warehouse Edition

○ D. DB2 Enterprise Server Edition

Question 7

What is the purpose of the Design Advisor?

○ A. To analyze workloads and make recommendations for indexes and MQTs

○ B. To present a graphical representation of a data access plan and recommend design changes that will improve performance

○ C. To replicate data between a DB2 database and another relational database

○ D. To configure clients so they can access databases stored on remote servers

Question 8

Which of the following tools can be used to catalog a database?

○ A. Visual Explain

○ B. Alert Center

○ C. Journal

○ D. Configuration Assistant

Question 9

Which of the following is used to create and debug user-defined functions?

○ A. SQL Assist

○ B. Control Center

○ C. Command Editor

○ D. Developer Workbench

Question 10

Which of the following DB2 tools allows a user to set DB2 registry parameters?

○ A. Task Center

○ B. Visual Explain

○ C. Configuration Assistant

○ D. Satellite Administration Center

Question 11

What is the SQL Performance Monitor used for?

○ A. To examine the health of a DB2 Database Manager instance

○ B. To visually construct complex DML statements and examine the results of their execution

○ C. To schedule tasks, run tasks, and send notifications about completed tasks to other users

○ D. To analyze database operations performed against a DB2 for i5/OS database

Question 12

Which two of the following allow you to perform administrative tasks against database objects?

❑ A. Control Center

❑ B. Journal

❑ C. Command Line Processor

❑ D. Task Center

❑ E. Health Center

Question 13

Which of the following tasks can NOT be performed using the Developer Workbench?

○ A. Develop and debug an SQL stored procedure
○ B. Develop and debug a user-defined data type
○ C. Develop and debug a user-defined function
○ D. Develop and run XML queries

Question 14

Which of the following tools can be used to automate table reorganization operations?

○ A. Control Center
○ B. Command Center
○ C. Command Line Processor
○ D. Task Center

Question 15

Which of the following can be viewed with the Journal?

○ A. Historical information about tasks, database changes, messages, and notifications
○ B. Information about licenses associated with each DB2 9 product installed on a particular system
○ C. Graphical representations of data access plans chosen for SQL statements
○ D. Warning and alarm thresholds for database indicators

Question 16

Which of the following is NOT a characteristic of a data warehouse?

○ A. Summarized queries that perform aggregations and joins
○ B. Heterogeneous data sources
○ C. Voluminous historical data
○ D. Sub-second response time

Question 17

Which of the following is NOT a characteristic of an OLTP database?

- ○ A. Granular transactions
- ○ B. Current data
- ○ C. Optimized for queries
- ○ D. Frequent updates

Question 18

Which of the following is true about XML columns?

- ○ A. XML columns are used to store XML documents as a hierarchical set of entities
- ○ B. Only XQuery can be used to retrieve an XML document from an XML column
- ○ C. XML columns must be altered to accommodate additional parent/child relationships if they are used in referential constraints
- ○ D. In order to access any portion of an XML document stored in an XML column, the entire document must be retrieved

Question 19

Which of the following products is used to shred extensible markup language documents?

- ○ A. DB2 AVI Extender
- ○ B. DB2 Text Extender
- ○ C. DB2 XML Extender
- ○ D. DB2 Spatial Extender

Question 20

Which of the following best describes the difference between the DB2 Spatial Extender and the DB2 Geodetic Extender?

- ○ A. The DB2 Spatial Extender uses a latitude-longitude coordinate system; the DB2 Geodetic Extender uses a planar, x- and y-coordinate system

- ○ B. The DB2 Geodetic Extender is used to describe points, lines, and polygons; the DB2 Spatial Extender is used to find area, endpoints, and intersects

- ○ C. The DB2 Spatial Extender treats the world as a flat map; the DB2 Geodetic Extender treats the world as a round globe

- ○ D. The DB2 Geodetic Extender can be used to manage information like the locations of office buildings or the size of a flood zone; the DB2 Spatial Extender can be used for calculations and visualizations in disciplines like military command/control and asset management, meteorology and oceanography

Question 21

Which of the following is the major difference between relational data and XML data?

- ○ A. Relational data is self-describing; XML data is not
- ○ B. Relational data has inherent ordering; XML data does not
- ○ C. Relational data must be tabular; XML data does not have to be tabular
- ○ D. Relational data is comprised of entities; XML data is comprised of numbers, characters, and dates

Security

Question 22

Which of the following is NOT a valid method of authentication that can be used by DB2 9?

- ○ A. SERVER
- ○ B. SERVER_ENCRYPT
- ○ C. CLIENT
- ○ D. DCS

Question 23

In a client-server environment, which two of the following can be used to verify passwords?

❑ A. System Catalog

❑ B. User ID/password file

❑ C. Client Operating System

❑ D. Communications layer

❑ E. Application Server

Question 24

A table named DEPARTMENT has the following columns:

```
DEPT_ID
DEPT_NAME
MANAGER
AVG_SALARY
```

Which of the following is the best way to prevent most users from viewing AVG_SALARY data?

○ A. Encrypt the table's data

○ B. Create a view that does not contain the AVG_SALARY column

○ C. Revoke SELECT access for the AVG_SALARY column from users who should not see AVG_SALARY data

○ D. Store AVG_SALARY data in a separate table and grant SELECT privilege for that table to the appropriate users

Question 25

Which authority or privilege is granted by the DB2 Database Manager configuration file?

○ A. CONNECT

○ B. CONTROL

○ C. SYSMAINT

○ D. EXECUTE

Question 26

Which two of the following authorities allow a user to create a new database?

- ❏ A. SYSADMN
- ❏ B. SYSCTRL
- ❏ C. SYSMAINT
- ❏ D. DBADM
- ❏ E. CREATEDB

Question 27

Assuming USER1 has no authorities or privileges, which of the following will allow USER1 to create a view named VIEW1 that references two tables named TAB1 and TAB2?

- ○ A. CREATEIN privilege on the database
- ○ B. REFERENCES privilege on TAB1 and TAB2
- ○ C. CREATE_TAB privilege on the database
- ○ D. SELECT privilege on TAB1 and TAB2

Question 28

Which of the following will allow user USER1 to change the comment associated with a table named TABLE1?

- ○ A. GRANT UPDATE ON TABLE table1 TO user1
- ○ B. GRANT CONTROL ON TABLE table1 TO user1
- ○ C. GRANT ALTER ON TABLE table1 TO user1
- ○ D. GRANT REFERENCES ON TABLE table1 TO user1

Question 29

A table called DEPARTMENT has the following columns:

```
DEPT_ID
DEPT_NAME
MANAGER
```

Which of the following statements will ONLY allow user USER1 to modify the DEPT_NAME column?

- ○ A. GRANT ALTER ON TABLE department TO user1
- ○ B. GRANT ALTER (dept_name) ON TABLE department TO user1
- ○ C. GRANT UPDATE ON TABLE department TO user1
- ○ D. GRANT UPDATE (dept_name) ON TABLE department TO user1

Question 30

An index named EMPID_X exists for a table named EMPLOYEE. Which of the following will allow user USER1 to drop the EMPID_X index?

- ○ A. GRANT DROP ON INDEX empid_x TO user1
- ○ B. GRANT DELETE ON INDEX empid_x TO user1
- ○ C. GRANT INDEX ON TABLE employee TO user1
- ○ D. GRANT CONTROL ON INDEX empid_x TO user1

Question 31

On which two of the following database objects may the SELECT privilege be controlled?

- ❑ A. Sequence
- ❑ B. Nickname
- ❑ C. Schema
- ❑ D. View
- ❑ E. Index

Question 32

User USER1 wants to utilize an alias to remove rows from a table. Assuming USER1 has no authorities or privileges, which of the following privileges are needed?

- ○ A. DELETE privilege on the table
- ○ B. DELETE privilege on the alias
- ○ C. DELETE privilege on the alias; REFERENCES privilege on the table
- ○ D. REFERENCES privilege on the alias; DELETE privilege on the table

Question 33

User USER1 holds CONTROL privilege on table TABLE1. Which two of the following statements is user USER1 allowed to execute?

- ❑ A. GRANT CONTROL ON table1 TO user2
- ❑ B. GRANT LOAD ON table1 TO user2
- ❑ C. GRANT INSERT, UPDATE ON table1 TO user2 WITH GRANT OPTION
- ❑ D. GRANT BINDADD ON table1 TO PUBLIC
- ❑ E. GRANT ALL PRIVILEGES ON table1 TO PUBLIC

Question 34

A user wishing to invoke an SQL stored procedure that queries a table must have which of the following privileges?

- ○ A. CALL privilege on the procedure; SELECT privilege on the table
- ○ B. CALL privilege on the procedure; REFERENCES privilege on the table
- ○ C. EXECUTE privilege on the procedure; SELECT privilege on the table
- ○ D. EXECUTE privilege on the procedure; REFERENCES privilege on the table

Question 35

After the following SQL statement is executed:

```
GRANT ALL PRIVILEGES ON TABLE employee TO USER user1
```

Assuming user USER1 has no other authorities or privileges, which of the following actions is user USER1 allowed to perform?

- ○ A. Drop an index on the EMPLOYEE table
- ○ B. Grant all privileges on the EMPLOYEE table to other users
- ○ C. Alter the table definition
- ○ D. Drop the EMPLOYEE table

Question 36

Which two of the following privileges is required in order to use a package?

- ❏ A. BINDADD
- ❏ B. BIND
- ❏ C. CONNECT
- ❏ D. EXECUTE
- ❏ E. USE

Question 37

Which of the following statements allows user USER1 to take the ability to create packages in a database named SAMPLE away from user USER2?

- ○ A. REVOKE CONNECT ON DATABASE FROM user2
- ○ B. REVOKE CREATETAB ON DATABASE FROM user2
- ○ C. REVOKE BIND ON DATABASE FROM user2
- ○ D. REVOKE BINDADD ON DATABASE FROM user2

Question 38

Which of the following will provide user USER1 and all members of the group GROUP1 with the ability to perform DML, but no other operations on table TABLE1?

○ A. GRANT INSERT, UPDATE, DELETE, SELECT ON TABLE table1 TO user1 AND group1

○ B. GRANT INSERT, UPDATE, DELETE, SELECT ON TABLE table1 TO USER user1, GROUP group1

○ C. GRANT ALL PRIVILEGES EXCEPT ALTER, INDEX, REFERENCES ON TABLE table1 TO USER user1, GROUP group1

○ D. GRANT CONTROL ON TABLE table1 TO user1 AND group1

Question 39

What does the following statement do?

```
GRANT REFERENCES (col1, col2) ON TABLE table1 TO user1 WITH
GRANT OPTION
```

○ A. Gives user USER1 the ability to refer to COL1 and COL2 of table TABLE1 in queries, along with the ability to give this authority to other users and groups.

○ B. Gives user USER1 the ability to refer to COL1 and COL2 of table TABLE1 in views, along with the ability to give this authority to other users and groups.

○ C. Gives user USER1 the ability to define a referential constraint on table TABLE1 using columns COL1 and COL2 as the parent key of the constraint.

○ D. Gives user USER1 the ability to define a referential constraint on table TABLE1 using columns COL1 and COL2 as the foreign key of the constraint.

Question 40

User USER1 is the owner of TABLE1. Assuming user USER1 only holds privileges for TABLE1, which of the following is the best way to remove all privileges user USER1 holds?

○ A. REVOKE CONTROL ON table1 FROM user1

○ B. REVOKE ALL PRIVILEGES ON table1 FROM user1

○ C. REVOKE CONTROL ON table1 FROM user1;
    REVOKE ALL PRIVILEGES ON table1 FROM user1;

○ D. REVOKE CONTROL, ALL PRIVILEGES ON table1 FROM user1

Question 41

User USER1 has the privileges needed to invoke a stored procedure named GEN_RESUME. User USER2 needs to be able to call the procedure – user USER1 and all members of the group PUBLIC should no longer be allowed to call the procedure. Which of the following statement(s) can be used to accomplish this?

○ A. GRANT EXECUTE ON ROUTINE gen_resume TO user2 EXCLUDE user1, PUBLIC

○ B. GRANT EXECUTE ON PROCEDURE gen_resume TO user2;
REVOKE EXECUTE ON PROCEDURE gen_resume FROM user1, PUBLIC;

○ C. GRANT CALL ON ROUTINE gen_resume TO user2 EXCLUDE user1 PUBLIC

○ D. GRANT CALL ON PROCEDURE gen_resume TO user2;
REVOKE CALL ON PROCEDURE gen_resume FROM user1, PUBLIC;

Question 42

A view named V.VIEW1 is based on a table named T.TABLE1. A user with DBADM authority issues the following statement:

```
GRANT INSERT ON v.view1 TO user1 WITH GRANT OPTION
```

Which of the following statements is USER1 authorized to execute?

○ A. GRANT INSERT ON t.table1 TO user2
○ B. GRANT CONTROL ON v.view1 TO user2
○ C. GRANT ALL PRIVILEGES ON v.view1 TO user2
○ D. GRANT INSERT ON v.view1 TO user2

Question 43

What does the following statement do?

```
GRANT ALTER ON SEQUENCE gen_empid TO user1 WITH GRANT OPTION
```

○ A. Gives USER1 the ability to change the comment associated with a sequence named GEN_EMPID, along with the ability to give this CONTROL authority for the sequence to other users and groups.

○ B. Gives USER1 the ability to change the values returned by the PREVIOUS_VALUE and NEXT_VALUE expressions associated with a sequence named GEN_EMPID, along with the ability to give CONTROL authority for the sequence to other users and groups.

○ C. Gives USER1 the ability to change the comment associated with a sequence named GEN_EMPID, along with the ability to give this authority to other users and groups.

○ D. Gives USER1 the ability to change the values returned by the PREVIOUS_VALUE and NEXT_VALUE expressions associated with a sequence named GEN_EMPID, along with the ability to give this authority to other users and groups.

Working with Databases and Database Objects

Question 44

While attempting to connect to a database stored on an iSeries server from a Windows client, the following message was displayed:

SQL1013N The database alias name or database name "TEST_DB" could not be found.

Which of the following actions can be used to help determine why this message was displayed?

○ A. Execute the LIST REMOTE DATABASES command on the server; look for an entry for the TEST_DB database

○ B. Execute the LIST DCS DIRECTORY command on the server; look for an entry for the TEST_DB database

○ C. Execute the LIST REMOTE DATABASES command on the client; look for an entry for the TEST_DB database

○ D. Execute the LIST DCS DIRECTORY command on the client; look for an entry for the TEST_DB database

Question 45

A database named TEST_DB resides on a z/OS system and listens on port 446. The TCP/IP address for this system is 192.168.10.20 and the TCP/IP host name is MYHOST. Which of the following commands is required to make this database accessible to a Linux client?

○ A. CATALOG TCPIP NODE zos_srvr REMOTE myhost SERVER 192.168.10.20;
       CATALOG DATABASE zos_db AS test_db AT NODE zos_srvr;
       CATALOG DCS DATABASE zos_db AS test_db;

○ B. CATALOG TCPIP NODE zos_srvr REMOTE myhost SERVER 192.168.10.20;
       CATALOG DCS DATABASE zos_db AS test_db AT NODE zos_srvr;

○ C. CATALOG TCPIP NODE zos_srvr REMOTE myhost SERVER 446;
       CATALOG DCS DATABASE zos_db AS test_db AT NODE zos_srvr;

○ D. CATALOG TCPIP NODE zos_srvr REMOTE myhost SERVER 446;
       CATALOG DATABASE zos_db AS test_db AT NODE zos_srvr;
       CATALOG DCS DATABASE zos_db AS test_db;

Question 46

Which of the following statements will catalog the database MYDB on the node MYNODE and assign it the alias MYNEWDB?

○ A. CATALOG DATABASE mynewdb AT NODE mynode

○ B. CATALOG DATABASE mynewdb AS mydb AT NODE mynode

○ C. CATALOG DATABASE mydb AT NODE mynode

○ D. CATALOG DATABASE mydb AS mynewdb AT NODE mynode

Question 47

Which of the following are NOT stored in the system catalog tables?

○ A. SQL statements used to create views

○ B. SQL statements used to create triggers

○ C. SQL statements used to create constraints

○ D. Table names

Question 48

Which of the following tools can NOT be used to catalog a database?

○ A. Control Center

○ B. SQL Assist

○ C. Configuration Assistant

○ D. Command Line Processor

Question 49

In which of the following scenarios would a stored procedure be beneficial?

○ A. An application running on a remote client needs to be able to convert degrees Celsius to degrees Fahrenheit and vice versa

○ B. An application running on a remote client needs to collect three input values, perform a calculation using the values provided, and store the input data, along with the results of the calculation in two different base tables

○ C. An application running on a remote client needs to track every modification made to a table that contains sensitive data

○ D. An application running on a remote client needs to ensure that every new employee that joins the company is assigned a unique, sequential employee number

Question 50

If the following SQL statements are executed in the order shown:

```
CREATE TABLE orders
      (order_num      INTEGER NOT NULL,
       buyer_name     VARCHAR(35),
       amount         NUMERIC(5,2));

CREATE UNIQUE INDEX idx_orderno ON orders(order_num);
```

Which of the following describes the resulting behavior?

○ A. Every ORDER_NUM value entered must be unique; whenever the ORDERS table is queried rows should be displayed in order of increasing ORDER_NUM values

○ B. Every ORDER_NUM value entered must be unique; whenever the ORDERS table is queried rows will be displayed in no particular order

○ C. Duplicate ORDER_NUM values are allowed; no other index can be created for the ORDERS table that reference the ORDER_NUM column

○ D. Every ORDER_NUM value entered must be unique; no other index can be created for the ORDERS table that reference the ORDER_NUM column

Question 51

An alias can be an alternate name for which two of the following DB2 objects?

- ❑ A. Sequence
- ❑ B. Trigger
- ❑ C. View
- ❑ D. Schema
- ❑ E. Table

Question 52

Which of the following events will NOT cause a trigger to be activated?

- ○ A. A select operation
- ○ B. An insert operation
- ○ C. An update operation
- ○ D. A delete operation

Question 53

If a view named V1 is created in such a way that it references every column in a table named EMPLOYEE except a column named SALARY, which of the following is NOT an accurate statement?

- ○ A. View V1 can be used in the same context as the EMPLOYEE table for all data retrieval operations that do not acquire SALARY information
- ○ B. View V1 can be used as a data source for other views
- ○ C. View V1 does not have to reside in the same schema as the EMPLOYEE table
- ○ D. All data, except SALARY data that is stored in the EMPLOYEE table is copied to the physical location associated with view V1

Question 54

Which of the following would NOT provide access to data stored in table TABLE1 using the name T1?

- ○ A. An alias named T1 that references table TABLE1
- ○ B. A view named T1 that references table TABLE1
- ○ C. A schema named T1 that references table TABLE1
- ○ D. An alias named T1 that references a view named V1 that references table TABLE1

Question 55

Which of the following DB2 objects can be referenced by an INSERT statement to generate values for a column?

○ A. Sequence
○ B. Identity column
○ C. Trigger
○ D. Table function

Question 56

A sequence was created with the DDL statement shown below:

```
CREATE SEQUENCE my_seq START WITH 10 INCREMENT BY 10 CACHE 10
```

User USER1 successfully executes the following statements in the order shown:

```
VALUES NEXT VALUE FOR my_seq INTO :hvar;
VALUES NEXT VALUE FOR my_seq INTO :hvar;
```

User USER2 successfully executes the following statements in the order shown:

```
ALTER SEQUENCE my_seq RESTART WITH 5 INCREMENT BY 5 CACHE 5;
VALUES NEXT VALUE FOR my_seq INTO :hvar;
```

After users USER1 and USER2 are finished, user USER3 executes the following query:

```
SELECT NEXT VALUE FOR my_seq FROM sysibm.sysdummy1
```

What value will be returned by the query?

○ A. 5
○ B. 10
○ C. 20
○ D. 30

Question 57

Given the following statements:

```
CREATE TABLE tab1 (c1 INTEGER, c2 CHAR(5));
CREATE VIEW view1 AS SELECT c1, c2 FROM tab1 WHERE c1 < 100;
CREATE VIEW view2 AS SELECT c1, c2 FROM view1
        WITH CASCADED CHECK OPTION;
```

Which of the following INSERT statements will fail to execute?

○ A. INSERT INTO view2 VALUES(50, 'abc')
○ B. INSERT INTO view1 VALUES (100, 'abc')
○ C. INSERT INTO view2 VALUES(150, 'abc')
○ D. INSERT INTO view1 VALUES(100, 'abc')

Question 58

Given the following statements:

```
CREATE TABLE t1 (c1 INTEGER, c2 CHAR(5));
CREATE TABLE t1audit (user VARCHAR(20), date DATE, action
VARCHAR(20));

CREATE TRIGGER trig1 AFTER INSERT ON t1
FOR EACH ROW
MODE DB2SQL
INSERT INTO t1audit VALUES (CURRENT USER, CURRENT DATE,
'Insert');
```

If user USER1 executes the following statements:

```
INSERT INTO t1 VALUES (1, 'abc');
INSERT INTO t1 (c1) VALUES (2);
UPDATE t1 SET c2 = 'ghi' WHERE c1 = 1;
```

How many new records will be written to the database?

○ A. 0

○ B. 2

○ C. 3

○ D. 4

Question 59

Which of the following is NOT an attribute of Declared Global Temporary Tables (DGTTs)?

○ A. Each application that defines a DGTT has its own instance of the DGTT

○ B. Two different applications cannot create DGTTs that have the same name

○ C. DGTTs can only be used by the application that creates them, and only for the life of the application

○ D. Data stored in a DGTT can exist across transaction boundaries

Question 60

Which of the following is an accurate statement about packages?

○ A. Packages provide a logical grouping of database objects.

○ B. Packages contain control structures that are considered the bound form for SQL statements

○ C. Packages describe the objects in a DB2 database and their relationship to each other

○ D. Packages may be used during query optimization to improve the performance for a subset of SELECT queries

Question 61

Given the following information:

```
Protocol: TCP/IP
Port Number: 5000
Host Name: DB_SERVER
Database Name: TEST_DB
Database Server Platform: Linux
```

Which of the following will allow a client to access the database stored on the server?

○ A. CATALOG DATABASE test_db AS test_db REMOTE TCPIP SERVER
      db_server PORT 5000 OSTYPE LINUX;

○ B. CATALOG TCPIP NODE 5000 REMOTE SERVER db_server
      OSTYPE LINUX;
      CATALOG DATABASE test_db AS test_db AT NODE db_server
      AUTHENTICATION SERVER;

○ C. CATALOG TCPIP NODE db_server REMOTE db_server SERVER 5000
      OSTYPE LINUX;
      CATALOG DATABASE test_db AS test_db AT NODE db_server
      AUTHENTICATION SERVER;

○ D. CATALOG TCPIP NODE db_server REMOTE db_server PORT 5000
      OSTYPE LINUX;
      CATALOG DATABASE test_db AS test_db AT NODE db_server
      AUTHENTICATION SERVER;

Question 62

A declared temporary table is used for which of the following purposes?

○ A. Backup purposes

○ B. Storing intermediate results

○ C. Staging area for load operations

○ D. Sharing result data sets between applications

Question 63

Which of the following DB2 objects is NOT considered executable using SQL?

○ A. Routine

○ B. Function

○ C. Procedure

○ D. Trigger

Question 64

Which of the following is NOT an accurate statement about views?

○ A. Views are publicly referenced names and no special authority or privilege is needed to use them.

○ B. Views can be used to restrict access to columns in a base table that contain sensitive data

○ C. Views can be used to store queries that multiple applications execute on a regular basis in a database

○ D. Views support INSTEAD OF triggers

Question 65

Which of the following SQL statements can be used to create a DB2 object to store numerical data as EURO data?

○ A. CREATE NICKNAME euro FOR DECIMAL (9,3)

○ B. CREATE ALIAS euro FOR DECIMAL (9,3)

○ C. CREATE DISTINCT TYPE euro AS DECIMAL (9,3)

○ D. CREATE DATA TYPE euro AS DECIMAL (9,3)

Working with DB2 Data Using SQL and XQuery

Question 66

Given the following two tables:

```
            NAMES
----------------------------------
NAME                    NUMBER
----------              ------
Wayne Gretzky           99
Jaromir Jagr            68
Bobby Orr               4
Bobby Hull              23
Mario Lemieux           66

            POINTS
----------------------------------
NAME                    POINTS
----------              ------
Wayne Gretzky           244
Bobby Orr               129
Brett Hull              121
Mario Lemieux           189
Joe Sakic               94
```

How many rows would be returned using the following statement?

    SELECT name FROM names, points

○ A. 0

○ B. 5

○ C. 10

○ D. 25

Question 67

Given the following CREATE TABLE statement:

```
CREATE TABLE EMPLOYEE
  (EMPNO      CHAR(3) NOT NULL,
   FIRSTNAME  CHAR(20) NOT NULL,
   MIDINIT    CHAR(1),
   LASTNAME   CHAR(20) NOT NULL,
   SALARY     DECIMAL(10, 2))
```

Which of the following will retrieve the rows that have a missing value in the MIDINIT column?

○ A. SELECT * FROM employee WHERE midinit = ' '

○ B. SELECT * FROM employee WHERE midinit = NULL

○ C. SELECT * FROM employee WHERE midinit = " "

○ D. SELECT * FROM employee WHERE midinit IS NULL

Question 68

Given the following two tables:

```
          TAB1
------------------------
COL_1             COL_2
-----             -----
A                 10
B                 12
C                 14

          TAB2
------------------------
COL_A             COL_B
-----             -----
A                 21
C                 23
D                 25
```

Assuming the following results are desired:

COL_1	COL_2	COL_A	COL_B
A	10	A	21
B	12	–	–
C	14	C	23
–	–	D	25

Which of the following joins will produce the desired results?

○ A. SELECT * FROM tab1 INNER JOIN tab2 ON col_1 = col_a

○ B. SELECT * FROM tab1 LEFT OUTER JOIN tab2 ON col_1 = col_a

○ C. SELECT * FROM tab1 RIGHT OUTER JOIN tab2 ON col_1 = col_a

○ D. SELECT * FROM tab1 FULL OUTER JOIN tab2 ON col_1 = col_a

Question 69

If the following SQL statements are executed in the order shown:

```
CREATE TABLE table1 (c1  INTEGER, c2  INTEGER);
INSERT INTO table1 VALUES (123, 456);
UPDATE table1 SET c1 = NULL;
```

What will be the result of the following statement?

```
SELECT * FROM table1;
```

○ A. C1   C2
```
   ---      ---
   123      456
   1 record(s) selected.
```

○ B. C1   C2
```
   ---      ---
   NULL     456
   1 record(s) selected.
```

○ C. C1   C2
```
   ---      ---
    -       456
   1 record(s) selected.
```

○ D. C1   C2
```
   ---      ---
    0       456
   1 record(s) selected.
```

Question 70

Given the following table:

TAB1

COL1	COL2
A	10
B	20
C	30
A	10
D	40
C	30

Assuming the following results are desired:

TAB1

COL1	COL2
A	10
B	20
C	30
D	40

Which of the following statements will produce the desired results?

○ A. SELECT UNIQUE * FROM tab1

○ B. SELECT DISTINCT * FROM tab1

○ C. SELECT UNIQUE(*) FROM tab1

○ D. SELECT DISTINCT(*) FROM tab1

Question 71

Assuming table TAB1 contains 100 rows, which of the following queries will return only half of the rows available?

○ A. SELECT * FROM tab1 FIND FIRST 50 ROWS

○ B. SELECT * FROM tab1 FETCH FIRST 50 ROWS ONLY

○ C. SELECT * FROM tab1 WHILE ROW_NUM < 50

○ D. SELECT * FROM tab1 MAXROWS 50

Question 72

Given the following two tables:

```
EMPLOYEE

ID NAME                DEPTID
-- ------------------- ---
01 Mick Jagger         10
02 Keith Richards      20
03 Ronnie Wood         20
04 Charlie Watts       20
05 Bill Wyman          30
06 Brian Jones         -


DEPARTMENT

ID DEPTNAME
-- ---------------------
10 Executive Staff
20 Sales
30 Marketing
40 Engineering
50 Human Resources
```

Which two of the following queries will display the employee name and department name for all employees that are in Sales?

❑ A. SELECT e.name, d.deptname
      FROM employee e, department d
      WHERE e.deptid = d.id AND d.id = '20'

❑ B. SELECT e.name, d.deptname
      FROM employee e FULL OUTER JOIN department d
      ON e.deptid = d.id
      WHERE d.id = '20'

❑ C. SELECT e.name, d.deptname
      FROM employee e RIGHT OUTER JOIN department d
      ON e.deptid = d.id
      WHERE d.id = '20'

❑ D. SELECT e.name, d.deptname
      FROM employee e LEFT OUTER JOIN department d
      ON e.deptid = d.id
      WHERE d.id = '20'

❑ E. SELECT e.name, d.deptname
      FROM employee e INNER JOIN department d
      ON e.deptid = d.id
      WHERE d.id = '20'

Question 73

Given the following queries:

```
SELECT c1 FROM tab1;
SELECT c1 FROM tab2;
```

Which of the following set operators can be used to produce a result data set that contains only records that are not found in the result data set produced by each query after duplicate rows have been eliminated?

○ A. UNION

○ B. INTERSECT

○ C. EXCEPT

○ D. MERGE

Question 74

Given the following two tables:

NAMES

NAME	NUMBER
Wayne Gretzky	99
Jaromir Jagr	68
Bobby Orr	4
Bobby Hull	23
Brett Hull	16
Mario Lemieux	66
Mark Messier	11

POINTS

NAME	POINTS
Wayne Gretzky	244
Jaromir Jagr	168
Bobby Orr	129
Brett Hull	121
Mario Lemieux	189
Joe Sakic	94

Which of the following statements will display the player name, number, and points for all players that have scored points?

○ A. SELECT p.name, n.number, p.points FROM names n INNER JOIN points p ON n.name = p.name

○ B. SELECT p.name, n.number, p.points FROM names n LEFT OUTER JOIN points p ON n.name = p.name

○ C. SELECT p.name, n.number, p.points FROM names n RIGHT OUTER JOIN points p ON n.name = p.name

○ D. SELECT p.name, n.number, p.points FROM names n FULL OUTER JOIN points p ON n.name = p.name

Question 75

Which of the following is a valid wildcard character in a LIKE clause of a SELECT statement?

○ A. %

○ B. *

○ C. ?

○ D. \

Question 76

Given the following tables:

YEAR_2007

EMPID	NAME
1	Jagger, Mick
2	Richards, Keith
3	Wood, Ronnie
4	Watts, Charlie
5	Jones, Darryl
6	Leavell, Chuck

YEAR_1962

EMPID	NAME
1	Jagger, Mick
2	Richards, Keith
3	Jones, Brian
4	Wyman, Bill
5	Watts, Charlie
6	Stewart, Ian

If the following SQL statement is executed, how many rows will be returned?

```
SELECT name FROM year_2007
UNION ALL
SELECT name FROM year_1962
```

○ A. 6

○ B. 9

○ C. 10

○ D. 12

Question 77

Given the following table definition:

```
SALES
-------------------------------------------------
INVOICE_NO          CHAR(20) NOT NULL
SALES_DATE          DATE
SALES_PERSON        VARCHAR(25)
REGION              CHAR(20)
SALES_AMT           DECIMAL(9,2)
```

Which of the following queries will return SALES information, sorted by SALES_PERSON, from A to Z, and SALES_DATE, from most recent to earliest?

- ○ A. SELECT invoice_no, sales_person, sales_date, sales_amt FROM sales
     SORT BY sales_person, sales_date DESC

- ○ B. SELECT invoice_no, sales_person, sales_date, sales_amt FROM sales
     SORT BY sales_person DESC, sales_date

- ○ C. SELECT invoice_no, sales_person, sales_date, sales_amt FROM sales
     ORDER BY sales_person, sales_date DESC

- ○ D. SELECT invoice_no, sales_person, sales_date, sales_amt FROM sales
     ORDER BY sales_person DESC, sales_date

Question 78

Given the following statement:

```
SELECT hyear, AVG(salary)
FROM (SELECT YEAR(hiredate) AS hyear, salary
            FROM employee WHERE salary > 30000
GROUP BY hyear
```

Which of the following describes the result if this statement is executed?

- ○ A. The statement will return the year and average salary for all employees that have a salary greater than $30,000, sorted by year.

- ○ B. The statement will return the year and average salary for all employees hired within a given year that have a salary greater than $30,000.

- ○ C. The statement will return the year and average salary for all years that every employee hired had a salary greater than $30,000.

- ○ D. The statement will return the year and average salary for all years that any employee had a salary greater than $30,000.

Question 79

Which two of the following statements are true about the HAVING clause?

- ❏ A. The HAVING clause is used in place of the WHERE clause.
- ❏ B. The HAVING clause uses the same syntax as the WHERE clause.
- ❏ C. The HAVING clause can only be used with the GROUP BY clause.
- ❏ D. The HAVING clause accepts wildcards.
- ❏ E. The HAVING clause uses the same syntax as the IN clause.

Question 80

Given the following table definitions:

```
DEPARTMENT
------------------------------
DEPTNO       CHAR(3)
DEPTNAME     CHAR(30)
MGRNO        INTEGER
ADMRDEPT     CHAR(3)


EMPLOYEE
------------------------------
EMPNO        INTEGER
FIRSTNAME    CHAR(30)
MIDINIT      CHAR
LASTNAME     CHAR(30)
WORKDEPT     CHAR(3)
```

Which of the following statements will list every employee number and last name, along with the employee number and last name of their manager, including employees that have not been assigned to a manager?

- ○ A. SELECT e.empno, e.lastname, m.empno, m.lastname FROM employee e
  LEFT INNER JOIN department INNER JOIN employee m ON
  mgrno=m.empno ON e.workdept=deptno
- ○ B. SELECT e.empno, e.lastname, m.empno, m.lastname FROM employee e
  LEFT OUTER JOIN department INNER JOIN employee m ON
  mgrno=m.empno ON e.workdept=deptno
- ○ C. SELECT e.empno, e.lastname, m.empno, m.lastname FROM employee e
  RIGHT OUTER JOIN department INNER JOIN employee m ON
  mgrno=m.empno ON e.workdept=deptno
- ○ D. SELECT e.empno, e.lastname, m.empno, m.lastname FROM employee e
  RIGHT INNER JOIN department INNER JOIN employee m ON
  mgrno=m.empno ON e.workdept=deptno

Question 81

Given the following table:

```
EMPLOYEE

EMPID    NAME                  INSTRUMENT
---      ------------------    -----
1        Jagger, Mick          01
2        Richards, Keith       02
3        Wood, Ronnie          02
4        Watts, Charlie        03
5        Jones, Darryl         04
6        Leavell, Chuck        05
```

If the following query is executed:

```
SELECT name,
    CASE WHEN instrument = '01' THEN 'HARMONICA'
         WHEN instrument = '02' THEN 'GUITAR'
         WHEN instrument = '03' THEN 'DRUMS'
         ELSE 'UNKNOWN'
    END AS instrument
FROM employee
```

What will be the results?

○ A.
```
NAME                  INSTRUMENT
------------------    ---------
Jagger, Mick          HARMONICA
Richards, Keith       GUITAR
Wood, Ronnie          GUITAR
Watts, Charlie        DRUMS
Jones, Darryl         ERROR
Leavell, Chuck        ERROR
```

○ B.
```
NAME                  INSTRUMENT
------------------    ---------
Jagger, Mick          HARMONICA
Richards, Keith       GUITAR
Wood, Ronnie          GUITAR
Watts, Charlie        DRUMS
Jones, Darryl         04
Leavell, Chuck        05
```

○ C.
```
NAME                  INSTRUMENT
------------------    ---------
Jagger, Mick          HARMONICA
Richards, Keith       GUITAR
Wood, Ronnie          GUITAR
Watts, Charlie        DRUMS
Jones, Darryl         UNKNOWN
Leavell, Chuck        UNKNOWN
```

○ D.
```
NAME                  INSTRUMENT
------------------    ---------
Jagger, Mick          HARMONICA
Richards, Keith       GUITAR
Wood, Ronnie          GUITAR
Watts, Charlie        DRUMS
Jones, Darryl         -
Leavell, Chuck        -
```

Question 82

If the following statement is executed:

```
UPDATE employees SET workdept =
(SELECT deptno FROM department WHERE deptno = 'A01')
WHERE workdept IS NULL
```

Which of the following describes the results?

○ A. The statement will fail because an UPDATE statement cannot contain a subquery.

○ B. The statement will only succeed if the data retrieved by the subquery does not contain multiple records.

○ C. The statement will succeed; if the data retrieved by the subquery contains multiple records, only the first record will be used to perform the update.

○ D. The statement will only succeed if every record in the EMPLOYEES table has a null value in the WORKDEPT column.

Question 83

Given the following table:

```
CURRENT_EMPLOYEES
————————————————————————————
EMPID       INTEGER NOT NULL
NAME        CHAR(20)
SALARY      DECIMAL(10,2)

PAST_EMPLOYEES
————————————————————————————
EMPID       INTEGER NOT NULL
NAME        CHAR(20)
SALARY      DECIMAL(10,2)
```

Assuming both tables contain data, which of the following statements will NOT successfully add data to table CURRENT_EMPLOYEES?

○ A. INSERT INTO current_employees (empid) VALUES (10)

○ B. INSERT INTO current_employees VALUES (10, 'JAGGER', 85000.00)

○ C. INSERT INTO current_employees SELECT empid, name, salary FROM past_employees WHERE empid = 20

○ D. INSERT INTO current_employees (name, salary) VALUES (SELECT name, salary FROM past_employees WHERE empid = 20)

Question 84

Given the following table definition:

```
SALES
---------------------------
SALES_DATE      DATE
SALES_PERSON    CHAR(20)
REGION          CHAR(20)
SALES           INTEGER
```

Which of the following SQL statements will remove all rows that had a SALES_DATE in the year 1995?

○ A.   DELETE * FROM sales WHERE YEAR(sales_date) = 1995

○ B.   DELETE FROM sales WHERE YEAR(sales_date) = 1995

○ C.   DROP * FROM sales WHERE YEAR(sales_date) = 1995

○ D.   DROP FROM sales WHERE YEAR(sales_date) = 1995

Question 85

Given the following table definition:

```
EMPLOYEES
---------------------------
EMPID        INTEGER
NAME         CHAR(20)
DEPT         CHAR(10)
SALARY       DECIMAL(10,2)
COMMISSION   DECIMAL(8,2)
```

Assuming the DEPT column contains the values 'ADMIN', 'PRODUCTION', and 'SALES', which of the following statements will produce a result data set in which all ADMIN department employees are grouped together, all PRODUCTION department employees are grouped together, and all SALES department employees are grouped together?

○ A.   SELECT name, dept FROM employees ORDER BY dept

○ B.   SELECT name, dept FROM employees GROUP BY dept

○ C.   SELECT name, dept FROM employees GROUP BY ROLLUP (dept)

○ D.   SELECT name, dept FROM employees GROUP BY CUBE (dept)

Question 86

The following SQL statement:

```
DELETE FROM tab1 WHERE CURRENT OF csr1 WITH RR
```

Is used to perform which type of delete operation?

○ A. Positioned

○ B. Searched

○ C. Embedded

○ D. Dynamic

Question 87

Given the following data:

```
TAB1

C1   C2
--   --
200  abc
250  abc
150  def
300  ghi
175  def
```

If the following query is executed:

```
WITH subset (col1, col2) AS
    (SELECT c1, c2 FROM tab1 WHERE c1 > 150)
SELECT col2, SUM(col1) AS col1_sum
  FROM subset
  GROUP BY col2
  ORDER BY col2
```

Which of the following result data sets will be produced?

○ A.
```
COL2      COL1_SUM
----      --------
abc            200
abc            250
def            175
ghi            300

4 record(s) selected.
```

○ B.
```
COL2      COL1_SUM
----      --------
abc            450
def            175
ghi            300

3 record(s) selected.
```

○ C.
```
COL2      COL1_SUM
----      --------
abc            450
def            325
ghi            300

3 record(s) selected.
```

○ D.
```
COL2  COL1_SUM
----      --------
abc            450
abc            450
def            175
def            175
ghi            300

5 record(s) selected.
```

Question 88

Given the following table definitions:

```
TABLE1
---------------------
ID          INT
NAME        CHAR(30)
PERSON      INT
CITIES      INT


TABLE2
---------------------
ID          INT
LASTNAME    CHAR(30)
```

Which of the following statements will remove all rows in table TABLE1 that have matching PERSONs in table TABLE2?

○ A. DELETE FROM table1 WHERE id IN (SELECT id FROM table2)

○ B. DELETE FROM table1 WHERE id IN (SELECT person FROM table2)

○ C. DELETE FROM table1 WHERE person IN (SELECT id FROM table2)

○ D. DELETE FROM table1 WHERE person IN (SELECT person FROM table2)

Question 89

Given the following two tables:

NAMES

NAME	NUMBER
Wayne Gretzky	99
Jaromir Jagr	68
Bobby Orr	4
Bobby Hull	23
Brett Hull	16
Mario Lemieux	66
Mark Messier	11

POINTS

NAME	POINTS
Wayne Gretzky	244
Jaromir Jagr	168
Bobby Orr	129
Brett Hull	121
Mario Lemieux	189
Joe Sakic	94

Which of the following statements will display the player name, number, and points for all players that have scored points?

- ○ A. SELECT p.name, n.number, p.points FROM names n INNER JOIN points p ON n.name = p.name

- ○ B. SELECT p.name, n.number, p.points FROM names n LEFT OUTER JOIN points p ON n.name = p.name

- ○ C. SELECT p.name, n.number, p.points FROM names n RIGHT OUTER JOIN points p ON n.name = p.name

- ○ D. SELECT p.name, n.number, p.points FROM names n FULL OUTER JOIN points p ON n.name = p.name

Question 90

Given the following table definitions:

EMPLOYEES

EMPID	INTEGER	
NAME	CHAR(20)	
DEPTID		CHAR(3)
SALARY	DECIMAL(10,2)	
COMMISSION	DECIMAL(8,2)	

DEPARTMENTS

DEPTNO	INTEGER
DEPTNAME	CHAR(20)

Question 90 *continued*

Which of the following statements will produce a result data set that satisfies all of these conditions:

> Displays the total number of employees in each department

> Displays the corresponding department name for each department ID

> Sorted by department employee count, from greatest to least

- ○ A. SELECT *, COUNT(empno) FROM departments, employees
  WHERE deptid = deptno GROUP BY deptname ORDER BY 2 DESC
- ○ B. SELECT deptname, COUNT(empno) FROM departments, employees
  WHERE deptid = deptno GROUP BY deptname ORDER BY 2 DESC
- ○ C. SELECT deptname, COUNT(empno) FROM departments, employees
  WHERE deptid = deptno GROUP BY deptname ORDER BY 2 ASC
- ○ D. SELECT deptname, COUNT(*) FROM departments, employees
  WHERE deptid = deptno GROUP BY deptname ORDER BY 2

Question 91

Given the following table:

```
CURRENT_EMPLOYEES

-----------------------------
EMPID       INTEGER NOT NULL
NAME        CHAR(20)
SALARY      DECIMAL(10,2)


PAST_EMPLOYEES

-----------------------------
EMPID       INTEGER NOT NULL
NAME        CHAR(20)
SALARY      DECIMAL(10,2)
```

Assuming both tables contain data, which of the following statements will NOT successfully add data to table CURRENT_EMPLOYEES?

- ○ A. INSERT INTO current_employees (empid) VALUES (10)
- ○ B. INSERT INTO current_employees VALUES (10, 'JAGGER', 85000.00)
- ○ C. INSERT INTO current_employees SELECT empid, name, salary
  FROM past_employees WHERE empid = 20
- ○ D. INSERT INTO current_employees (name, salary) VALUES
  (SELECT name, salary FROM past_employees WHERE empid = 20)

Question 92

Given the following table:

```
STOCK
-------------------
CATEGORY      CHAR(1)
PARTNO        CHAR(12)
DESCRIPTION   VARCHAR(40)
QUANTITY      INTEGER
PRICE         DEC(7,2)
```

If items are indicated to be out of stock by setting DESCRIPTION to NULL and QUANTITY and PRICE to zero, which of the following statements updates the STOCK table to indicate that all items except those with CATEGORY of 'S' are temporarily out of stock?

- A. UPDATE stock SET description = 'NULL', quantity = 0, price = 0
     WHERE category 'S'
- B. UPDATE stock SET description = NULL, SET quantity = 0, SET price = 0
     WHERE category 'S'
- C. UPDATE stock SET (description, quantity, price) = ('null', 0, 0)
     WHERE category 'S'
- D. UPDATE stock SET (description, quantity, price) = (NULL, 0, 0)
     WHERE category 'S'

Question 93

Given the following SQL statements:

```
CREATE TABLE tab1 (col1  INTEGER)
INSERT INTO tab1 VALUES (NULL)
INSERT INTO tab1 VALUES (1)

CREATE TABLE tab2 (col2 INTEGER)
INSERT INTO tab2 VALUES (NULL)
INSERT INTO tab2 VALUES (1)
INSERT INTO tab2 VALUES (2)
```

What will be the result when the following statement is executed?

```
SELECT * FROM tab1 WHERE col1 IN (SELECT col2 FROM tab2)
```

- A. COL1

     1
     1 record(s) selected.

- B. COL1

     NULL
     1
     2 record(s) selected.

- C. COL1

     -
     1
     2 record(s) selected.

- D. COL1

     -
     1 record(s) selected.

Question 94

Given the following table definition:

```
SALES
----------------------------------------
INVOICE_NO        CHAR(20) NOT NULL
SALES_DATE        DATE
SALES_PERSON      CHAR(20)
REGION            CHAR(20)
SALES             INTEGER
```

If the following SELECT statement is executed, which of the following describes the order of the rows in the result data set produced?

```
SELECT * FROM sales
```

○ A. The rows are sorted by INVOICE_NO in ascending order.

○ B. The rows are sorted by INVOICE_NO in descending order.

○ C. The rows are ordered based on when they were inserted into the table.

○ D. The rows are not sorted in any particular order.

Question 95

Given the following tables:

```
YEAR_2007
EMPID NAME
----- ------------------
1     Jagger, Mick
2     Richards, Keith
3     Wood, Ronnie
4     Watts, Charlie
5     Jones, Darryl
6     Leavell, Chuck


YEAR_1962
EMPID NAME
----- ------------------
1     Jagger, Mick
2     Richards, Keith
3     Jones, Brian
4     Wyman, Bill
5     Chapman, Tony
6     Stewart, Ian
```

If the following SQL statement is executed, how many rows will be returned?

```
SELECT name FROM year_2006
UNION
SELECT name FROM year_1962
```

○ A. 0

○ B. 6

○ C. 10

○ D. 12

Question 96

Which of the following best describes a unit of work?

○ A. It is a recoverable sequence of operations whose point of consistency is established when a connection to a database has been established or when a mechanism known as a savepoint is created.

○ B. It is a recoverable sequence of operations whose current point of consistency can be determined by querying the system catalog tables.

○ C. It is a recoverable sequence of operations whose point of consistency is established when an executable SQL statement is processed after a connection to a database has been established or a previous transaction has been terminated.

○ D. It is a recoverable sequence of operations whose point of consistency is only established if a mechanism known as a savepoint is created.

Question 97

Given the following set of statements:

```
CREATE TABLE tab1 (col1 INTEGER, col2 CHAR(20));
COMMIT;
INSERT INTO tab1 VALUES (123, 'Red');
INSERT INTO tab1 VALUES (456, 'Yellow');
SAVEPOINT s1 ON ROLLBACK RETAIN CURSORS;
DELETE FROM tab1 WHERE col1 = 123;
INSERT INTO tab1 VALUES (789, 'Blue');
ROLLBACK TO SAVEPOINT s1;
INSERT INTO tab1 VALUES (789, 'Green');
UPDATE tab1 SET col2 = NULL WHERE col1 = 789;
COMMIT;
```

Which of the following records would be returned by the following statement?

```
SELECT * FROM tab1
```

○ A.
```
COL1      COL2
----      ----
123       Red
456       Yellow
2 record(s) selected.
```

○ B.
```
COL1      COL2
----      ----
456       Yellow
1 record(s) selected.
```

○ C.
```
COL1      COL2
----      ----
123       Red
456       Yellow
789       -
3 record(s) selected.
```

○ D.
```
COL1      COL2
----      ----
123       Red
456       Yellow
789       Green
3 record(s) selected.
```

Question 98

Given the following table:

```
TAB1

COL1          COL2
-----         -----
A             10
B             20
C             30
D             40
E             50
```

And the following SQL statements:

```
DECLARE c1 CURSOR WITH HOLD FOR
     SELECT * FROM tab1 ORDER BY col_1;
OPEN c1;
FETCH c1;
FETCH c1;
FETCH c1;
COMMIT;
FETCH c1;
CLOSE c1;
FETCH c1;
```

Which of the following is the last value obtained for COL_2?

○ A. 20

○ B. 30

○ C. 40

○ D. 50

Question 99

A stored procedure has been created with the following statement:

```
CREATE PROCEDURE proc1 (IN var1 VARCHAR(10), OUT rc INTEGER)
SPECIFIC myproc LANGUAGE SQL …
```

What is the correct way to invoke this procedure from the command line processor (CLP)?

○ A. CALL proc1 ('SALES', ?)

○ B. CALL myproc ('SALES', ?)

○ C. CALL proc1 (SALES, ?)

○ D. RUN proc1 (SALES, ?)

Question 100

Given the following table:

TEMP_DATA

```
TEMP   DATE
-----  -----
45    12/25/2006
51    12/26/2006
67    12/27/2006
72    12/28/2006
34    12/29/2006
42    12/30/2006
```

And the following SQL statement:

```
CREATE FUNCTION degf_to_c (temp INTEGER)
    RETURNS INTEGER
    LANGUAGE SQL
    CONTAINS SQL
    NO EXTERNAL ACTION
    DETERMINISTIC
    BEGIN ATOMIC
        DECLARE newtemp INTEGER;
        SET newtemp = temp - 32;
        SET newtemp = newtemp * 5;
        RETURN newtemp / 9;
    END
```

Which two of the following SQL statements illustrate the proper way to invoke the scalar function DEGF_TO_C?

❑ A. VALUES degf_to_c(32)

❑ B. SELECT date, degf_to_c(temp) AS temp_c FROM temp_data

❑ C. CALL degf_to_c(32)

❑ D. SELECT * FROM TABLE(degf_to_c(temp)) AS temp_c

Question 101

Given the following CREATE TABLE statement:

```
CREATE TABLE customer(custid INTEGER, info XML)
```

And the following INSERT statements:

```
INSERT INTO customer VALUES (1000,
'<customerinfo xmlns="http://custrecord.dat" custid="1000">
  <name>John Doe</name>
  <addr country="United States">
    <street>25 East Creek Drive</street>
    <city>Raleigh</city>
    <state-prov>North Carolina</state-prov>
    <zip-pcode>27603</zip-pcode>
  </addr>
  <phone type="work">919-555-1212</phone>
  <email>john.doe@abc.com</email>
</customerinfo>');

INSERT INTO customer VALUES (1000,
'<customerinfo xmlns="http://custrecord.dat" custid="1001">
  <name>Paul Smith</name>
  <addr country="Canada">
    <street>412 Stewart Drive</street>
    <city>Toronto</city>
    <state-prov>Ontario</state-prov>
    <zip-pcode>M8X-3T6</zip-pcode>
  </addr>
  <phone type="work">919-555-4444</phone>
  <email>psmith@xyz.com</email>
</customerinfo>');
```

What is the result of the following XQuery expression?

```
XQUERY declare default element namespace
"http://custrecord.dat"; for $info in
db2-fn:xmlcolumn('CUSTOMER.INFO')/customerinfo where
$info/addr/state-prov="Ontario" return $info/name/text();
```

◯ A. Paul Smith

◯ B. <name xmlns="http://custrecord.dat">Paul Smith</name>

◯ C. <customerinfo xmlns="http://custrecord.dat" custid="1001"><name xmlns="http://custrecord.dat">Paul Smith</name>

◯ D. <customerinfo xmlns="http://custrecord.dat" custid="1001">Paul Smith</customerinfo>

Working with DB2 Tables, Views, and Indexes

Question 102

Which of the following is a valid DB2 data type?

○ A. NUMBER

○ B. INTERVAL

○ C. BYTE

○ D. NUM

Question 103

Which of the following DB2 data types does NOT have a fixed length?

○ A. INT

○ B. CHAR

○ C. XML

○ D. DOUBLE

Question 104

Which of the following is the best statement to use to create a user-defined data type that can be used to store currency values?

○ A. CREATE DISTINCT TYPE currency AS NUMERIC(7,2)

○ B. CREATE DISTINCT TYPE currency AS SMALLINT

○ C. CREATE DISTINCT TYPE currency AS BIGINT

○ D. CREATE DISTINCT TYPE currency AS DOUBLE

Question 105

Which of the following DB2 data types can be used to store 1000 MB of single-byte character data?

○ A. BLOB

○ B. CLOB

○ C. DBCLOB

○ D. GRAPHIC

Question 106

Which of the following DB2 data types CANNOT be used to create an identity column?

○ A. SMALLINT

○ B. INTEGER

○ C. NUMERIC

○ D. DOUBLE

Question 107

Given the requirements to store employee names, employee numbers, and when employees were hired, which of the following built-in data types CANNOT be used to store the day an employee was hired?

○ A. Character Large Object

○ B. Time

○ C. Varying-Length Character String

○ D. Timestamp

Question 108

Given the requirements to store customer names, billing addresses, and telephone numbers, which of the following would be the best way to define the telephone number column for a table if all customers were located in the same country?

○ A. PHONE   CHAR(15)

○ B. PHONE   VARCHAR(15)

○ C. PHONE   LONG VARCHAR

○ D. PHONE   CLOB(1K)

Question 109

Which of the following strings can NOT be inserted into an XML column using XMLPARSE()?

○ A. "<employee />"

○ B. "<name>John Doe</name>"

○ C. "<?xml version='1.0' encoding='UTF-8' ?>"

○ D. "<p></p>"

Question 110

Which two of the following are optional and do not have to be specified when creating a table?

❏   A.   Table name

❏   B.   Column name

❏   C.   Default constraint

❏   D.   Column data type

❏   E.   NOT NULL constraint

Question 111

Which of the following is a NOT a valid reason for defining a view on a table?

○   A.   Restrict users' access to a subset of table data

○   B.   Ensure that rows inserted remain within the scope of a definition

○   C.   Produce an action as a result of a change to a table

○   D.   Provide users with an alternate view of table data

Question 112

Given the following CREATE TABLE statement:

```
CREATE TABLE table2 LIKE table1
```

Which two of the following will NOT occur when the statement is executed?

❏   A.   TABLE2 will have the same column names and column data types as TABLE1

❏   B.   TABLE2 will have the same column defaults as TABLE1

❏   C.   TABLE2 will have the same nullability characteristics as TABLE1

❏   D.   TABLE2 will have the same indexes as TABLE1.

❏   E.   TABLE2 will have the same referential constraints as TABLE1

Question 113

If the following SQL statements are executed:

```
CREATE TABLE tab1 (id SMALLINT NOT NULL PRIMARY KEY,
                   name  VARCHAR(25));

CREATE TABLE tab2 (empid   SMALLINT,
                   weekno  SMALLINT,
                   payamt  DECIMAL(6,2),
        CONSTRAINT const1 FOREIGN KEY (empid)
            REFERENCES taba(id) ON UPDATE NO ACTION);
```

Which of the following statements is true?

- ○ A. Only values that exist in the ID column of table TAB1 are allowed to be inserted in the EMPID column of table TAB2
- ○ B. The updating of values in the ID column of table TAB1 is not allowed
- ○ C. Only values that do not already exist in the ID column of table TAB1 are allowed to be inserted in the EMPID column of table TAB2
- ○ D. When values that exist in the ID column of table TAB1 are updated, corresponding values in the EMPID column of table TAB2 are updated as well

Question 114

Which of the following CANNOT be used to restrict specific values from being inserted into a column in a particular table?

- ○ A. Index
- ○ B. Check constraint
- ○ C. Referential constraint
- ○ D. Default constraint

Question 115

If table TAB1 is created using the following statement:

```
CREATE TABLE tab1 (col1  INTEGER NOT NULL,
                   col2  CHAR(5),
        CONSTRAINT cst1 CHECK (col1 in (1, 2, 3)))
```

Which of the following statements will successfully insert a record into table TAB1?

- ○ A. INSERT INTO tab1 VALUES (0, 'abc')
- ○ B. INSERT INTO tab1 VALUES (NULL, 'abc')
- ○ C. INSERT INTO tab1 VALUES (ABS(2), 'abc')
- ○ D. INSERT INTO tab1 VALUES (DEFAULT, 'abc')

Question 116

Given the following table definition:

```
EMPLOYEES
-------------------------
EMPID .      INTEGER
NAME         CHAR(20)
SALARY       DECIMAL(10,2)
```

If the following SQL statement is executed:

```
CREATE UNIQUE INDEX empid_ui ON employees (empid)
```

Which two of the following statements are true?

❑ A. Multiple null values are allowed in the EMPID column of the EMPLOYEES table.

❑ B. No null values are allowed in the EMPID column of the EMPLOYEES table.

❑ C. One (and only one) null value is allowed in the EMPID column of the EMPLOYEES table.

❑ D. No other unique indexes can be created on the EMPLOYEES table.

❑ E. Every value found in the EMPID column of the EMPLOYEES table will be different.

Question 117

If the following SQL statements are executed:

```
CREATE TABLE make (makeid SMALLINT NOT NULL PRIMARY KEY,
                   make   VARCHAR(25));

CREATE TABLE model (modelid  SMALLINT,
                    model    VARCHAR(25),
                    makeid   SMALLINT,
         CONSTRAINT const1 FOREIGN KEY (makeid)
             REFERENCES make(makeid) ON DELETE RESTRICT);
```

And each table created is populated as follows:

```
MAKE

MAKEID   MAKE
------   ------
1        Ford
2        Chevrolet
3        Toyota

MODEL

MODELID   MODEL     MAKEID
-------   -------   ------
1         Mustang   1
2         Escort    1
3         Malibu    2
4         Camry     3
```

Question 117 *continued*

If the following SQL statement is executed:

    DELETE FROM make WHERE makeid = 1

What is the total number of rows that will be deleted?

○ A. 0
○ B. 1
○ C. 2
○ D. 3

Question 118

Given the statement:

    CREATE TABLE tablea (col1 INTEGER NOT NULL,
        CONSTRAINT const1 CHECK (col1 in (100, 200, 300))

Which of the following can be inserted into TABLEA?

○ A. 0
○ B. NULL
○ C. 100
○ D. '100'

Question 119

Which of the following deletion rules on CREATE TABLE will allow parent table rows to be deleted if a dependent row exists?

○ A. ON DELETE RESTRICT

○ B. ON DELETE NO ACTION

○ C. ON DELETE SET NO VALUE

○ D. ON DELETE CASCADE

Question 120

Which of the following is NOT a characteristic of a unique index?

○ A. Each column in a base table can only participate in one unique index, regardless of how the columns are grouped (the same column cannot be used in multiple unique indexes)

○ B. In order for an index to be used to support a unique constraint, it must have been defined with the UNIQUE attribute

○ C. A unique index cannot be created for a populated table if the key column specified contains more than one NULL value

○ D. A unique index can only be created for a non-nullable column

Question 121

If the following statement is executed:

```
CREATE TABLE employee
    (empid      INT NOT NULL GENERATED BY DEFAULT
         AS IDENTITY (START WITH 1, INCREMENT BY 5),
    name       VARCHAR(20),
    dept       INT CHECK (dept BETWEEN 1 AND 20),
    hiredate   DATE WITH DEFAULT CURRENT DATE,
    salary     DECIMAL(7,2),
    PRIMARY KEY(empid),
     CONSTRAINT cst1 CHECK (YEAR(hiredate) > 2006 OR
        Salary > 60500));
```

Which of the following INSERT statements will fail?

○ A. INSERT INTO employee VALUES (15, 'Smith', 5, '01/22/2004', 92500.00)

○ B. INSERT INTO employee VALUES (DEFAULT, 'Smith', 2, '10/07/2002', 80250.00)

○ C. INSERT INTO employee VALUES (20, 'Smith', 5, NULL, 65000.00)

○ D. INSERT INTO employee VALUES (DEFAULT, 'Smith', 10, '11/18/2004', 60250.00)

Question 122

Which of the following is used to indicate a column will not accept NULL values and can be referenced in another table's foreign key specification?

○ A. Check constraint

○ B. Unique constraint

○ C. Default constraint

○ D. Informational constraint

Question 123

Given the following scenario:

Table TABLE1 needs to hold specific numeric values up to 9999999.999 in column COL1. Once TABLE1 is populated, arithmetic operations will be performed on data stored in column COL1.

Which of the following would be the most appropriate DB2 data type to use for column COL1?

○ A. INTEGER

○ B. REAL

○ C. NUMERIC(7, 3)

○ D. DECIMAL(10, 3)

Question 124

Given the following statement:

```
CREATE TABLE  tab1
       (col1   SMALLINT NOT NULL PRIMARY KEY,
        col2   VARCHAR(200) NOT NULL WITH DEFAULT NONE,
        col3   DECIMAL(5,2) CHECK (col3 >= 100.00),
        col4   DATE NOT NULL WITH DEFAULT)
```

Which of the following definitions will cause the CREATE TABLE statement to fail?

○ A. COL1

○ B. COL2

○ C. COL3

○ D. COL4

Question 125

Which type of key is defined on the child table to implement a referential constraint?

○ A. Unique key

○ B. Primary key

○ C. Foreign key

○ D. Composite key

Question 126

Which of the following is NOT true about schemas?

○ A. If a schema name is not specified, either by qualifying a database object name or by executing the SET CURRENT SCHEMA statement, the authorization ID of the current session user is used as the schema name by default

○ B. The value assigned to the CURRENT SCHEMA special register is persistent across database restarts

○ C. A schema enables the creation of multiple objects in a database without encountering namespace collisions

○ D. When most database objects are created, they are either implicitly or explicitly assigned to a schema

Question 127

If the following statement is executed:

```
CREATE TABLE tab1 (col1 INTEGER NOT NULL,
                   col2 INTEGER,
         CONSTRAINT const1 FOREIGN KEY (col2)
             REFERENCES tab1(col1));
```

How many unique indexes are defined for table TAB1?

○ A. 0

○ B. 1

○ C. 2

○ D. 3

Question 128

When does a view get populated?

○ A. When it is created

○ B. When it is referenced in an INSERT statement

○ C. The first time any executable SQL statement references it

○ D. Any time an executable SQL statement references it

Question 129

Given the following statements:

```
CREATE TABLE table1 (col1 INTEGER, col2 CHAR(3));
CREATE VIEW view1 AS
    SELECT col1, col2 FROM table1
    WHERE col1 < 100
    WITH LOCAL CHECK OPTION;
```

Which of the following INSERT statements will execute successfully?

○ A. INSERT INTO view1 VALUES (50, abc)

○ B. INSERT INTO view1 VALUES(100, abc)

○ C. INSERT INTO view1 VALUES(50, 'abc')

○ D. INSERT INTO view1 VALUES(100, 'abc')

Question 130

Given the following tables:

TABLEA

EMPID NAME
————— ———————
1   USER1
2   USER2

TABLEB

EMPID WEEKNO PAYAMT
————— ——————— ———————
1   1   1000.00
1   2   1000.00
2   1   2000.00

and the fact that TABLEB was defined as follows:

```
CREATE TABLE tableb (empid  SMALLINT,
                     weekno SMALLINT,
                     payamt DECIMAL(6,2),
    CONSTRAINT const1 FOREIGN KEY (empid)
    REFERENCES tablea(empid)
    ON DELETE NO ACTION)
```

If the following command is issued:

```
DELETE FROM tablea WHERE empid=2
```

How many rows will be deleted from TABLEA and TABLEB?

○ A. TABLEA - 0, TABLEB - 0

○ B. TABLEA - 0, TABLEB - 1

○ C. TABLEA - 1, TABLEB - 0

○ D. TABLEA - 1, TABLEB - 1

Question 131

Which of the following actions will NOT cause a trigger to be fired?

○ A. INSERT

○ B. DELETE

○ C. ALTER

○ D. UPDATE

Question 132

The following triggers were defined for a table named SALES in the order shown:

```
CREATE TRIGGER trigger_a
NO CASCADE BEFORE INSERT ON sales
REFERENCING NEW AS new
FOR EACH ROW
SET new.commission = sale_amt * .05
   WHERE invoice = n.invoice;

CREATE TRIGGER trigger_b
AFTER INSERT ON sales
REFERENCING NEW AS new
FOR EACH ROW
UPDATE sales SET bill_date = CURRENT DATE + 30 DAYS
   WHERE invoice = n.invoice;

CREATE TRIGGER trigger_c
NO CASCADE BEFORE DELETE ON sales
FOR EACH ROW
SIGNAL SQLSTATE '75005'
   SET MESSAGE_TEXT = 'Deletes not allowed!';
```

Which of the following statements is NOT true?

○ A. Once a row has been added to the SALES table, it cannot be removed

○ B. Whenever a row is inserted into the SALES table, the value in the BILL_DATE column is automatically set to 30 days from today

○ C. Each time a row is inserted into the SALES table, trigger TRIGGER_A is fired first, followed by trigger TRIGGER_B

○ D. Whenever a row in the SALES table is updated, all three triggers are fired but nothing happens because none of the triggers have been coded to trap update operations

Question 133

Which of the following is NOT a difference between a unique index and a primary key?

○ A. A primary key is a special form of a unique constraint; both use a unique index.

○ B. Unique indexes can be defined over one or more columns; primary keys can only be defined on a single column.

○ C. A table can have many unique indexes but only one primary key.

○ D. Unique indexes can be defined over one or more columns that allow null values; primary keys cannot contain null values.

Question 134

Which of the following CREATE TABLE statements will NOT be successful?

○ A. CREATE TABLE t1 (c1 XML NOT NULL UNIQUE, c2 INT)

○ B. CREATE TABLE t1 (c1 XML NOT NULL, c2 CHAR(20))

○ C. CREATE TABLE t1 (c1 XML CHECK (c1 IS VALIDATED), c2 INT)

○ D. CREATE TABLE t1 (c1 XML, c2 XML)

Question 135

If the following SQL statement is executed:

```
CREATE TABLE sales
     (invoice_no   NOT NULL PRIMARY KEY,
      sales_date   DATE,
      sales_amt    NUMERIC(7,2))
     IN tbsp0, tbsp1, tbsp2, tbsp3
     PARTITION BY RANGE (sales_date NULLS FIRST)
        (STARTING '1/1/2007' ENDING '12/31/2007'
         EVERY 3 MONTHS)
```

Which of the following statements is true?

○ A. Administrative tasks such as backing up, restoring, and reorganizing data stored in the SALES table must be done at the table level; not at the partition level

○ B. Data can be quickly rolled in and out of the SALES table by using the ATTACH PARTITION and DETACH PARTITION clauses of the ALTER TABLE statement

○ C. If an index is created for the SALES table, its data must be stored in table space TBSP0

○ D. When resolving queries against the SALES table, each partition used is scanned asynchronously and the results of each partition scan are merged to produce the result data set returned

Question 136

Which of the following is NOT a characteristic of a declared temporary table?

- ○ A. Declared temporary tables are not persistent and can only be used by the application that creates them
- ○ B. It is possible for many applications to create declared temporary tables that have the same name
- ○ C. Declared temporary tables are created by executing a CREATE TABLE statement with the DECLARED GLOBAL TEMPORARY clause specified
- ○ D. Once the application that created a global temporary table is terminated, any records in the table are deleted and the table is automatically destroyed

Data Concurrency

Question 137

Which of the following isolation levels will lock all rows scanned to build a result data set?

- ○ A. Uncommitted Read
- ○ B. Cursor Stability
- ○ C. Read Stability
- ○ D. Repeatable Read

Question 138

Application A holds an Exclusive lock on table TAB1 and needs to acquire an Exclusive lock on table TAB2. Application B holds an Exclusive lock on table TAB2 and needs to acquire an Exclusive lock on table TAB1. If lock timeout is set to -1 and both applications are using the Read Stability isolation level, which of the following will occur?

- ○ A. Applications A and B will cause a deadlock situation
- ○ B. Application B will read the copy of table TAB1 that was loaded into memory when Application A first read it
- ○ C. Application B will read the data in table TAB1 and see uncommitted changes made by Application A
- ○ D. Application B will be placed in a lock-wait state until Application A releases its lock

Question 139

A transaction using the Read Stability isolation level scans the same table multiple times before it terminates. Which of the following can occur within this transaction's processing?

- ○ A. Uncommitted changes made by other transactions can be seen from one scan to the next.
- ○ B. Rows removed by other transactions that appeared in one scan will no longer appear in subsequent scans.
- ○ C. Rows added by other transactions that did not appear in one scan can be seen in subsequent scans.
- ○ D. Rows that have been updated can be changed by other transactions from one scan to the next.

Question 140

Two applications have created a deadlock cycle in the locking subsystem. If lock timeout is set to 30 and both applications were started at the same time, what action will the deadlock detector take when it "wakes up" and discovers the deadlock?

- ○ A. It will randomly pick an application and rollback its current transaction
- ○ B. It will rollback the current transactions of both applications
- ○ C. It will wait 30 seconds, then rollback the current transactions of both applications if the deadlock has not been resolved
- ○ D. It will go back to sleep for 30 seconds, then if the deadlock still exists, it will randomly pick an application and rollback its current transaction

Question 141

Application A is running under the Repeatable Read isolation level and holds an Update lock on table TAB1. Application B wants to query table TAB1 and cannot wait for Application A to release its lock. Which isolation level should Application B run under to achieve this objective?

- ○ A. Repeatable Read
- ○ B. Read Stability
- ○ C. Cursor Stability
- ○ D. Uncommitted Read

Question 142

Which of the following DB2 UDB isolation levels will only lock rows during read processing if another transaction tries to drop the table the rows are being read from?

- ○ A. Repeatable Read
- ○ B. Read Stability
- ○ C. Cursor Stability
- ○ D. Uncommitted Read

Question 143

Application A holds a lock on a row in table TAB1. If lock timeout is set to 20, what will happen when Application B attempts to acquire a compatible lock on the same row?

- ○ A. Application B will acquire the lock it needs
- ○ B. Application A will be rolled back if it still holds its lock after 20 seconds have elapsed
- ○ C. Application B will be rolled back if Application A still holds its lock after 20 seconds have elapsed
- ○ D. Both applications will be rolled back if Application A still holds its lock after 20 seconds have elapsed

Question 144

To which of the following resources can a lock NOT be applied?

- ○ A. Table spaces
- ○ B. Buffer pools
- ○ C. Tables
- ○ D. Rows

Question 145

Which of the following causes a lock that is being held by an application using the Cursor Stability isolation level to be released?

- ○ A. The cursor is moved to another row
- ○ B. The row the cursor is on is deleted by the application
- ○ C. The row the cursor is on is deleted by another application
- ○ D. The row the cursor is on needs to be updated by another application

Question 146

Which of the following modes, when used with the LOCK TABLE statement, will cause the DB2 Database Manager to acquire a table-level lock that prevents other concurrent transactions from accessing data stored in the table while the owning transaction is active?

○ A. SHARE MODE

○ B. ISOLATED MODE

○ C. EXCLUSIVE MODE

○ D. RESTRICT MODE

Question 147

An application has acquired a Share lock on a row in a table and now wishes to update the row. Which of the following statements is true?

○ A. The application must release the row-level Share lock it holds and acquire an Update lock on the row

○ B. The application must release the row-level Share lock it holds and acquire an Update lock on the table

○ C. The row-level Share lock will automatically be converted to a row-level Update lock

○ D. The row-level Share lock will automatically be escalated to a table-level Update lock

Question 148

Application A wants to read a subset of rows from table TAB1 multiple times. Which of the following isolation levels should Application A use to prevent other users from making modifications and additions to table TAB1 that will affect the subset of rows read?

○ A. Repeatable Read

○ B. Read Stability

○ C. Cursor Stability

○ D. Uncommitted Read

Question 149

Application A issues the following SQL statements within a single transaction using the Uncommitted Read isolation level:

```
SELECT * FROM department WHERE deptno = 'A00';
UPDATE department SET mgrno = '000100' WHERE deptno = 'A00';
```

As long as the transaction is not committed, which of the following statements is FALSE?

○ A. Other applications not running under the Uncommitted Read isolation level are prohibited from reading the updated row

○ B. Application A is allowed to read data stored in another table, even if an Exclusive lock is held on that table

○ C. Other applications running under the Uncommitted Read isolation level are allowed to read the updated row

○ D. Application A is not allowed to insert new rows into the DEPARTMENT table as long as the current transaction remains active

Question 150

A table contains a list of all seats available at a football stadium. A seat consists of a section number, a seat number, and whether or not the seat has been assigned. A ticket agent working at the box office generates a list of all unassigned seats. When the agent refreshes the list, it should only change if another agent assigns one or more unassigned seats. Which of the following is the best isolation level to use for this application?

○ A. Repeatable Read

○ B. Read Stability

○ C. Cursor Stability

○ D. Uncommitted Read

Answers

Planning

Question 1

The correct answer is **B**. DB2 Express Edition (or DB2 Express) is an entry-level data server that is designed to be used on microcomputers that have up to 2 CPUs (a dual-core processor is treated as a single CPU), up to 4 GB of memory, and are running a supported version of Linux, Solaris, or Windows. DB2 Everyplace is a small footprint (approximately 350 KB) relational database and a high performance data synchronization solution that allows enterprise applications and data to be extended to mobile devices like personal digital assistants (PDAs), handheld personal computers (HPCs), and smart phones; DB2 Workgroup Server Edition (WSE) is a multi-user, full-function, client/server database management system designed to be used on microcomputers that have up to 4 CPUs, up to 16 GB of memory, and are running any of the following operating systems: AIX, HP-UX, Solaris, Linux, and Windows; and DB2 Enterprise Server Edition (ESE) is a multi-user, full-function, Web-enabled client/server database management system that is designed to be used on any size server (from one to hundreds of CPUs) that is running any of the following operating systems: AIX, HP-UX, Solaris, Linux, and Windows.

Question 2

The correct answer is A. DB2 Personal Edition can be used as a remote client to other DB2 servers; however, it can only accept requests from local applications.

Question 3

The correct answer is **C**. DB2 Connect Enterprise Edition is an add-on product for DB2 that allows data to be moved between Linux, UNIX, and Windows DB2 servers and iSeries- and zSeries-based DB2 servers. Because some editions of DB2 must be installed before DB2 Connect can be used, and because DB2 Connect is needed in this case to provide communications between the Solaris server and the z/OS client, answers A and B are both wrong. The question states "at a minimum, which … products must be installed …" and since DB2 Enterprise Server Edition comes packaged with a limited version of DB2 Connect, DB2 Connect does not need to be installed with DB2 Enterprise Server Edition, so answer D is also incorrect.

Question 4

The correct answer is **D**. DB2 Enterprise Server Edition is designed to be used on a server that is running any of the following operating systems: AIX, HP-UX, Solaris, Linux, and Windows. DB2 Express-C is designed to be used on microcomputers that are running a supported version of Linux or Windows; DB2 Express is designed to be used on microcomputers that are running a supported version of Linux, Solaris, or Windows; and DB2 Personal Edition can be deployed on any Personal Computer (PC) that is running Linux or Windows.

Question 5

The correct answer is **C**. DB2 Universal Developer's Edition contains both the tools to build applications for supported Linux, UNIX, and Windows servers, and a DRDA Application Requestor. DB2 Personal Developer's Edition does not provide a DRDA Application Requestor.

Question 6

The correct answer is **B**. DB2 for i5/OS is an advanced, 64-bit relational database management system that leverages the On-Demand capabilities of System i to quickly respond to changing workloads. DB2 for z/OS is a multi-user, full-function, database management system that has been designed specifically for z/OS, IBM's flagship mainframe operating system. DB2 Data Warehouse Edition (DWE) is comprised of, among other things, DB2 Enterprise Server Edition and the DB2 Data Partitioning Feature – DB2 Enterprise Server Edition (ESE) is designed to be used on a server that is running any of the following operating systems: AIX, HP-UX, Solaris, Linux, and Windows.

Question 7

The correct answer is **A**. The Design Advisor is a special tool that is designed to capture specific information about typical workloads (queries or sets of SQL operations) performed against your database and recommend changes based upon the information provided. When given a set of SQL statements in a workload, the Design Advisor will make recommendations for new indexes, new materialized query tables (MQTs), conversions of base tables to multidimensional clustering (MDC) tables, redistribution of table data, and deletion of indexes and MQTs that are not being used by the workload specified. Visual Explain is used to present a graphical representation of a data access plan but it does not recommend design changes; the Replication Center allows users to administer data replication between a DB2 database and any other relational database; and the Configuration Assistant allows users to configure clients so they can access databases stored on remote DB2 servers.

Question 8

The correct answer is D. One of the primary uses of the Configuration Assistant is to catalog remote server databases on client workstations.

Question 9

The correct answer is **D**. The Developer Workbench is an interactive GUI application that can be used to create, build, debug, and deploy stored procedures, structured data types, and user-defined functions.

Question 10

The correct answer is **C**. The Configuration Assistant is an interactive GUI application that allows users to configure clients so they can access databases stored on remote DB2 servers. From the Configuration Assistant, users can: catalog new databases, work with or uncatalog existing databases, bind applications, *set DB2 environment/registry variables*, configure the DB2 Database Manager instance, configure ODBC/CLI parameters, import and export configuration information, change passwords, and test database connections. The Task Center allows users to schedule tasks, run tasks, and send notifications about completed tasks to other users; Visual Explain provides database administrators and application developers with the ability to view a graphical representation of the access plan that has been chosen by the DB2 Optimizer for a particular SQL statement; and the Satellite Administration Center is a GUI application that allows users to set up and administer a group of DB2 servers that perform the same business function.

Question 11

The correct answer is **D**. If you are running DB2 for i5/OS, the SQL Performance Monitor is a valuable tool that can be used to keep track of the resources SQL statements use. The Health Monitor is a server-side tool that constantly monitors the health of a DB2 Database Manager instance without a need for user interaction; SQL Assist is an interactive GUI application that allows users to visually construct complex SELECT, INSERT, UPDATE, and DELETE SQL statements and examine the results of their execution; and the Task Center is allows users to schedule tasks, run tasks, and send notifications about completed tasks to other users.

Question 12

The correct answers are **A** and **C**. The Control Center presents a clear, concise view of an entire system, and it serves as the central point for managing systems and performing common administration tasks. The Command Line Processor (CLP) is a text-oriented application that allows users to issue DB2 commands, system commands, and SQL statements, as well as view the results of the statements/commands executed. Because most of the tasks that can be performed with the Control Center have corresponding DB2 commands, both the Control Center and the Command Line Processor can be used to perform administrative tasks against a database and its objects.

Question 13

The correct answer is **B**. The Developer Workbench is a comprehensive development environment that can be used to create, edit, debug, deploy, and test DB2 stored procedures and user-defined functions. The Developer Workbench can also be used to develop SQLJ applications, and to create, edit, and run SQL statements and XML queries.

Question 14

The correct answer is **D**. The Task Center allows users to schedule tasks, run tasks, and send notifications about completed tasks to other users. Users can create a task within the Task Center, generate a task by saving the results from a DB2 dialog or wizard, create a script within another tool and save it to the Task Center, or import an existing script. Thus, it is possible to create a script that calls the REORG command and have the Task Center to execute that script on a routine basis.

Question 15

The correct answer is **A**. The Journal is an interactive GUI application that tracks historical information about tasks, database actions and operations, Control Center actions, messages, and alerts. The License Center allows users to view information about the license associated with each DB2 9 product installed on a particular system; Visual Explain provides database administrators and application developers with the ability to view a graphical representation of the access plan that has been chosen by the DB2 Optimizer for a particular SQL statement; and the Health Center is used to select the instance and database objects that you want to monitor, customize the threshold settings of any health indicator, and specify where notifications are to be sent and what actions are to be taken if an alert is issued.

Question 16

The correct answer is **D**. Data Warehousing involves storing and managing large volumes of data (often historical in nature) that is used primarily for analysis. Workloads in a data warehouse vary; they can consist of bulk load operations, short running queries, long running complex queries, random queries, occasional updates to data, and the execution of online utilities. OLTP workloads, on the other hand, tend to be a mix of real-time DML operations (inserts, updates, and deletes) and often require sub-second end-user response time.

Question 17

The correct answer is **C**. OLTP systems are designed to support day-to-day, mission-critical business activities such as order entry, stock trading, inventory management, and banking. This typically involves hundreds to thousands of users issuing millions of transactions per day against databases that vary in size. Response time requirements tend to be sub-second and workloads tend to be a mix of real-time DML operations (inserts, updates, and deletes). Workloads in a data warehouse can consist of bulk load operations, short running queries, long running complex queries, random queries, occasional updates to data, and the execution of online utilities. Thus, data warehouses are optimized for queries.

Question 18

The correct answer is **A**. With DB2 9, XML documents are stored in tables that contain one or more columns that are based on the new XML data type. Along with the XML data type, support for XML data includes new storage techniques for efficient management of the hierarchical entities that are inherent in XML documents, new indexing technology to speed up retrieval of subsets of XML documents (entire documents do not have to be read in order to retrieve specific information), new capabilities for validating XML data and managing changing XML schemas, new query language support (including native support for XQuery as well as new SQL/XML enhancements), new query optimization techniques, integration with popular application programming interfaces (APIs), and extensions to popular database utilities.

Question 19

The correct answer is **C**. The DB2 XML Extender can be used to decompose (shred) XML elements from a document and store them in columns and tables; it can also compose (create) new XML documents from existing character and numerical data or previously shredded XML documents. (If the DB2 XML extender is not used, XML documents are stored hierarchically in columns with the XML data type.) The DB2 Audio, Video, and Image (AVI) Extender contains a set of data types and functions that can be used to store and manipulate nontraditional data such as audio clips, movies, and pictures in a DB2 UDB database; the DB2 Text Extender contains a set of data types and functions that can be used to store complex text documents in a DB2 UDB database and to extract key information from such documents; and the DB2 Spatial Extender contains a set of user-defined data types that can be used to describe spatial data (for example, points, lines, and polygons) and a set of user-defined functions that can be used to query spatial objects (for example, to find area, endpoints, and intersects).

Question 20

The correct answer is **C**. The DB2 Spatial Extender contains a set of user-defined data types that can be used to describe spatial data (for example, points, lines, and polygons) and a set of user-defined functions that can be used to query spatial objects (for example, to find area, endpoints, and intersects). With this capability, you can generate, analyze, and exploit spatial information about geographic features, such as the locations of office buildings or the size of a flood zone and present it in a three-dimensional format. The DB2 Geodetic Extender contains a set of user-defined data types and functions that treat the Earth like a globe rather than a flat map (it can construct a virtual globe at any scale); a round earth is paramount for calculations and visualizations for users in disciplines like military command/control and asset management, meteorology and oceanography (scientific, government, and commercial), and satellite imagery. The DB2 Geodetic Extender has the capability to manage geospatial information referenced by latitude-longitude coordinates and support global spatial queries without the limitations inherent in map projections. To handle objects defined on the earth's surface with precision, the DB2 Geodetic Extender uses a latitude-longitude coordinate system on an ellipsoidal earth model—or geodetic datum—rather than a planar, x- and y-coordinate system.

Question 21

The correct answer is **C**. Extensible Markup Language (XML) is a simple, very flexible text format that provides a neutral, flexible way to exchange data between different devices, systems, and applications because data is maintained in a self-describing format. XML documents are comprised of a hierarchical set of entities and many XML documents contain heavily nested parent/child relationships and/or irregular structures. Relational data, on the other hand, is a collection of numeric values, character strings, and date/time/timestamp values that must be stored in a tabular format. (XML documents can be "shredded" or decomposed and their contents stored across multiple columns in one or more tables and this approach is ideal if the XML data being stored is tabular in nature. However, the cost associated with decomposing XML data often depends on the structure of the underlying XML document and may require a large number of tables, some of which may need to have values generated for foreign keys in order to capture the relationships and ordering that is inherent in the original documents.)

Security

Question 22

The correct answer is **D**. In DB2 9, the following authentication types are available: SERVER, SERVER_ENCRYPT, CLIENT, KERBEROS, KRB_SERVER_ENCRYPT, DATA_ENCRYPT, DATA_ENCRYPT_CMP, GSSPLUGIN, and GSS_SERVER_ENCRYPT. (Although DCS was a valid method of authentication in DB2 UDB Version 7.x, it is no longer supported.)

Question 23

The correct answers are **C** and **E**. Authentication is usually performed by an external security facility that is not part of DB2. This security facility may be part of the operating system (as is the case with AIX, Solaris, Linux, HP-UX, Windows 2000/NT, and many others), may be a separate add-on product (for example, Distributed Computing Environment (DCE) Security Services), or may not exist at all (which is the case with Windows 95, Windows 98, and Windows Millennium Edition). The combination of authentication types specified at both the client and the server determine which authentication method is actually used.

Question 24

The correct answer is **B**. A view is a virtual table residing in memory that provides an alternative way of working with data that resides in one or more base tables. For this reason, views can be used to prevent access to select columns in a table. While it is possible to encrypt the data stored in the DEPARTMENT table or move the AVG_SALARY data to a separate table (you cannot revoke SELECT privilege for a column), the best solution is to create a view for the DEPARTMENT table that does not contain the AVG_SALARY column, revoke SELECT privilege on the DEPARTMENT table from users who are not allowed to see AVG_SALARY data, and grant SELECT privilege on the new view to users who need to access the rest of the data stored in the DEPARTMENT table.

Question 25

The correct answer is **C**. The instance-level authorities available (SYSADM, SYSCTRL, SYSMAINT, and SYSMON) can only be given to a group of users and the names of the groups that have been given these authorities are recorded in the DB2 Database Manager configuration files that are associated with each instance.

Question 26

The correct answers are **A** and **B**. Only users with System Administrator (SYSADM) authority or System Control (SYSCTRL) authority are allowed to create new databases.

Question 27

The correct answer is **D**. In order to create a view, a user must hold appropriate privileges (at a minimum, SELECT privilege) on each base table the view references. CREATEIN is a schema privilege—not a database privilege; REFERENCES privilege allows a user to create and drop foreign key constraints that reference the table in a parent relationship; and CREATETAB privilege allows a user to create new tables in the database (there is no CREATE_TAB privilege).

Question 28

The correct answer is **C**. The ALTER table privilege allows a user to add columns to the table, *add or change comments associated with the table and/or any of its columns,* create a primary key for the table, create a unique constraint for the table, create or drop a check constraint for the table, and create triggers for the table (provided the user holds the appropriate privileges for every object referenced by the trigger). The UPDATE table privilege allows a user to modify data in a table; the CONTROL table privilege allows a user to remove (drop) a table from a database and gives the user the ability to grant and revoke one or more table privileges (except the CONTROL privilege) to/from other users and groups; the REFERENCES table privilege allows a user to create and drop foreign key constraints that reference the table in a parent relationship.

Question 29

The correct answer is **D**. The first GRANT statement (Answer A) provides USER1 with the ability to alter the table definition for the DEPARTMENT table; the second GRANT statement (Answer B) is not valid because you can only specify column names with the UPDATE and REFERENCES privilege; and the third GRANT statement (Answer C) provides user USER1 with the ability to change the data stored in any column of the UPDATE table.

Question 30

The correct answer is **D**. The first GRANT statement (Answer A) is not valid because there is no DROP privilege; the second GRANT statement (Answer B) is not valid because DELETE is not an index privilege (DELETE is a table or view privilege); and the third GRANT statement (Answer C) provides user USER1 with the ability to create indexes for the EMPLOYEE table. The only thing that a person who has CONTROL privilege for an index can do with that index is delete (drop) it.

Question 31

The correct answers are **B** and **D**. SELECT privilege is available for tables, views, and nicknames. The SELECT table privilege allows a user to retrieve data from a table, create a view that references the table, and run the EXPORT utility against the table; the SELECT view privilege allows a user to retrieve data from a view, create a second view that references the view, and run the EXPORT utility against the view; and the SELECT privilege for a nickname allows a user to retrieve data from the table or view within a federated data source that the nickname refers to.

Question 32

The correct answer is **A**. The DELETE table privilege allows a user to remove rows of data from a table. Aliases are publicly referenced names, so no special authority or privilege is required to use them. However, tables or views referred to by an alias have still have the authorization requirements that are associated with these types of objects.

Question 33

The correct answers are **C** and **E**. The first GRANT statement (Answer A) is not valid because only users with System Administrator (SYSADM) authority or Database Administrator

(DBADM) authority are allowed to explicitly grant CONTROL privilege on any object; the second GRANT statement (Answer B) is not valid because LOAD is not a table privilege (LOAD is a database privilege); and the fourth GRANT statement (Answer D) is not valid because BINDADD is not a table privilege (BINDADD is a database privilege). However, a user with CONTROL privilege on a table can grant any table privilege (except the CONTROL privilege), along with the ability to give that privilege to other users and/or groups to anyone—including the group PUBLIC.

Question 34

The correct answer is **C**. The EXECUTE privilege, when granted, allows a user to invoke a routine (a routine can be a user-defined function, a stored procedure, or a method that can be invoked by several different users), create a function that is sourced from the routine (provided the routine is a function), and reference the routine in a Data Definition Language SQL statement (for example, CREATE VIEW and CREATE TRIGGER) statement. When the EXECUTE privilege is granted for a routine, any privileges needed by the routine must also be granted—in this case, the SELECT privilege is needed for the table the procedure will query.

Question 35

The correct answer is **C**. The GRANT ALL PRIVILEGES statement gives USER1 the following privileges for the EMPLOYEE table: ALTER, SELECT, INSERT, UPDATE, DELETE, INDEX, and REFERENCES. To drop an index, USER1 would need CONTROL privilege on the index – not the table the index is based on; USER1 cannot grant privileges to other users because the WITH GRANT OPTION clause was not specified with the GRANT ALL PRIVILEGES statement used to give USER1 table privileges; and in order to drop the EMPLOYEE table, USER1 would have to have CONTROL privilege on the table—CONTROL privilege is not granted with the GRANT ALL PRIVILEGES statement.

Question 36

The correct answers are **C** and **D**. Users must be able to connect to a database before they can use a package and they need to be able to execute the package once they are connected; therefore both CONNECT and EXECUTE privileges are required if the user does not have SYSADM authority

Question 37

The correct answer is **D**. The BINDADD database privilege allows a user to create packages in a database by precompiling embedded SQL application source code files against the database and/or by binding application bind files to the database. The CONNECT database privilege allows a user to establish a connection to a database and the CREATETAB database privilege allows a user to create new tables in the database. The BIND privilege is a package privilege—not a database privilege—and it allows a user to rebind a package that has already been bound to a database.

Question 38

The correct answer is **B**. The syntax used to grant table privileges is:

```
GRANT [ALL <PRIVILEGES> |
        Privilege <( ColumnName, ... )> , ...]
ON TABLE [TableName]
TO [Recipient, ...]
<WITH GRANT OPTION>
```

where:

Privilege   Identifies one or more table privileges that are to be given to one or more users and/or groups. The following values are valid for this parameter: CONTROL, ALTER, SELECT, INSERT, UPDATE, DELETE, INDEX, and REFERENCES. (CONTROL privilege is not recognized by DB2 for iSeries and DB2 for zSeries.)

ColumnName   Identifies by name one or more specific columns that UPDATE or REFERENCES privileges are to be associated with. This option is only used when Privilege contains the value UPDATE or REFERENCES.

TableName   Identifies by name the table that all table privileges specified are to be associated with.

Recipient   Identifies the name of the user(s) and/or group(s) that are to receive the table privileges specified. The value specified for the Recipient parameter can be any combination of the following: <USER> [*UserName*], <GROUP> [*GroupName*], and PUBLIC.

CONTROL privilege allows a user to remove (drop) a table from a database and gives the user the ability to grant and revoke one or more table privileges (except the CONTROL privilege) to/from other users and groups; granting ALL PRIVILEGES gives a user the right to perform other operations besides DML operations.

Question 39

The correct answer is **C**. The REFERENCES table privilege allows a user to create and drop foreign key constraints that reference a table in a parent relationship. This privilege can be granted for the entire table or limited to one or more columns within the table, in which case only those columns can participate as a parent key in a referential constraint. (This particular GRANT statement also gives USER1 the ability the ability to give the REFERENCES privilege for columns COL1 and COL2 to other users and groups.)

Question 40

The correct answer is **C**. The owner of a table automatically receives CONTROL privilege, along with all other table privileges available for that table. If the CONTROL privilege is later revoked from the table owner, all other privileges that were automatically granted to the owner when the table was created are not automatically revoked. Instead, they must be explicitly revoked in one or more separate operations. Therefore, both REVOKE statements shown in answer C must be executed in order to completely remove all privileges user USER1 holds on table TABLE1. If an attempt is made to try to combine both operations in a single statement as shown in answer D, an error will be generated.

Question 41

The correct answer is **B**. The syntax used to grant the only stored procedure privilege available is:

```
GRANT EXECUTE ON [RoutineName] |[PROCEDURE <SchemaName.> *]
TO [Recipient, ...]
<WITH GRANT OPTION>
```

The syntax used to revoke the only stored procedure privilege available is:

```
REVOKE EXECUTE ON [RoutineName | [PROCEDURE <SchemaName.> *]
FROM [Forfeiter, ...] <BY ALL>
RESTRICT
```

where:

RoutineName	Identifies by name the routine (user-defined function, method, or stored procedure) that the EXECUTE privilege is to be associated with.
TypeName	Identifies by name the type in which the specified method is found.
SchemaName	Identifies by name the schema in which all functions, methods, or procedures—including those that may be created in the future—are to have the EXECUTE privilege granted on.
Recipient	Identifies the name of the user(s) and/or group(s) that are to receive the EXECUTE privilege. The value specified for the Recipient parameter can be any combination of the following: <USER> [UserName], <GROUP> [GroupName], and PUBLIC.
Forfeiter	Identifies the name of the user(s) and/or group(s) that are to lose the routine privileges specified. The value specified for the Forfeiter parameter can be any combination of the following: <USER> [*UserName*], <GROUP> [*GroupName*], and PUBLIC.

Thus, the proper way to grant and revoke stored procedure privileges is by executing the GRANT EXECUTE … and REVOKE EXECUTE … statements.

Question 42

The correct answer is **D**. The first GRANT statement (Answer A), when executed, would attempt to give user USER2 INSERT privilege on table T.TABLE1—since user USER1 does not have the authority needed to grant this privilege, this statement would fail; the second GRANT statement (Answer B) is not valid because only users with System Administrator (SYSADM) authority or Database Administrator (DBADM) authority are allowed to explicitly grant CONTROL privilege on any object—again, user USER1 does not have the authority needed to grant this privilege; and the third GRANT statement (Answer C), when executed, would attempt to give user USER2 every view privilege available (except the CONTROL privilege) on view V.VIEW1—since user USER1 does not have the authority needed to grant these privileges, this statement would also fail.

Question 43

The correct answer is **C**. The ALTER sequence privilege allows a user to perform administrative tasks like restarting the sequence, changing the increment value for the sequence, and add or change the comment associated with the sequence. And when the GRANT statement is executed with the WITH GRANT OPTION clause specified, the user/group receiving privileges is given the ability to grant the privileges received to others. There is no CONTROL privilege for a sequence and the USAGE privilege is the sequence privilege that allows a user to use the PREVIOUS VALUE and NEXT VALUE expressions that are associated with the sequence. (The PREVIOUS VALUE expression returns the most recently generated value for the specified sequence; the NEXT VALUE expression returns the next value for the specified sequence.)

Working with Databases and Database Objects

Question 44

The correct answer is **D**. In order to access a remote database from a client workstation, the database must be cataloged in the system database directory of both the client and the server and the server workstation must be cataloged in the client's node directory. (The entry in the node directory tells the DB2 Database Manager how to connect to the server to get access to the database stored there.) Because the information needed to connect to DRDA host databases is different from the information used to connect to LAN-based databases, information about remote host or iSeries databases is kept in a special directory known as the Database Connection Services (DCS) directory. If an entry in the DCS directory has a database name that corresponds to the name of a database stored in the system database directory, the specified Application Requester (which in most cases is DB2 Connect) can forward SQL requests to the database that resides on a remote DRDA server. The contents of the DCS directory file can be viewed by executing the LIST DCS DIRECTORY command. If there is no record for a zSeries or iSeries database in the DCS directory, no database connection can be established.

Question 45

The correct answer is **D**. In order to access a remote database on a z/OS server, the database must be cataloged in the system database directory of the client, the server must be cataloged in the client's node directory, and an entry for the database must exist in the DCS directory. Answer D illustrates the proper way to catalog the server, the DCS database, and create a corresponding entry for the DCS database in the system database directory.

Question 46

The correct answer is **D**. The correct syntax for the CATALOG DATABASE command is:

```
CATALOG [DATABASE | DB] [DatabaseName]
<AS [Alias]>
<ON [Path] | AT NODE [NodeName]>
<AUTHENTICATION [AuthenticationType]>
<WITH "[Description]">
```

where:

DatabaseName	Identifies the name that has been assigned to the database to be cataloged.
Alias	Identifies the alias that is to be assigned to the database when it is cataloged.
Path	Identifies the location (drive and/or directory) where the directory hierarchy and files associated with the database to be cataloged are physically stored.
NodeName	Identifies the node where the database to be cataloged resides. The node name specified should match an entry in the node directory file (i.e., should correspond to a node that has already been cataloged).
AuthenticationType	Identifies where and how authentication is to take place when a user attempts to access the database. The following values are valid for this parameter: SERVER, CLIENT, SERVER_ENCRYPT, KERBEROS TARGET PRINCIPAL [*PrincipalName*] (where *PrincipalName* is the fully qualified Kerberos principal name for the target server), DATA_ENCRYPT, and GSSPLUGIN.
Description	A comment used to describe the database entry that will be made in the database directory for the database to be cataloged. The description must be enclosed by double quotation marks.

Question 47

The correct answer is **A**. The system catalog tables are used to keep track of information like database object definitions, database object dependencies, database object privileges, column data types, and table constraints. In most cases, the complete characteristics of a database object are stored in one or more system catalog tables when the object is created. However in some cases, such as when triggers and constraints are defined, the actual SQL used to create the object is stored instead. Characteristics of views, *not* the SQL used to create them, are stored in the system catalog tables.

Question 48

The correct answer is **B**. The Control Center and the Configuration Assistant provide visual tools for cataloging databases while the CATALOG DATABASE command can be executed from the Command Line Processor. Since the CATALOG DATABASE command is a command and not an SQL statement, it cannot be issued from the SQL Assist utility.

Question 49

The correct answer is **B**. A scalar user-defined function would be the best option for the requirements outlined in answer A; an UPDATE trigger and a DELETE trigger that inserts records into an activity table every time update and delete operations are performed on a table containing sensitive data would be the best way to accomplish the requirements outlined in answer C; and an identity column or sequence could be used to address the requirements shown in answer D.

Question 50

The correct answer is **A**. If the UNIQUE clause is specified when the CREATE INDEX statement is executed, rows in the table associated with the index will not have two or more occurrences of the same values in the set of columns that make up the index key. Furthermore, the creation of an index provides a logical ordering of the rows of a table so in this example, rows inserted into the ORDERS table will be ordered ORDER_NUM values, in ascending order.

Question 51

The correct answers are **C** and **E**. An alias is simply an alternate name for a table or view. (Aliases can also be created for nicknames that refer to tables or views found on federated systems.) Once created, an alias can be referenced the same way the table or view the alias refers to can be referenced.

Question 52

The correct answer is **A**. A trigger can be activated whenever an insert, update, or delete operation is performed against the subject table that is associated with the trigger.

Question 53

The correct answer is **D**. Although a view looks like a base table, it does not exist as a table in physical storage; therefore, it does not contain data. Instead, a view refers to data that is stored in other base tables so data stored in the EMPLOYEE table would not be copied to view V1.

Question 54

The correct answer is **C**. An alias is an alternate name for a table or view; therefore, it is possible to create an alias named T1 for the table TABLE1, and it is possible to create an alias named T1 for a view named V1. Views are used to provide a different way of looking at the data stored in one or more base tables. Schemas, on the other hand, are used to logically group data; therefore, a schema named T1 could be used to group aliases and views that reference table TABLE1, but it could not be used to provide access to the data stored in table TABLE1.

Question 55

The correct answer is **A**. Sequences, identity columns, and triggers can be used to automatically generate values for columns. However, only sequences can be referenced in an INSERT statement.

Question 56

The correct answer is D. The first VALUES statement executed by user USER1 will return the value 10; the second will return the value 20. The ALTER statement changes the behavior of the sequence and the VALUES statement executed by user USER2 will return the value 5. When user USER3 executes queries the database to obtain the next sequence number, the value 30 is returned. Why? Because when user USER2 obtained a value from the sequence, four more values were generated and cached since a cache value of 5 was specified for the sequence. Since an increment value of 5 was also used, the numbers cached were: 10, 15, 20, and 25. But none of the cached values were used—they were discarded when user USER2 terminated his database connection. Then, when user USER3 queried the sequence for the next number available, he received the number 30 because that was, in fact, the next number in the sequence.

Question 57

The correct answer is **C**. The statement "INSERT INTO view2 VALUES(150, 'abc')" will fail because the value 150 is greater than 100; because view VIEW2 was created with the WITH CASCADED CHECK OPTION specified, the "WHERE c1 < 100" clause used to create view VIEW1 became a constraint that is used to validate insert and update operations that are performed against view VIEW2 to ensure that all rows inserted into or updated in the base table the view refers to conform to the view's definition.

Question 58

The correct answer is **D**. Each time a record is inserted into table T1, trigger TRIG1 is fired and a record is written to the table T1AUDIT. If both tables were queried after the update operation completes, the results would look something like this:

```
SELECT
 * FROM t1
C1         C2
----------------
1          ghi
2          -
  2 record(s) selected.

SELECT * FROM t1audit
USER                 DATE            ACTION
---------------------------------------------------
RSANDERS             01/20/2007      Insert
RSANDERS             01/20/2007      Insert
  2 record(s) selected.
```

In order to track update and delete operations performed against table T1, similar UPDATE and DELETE triggers would need to be created.

Question 59

The correct answer is **B**. Unlike base tables, whose descriptions and constraints are stored in the system catalog tables of the database to which they belong, declared temporary tables are not persistent and can only be used by the application that creates them—and only for the life of the application. When the application that creates a declared temporary table terminates, the rows of the table are deleted, and the description of the table is dropped. (However, data stored in a temporary table can exist across transaction boundaries.) Another significant difference focuses on naming conventions: Base table names must be unique within a schema, but because each application that defines a declared temporary table has its own instance of that table, it is possible for many applications to create declared temporary tables that have the same name.

Question 60

The correct answer is **B**. A package is an object that contains the information needed to process SQL statements associated with a source code file of an application program. When an Embedded SQL source code file is precompiled, a corresponding package that contains, among other things, the access plans that will be used to process each SQL statement embedded in the source code file is produced. (Access plans contain optimized information that the DB2 Database Manager uses to execute SQL statements.) This package must reside in a DB2 database that contains the data objects referenced by the package before the corresponding application can be executed against that database. The process of creating and storing a package in a DB2 database is known as "binding," and by default, packages are automatically bound to a database during the precompile process.

Schemas provide a logical grouping of database objects; the system catalog describes the objects in a DB2 database and their relationship to each other; and Multi-dimensional Clustering Tables (MCDs) may be used during query optimization to improve the performance for a subset of SELECT queries.

Question 61

The correct answer is **C**. In this case, both the node and the database must be cataloged by executing the CATALOG ... NODE and CATALOG DATABASE commands. Answer C is the only answer that uses the correct syntax for these two commands.

Question 62

The correct answer is **B**. Declared temporary tables are used to hold temporary data on behalf of a single application and are automatically destroyed when the application that declared them disconnects from the database. Declared temporary tables are not used for backup purposes, to save data for load operations, or to share result data sets between applications.

Question 63

The correct answer is **D**. Routines are a type of database object that you can use to encapsulate logic that can be invoked like a programming sub-routine. There are many different types of routines available; routines can be grouped in different ways, but are primarily grouped by their system or user definitions, by their functionality, and by their implementation. The supported routine definitions are:

- System-defined routines
- User-defined routines

The supported functional types of routines are:

- Procedures (also called stored procedures)
- Functions
- Methods

The supported routine implementations are:

- Built-in routines
- Sourced routines
- SQL routines
- External routines

Question 64

The correct answer is **A**. Views can be used to restrict access to columns in a base table that contain sensitive data, views can be used to store queries that multiple applications execute on a regular basis in a database, and views support INSTEAD OF triggers. Aliases are publicly referenced names that require no special authority or privilege to use.

Question 65

The correct answer is **C**. A distinct data type is a user-defined data type that is derived from one of the built-in data types available with DB2. Although a distinct data type shares a common internal representation with a built-in data type, it is considered a separate data type that is distinct from any other data type (hence, the "distinct" in the name). Distinct user-defined data types can be created by executing the CREATE DISTINCT TYPE SQL statement. The basic syntax for this statement is:

```
CREATE DISTINCT TYPE [TypeName]
AS [SourceDataType]
<WITH COMPARISONS>
```

where:

TypeName   Identifies the name that is to be assigned to the distinct data type to be created.

SourceDataType   Identifies the built-in data type that the distinct data type to be created is to be based on.

Thus, if you wanted to create a distinct data type to store EURO data, you could do so by executing an SQL statement like that in answer C.

Working with DB2 Data Using SQL and XQuery

Question 66

The correct answer is **D**. When a SELECT statement such as the one shown is executed, the result data set produced will contain all possible combinations of the rows found in each table specified (otherwise known as the Cartesian product). Every row in the result data set produced is a row from the first table referenced concatenated with a row from the second table referenced, concatenated in turn with a row from the third table referenced, and so on. The total number of rows found in the result data set produced is the product of the number of rows in all the individual table-references; in this case, 5 x 5 = 25.

Question 67

The correct answer is **D**. The proper way to test for a missing value (or null) is by using the NULL predicate with a WHERE clause, and answer D shows the correct way to construct such a

WHERE clause. Keep in mind that NULL, zero (0), and blank (" ") are not the same value. NULL is a special marker used to represent missing information, while zero and blank (empty string) are actual values that can be stored in a column to indicate a specific value (or lack thereof).

Question 68

The correct answer is **D**. When a full outer join operation is performed, rows that would have been returned by an inner join operation, together with all rows stored in both tables of the join operation that would have been eliminated by the inner join operation are returned in the result data set produced. An inner join can be thought of as the cross product of two tables, in which every row in one table that has a corresponding row in another table is combined with that row to produce a new record. When a left outer join operation is performed, rows that would have been returned by an inner join operation, together with all rows stored in the left-most table of the join operation (i.e., the table listed first in the OUTER JOIN clause) that would have been eliminated by the inner join operation, are returned in the result data set pro-duced. When a right outer join operation is performed, rows that would have been returned by an inner join operation, together with all rows stored in the rightmost table of the join opera-tion (i.e., the table listed last in the OUTER JOIN clause) that would have been eliminated by the inner join operation, are returned in the result data set produced.

Question 69

The correct answer is **C**. The UPDATE statement assigns a NULL value to column C1 and NULL values are displayed as a dash (-).

Question 70

The correct answer is **B**. If the DISTINCT clause is specified with a SELECT statement, duplicate rows are removed from the final result data set returned. Two rows are considered to be duplicates of one another if the value of every column of the first row is identical to the value of the corresponding column of the second row.

Question 71

The correct answer is **B**. The FETCH FIRST clause is used to limit the number of rows that are returned to the result data set produced in response to a query. When used, the FETCH FIRST clause is followed by a positive integer value and the words ROWS ONLY. This tells the DB2 Database Manager that the user/application executing the query does not want to see more than n number of rows, regardless of how many rows might exist in the result data set that would be produced were the FETCH FIRST clause not specified.

Question 72

The correct answers are **A** and **E**. An inner join can be thought of as the cross product of two tables, in which every row in one table that has a corresponding row in another table is combined with that row to produce a new record. The syntax for a SELECT statement that performs an inner join operation is:

```
SELECT
[* | [Expression] <<AS> [NewColumnName]> ,...]
FROM [[TableName] <<AS> [CorrelationName]> ,...]
[JoinCondition]
```

where:

Expression Identifies one or more columns whose values are to be returned when the SELECT statement is executed. The value specified for this option can be any valid SQL language element; however, corresponding table or view column names are commonly used.

NewColumnName Identifies a new column name that is to be used in place of the corresponding table or view column name specified in the result data set returned by the SELECT statement.

TableName Identifies the name(s) assigned to one or more tables that data is to be retrieved from.

CorrelationName Identifies a shorthand name that can be used when referencing the table name specified in the *TableName* parameter.

JoinCondition Identifies the condition to be used to join the tables specified. Typically, this is a WHERE clause in which the values of a column in one table are compared with the values of a similar column in another table.

The following syntax can also be used to create a SELECT statement that performs an inner join operation:

```
SELECT
[* | [Expression] <<AS> [NewColumnName]> ,...]
FROM [[TableName1] <<AS> [CorrelationName1]>]
<INNER> JOIN
[[TableName2] <<AS> [CorrelationName2]>]
ON [JoinCondition]
```

where:

Expression	Identifies one or more columns whose values are to be returned when the SELECT statement is executed. The value specified for this option can be any valid SQL language element; however, corresponding table or view column names are commonly used.
NewColumnName	Identifies a new column name to be used in place of the corresponding table or view column name specified in the result data set returned by the SELECT statement.
TableName1	Identifies the name assigned to the first table data is to be retrieved from.
CorrelationName1	Identifies a shorthand name that can be used when referencing the leftmost table of the join operation.
TableName2	Identifies the name assigned to the second table data is to be retrieved from.
CorrelationName2	Identifies a shorthand name that can be used when referencing the rightmost table of the join operation.
JoinCondition	Identifies the condition to be used to join the two tables specified.

Question 73

The correct answer is **C**. When the EXCEPT set operator is used, the result data sets produced by each individual query are combined, all duplicate rows found are eliminated, and all records found in the first result data set that have a corresponding record in the second result data set are eliminated, leaving just the records that are not found in both result data sets. When the UNION set operator is used, the result data sets produced by each individual query are combined and all duplicate rows are eliminated; when the INTERSECT set operator is used, the result data sets produced by each individual query are combined, all duplicate rows found are eliminated, and all records found in the first result data set that do not have a corresponding record in the second result data set are eliminated, leaving just the records that are found in both result data sets; and MERGE is not a set operator.

Question 74

The correct answer is **C**. When a right outer join operation is performed, rows that would have been returned by an inner join operation, together with all rows stored in the rightmost table of the join operation (i.e., the table listed last in the OUTER JOIN clause) that would have been eliminated by the inner join operation are returned in the result data set produced. In this case, we want to see all records found in the POINTS table, along with any corresponding records found in the NAMES table, so a right outer join is the appropriate join operation to use.

Question 75

The correct answer is **A**. The pattern of characters specified with the LIKE clause of a SELECT statement can consist of regular alphanumeric characters and/or special metacharacters that are interpreted as follows:

- The underscore character (_) is treated as a wild card character that stands for any single alphanumeric character.
- The percent character (%) is treated as a wild card character that stands for any sequence of alphanumeric characters.

Question 76

The correct answer is **D**. When the UNION ALL set operator is used, the result data sets produced by each individual query are combined; all duplicate rows found are retained. Thus with this example, the results of both tables are combined (6 rows + 6 rows = 12 rows) and the duplicate rows for "Jagger, Mick", "Richards, Keith", and "Watts, Charlie" are retained. Had the UNION set operator been used instead, the result data sets produced by each individual query would have been combined, all duplicate rows would have been eliminated, and the answer would have been 9 (12 – 3 = 9 rows).

Question 77

The correct answer is **C**. Data is stored in a table in no particular order, and unless otherwise specified, a query only returns data in the order in which it is found. The ORDER BY clause is used to tell the DB2 Database Manager how to sort and order the rows that are to be returned in a result data set produced in response to a query. When specified, the ORDER BY clause is followed by the name of one or more column(s) whose data values are to be sorted and a keyword that indicates the desired sort order. If the keyword ASC follows the column's name, ascending order is used, and if the keyword DESC follows the column name, descending order is used. If no keyword is specified, ascending order is used by default.

Question 78

The correct answer is **B**. The subselect produces a result data set that contains hire year and salary information for each employee whose salary is greater than $30,000.00. The GROUP BY clause is used to tell the DB2 Database Manager how to organize rows of data returned in the result data set produced in response to a query. (The GROUP BY clause specifies an intermediate result table consisting of a group of rows.) In this example, the GROUP BY clause tells the outer SELECT to calculate and group average salary information by hire year.

Question 79

The correct answers are **B** and **C**. The HAVING clause is used to apply further selection criteria to columns that are referenced in a GROUP BY clause. This clause behaves like the WHERE clause, except that it refers to data that has already been grouped by a GROUP BY clause (the HAVING clause is used to tell the DB2 Database Manager how to select the rows that are to be returned in a result data set from rows that have already been grouped.) And like the WHERE clause, the HAVING clause is followed by a search condition that acts as a simple test that, when applied to a row of data, will evaluate to TRUE, FALSE, or Unknown.

Question 80

The correct answer is **B**. There is no such thing as a RIGHT INNER JOIN or a LEFT INNER JOIN so the statements shown in Answers A and D are invalid. Because we want to get employee records for employees who do not have a manager and because the EMPLOYEE table is listed before the OUTER JOIN clause, the LEFT OUTER JOIN is the correct join to use.

Question 81

The correct answer is **C**. One efficient and concise way to display coded values in a readable format is to use one or more CASE expressions in the selection list of a query. Each CASE operation evaluates a specified expression and supplies a different value, depending on whether a certain condition is met. A CASE expression can take one of two forms: simple or searched. The CASE statement presented in the question is a searched CASE expression; in this example, if the INSTRUMENT column contains the value '01', the word 'HARMONICA' is returned, if the INSTRUMENT column contains the value '02', the word 'GUITAR' is returned, if the INSTRUMENT column contains the value '03', the word 'DRUMS' is returned, and if the INSTRUMENT column contains any other value, the word 'UNKNOWN' is returned.

Question 82

The correct answer is **B**. When the results of a query, or subselect, are used to provide values for one or more columns identified in the column name list provided for an UPDATE statement, the values retrieved from one base table or view are used to modify values stored in another. The number of values returned by the subselect must match the number of columns provided in the column name list specified, and only one record can be returned.

Question 83

The correct answer is **D**. Because the EMPID column in each table was defined in such a way that it does not allow null values, a non-null value must be provided for this column anytime data is inserted into either table. The INSERT statement shown in answer D does not provide a value for the EMPID column of the CURRENT_EMPLOYEES table, so the statement will fail.

Question 84

The correct answer is **B**. The DELETE statement is used to remove specific records from a table (the DROP statement completely destroys the table object), and the correct syntax for the DELETE statement is DELETE FROM [*TableName*] ...

Question 85

The correct answer is **A**. The ORDER BY clause is used to tell the DB2 Database Manager how to sort and order the rows that are to be returned in a result data set produced in response to a query. In this example, all rows containing the value "ADMIN" in the DEPT column would be listed first, followed by all rows containing the value "PRODUCTION", followed by all rows containing the value "SALES".

Question 86

The correct answer is **A**. Delete operations can be conducted in one of two ways: as *searched delete* operations or as positioned delete operations. To perform a positioned delete, a cursor must first be created, opened, and positioned on the row to be deleted. Then, the DELETE statement used to remove the row must contain a WHERE CURRENT OF [*CursorName*] clause (*CursorName* identifies the cursor being used). Because of their added complexity, *positioned delete* operations are typically performed by embedded SQL applications.

Question 87

The correct answer is **B**. Common table expressions are mechanisms that are used to construct local temporary tables that reside in memory and only exist for the life of the SQL statement that defines them. The syntax used to construct a common table expression is:

```
WITH [TableName] <( [ColumnName] ,...] )>
AS ( [SELECTStatement] )
```

where:

TableName   Specifies the name that is to be assigned to the temporary table to be created.

ColumnName   Specifies the name(s) to be assigned to one or more columns that are to be included in the temporary table to be created. Each column name specified must be unique and unqualified; if no column names are specified, the names derived from the result data set produced by the SELECT Statement specified will be used. If a list of column names is specified, the number of column names provided must match the number of columns that will be returned by the SELECT statement used to.create the temporary table. If a common table expression is recursive, or if the result data set produced by the SELECT statement specified contains duplicate column names, column names must be specified.

SELECTStatement   Identifies a SELECT SQL statement that, when executed, will produce the data values to be added to the column(s) in the temporary table to be created.

So in this example, all of the data stored in table TAB1, with the exception of the record "150 - def" is copied to a common table named SUBSET, and then a query is run against this common table.

Question 88

The correct answer is **C**. Since we are looking for values in the PERSON column of TABLE1 that have a matching value in the ID column of TABLE2, the statement shown in Answer C is the only statement that is correct. (The SQL statements shown in Answers B and D are incorrect because there is no PERSON column in TABLE2; the statement shown in Answer A is incorrect because it is looking for values that match those in the ID column in TABLE1, not the PERSON column.)

Question 89

The correct answer is **C**. When a right outer join operation is performed, rows that would have been returned by an inner join operation, together with all rows stored in the rightmost table of the join operation (i.e., the table listed last in the OUTER JOIN clause) that would have been eliminated by the inner join operation are returned in the result data set produced. In this case, we want to see all records found in the POINTS table, along with any corresponding records found in the NAMES table, so a right outer join is the appropriate join operation to use.

Question 90

The correct answer is **B**. COUNT(empno) together with GROUP BY deptname displays the total number of employees in each department; SELECT deptname displays the corresponding department name for each department ID, and ORDER BY 2 DESC sorts the data by employee count (which is column 2) from greatest to least.

Question 91

The correct answer is **D**. Because the EMPID column was defined in such a way that it does not allow null values, a non-null value must be provided for this column anytime data is inserted into either table. The INSERT statement shown in Answer D does not provide a value for the EMPID column of the CURRENT_EMPLOYEES table, so the statement will fail.

Question 92

The correct answer is **D**. Because 'NULL' is treated as a string instead of a NULL value, the SQL statements shown in Answers A and C would not set the STATUS to NULL; the statement shown in Answer B is invalid because the SET keyword is only used once in the UPDATE statement. Therefore, statement D is the only UPDATE statement shown that will accomplish the desired task.

Question 93

The correct answer is **A**. The IN predicate is used to define a comparison relationship in which a value is checked to see whether or not it matches a value in a finite set of values. This finite set of values can consist of one or more literal values coded directly in the SELECT statement, or it can be composed of the non-null values found in the result data set generated by a subquery. So in this example, the non-null values that appear in the result data set produced by the subquery are the values 1 and 2, and the only row in TAB1 that has a matching value in COL1 is the row with the value 1 in it.

Question 94

The correct answer is **D**. Data is stored in a table in no particular order, and unless otherwise specified (with an ORDER BY clause), a query only returns data in the order in which it is found.

Question 95

The correct answer is **C**. When the UNION set operator is used, the result data sets produced by each individual query are combined and all duplicate rows are eliminated. Thus with this example, the results of both tables are combined (6 rows + 6 rows = 12 rows) and the duplicate rows for Jagger, Mick and Richards, Keith are removed (12 – 2 = 10 rows). So 10 rows are returned.

Question 96

The correct answer is **C**. A *transaction* (also known as a *unit of work*) is a sequence of one or more SQL operations grouped together as a single unit, usually within an application process. A given transaction can perform any number of SQL operations—from a single operation to many hundreds or even thousands, depending on what is considered a "single step" within your business logic. The initiation and termination of a single transaction defines points of data consistency within a database; either the effects of all operations performed within a transaction are applied to the database and made permanent (committed), or the effects of all operations performed are backed out (rolled back) and the database is returned to the state it was in before the transaction was initiated. In most cases, transactions are initiated the first time an executable SQL statement is executed after a connection to a database has been made or immediately after a preexisting transaction has been terminated. Once initiated, transactions can be implicitly terminated using a feature known as "automatic commit" (in this case, each executable SQL statement is treated as a single transaction, and any changes made by that statement are applied to the database if the statement executes successfully or discarded if the statement fails) or they can be explicitly terminated by executing the COMMIT or the ROLLBACK SQL statement.

Question 97

The correct answer is **C**. DB2 uses a mechanism known as a savepoint to allow an application to break the work being performed by a single large transaction into one or more subsets. Once created, a savepoint can be used in conjunction with a special form of the ROLLBACK SQL statement to return a database to the state it was in at the point in time a particular savepoint was created. The syntax for this form of the ROLLBACK statement is:

```
ROLLBACK <WORK> TO SAVEPOINT <[SavepointName]>
```

where:

SavepointName   Identifies the name assigned to the savepoint that indicates the point in time that operations performed against the database are to be rolled back (backed out) to.

So, in this example, every operation performed between the time savepoint S1 was created and the ROLLBACK TO SAVEPOINT statement was executed was undone.

Question 98

The correct answer is **C**. When a cursor that has been declared with the WITH HOLD option specified (as in the example shown) is opened, it will remain open across transaction boundaries until it is explicitly closed; otherwise, it will be implicitly closed when the transaction that opens it is terminated. In this example, the cursor is opened, the first three rows are fetched from it, the transaction is committed (but the cursor is not closed), another row is fetched from it, and then the cursor is closed. Thus, the last value obtained will be:

```
              TAB1
--------------------------------
COL1                COL2
---                 ----
D                   40
```

Question 99

The correct answer is **A**. The CALL statement is used to invoke a stored procedure, so answer D is wrong; because a stored procedure cannot be invoked using its specific name, answer B is wrong; and since SALES is a character string value that is being passed to the procedure, it must be enclosed in single quotes. Therefore, answer C is wrong.

Question 100

The correct answers are **A** and **B**. How a user-defined function is invoked depends a lot on what it has been designed to do; scalar user-defined functions can be invoked as an expression in the select list of a query while table and row functions must be referenced by the FROM clause. Because the user-defined function used in this example is a scalar function that only returns a single value, answer B is the correct way to call it. A scalar function can also be invoked by executing a VALUES statement that looks something like the one shown in answer A.

Question 101

The correct answer is **A**. In XQuery, expressions are the main building blocks of a query. Expressions can be nested and form the body of a query. A query can also have a prolog that contains a series of declarations that define the processing environment for the query. Thus, if you wanted to retrieve customer names for all customers who reside in North Carolina from XML documents stored in the CUSTINFO column of a table named CUSTOMER (assuming this table has been populated with the INSERT statement we looked at earlier), you could do so by executing an XQuery expression that looks something like this:

```
XQUERY declare default element namespace "http://custrecord.dat"; for $info
in db2-fn:xmlcolumn('CUSTOMER.CUSTINFO')/customerinfo where
$info/addr/state-prov="North Carolina" return $info/name
```

And when this XQuery expression is executed from the Command Line Processor, it should return information that looks like this (again, assuming this table has been populated with the INSERT statement we looked at earlier):

```
1
```

```
<name xmlns="http://custrecord.dat">John Doe</name>
```

If you wanted to remove the XML tags and just return the customer name, you could do so by executing an XQuery expression that looks like this instead:

```
XQUERY declare default element namespace "http://custrecord.dat"; for $info
in db2-fn:xmlcolumn('CUSTOMER.CUSTINFO')/customerinfo where
$info/addr/state-prov="North Carolina" return $info/name/text()
```

Now, when the XQuery expression is executed from the Command Line Processor, it should return information that looks like this:

```
1
```

```
John Doe
```

Working with DB2 Tables, Views, and Indexes

Question 102

The correct answer is **D**. NUMBER, INTERVAL, and BYTE are not valid DB2 data types. The terms DECIMAL, DEC, NUMERIC, and NUM are used to denote the decimal data type. The decimal data type is used to store numeric values that contain both whole and fractional parts, separated by a decimal point. The exact location of the decimal point is determined by the precision and the scale of the value (the scale is the number of digits used by the fractional part). The maximum precision allowed for decimal values is 31 digits, and the corresponding scale must be a positive number less than the precision of the number. If no precision or scale is specified, a scale of 5 and a precision of 0 is used by default – DECIMAL(5,0).

Question 103

The correct answer is **C**. The XML data type is used to store XML documents in their native format. The amount of storage space set aside to store an XML document varies and is determined in part, by the size and characteristics of the XML document being stored.

The integer data type is used to store numeric values that have a precision of 10 digits. The range for integer values is –2,147,483,648 to 2,147,483,647, and 4 bytes of storage space is required for every integer value stored. The terms INTEGER and INT are used to denote the integer data type.

The fixed-length character string data type is used to store character string values that are between 1 and 254 characters in length. The amount of storage space needed to store a fixed-length character string value can be determined by solving the following equation: (Number of characters x 1) = Bytes required. (A fixed amount of storage space is allocated, even if all of the space allocated is not needed—short strings are padded with blanks.) The terms CHARACTER and CHAR are used to denote the fixed-length character string data type.

The double-precision floating-point data type is used to store a 64-bit approximation of a real number. This number can be zero, or it can fall within the range –1.79769E+308 to –2.225E–307 or 2.225E–307 to 1.79769E+308. Each double-precision floating-point value can be up to 53 digits in length, and 8 bytes of storage space is required for every value stored. The terms DOUBLE, DOUBLE PRECISION, and FLOAT are used to denote the double-precision floating-point data type.

Question 104

The correct answer is **A**. The decimal data type is used to store numeric values that contain both whole and fractional parts, separated by a decimal point. The terms DECIMAL, DEC, NUMERIC, and NUM are used to denote the decimal data type. Since currency values contain both whole and fractional parts, the decimal data type is the best choice to base a user-defined data type on. And to create a distinct data type named CURRENCY that can be used to store numeric data you would execute a CREATE DISTINCT TYPE SQL statement that looks like the one shown in Answer A.

Question 105

The correct answer is **B**. The character large object (CLOB) data type is used to store single-byte character data. The binary large object (BLOB) data type is used to store binary data; the double-byte character large object (DBCLOB) data type is used to store double-byte character data; and the fixed-length double-byte character string (GRAPHIC) data type is used to store double-byte character data strings.

Question 106

The correct answer is **D**. The data type assigned to an identity column must be a numeric data type with a scale of 0; therefore, the only data types that can be assigned to an identity column are: SMALLINT, INTEGER, BIGINT, DECIMAL/NUMERIC, or a user-defined data type that is based on one of these data types.

Question 107

The correct answer is **B**. A date value can be stored using a date (DATE), timestamp (TIMESTAMP), or character string (CHAR) data type. The time (TIME) data type, on the other hand, can only be used to store a time value.

Question 108

The correct answer is **A**. Although each data type specified is valid, the CHAR(15) data type will only require 16 bytes of storage whereas the VARCHAR(15) data type will need 20 bytes of storage, the LONG VARCHAR data type will need 40 bytes, and the CLOB(1K) data type will require over 1024 bytes of storage space.

Question 109

The correct answer is **C**. The XMLPARSE function parses a character string and returns an XML value; the character string expression to be parsed must evaluate to a well-formed XML document that conforms to XML 1.0, as modified by the XML Namespaces recommendation. Answers A, B, and D are character strings that are comprised of a starting tag, an optional value, and a corresponding ending tag. As a result, these strings can be converted into a well-formed, but small, XML documents.

Question 110

The correct answers are **C** and **E**. At a minimum, when a new table is created, a table name, one or more column names, and corresponding column data types must be specified. Primary keys, constraints (NOT NULL, default, check, unique, referential integrity, and informational), and table space information is optional and is not required.

Question 111

The correct answer is **C**. A trigger is used to produce an action as a result of a change to a table. Views provide users with alternate ways to see table data. And because a view can reference the data stored in any number of columns found in the base table it refers to, views can be used, together with view privileges, to control what data a user can and cannot see. Furthermore, if a view is created with the WITH [LOCAL | CASCADED] CHECK OPTION specified, it can be used to ensure that all rows added to a table through it conform to its definition.

Question 112

The correct answers are **D** and **E**. When the CREATE TABLE ... LIKE ... statement is executed, each column of the table that is created will have exactly the same name, data type and nullability characteristic as the columns of the source table used to create the new table. Furthermore, if the EXCLUDING COLUMN DEFAULTS option is not specified (which is the case in this example), all column defaults will be copied as well. However, the new table will not contain any unique constraints, foreign key constraints, triggers, or indexes that exist in the original.

Question 113

The correct answer is **A**. The Insert Rule for a referential constraint guarantees that a value can never be inserted into the foreign key of a child table unless a matching value can be found in the corresponding parent key of the associated parent table. Any attempt to insert records into a child table that violates this rule will result in an error, and the insert operation will fail. The Insert Rule for a referential constraint is implicitly created when the referential constraint itself is created. In this example, the EMPID column of table TAB2 is a foreign key (in a child table) that references the ID column (the parent key) of table TAB1 (the parent table). Therefore, because of the Insert Rule, values cannot be added to the EMPID column of table TAB2 that do not already exist in the ID column of table TAB1.

Question 114

The correct answer is **D**. A unique index, a check constraint, and a referential constraint place restrictions on what can and cannot be stored in the column(s) they are associated with. A default constraint, however, is used to provide a default value for a particular column if no data is provided for that column when data is inserted into a table; if a value is provided for the column, the default value is ignored.

Question 115

The correct answer is **C**. A check constraint is used to ensure that a particular column in a base table is never assigned an unacceptable value—once a check constraint has been defined for a column, any operation that attempts to place a value in that column that does not meet specific criteria will fail. Check constraints are comprised of one or more predicates that collectively are known as the check condition. This check condition is compared with the data value provided and the result of this comparison is returned as the value TRUE, FALSE, or Unknown. If the check constraint returns the value TRUE, the value is acceptable, so it is added to the database. If, on the other hand, the check constraint returns the value FALSE or Unknown, the operation attempting to place the value in the database fails, and all changes made by that operation are backed out.

In this example, the check constraint CST1 defined for table TAB1 only allows the values 1, 2, or 3 to be entered into column COL1. The INSERT statement shown in Answer C is the only INSERT statement that has a valid value specified for column COL1.

Question 116

The correct answers are **C** and **E**. When a unique index is created for a column, every value found in that column must be unique, and one of the column's unique values can be the null value.

Question 117

The correct answer is **A**. The ON DELETE RESTRICT ensures that whenever a delete operation is performed on the parent table of a referential constraint, the value for the foreign key of each row in the child table will have the same matching value in the parent key of the parent table that it had before the delete operation was performed. Therefore, in this example no row will be deleted from the MAKE because two rows exist in the MODEL table that references the row the DELETE statement is trying to remove.

Had the ON DELETE CASCADE definition been used instead, the delete operation would have succeeded and the tables would have looked like this:

```
MAKE

MAKEID    MAKE
_____    _____

2         Chevrolet
3         Toyota
```

```
MODEL
MODELID   MODEL      MAKEID
_____    _____   _____

3         Malibu     2
4         Camry      3
```

On the other hand, if the ON DELETE SET NULL definition had been used, the delete operation would have succeeded and the tables would have looked like this:

```
MAKE
MAKEID    MAKE
_____     _____

2         Chevrolet
3         Toyota
```

```
MODEL
MODELID   MODEL      MAKEID
_____   _____   _____

1         Mustang    _
2         Escort     _
3         Malibu     2
4         Camry      3
```

Question 118

The correct answer is **C**. The check constraint (CONST1) for TABLEA will only allow the values 1, 2, or 3 to be entered into column COL1. The NOT NULL constraint prohibits null values, the value 0 is not a valid value, and the value '1' is a character value (the column COL1 was defined using a numeric data type).

Question 119

The correct answer is **D**. The ON DELETE RESTRICT delete rule and the ON DELETE NO ACTION delete rule prevent the deletion of parent rows in a parent table if dependent rows that reference the primary row being deleted exist in the corresponding child table, and the ON DELETE SET NO VALUE delete rule is an invalid rule. On the other hand, the ON DELETE CASCADE delete rule will allow rows in the parent table to be deleted; if dependent rows that reference the primary row being deleted exist in the corresponding child table, they will be deleted as well.

Question 120

The correct answer is **D**. A unique index allows one and only one NULL value; the value "NULL" means a column's value is undefined and distinct from any other value. The remaining characteristics are true for unique indexes.

Question 121

The correct answer is **D**. In this example, the statement "INSERT INTO employee VALUES (DEFAULT, 'Smith', 10, '11/18/2004', 60250.00)" will fail because the hire date and the salary specified violates check constraint CST1 – YEAR(hiredate) > 2006 OR salary > 60500).

Question 122

The correct answer is **B**. A unique constraint can be used to ensure that the value(s) assigned to one or more columns when a record is added to a base table are always unique; once a unique constraint has been defined for one or more columns, any operation that attempts to place duplicate values in those columns will fail. Although a unique, system-required index is used to enforce a unique constraint, there is a distinction between defining a unique constraint and creating a unique index; even though both enforce uniqueness, a unique index allows NULL values and generally cannot be used in a referential constraint. A unique constraint on the other hand, does not allow NULL values and can be referenced in a foreign key specification. (The value "NULL" means a column's value is undefined and distinct from any other value, including other NULL values).

A check constraint (also known as a table check constraint) can be used to ensure that a particular column in a base table is never assigned an unacceptable value—once a check constraint has been defined for a column, any operation that attempts to place a value in that column that does not meet specific criteria will fail. The default constraint can be used to ensure that a particular column in a base table is assigned a predefined value (unless that value is overridden) each time a record is added to the table. The predefined value provided could be null (if the NOT NULL constraint has not been defined for the column), a user-supplied value compatible with the column's data type, or a value furnished by the DB2 Database Manager. Unlike other constraints, informational constraints are not enforced during insert and update processing. However, the DB2 SQL Optimizer will evaluate information provided by an informational constraint when considering the best access plan to use to resolve a query. As a result, an informational constraint may result in better query performance even though the constraint itself will not be used to validate data entry/modification.

Question 123

The correct answer is **D**. The decimal (DECIMAL or NUMERIC) data type is used to hold the number—the precision is 10 because 10 numbers will be displayed and the scale is 3 because the number contains three decimal places.

Question 124

The correct answer is **B**. Because column COL2 was defined using a varying-length character string (VARCHAR) data type, the default value provided for the default constraint must be enclosed in single quotes. Had the value 'NONE' been provided instead of the value NONE, the column COL2 would have been created. Instead, because column COL2 could not be created, the table TAB1 was not created.

Question 125

The correct answer is **C**. To create a referential constraint, you define a primary key, using one or more columns in the parent table, and you define a foreign key for one or more corresponding columns in the child table that reference the parent table's primary key. (The list of column names in the foreign key clause must be identical to the list of column names specified in the primary key OR a unique constraint for the columns in the parent table that are referenced by the foreign key in the child must exist in order for a referential constraint to be successfully created.)

Question 126

The correct answer is C. The value assigned to the CURRENT SCHEMA special register is not persistent across database restarts. Therefore, if you assign a value to the CURRENT SCHEMA special register, disconnect from the database, and reconnect, the CURRENT SCHEMA special register will contain your authentication ID – not the value you assigned it earlier.

Question 127

The correct answer is **A**. Since no unique or primary constraints were included in the table definition, no unique indexes are created.

Question 128

The correct answer is **D**. A view is a named specification of a result table that is populated whenever the view is referenced in an SQL statement. (Each time a view is referenced, a query is executed and the results are retrieved from the underlying table and returned in a table-like format.) Like base tables, views can be thought of as having columns and rows. And in most cases, data can be retrieved from a view the same way it can be retrieved from a table.

Question 129

The correct answer is **C**. If the WITH LOCAL CHECK OPTION clause of with the CREATE VIEW SQL statement is specified, insert and update operations performed against the view that is created are validated to ensure that all rows being inserted into or updated in the base table the view refers to conform to the view's definition (otherwise, the insert/update operation will fail). So what exactly does this mean? Suppose a view was created using the following CREATE VIEW statement:

```
CREATE VIEW priority_orders
AS SELECT * FROM orders WHERE response_time < 4
WITH LOCAL CHECK OPTION
```

Now, suppose a user tries to insert a record into this view that has a RESPONSE_TIME value of 6. The insert operation will fail because the record violates the view's definition. Had the view not been created with the WITH LOCAL CHECK OPTION clause, the insert operation would have been successful, even though the new record would not be visible to the view that was used to add it.

Because VIEW1 was created using a SELECT statement that only references rows that have a value less than 100 in COL1 and because VIEW1 was created with the WITH LOCAL CHECK OPTION specified, each value inserted into COL1 (using VIEW1) must be less than 100. In addition, because COL2 was defined using a character data type, all values inserted into COL2 must be enclosed in single quotes. The INSERT statements shown in Answers B and D will fail because the value to be assigned to COL1 exceeds 100; the INSERT statement shown in Answer A will fail because the value "abc" is not enclosed in single quotation marks.

Question 130

The correct answer is **A**. The ON DELETE NO ACTION definition ensures that whenever a delete operation is performed on the parent table in a referential constraint, the value for the foreign key of each row in the child table will have a matching value in the parent key of the parent table (after all other referential constraints have been applied). Therefore, no row will be deleted from TABLEA because a row exists in TABLEB that references the row the DELETE statement is trying to remove. And because the ON DELETE CASCADE definition was not used, no row will be deleted from TABLEB.

Question 131

The correct answer is **C**. Whenever an insert operation, an update operation, or a delete operation is performed against the subject table or view, a trigger can be activated (fired).

Question 132

The correct answer is **D**. Triggers are only fired if the trigger event they have been designed to watch for takes place against the subject table they are designed to interact with. In this example, no UPDATE trigger was defined; therefore, no triggers are fired when the sales table is updated.

Trigger TRIGGER_C will be fired anytime a delete operation is performed against the SALES table and triggers TRIGGER_A and TRIGGER_B will be fired in the order they were created whenever an insert operation is performed against the SALES table. Trigger TRIGGER_A is designed to calculate a sales commission for an invoice based on the sale amount; trigger TRIGGER_B is designed to assign a value to the BILL_DATE column that is 30 days from today; and trigger TRIGGER_C is designed to display an error message whenever anyone tries to delete records from the SALES table.

Question 133

The correct answer is **B**. Both primary keys and unique indexes can be defined over one or more columns in a table.

Question 134

The correct answer is **A**. The XML data type can be used to store well-formed XML documents in their native format. A table can contain any number of XML columns; however each XML column used has the following restrictions:

- It cannot be part of any index except an XML index.
- It cannot be included as a column of a primary key or unique constraint.
- It cannot be a foreign key of a referential constraint.
- It cannot have a specified default value or a WITH DEFAULT clause—if the column is nullable, the default value for the column is the null value.
- It cannot be used in a table with a distribution key.
- It cannot be used in range-clustered or range-partitioned tables.

In addition, XML columns can only be referenced in a check constraint if the check constraint contains the VALIDATED predicate. (The VALIDATED predicate checks to see if an XML value has been validated using the XMLVALIDATE() function. The XMLVALIDATE() function returns a copy of the input XML value, augmented with information obtained from XML schema validation, including default values and type annotations. If the value of the column is null, the result of the VALIDATED predicate is unknown; otherwise, the result is either TRUE or FALSE.)

Question 135

The correct answer is **B**. The SALES table in the example is partitioned such that each quarter's data is stored in a different data partition, and each partition resides in a different table space. Advantages of using table partitioning include:

Easy roll-in and roll-out of data. Rolling in partitioned table data allows a new range to be easily incorporated into a partitioned table as an additional data partition. Rolling out partitioned table data allows you to easily separate ranges of data from a partitioned table for subsequent purging or archiving. Data can be quickly rolled in and out by using the ATTACH PARTITION and DETACH PARTITION clauses of the ALTER TABLE statement.

Easier administration of large tables. Table level administration becomes more flexible because administrative tasks can be performed on individual data partitions. Such tasks include: detaching and reattaching of a data partition, backing up and restoring individual data partitions, and reorganizing individual indexes. In addition, time consuming maintenance operations can be shortened by breaking them down into a series of smaller operations. For example, backup operations can be performed at the data partition level when the each data partition is placed in separate table space. Thus, it is possible to backup one data partition of a partitioned table at a time.

Flexible index placement. With table partitioning, indexes can be placed in different table spaces allowing for more granular control of index placement.

Better query processing. When resolving queries, one or more data partitions may be automatically eliminated, based on the query predicates used. This functionality, known as Data Partition Elimination, improves the performance of many decision support queries because less data has to be analyzed before a result data set can be returned.

Question 136

The correct answer is **C**. Unlike base tables, whose descriptions and constraints are stored in the system catalog tables of the database to which they belong, declared temporary tables are not persistent and can only be used by the application that creates them—and only for the life of the application. (Once the application that created the global temporary table is terminated, any records in the table are deleted and the table itself is destroyed.) When the application that creates a declared temporary table terminates, the rows of the table are deleted, and the definition of the table is dropped. (However, data stored in a temporary table can exist across transaction boundaries.) Another significant difference between the two centers around naming conventions: Base table names must be unique within a schema, but because each application that defines a declared temporary table has its own instance of that table, it is possible for many applications to create declared temporary tables that have the same name. And where base tables are created with the CREATE TABLE SQL statement, declared temporary tables are created with the DECLARE GLOBAL TEMPORARY TABLE statement.

Data Concurrency

Question 137

The correct answer is **D**. The Repeatable Read isolation level will lock all rows scanned in response to a query. (The Read Stability isolation level will only lock the rows returned in the result data set; the Cursor Stability isolation level will only lock the row in the result data set that the cursor is currently pointing to; and the Uncommitted Read isolation level will not lock any rows during normal read processing.)

Question 138

The correct answer is **A**. If Application B did not already have an Exclusive lock on table TAB2, Application B would be placed in a lock-wait state until Application A released its locks. However, because Application B holds an Exclusive lock on table TAB2, when Application A tries to acquire an Exclusive lock on table TAB2 and Application B tries to acquire an Exclusive lock on table TAB1, a deadlock will occur – processing by both transactions will be suspended until their second lock request is granted. Because neither lock request can be granted until one of the owning transactions releases the lock it currently holds (by performing a commit or rollback operation), and because neither transaction can perform a commit or rollback operation because they both have been suspended (and are waiting on locks), a deadlock has occurred.

Question 139

The correct answer is **C**. When the Read Stability isolation level is used by a transaction that executes a query, locks are acquired on all rows returned to the result data set produced, and other transactions cannot modify or delete the locked rows; however, they can add new rows to the table that meet the query's search criteria. If that happens, and the query is run again, these new rows will appear in the new result data set produced.

Question 140

The correct answer is **A**. When a deadlock cycle occurs, all transactions involved will wait indefinitely for a lock to be released unless some outside agent steps in and breaks the cycle. With DB2, this agent is a background process, known as the deadlock detector, and its sole responsibility is to locate and resolve any deadlocks found in the locking subsystem. Each database has its own deadlock detector, which is activated as part of the database initialization process. Once activated, the deadlock detector stays "asleep" most of the time but "wakes up" at preset intervals and examines the locking subsystem to determine whether a deadlock situation exists. If the deadlock detector discovers a deadlock cycle, it randomly selects one of the transactions involved to roll back and terminate; the transaction chosen (referred to as the victim process) is then sent an SQL error code, and every lock it had acquired is released. The remaining transaction(s) can then proceed, because the deadlock cycle has been broken.

Question 141

The correct answer **D**. Typically, locks are not acquired during processing when the Uncommitted Read isolation level is used. Therefore, if Application B runs under this isolation level, it will be able to retrieve data from table TAB1 immediately – lock compatibility is not an issue that will cause Application B to wait for a lock.

Question 142

The correct answer is **D**. Usually locks are not acquired during processing when the Uncommitted Read isolation level is used. However, rows that are retrieved by a transaction using the Uncommitted Read isolation level will be locked if another transaction attempts to drop or alter the table from which the rows were retrieved.

Question 143

The correct answer is **A**. Any time one transaction holds a lock on a data resource and another transaction attempts to acquire a lock on the same resource, the DB2 Database Manager will examine each lock's state and determine whether they are compatible. If the state of a lock placed on a data resource by one transaction is such that another lock can be placed on the same resource by another transaction before the first lock acquired is released, the locks are said to be compatible and the second lock will be acquired. However, if the locks are not compatible, the transaction requesting the incompatible lock must wait until the transaction holding the first lock is terminated before it can acquire the lock it needs. If the requested lock is not acquired before the time interval specified in the locktimeout configuration parameter has elapsed, the waiting transaction receives an error message and is rolled back.

Question 144

The correct answer is **B**. Locks can only be acquired for table spaces, tables, and rows.

Question 145

The correct answer is A. If a row level lock is held by a application using the Cursor Stability isolation level, that lock remains in effect until either the cursor is moved to a new row (at which time the lock for the old row is released – if possible, and a new lock for the current row is acquired) or the transaction holding the lock is terminated.

Question 146

The correct answer is **C**. The LOCK TABLE statement allows a transaction to explicitly acquire a table-level lock on a particular table in one of two modes: SHARE and EXCLUSIVE. If a table is locked using the SHARE mode, a table-level Share (S) lock is acquired on behalf of the transaction, and other concurrent transactions are allowed to read, but not change, the data stored in the locked table. If a table is locked using the EXCLUSIVE mode, a table-level Exclusive (X) lock is acquired, and other concurrent transactions can neither access nor modify data stored in the locked table.

Question 147

The correct answer is **C**. If a transaction holding a lock on a resource needs to acquire a more restrictive lock on the same resource, the DB2 Database Manager will attempt to change the state of the existing lock to the more restrictive state. The action of changing the state of an existing lock to a more restrictive state is known as *lock conversion*. Lock conversion occurs because a transaction can hold only one lock on a specific data resource at any given time. In most cases, lock conversion is performed on row-level locks, and the conversion process is fairly straightforward. For example, if an Update (U) lock is held and an Exclusive (X) lock is needed, the Update (U) lock will be converted to an Exclusive (X) lock.

Question 148

The correct answer is **A**. When the Repeatable Read isolation level is used, the effects of one transaction are completely isolated from the effects of other concurrent transactions; when this isolation level is used, every row that's referenced in any manner by the owning transaction is locked for the duration of that transaction. As a result, if the same SELECT SQL statement is issued multiple times within the same transaction, the result data sets produced are guaranteed to be the identical. Other transaction are prohibited from performing insert, update, or delete operations that would affect any row that has been accessed by the owning transaction as long as that transaction remains active.

Question 149

The correct answer is **D**. When the Uncommitted Read isolation level is used, rows retrieved by a transaction are only locked if the transaction modifies data associated with one or more rows retrieved or if another transaction attempts to drop or alter the table the rows were retrieved from.) As the name implies, transactions running under the uncommitted read isolation level can see changes made to rows by other transactions before those changes have been committed. On the other hand, transactions running under the Repeatable Read, Read Stability, or Cursor Stability isolation level are prohibited from seeing uncommitted data. Therefore, applications running under the Uncommitted Read isolation level can read the row Application A updated while applications running under a different isolation level cannot. Because no locks are needed in order for Application A to read data stored in other tables, it can do so – even if a restrictive lock is held on that table. However, there is nothing that prohibits Application A from performing an insert operation from within the open transaction.

Question 150

The correct answer is **C**. If the Repeatable Read isolation level is used, other agents will be unable to assign seats as long as the transaction that generated the list remains active; therefore, the list will not change when it is refreshed. If the Read Stability isolation level is used, other agents will be able to unassign currently assigned seats (and these unassigned seats will show up when the list is refreshed), but they will not be able to assign any seat that appears in the list as long as the transaction that generated the list remains active. If the Uncommitted Read isolation level is used, other agents will be able to unassign currently assigned seats, as well as assign unassigned seats; however, uncommitted seat unassignments/assignments will show up when the list is refreshed, and the agent may make an inappropriate change based on this data. Therefore, the best isolation level to use for this particular application is the Cursor Stability isolation level.

Index

A

Access control, 4, 12, 97, 98
  Advanced Access Control Feature in, 44
  Label Based Access Control (LBAC) in, 44, 105, 110, 111
Access plans, 251, 585
Action, trigger, 439
Activation time, trigger, 220–221, 438–439
Activity Monitor, 81
Add Database dialog, 182, **183**
Administration Console, DWE, 46
ADO/ADO.NET, 52, 54
Advanced Access Control Feature, 44
AFTER trigger, 220–221, 439, 440, 442
Aggregations, 13
AIX, 8, 11, 36, 41, 42, 98, 155, 567, 568, 573
Alerts, Health Center, 73
Aliases, 179, 180, 192, 214–217, 245, 250, 575, 582–583, 586
  chaining and, 214
  constraints and, 214
  Control Center to create, 215, **216**
  Create Alias dialog for, 215, **216**
  CREATE ALIAS for, 214–215
  nicknames vs., 122, 214
  SQL and, 172
  uses for, 216–217
ALL PRIVILEGES clause, 129, 130, 134–136, 139, 144, 159
Alphablox Analytics, 47
ALTER, 7, 116, 119, 122, 129, 131, 134, 139, 141, 144, 156, 158, 159, 574, 576, 577, 580, 583–585
ALTER TABLE, 416, 491
  locks and, 483, 485
ALTERIN privilege, 115, 128, 138–139
Ambiguous cursors, 315
Analytics, 12, 13
APPC support, 40
Application Developer/Programmer, authorities and privileges using, 150*t*
Application programming interfaces (APIs), 48, 60

Application Requestor (AR), 43, 568
Application Server (AS), 43, 568
Arranging to take a certification exam, 17–19
AS/400, 8, 36, 102
ASC (ascending) sort, 592
Atomic nature of transactions, 322
ATTACH PARTITION, 416, 609
Audio, Video, and Image (AVI) extender, 55–56, 572
Authentication, 12, 98–103, 150, 190, 191, 573, 581
  client-based, 100, 155
  DATA_ENCRYPT, 101, 155, 573, 581
  DATA_ENCRYPT_CMP, 101, 155, 573
  Database Manager and, 99, 102–103, 155
  Distributed Computing Environment (DCE) security services and, 98, 155
  encryption and, 100, 101, 102, 155
  external vs. internal facilities for, 98–99, 155
  Generic Security Service Application Program Interface (GSS-API) and, 101, 155
  GSS_Server_Encrypt and, 101, 155, 573
  Kerberos for, 100, 155, 573, 581
  KRB_Server_Encrypt and, 100, 155, 573
  passwords in, 98–99
  Server_Encrypt and, 100, 155, 573, 581
  server-based, 99, 155
  trusted vs. untrusted clients and, 102–103
  type of, 99
  user IDs in, 98–99
  where performed, 99–102
Authorities, 103–113, **104**, 151, 574. *See also* privileges
  BINDADD, 113, 127, 137, 149*t*, 157, 171, 576, 577
  BY ALL clause in, 138
  common jobs and, required for, 148, 148–149*t*
  CONNECT, 127, 137. *See also* CONNECT
  CONNECT_QUIESCE, 127, 137
  Control Center and, granting/revoking of, 125–126, **125**, **126**
  CREATE_EXTERNAL_ROUTINE, 113, 127, 137, 149*t*